THE HOUSE THAT TRANE BUILT

ALSO BY ASHLEY KAHN

A Love Supreme: The Story of John Coltrane's Signature Album

Kind of Blue: The Making of the Miles Davis Masterpiece

Rolling Stone: The Seventies (editor)

impulse!

The House That Trane Built

The Story of Impulse Records

ASHLEY KAHN

W. W. NORTON & COMPANY ■ NEW YORK LONDON

Photograph credits: Pages 9, 55, 75, 76, 99, 110–11: Joe Alper Photo Collection LLC; **252:** George Avakian; **235:** Steve Backer; **16, 28, 38, 266:** Copyright VNU Business Media, Inc., used with permission from *Billboard*; **72:** Blue Note/EMI; **26, 63:** Sid Feller/Verve Music Group; **122, 125, 126, 127, 186 [top]:** Jowcol Music and the Estate of John Coltrane; **2, 6:** Jim Marshall; **238, 267:** Michael Ochs Archives.com; **15:** Rhino Music/Warner Music Group; **60, 61, 208:** Sony/BMG; **iv, 41, 45, 81, 91, 118, 121 [both], 142, 149, 150, 161 [middle], 165 [both], 166, 173, 175, 188 [both], 191,193, 195, 202 [top], 203, 207 [both], 213, 216, 229 [all], 240 [top], 241:** Chuck Stewart; **14, 18:** Creed Taylor; **v, x, 24 [both], 25, 40, 44, 52, 68, 73, 82, 84, 90, 94, 95, 96, 98, 101 [all], 104 [both], 108, 114, 120, 124, 128, 136, 144, 148, 151, 152, 154, 159, 160 [both], 161 [top, bottom], 169, 172, 176, 177, 178, 184, 186 [bottom], 190, 194, 202 [bottom], 204–5 [all], 206, 209, 219, 220, 221, 224, 227, 228, 232, 236, 237, 240 [bottom], 242, 247 [all], 250, 251, 254, 258, 262, 268, 269, 271, 272, 279, 280:** Verve Music Group; **12, 58, 92, 130, 164, 182, 210, 264:** Jack Vartoogian and the Verve Music Group; **281:** Author's collection.

Text credits: Pages 232–33: Howard Rosen/Evidence Music and Ed Michel.

Printed in the United States of America
First Edition

Manufacturing by Maple-Vail Book Manufacturing Group
Book design by Dana Sloan
Production manager: Julia Druskin

Library of Congress Cataloging-in-Publication Data
Kahn, Ashley.
The house that Trane built : the story of Impulse Records / Ashley Kahn
p. cm.
Includes bibliographical references, discography, and index.
ISBN-13: 978-0-393-05879-6 (hardcover)
ISBN-10: 0-393-05879-4 (hardcover)
1. Impulse records—History. 2. Sound recording industry—United States. 3. Jazz—History and criticism. 4. Coltrane, John, 1926–1967. I. Title.
ML3792.K34 2006
781.65'5—dc22 2005037218

W. W. Norton & Company, Inc.
500 Fifth Avenue, New York, N.Y. 10110
www.wwnorton.com

W. W. Norton & Company Ltd.
Castle House, 75/76 Wells Street, London W1T 3QT

1 2 3 4 5 6 7 8 9 0

CONTENTS

THE HOUSE THAT TRANE BUILT

THE HOUSE
THAT JAZZ BUILT
impulse!
SIMPÁTICO
Gary McFarland Gabor Szabo
A-9122
THE FURTHER ADVENTURES
OF EL CHICO
CHICO HAMILTON
A-9114
ROLL 'EM
SHIRLEY
SCOTT
PLAYS
THE BIG
BANDS
A-9119
RECORDED LIVE
Gary
McFarland:
Profiles
A-9112
MEDITATIONS
JOHN COLTRANE
A-9110
A flat,
G flat
and C
Yusef Lateef
A-9117
Benny
Carter
Additions to
Further Definitions
A-9116
impulse!
CONTINUES TO BUILD WITH NEW RELEASES
BY TODAY'S MOST VITAL ARTISTS
impulse!
IMPULSE RECORDS
NEW YORK
BEVERLY HILLS
A Subsidiary of ABC Records
A Subsidiary of American Broadcasting Companies, Inc.

INTRODUCTION

The music of a well-ordered age is calm and cheerful, and so is its government. The music of a restive age is excited and fierce, and its government is perverted. . . .

—*The Annals of Lu Buwei, quoted in Herman Hesse's* Magister Ludi

Orange and black. Fire and ebony. Fury and pride.

From 1961 through 1976, Impulse Records wore its signature colors proudly and raised its exclamation point high, producing albums with hinged, brightly hued covers that opened wide, attracting generations of listeners into an exciting and far-ranging world of improvised music. The sound in its grooves bristled with the spirit of the sixties, swinging with the musical experimentation and political outrage of the day. To many who made it through the era, the label was an inherent part of the velocity, keeping pace with—and at times predicting—the sound and politics that lay ahead.

"That's where it's at right now," explained Bob Thiele, the veteran record producer who headed Impulse through most of that period, in 1966. "Jazz music has always reflected the times. Today, there are violent social transitions taking place, and these changes that are sometimes confusing come out in musical expression."

But Impulse did so much more than reflect a revolutionary time. It fit perfectly into the golden age of jazz, that brief window from the late fifties to the seventies when more jazz players than ever before (or since) were alive and active, representing every era of the tradition. Think Armstrong to Ayler, swing to the "New Thing." No, Impulse didn't record them all. But it certainly tried harder than any other label, and managed to unify all these styles and approaches into a uniformly modern sensibility that has yet to fade.

Modern enough to still be a leading go-to record label for today's top mixers and hip-hop producers. The proof can be found in the orange-and-black spines peeping out of deejay record crates, and in the Impulse samples popping up in the freshest dance-floor grooves.

Invoke the label to anyone today who is music-aware, not only the jazz-savvy. The typical response mentions the music, the sixties-seventies overlap, and, just as often, fold-out covers and something about orange.

"In school, I could tell how much someone knew his music by the orange I saw on the shelf," states Daniel Richard, a record executive who, among other duties, is responsible for marketing Impulse recordings in France. "There was a certain mystery about those records," says jazz journalist and critic Gary Giddins. "When I was in high school, the question with Impulse was, did you alphabetize them with all the other albums or did you keep them together so you could have the big orange stripe on your wall?"

"The branding was terrific," offers Don Heckman, another veteran jazz critic. "I seem to recall that we were annoyed by the gatefolds initially because it took up more space on the shelves, but then you valued having that additional space for the liner notes and photographs and so forth."

It was branding that reached far beyond the jazz sphere, helped attract a whole new generation to jazz, and burned itself into the public consciousness. The rhythms and freedoms that resounded when Impulse LPs spun on turntables in the sixties and seventies resound as strongly today. In its

A new generation turns on to Trane: David Crosby of the Byrds (right) and brother Ethan with Coltrane's *Ballads* album.

© Jim Marshall

day, the Impulse logo promised forward-looking music in a design that was unforgettable—and functional.

"Those gatefolds were a wonderful development because they served as a deluxe rolling tray to manicure your marijuana," sixties political gadfly and jazz booster John Sinclair recalls. "The best Impulses had the most seeds stuck in the middle."

At the midpoint of the sixties most jazz record labels were identifiable by a consistent character and style. Columbia, the Tiffany of the lot, was really a general pop music label that boasted an upper tier of post-bebop jazz: Miles Davis, Thelonious Monk, and Dave Brubeck. Atlantic balanced modernists like the Modern Jazz Quartet and Rahsaan Roland Kirk with the soul- and blues-tinged sounds of David "Fathead" Newman and Hank Crawford. Verve specialized in vocals and well-crafted productions, finding commercial gold first in the bossa nova craze with Stan Getz and others, then with pop-friendly titles by the likes of Wes Montgomery. Prestige and Blue Note had come to rely primarily on the overlap of hard bop and soul-jazz stars like Gene Ammons, Jimmy Smith, and Lee Morgan. Finally, there was a new crop of experimentalists: Eric Dolphy and Sam Rivers on Blue Note; Albert Ayler and Pharoah Sanders on the tiny ESP label. From the early sixties on, they led a cadre of *avant-gardistas* (to borrow a term coined by Archie Shepp) who were building a more aggressive stratum atop the innovations laid down in the fifties by Ornette Coleman, Cecil Taylor, Charles Mingus, and John Coltrane.

Impulse stood out from the crowd in a number of significant ways.

Impulse was born fully mature, Athena-like, to the ABC-Paramount Record Corporation, unlike the many celebrated jazz independents like Blue Note and Riverside that struggled to distinction. Impulse rocked to life with a Top Ten pop hit, "One Mint Julep," courtesy of Ray Charles, and never felt dire financial pressures until well into the seventies. Those gatefold covers with glossy photographs did not come cheap—nor did the creative, large-budget recording projects for which the label became known. For Impulse—thinking like an independent and spending like a major—the support of a corporate parent was instrumental and distinctive.

While most groundbreaking labels stay sharp and modern for maybe four or five years, Impulse delivered a cutting edge for an impressive fifteen-year run, absorbing progressively new sounds and innovations, a restless rara avis in an industry where locking into formula is the rule and happens all too quickly. Much of Impulse's later output is still fanatically praised by a portion of fans and musicians, while remaining as divisively controversial today as it was when first released.

Impulse initially stood out from other labels of the day by covering a vast and variegated overview of the music, from swing to the extreme experimental edge of sixties jazz. Eventually, the label fine-tuned its focus almost exclusively on the avant-garde, and distinguished itself further by marketing that music successfully.

How the label was first perceived—and how that perception evolved—is one of the threads binding the Impulse story. At the outset, it was a glossy, well-packaged, and well-produced phenomenon generally hailed in the industry. By the mid-sixties, critics were praising its catholic taste and commercial triumphs, its ability, as one writer said, to "profitably encompass" the range of jazz talent. By the seventies, "it seemed as though Impulse became the label characterized by the angry black tenor man," says producer Ed Michel, who led the label into the rock era. "They weren't all angry, they weren't all black, and they weren't all tenor men, but that was kind of what it appeared to be."

The label's devotion to the mostly African-American, mostly avant-garde players collectively responsible for the last significant leap forward in modern jazz—the point where most jazz histories and timelines tend to end—stands today as one of its most important accomplishments.

"Impulse will always go down in history for having stuck its neck out," says vibraphonist Gary Burton, who saw Impulse recordings serve as primers for students when he was executive vice president of the Berklee College of Music. "It will be remembered for having made a commitment to artists like the Coltranes [John and Alice] and Pharoah Sanders and Archie Shepp and giving them a fair shot at establishing their music before a national audience—which is no small thing."

The label's commitment to music of apparently minimal commercial potential can be traced to the influence of one singular musician, a jazz player who could steer a major commercial enterprise like Impulse Records into its mission and musical identity. It is the most compelling aspect of the Impulse story. It is also the primary motivation for this book.

The name of the musician who proved to be Impulse's best-selling artist and remains its most enduring point of recognition: John Coltrane.

In 1967, the year the celebrated saxophonist died at forty, at the apogee of Impulse's fifteen-year arc, the label had already been dubbed "The House That Trane Built" by a coterie of musicians and music lovers. By then, Coltrane had far transcended mere jazz popularity. His distinctively dark, searching tone and frenetic delivery were reaching a wider range of ears than any other jazz player, save for his former boss, Miles Davis. His Impulse albums had sold tens of thousands of copies—over a hundred thousand in the case of *A Love Supreme*—attracting a younger generation that also gloried in the sound of rock, folk, electric blues, and other breaking styles of the period.

Could a label have asked for a more timely standard-bearer? Coltrane's breathtaking album-by-album progress matched the top-gear velocity that powered the age. Despite claims to the contrary, the screams and shrieks he summoned from his horn seemed one with the righteous rage and indignation blowing through the sixties. To many, it provided Impulse a political legitimacy and spiritual aura that no marketing department could have manufactured. The timing could not have been better.

"Impulse was there in the right place, at the right time," says Ed Michel. "We were the beneficiary of a cultural deep breath. The culture was very open to the music of Coltrane and his followers."

A majority of Impulse artists who followed Coltrane were in some manner or method swayed by his pioneering approach. One could measure it in the sound Charles Lloyd brought to Chico Hamilton's group, or in Sonny Rollins's edginess on *East Broadway Run Down* (recorded in the company of Coltrane's own sidemen—bassist Jimmy Garrison and drummer Elvin Jones). Another gauge was the sheer number of Impulse recordings that name-dropped the saxophonist: from the mid-sixties (Yusef Lateef's "Brother John," Elvin Jones's "Dear John C.," Albert Ayler's "For Coltrane") to the late sixties and into the seventies (Alice Coltrane's "Something About John Coltrane," Tom Scott's "With Respect to Coltrane," Michael White's "John Coltrane Was Here," Pharoah Sanders's "Memories of J. W. Coltrane"). Like their predecessor, these musicians were all avant-garde informed (if not outright avant-garde), they were all spirited (if not overtly spiritual), and they all added to Impulse's artistic credibility.

Such was the momentum of Coltrane's creative drive that it propelled Impulse along an experimental path for nearly a decade after his death. Where one had been, many were signed (and re-signed)—Archie Shepp,

Albert Ayler, Pharoah Sanders, Marion Brown, Dewey Redman, Gato Barbieri, John Klemmer, Sam Rivers. The label recruited a cadre of spiritually charged, free-blowing saxophonists, determined to keep his sound, and profitability, alive.

Excluding the world of artist-owned labels, there are few parallels in the jazz tradition to the Coltrane-Impulse symbiosis. Not Armstrong, Ellington, or Basie, whose careers spanned decades and multiple label deals. Not Monk, Gillespie, or Parker, whose velocity of stylistic change never matched, or established a body of work equal to, Coltrane's. Not Coltrane himself when, from 1955 to 1960, recording for Prestige, Blue Note, and Atlantic before joining Impulse.

Well, two do come close: it could be argued that a succession of amplified-jazz groups on Columbia Records in the seventies—Herbie Hancock's Head Hunters, Weather Report, the Mahavishnu Orchestra, Return to Forever—was a direct result of Miles Davis's shift to electric jazz in 1968. But that transpired almost two decades into the trumpeter's contract with Columbia, and the company's fascination with fusion did not last long. As well, Cannonball Adderley fulfilled an official artists-and-repertoire (A&R) role at Riverside, suggesting new signings, but his sound did not eventually define that of the label—not nearly as pervasively as Coltrane's did at Impulse.

A more quantifiable measure of Coltrane's stature at Impulse—how his sales figures compared to his labelmates', or to, say, Miles Davis's at Columbia—requires data that are sadly unavailable. During the golden years at Impulse, industry trackers like *Cash Box* and *Billboard* did not offer a jazz-specific chart, and any sales reports collected by the label itself are long lost. Nonetheless, through trade reports and anecdotes, musical analysis and historical context, it is possible to paint a vivid and accurate picture of what Impulse and Coltrane accomplished, and how one became the guide and the other followed.

To his fellow artists on Impulse, the man and the label are endurably linked and locked. "If there was an identity to Impulse, that identity for me was forged by Coltrane," states Archie Shepp. "John was the one from the beginning to the end there at Impulse," Alice Coltrane says of her late husband. "He would have recorded on for many more years. Once he had left it wasn't really over. It was never over."

When it comes to the business of recording music, no enterprise is immune to the lure or need of lucre. Record labels established with the purest of motivations learned fast about profit, loss, and keeping their creditors happy, or they just as rapidly disappeared. Conversely, even the most crass and commercial recording company has not been able to leave its mark without delivering music of some quality and value.

Ever since the first musician signed on the dotted line, the music business has been viewed with a wary eye. In a collective sense, the reputation has been earned. Too many tales of willful exploitation litter the history of the industry, too many examples of outright thievery still occur. The story of Impulse offers ample opportunity to commemorate and to criticize.

> The whole record industry is ambivalent to start with, because it's dealing in a commodity on a profit level, and yet it's also dealing with art, which is not a commodity, and which is not produced for the purpose of making a profit. I don't know how it can be reconciled, short of a revolution.

Those words belong not to a musician but to a recording industry insider: Bob Thiele. They were spoken in the heady days of 1971, with vocabulary more typical of late sixties *zeitgeist* than a man of Thiele's age. At the time, he was a forty-nine-year-old veteran of the business, an uncommonly open-minded A&R man and producer who had first fallen in love with jazz at the height of the swing era. He had pursued a career as a producer and developed into a hit-producing maven, guiding Hit Parade regulars like Pearl Bailey and the McGuire Sisters in the early fifties, then more rocking pioneers like Buddy Holly and Jackie Wilson by the end of the decade. But he never forgot his first love. He liked musicians and their world, and the affection was reciprocal. Most germane to the story at hand, he was the head of Impulse during most of Coltrane's glory days at the label.

The working relationship between Coltrane and Thiele is the primary thread in the Impulse saga, telling the unlikely tale of a musician who led and a producer who trusted instinct and learned to follow. In granting the star saxophonist rare license—Coltrane had the freedom to schedule his own recording sessions, while Thiele signed artists at his suggestion—Thiele crystallized the musical appeal and financial foundation that allowed Impulse to flourish.

A rare and fruitful partnership: Bob Thiele and John Coltrane in 1963.

Thiele was one of a series of determined producers who led the label between 1960 and 1977, and who are responsible for well over three hundred albums of lasting influence. Their names figure prominently in the production credits on LP or CD jackets. In the chronological order of their years at Impulse, they are Creed Taylor, Bob Thiele, Ed Michel, Steve Backer, and Esmond Edwards.

While in charge, each shaped the label in unique ways—in the roster of talent, in marketing strategies, in musical direction, in what each chose to do with the wealth of music produced by his predecessors. Most significantly, each wrote his own chapter to the Impulse story in how he took direction from, and found lasting value in, Coltrane's legacy. In a manner that prefigures the round-table approach of this book, the various Impulse heads provide their take on the legend and the label, beginning with Creed Taylor, the in-house producer at ABC who created Impulse and first signed Coltrane in 1960, only to depart a few months later:

> Coltrane was the jewel in Impulse's small catalog during the sixties. In terms of mass acceptance, only time could tell that story. I can only say that it took me years to really appreciate him. Not that I wasn't amazed by what he was doing at

that time, but to see how history has built this gigantic image of Coltrane . . . what other artist is around who is like that?

Thiele was already working for ABC in 1961, recording pop talent like Frankie Laine and Della Reese, when Creed Taylor departed. Thiele guided Impulse for the next eight years, through the middle of 1969. Michel joined ABC after the label moved to Los Angeles, steering the production side of Impulse for the next six years. Backer, hired in 1971 for his promotional abilities, proved his value and took over Impulse for the next two years. Edwards managed the label from 1975 to 1977, during the label's most transitional period, marking the end of an era.

I spoke with each member of this Impulse lineage—save for Thiele, who had passed away in 1996—and more than a hundred musicians, engineers, and industry professionals in researching this book. Ed Michel summed up the story best when he stated, with the inevitable pun, "Impulse was a record label that grew out of an aesthetic rather than out of a commercial impulse. It was born into a corporate environment and survived a corporate environment. It also went through phases. But everybody thought of Impulse as being John Coltrane's label . . . I mean, Impulse was the house that Trane built, as far as I was concerned, in the way that Atlantic was the house that Ray Charles built."

There are two things this book is not. It is not purely a discography—though one is supplied at the end, and much discographical data is used to tell the Impulse story, including catalog numbers in brackets, the "S" designating stereo, from the days when there was a choice. Nor is it a consumer's guide—though personal enthusiasm cannot be denied.

Because Impulse is remembered for its focus on design, many of the label's most eye-catching covers appear in the pages to follow, as do thirty-six album profiles scattered throughout this book, chosen both for their renown and for the revealing or unusual stories they yield—a studio triumph, a bold career move, a business stumble. Apologies for all the deserving titles passed over!

The fifty-year time frame of *The House That Trane Built* opens with the events leading to the establishment of Impulse, and ends in the present. In tracing the primary narrative—the story of the label—a strict timeline was bypassed in favor of a sectional approach, allowing full focus on major musicians and executives, and on certain subplots: Impulse's shifting stature in ABC's hierarchy. Bob Thiele's penchant for trend-chasing productions. The move west in 1969. The impact of the late-sixties rock explosion on Impulse, and the impact of the label on a new generation of listeners. The enduring popularity of John Coltrane. The enduring reputation of the label.

In its day, Impulse welcomed the rethinking of old formulas, prioritized new sounds and technologies, and treated all of its musicians as innovators, revolutionaries even. Perhaps that's the label's true calling card, the real reason behind the continued reverence. From the most traditional jazz to the most innovative and challenging, Impulse made it all sound equally, lastingly modern.

STEREO A-2
IMPULSE!
MONO A-3
IMPULSE!
STEREO A-4
IMPULSE!
STEREO A-5
IMPULSE!
IMPULSE!
STEREO A-7
IMPULSE!
STEREO A-8
STEREO A-9
IMPULSE!
STEREO A-10
IMPULSE!
STEREO A-11
IMPULSE!
ORCHESTRA
A-12
IMPULSE!
STEREO A-13
IMPULSE!
MONO A-14
IMPULSE!
IMPULSE!

CHAPTER 1

THE MAN BEHIND THE SIGNATURE: CREED TAYLOR (1954–1961)

Historians may remember the 1950s as the years of Eisenhower and Nixon. But in jazz, the image was different. Miles, Coltrane, Mingus, Sonny Rollins and Ornette helped set the tone . . . giants like Lester Young and Coleman Hawkins still walked the earth.

—The Jazz Word, *Burt Korall, Dom Cerulli, and Mort L. Nasatir*

He likes jazz, foreign films, Ivy League clothes, gin and tonic and pretty girls—the same sort of things *Playboy* readers like.

—Hugh Hefner, describing the height of hip in 1957

Impulse Records didn't just happen, despite the import of its name and all the spontaneous energy it eventually issued. Nor was it sudden in its conception. The label had its gestation process, one of patience, planning, and a confluence of circumstances, the product of an age when jazz enjoyed a substantial and growing audience, when the music business looked positively on recording and marketing jazz and saw the value of keeping the music in the catalog.

In the case of ABC-Paramount, the motivation to establish a separate, independent jazz division began with a quietly determined Southern-born trumpet player turned producer with an ear for well-produced recordings, and an eye for quality packaging: Creed Taylor.

Taylor was born in 1929 in Virginia. Like many of his generation, he grew up drawn equally to the notion of a sensible career and to the sound of swing. Music or medicine: the question would guide the young man's path until he reached

Future producer with horn: Creed Taylor (on trumpet) with the Five Dukes, Virginia Beach, 1949.

twenty-five. He chose Duke University, for example, both for its pre-med program and for its jazz group, the Duke Ambassadors, a farm team for the best big bands. When not in class or on the bandstand, Taylor was often in his dorm room, checking out the discs of the day, fine-tuning a musical philosophy that had begun during his early teens.

"I think the seed started about the time I was in high school," Taylor says, recalling that he would buy jazz records that "weren't being 'produced'—in quotes." While at Duke, he says, he bought all of producer Norman Granz's *Jazz at the Philharmonic* 78s. "I listened to those records that just went on and on—the tenor battles and the drum battles and da-da-da-da. I loved jazz but I said, 'Who needs this?' So I decided I'd like to get involved with that sort of thing and put together some carefully planned sessions and allocate free blowing space, but not interminable solos."

During his college years, Taylor visited New York City's vibrant jazz scene frequently, trips that fired his musical passion and introduced him to the latest innovations, including a style of small-group, soloist-centered jazz called bebop. After graduation and service with the Marines in the Korean War, Taylor moved to New York and labored to break into an overcrowded music business. By 1954, ready to call it quits and turn to a career in psychology, he found a gig with the equally struggling Bethlehem Records.

The small independent had been around for a year, trying to make it with popular singles but not succeeding. Its founder, Gus Wildi, was ready to try something new—and Taylor had an idea. The newly arrived laid-back West Coast style, collectively called "cool"—Stan Getz's whispered tenor sax, Paul Desmond's breezy alto (in Dave Brubeck's quartet), Chet Baker's languid trumpet (and vocals)—was proving immensely popular. With a hip, cool-friendly audience in mind, the fledgling producer combined an unknown smoky-voiced singer, a book of slow-burning ballads, and pianist Ellis Larkins's trio. The result was Chris Connor's *Sings Lullabys of Birdland,* which sold an unexpected 20,000 units—a healthy, profitable hit by '54 standards—saving the label and launching the careers of the singer and producer.

A cool start: the1955 album that helped launch Creed Taylor's career.

Taylor stuck with Bethlehem, producing a two-year stream of recordings by Connor and such wide-ranging talent as pianist Bobby Scott, flutist Herbie Mann, bassists Oscar Pettiford and Charles Mingus, and, significantly, the quintet co-led by trombonists J.J. Johnson and Kai Winding. It was a prolific period for Taylor, and it also afforded him his first chance to work with engineer Rudy Van Gelder, whose work with Blue Note and Prestige had impressed him. But Taylor was restless. In 1955, hoping for bigger challenges and budgets, he came across a trade-weekly report that led him to his next move.

> I read *Billboard* every week, and I found that ABC-Paramount was starting a record company. I wrote a letter to [the president] Sam Clark and got an interview. I said, "This is what I do very well," and that was it.

Founded in 1955, ABC-Paramount Records was the latest link in a chain of events brought on by federal antitrust decisions that rocked the entertainment industry in the early 1950s. Film studios like Paramount Pictures were separated from the theaters that formed their distribution divisions, while TV giant National Broadcasting Company was severed from its sister channel, the Blue Network. Blue was bought by the American Broadcasting Company, which later merged with the newly independent Paramount Theaters chain and moved its headquarters into 1501 Broadway, above New York's legendary Paramount Theater in Times Square.

Headed by former Paramount Pictures executive Leonard Goldenson, the new company, ABC-Paramount, sought to establish itself as a cross-media force in television, theaters, and sound recordings. A few years later, ABC-Paramount was still in the same cramped offices when, inspired by the success of *The Mickey Mouse Club,* a joint venture with the Disney corporation, Goldenson made the decision to launch a music division to release original music from the popular show. The Am-Par Record Corporation and its record label, ABC-Paramount Records, was born.

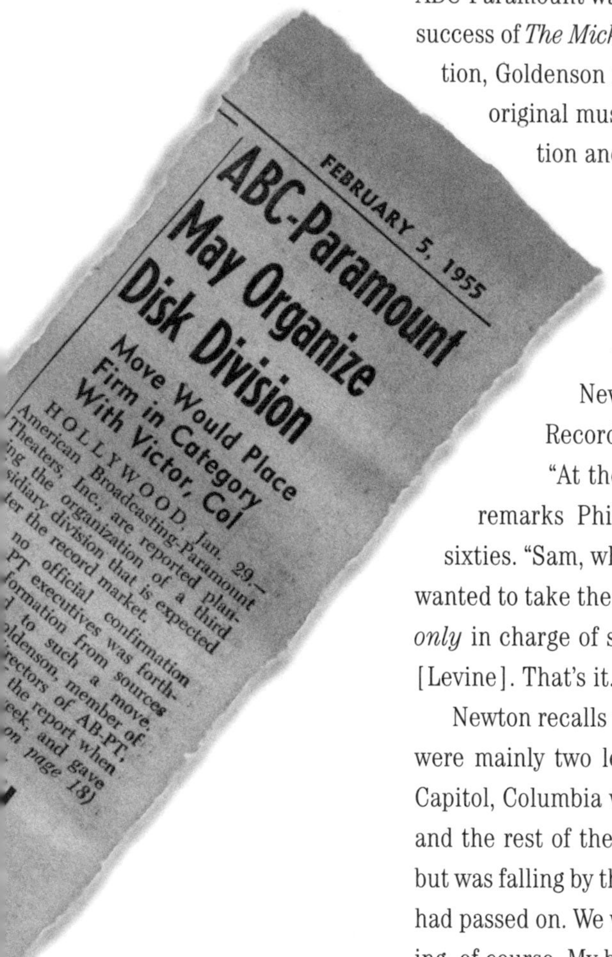
FEBRUARY 5, 1955

ABC-Paramount May Organize Disk Division

Move Would Place Firm in Category With Victor, Col

HOLLYWOOD, Jan. 29.—American Broadcasting-Paramount Theaters, Inc., are reported plan-ning the organization of a third ...sidiary division that is expected ...ter the record market. ...no official confirmation ...PT executives was forth- ...formation from sources ...d to such a move. ...oldenson, member of ...rectors of AB-PT, ...the report when ...eek, and gave ...on page 18)

Goldenson hired Sam Clark, a Boston-based record distributor, as the label's first president, and appointed Harry Levine, chief booker of live entertainment for the Paramount Theaters chain, to deal with the talent end of the business. Clark in turn recruited Larry Newton, who had run the rhythm and blues label Derby Records in Boston, to be his number two.

"At the start there were three people running that company," remarks Phil Kurnit, in-house counsel for the label in the mid-sixties. "Sam, who did a lot of the conceptual work in terms of where he wanted to take the company. Larry Newton, who was in charge of sales and *only* in charge of sales, and almost the whole company reported to Harry [Levine]. That's it."

Newton recalls the playing field they were entering. "In the fifties, there were mainly two levels of record companies. There were the big ones—Capitol, Columbia was big with Mitch Miller, and then you had RCA Victor, and the rest of the labels were indies. That was it. Decca was still strong, but was falling by the wayside, because the founder of that label, Jack Kapp, had passed on. We were shooting to be a major. We had good financial backing, of course. My boss, Leonard Goldenson, wanted to go all the way."

ABC-Paramount was determined from the outset to come across with the weight and impact of a major label—with a full catalog of singles and albums, and presence on the pop charts. Clark and Newton devised a two-part plan: hire in-house producers to develop recording projects and find new talent, and locate smaller record companies ripe for a partnership or a buyout. Creed Taylor was an example of the former, along with a more pop-oriented producer and arranger named Sid Feller.

"I started on July 14, 1955—the first salaried man," recalls Feller, who later gained notoriety as arranger on Ray Charles's sixties hits and long-running president of the Recording Industry Association of America. "We were in existence over five months before we issued our first record at the end of November 1955." ABC files show that the label's first single was "Siboney," by would-be teen idol Dick Duane, while the label's first recording session—on September 6, 1955—featured the Welsh-born pianist Alec Templeton.

"The first real artist we had as far as I can remember," reports Feller, "was Eydie Gormé." In fact, in its nascent years, ABC-Paramount saw little success with its album releases, with none of the first hundred making it onto any national charts save for a few by Gormé. "Not many companies could have continued with this type of success rate, but ABC-Paramount's pockets were apparently deep," notes the online *ABC-Paramount Album Discography*.

Around the same time Feller began at ABC, Don Costa was hired as the label's second pop producer; and shortly thereafter Creed Taylor walked into Clark's office and into his next job. Almost immediately, Taylor produced his first session for ABC, trombonist Urbie Green's *Blues and Other Shades of Green* [ABC 101], and dove immediately into a full schedule of recording sessions. Of ABC-Paramount's first hundred LPs, from 1955 to 1957, Taylor produced at least a third, utilizing many of the same jazzmen he had used at Bethlehem, including pianists Dave McKenna, Billy Taylor, and Bobby Scott, trumpeter Ruby Braff, saxophonists Zoot Sims and Lucky Thompson, bassist Oscar Pettiford, multi-instrumentalist Don Elliott, and arranger Quincy Jones. He used an all-star big band for an educational album titled *Know Your Jazz* [ABC-115].

Following the same formula of matching album to audience that had worked at Bethlehem, the producer conducted one-man marketing surveys, searching through bins in a little record store across the street from the Paramount building. "They sold everything from belly dance music to whatever; it was a very active barometer for me to find out what musical categories were not represented. For instance, they didn't have any Oriental music, so I did *Hi-Fi in an Oriental Garden,* and it really sold quite well."

Nevertheless, it was still popular singles that drove ABC-Paramount in its initial years. Feller remembers that starting off on a semi-major level allowed the company to deliver its first handful of teen-oriented hits.

"Paul Anka came to us in 1956, our second year in business, with a few million sellers. Then we had some good years with Lloyd Price, Steve Lawrence and Eydie Gormé, and that kept us in the major leagues." Other hitmakers from the late fifties included Danny and the Juniors, George

A young Creed Taylor in the studio, late fifties.

Hamilton IV, and, for a brief moment, Simon and Garfunkel, then recording under the name of Tom and Jerry.

There were growing pains.

"We spent a lot of money, and sold very little," notes Feller. "We were not Columbia, let's put it that way. Columbia had a dozen artists selling at that same time. Same with RCA and Capitol. We had one or two selling but we put out hundreds of other records which meant nothing. Was it a struggle? Yes, but we always had somebody who was selling."

Meanwhile, Newton spearheaded the licensing and label-buying drive with creative offers, as he recalls:

> It was similar to the motion picture business: I made a deal where ABC got twenty percent off the top, we paid all the expenses, and then we made a seventy-five/twenty-five split on the profits. And if they were going to sell out, I'd have the first option to buy the company. Early on, I made a deal with Philadelphia's Chancellor Records, which was a very important factor, because they had these two kids, Frankie Avalon and Fabian: we had some big records with them.

Another important money-making factor at ABC-Paramount was an early example of media synergy. As certain singers or groups captured the attention of a national television audience on such ABC programs as Dick Clark's *American Bandstand* or *The Mickey Mouse Club,* so their music would roll out on the ABC-Paramount label, or the short-lived Apt subsidiary. A variety of teen groups like the Sparkletones ("Black Slacks"), the Royal Teens ("Short Shorts"), and the Poni-Tails ("Just My Luck to Be Fifteen") were all beneficiaries of this formula.

Meanwhile Taylor, who was not making the numbers of such one-hit wonders, continued to produce albums that still moved enough copies to satisfy ABC's investment in his concept-driven approach. He expanded his efforts.

> I did a whole series of albums with songs, World War I songs, World War II songs, with just a barber shop quartet [and] jingle singers. I went to Yale and recorded bawdy drinking songs with a little remote recorder. I always liked Latin music, so I had a whole slate of flamenco stuff—Montoya and Sabicas—terribly dramatic music. I even took Kai Winding to Nashville and did a country album with Kai, [using] trombone as a voice that you don't normally hear with the repertoire of country music.

Despite the ecumenical projects, Taylor maintains, "Jazz was my mission before and after. [But] I didn't push it as a priority, I snuck it in because, as everybody in the business knows, the percentage of jazz sales is way down relative to pop sales. The big dollars were not coming from jazz."

Accordingly, Taylor made the most of the jazz sessions he was able to produce for ABC-Paramount, and true to his vision of full, premeditated production, they were all creatively conceived and rendered: Don Elliott's *The Voices of Don Elliott,* Billy Taylor's *My Fair Lady Loves Jazz,* and trumpeter Kenny Dorham's *Kenny Dorham and the Jazz Prophets,* the last of which "sold well for its time—about 10,000 copies."

A MORE ELEGANT LOOK

ABC's albums of the time—pop, jazz, other sounds—began to appear in striking, slick, full-color covers, an unusual (and relatively expensive) outlay for the mid-fifties. Driving the design effort was a closet jazz fan, Fran Attaway, then known as Fran Scott and the wife of clarinetist Tony Scott, who had been recommended to the label by Taylor.

"I started with Decca, and had also done some black-and-white line things for musicians, flyers and posters," recalls Attaway. "Creed liked the work I'd done for the Modern Jazz Quartet. But I didn't realize that he had sold me as somebody who would do the Dick Clark stuff—Fabian, Paul Anka, and all those other people. That was a surprise!"

Attaway took full advantage of the generous design budgets ABC was willing to outlay.

> I could spend any amount of money when I did the Dick Clark stuff. I could take a top photographer and go to Philadelphia and book a good hotel room and spend two days photographing. But the thing about the jazz musicians, to sell the four-color covers was tough.

Attaway persevered when her higher-ups questioned an expensive photo shoot in Central Park with a dancing couple for an Art Farmer album. Eyebrows were raised when she insisted on using an interracial couple. She stood fast, backed by her own convictions and, in boardroom meetings, by Taylor.

These meetings would have Sam, and the head of sales, the head of promotion, our top distributor too, sitting around, dressed in three-piece suits. Creed had this sense of how to appear to these really hard-type sales guys. He would usually sit a little back from the table—it was just a little trick, because, when you speak, it forced people to turn toward you a little bit more and pay attention. About three-quarters of the way through [the meeting], he would say quietly, "I have something I would like to introduce."

Let's say it was the Art Farmer album. He'd say, "And I'm bringing in a new arranger, by the name of Quincy Jones, and we'll call it his orchestra and Fran, why don't you say what you'd like to do." I'd describe a romantic scene on the front in full color. They'd all sit there and be very polite and listen. Then Sam would say, "Creed, are you sure this is a good idea—what's this man's name? Does he sing?" "Art Farmer. No, he plays trumpet." "Trumpet, hmmm. I don't know . . ."

They really had no idea what jazz was. I mean, they might have heard of Glenn Miller, Benny Goodman, and Satchmo, but they trusted Creed. He was the expert—very quiet, very controlled, very clear. He didn't promise anything he couldn't deliver.

The trust Taylor earned in-house at ABC-Paramount reached the jazz community as well. He continued to work with a growing coterie of respected players—Gerry Mulligan, Bob Brookmeyer, Tony Scott—while reaching to up-and-coming talent, as one future Impulse artist witnessed.

Trombonist Grachan Moncur III, while attending music school in Manhattan, secured an office job at ABC-Paramount tracking national sales. "This was around 1956—they didn't really have a big jazz department, but they were growing," he recalls. "It was funny, I remember when Cannonball and Nat [Adderley] came through the office one day—they had just migrated into town. Creed was giving them a tour of ABC and they looked into my office and saw me sitting there with a desk. They were so surprised to see a black dude with a desk, you know? Cannonball was very impressed. He said, 'Good to see you, my man.'"

Taylor could not have helped noticing that his mild-mannered, urbane approach to music-making did not exactly mesh with the more direct, eastern way of doing business around him. Others—like Alan Bergman, ABC's legal expert on music publishing in the mid-sixties—marked it as well. "Sam Clark, Harry Levine, Larry Newton—in his own crude kind of way Larry was a pretty good record man—they were kind of a rough crowd, not

Ivy League at all. Real upstarts compared to the real button-down atmosphere of Goddard Lieberson and Frank Stanton at CBS, or at RCA, or Capitol. They were all very corporate, CBS especially. ABC was run like a candy store."

"Sam was a classy guy but came up from the street," agrees Kurnit. "He was very, very bright and well dressed and had a very confident air. When I say the street, he was out there dealing with retailers all the time and all that stuff."

The man at the top who, when it came to music, seemed to get it was Levine. According to Kurnit, "Harry was worth his weight in gold. He was a bachelor for life and bright as can be. He had been dealing with managers—mainly agents—for the Paramount theater chain. He was Uncle Harry, very generous with everybody."

Taylor was one of the recipients of Levine's personal largess; soon the vivacious Broadway veteran and the quiet producer from the South cemented a working friendship. "Harry and I would have dinner, and he would tell me all these stories about what a jerk Harry James was, or when Sinatra came in and da-da-da-da-da," laughs Taylor. "He knew artists and their dynamic behavior. Sam was tough and he just wanted to see the bottom line. I really never knew what he liked musically."

VICTORY WITH VOCALESE

Levine's support would prove invaluable for many of Taylor's projects, including one he cooked up in late 1957, after being approached by the songwriter and singer Jon Hendricks with a bold proposal: re-create the big-band arrangements of, say, Count Basie, with a choir singing all the horn passages, individual singers handling the solos, plus a rhythm section. A witty lyricist, Hendricks would provide the words; all that was needed was enough jazz-savvy vocalists who could sing and swing, and Hendrick's friend Dave Lambert was one.

> They came by thinking I'd be the likeliest guy in town to hit with that kind of weird idea. Originally, we did highlight Basie songs all with studio singers. But it sounded stiff as a board because the studio singers were very precise and didn't fit the mold.

The solution? Utilizing the then-young studio technique of multitracking, recording and re-recording different performances onto the same reel of tape, the album was built around the trio of Lambert, Hendricks, and another bop-flavored singer named Annie Ross.

> We came up with the overdubbing idea. I wasn't worried so much about being technically clean—I was concerned about the feel and the overall sound, and the hiss couldn't have bothered me less. So what do you do? You roll off the top a little bit [filtering the resulting tape hiss], you make it a mono release, with four trumpets being sung by Annie Ross, Dave Lambert being the trombone section, and Jon Hendricks the saxophone section.

Fortunately, as Taylor remembers, approval for the not-inexpensive sixty hours of studio time had to come from Levine.

> He would say—he had a sense of humor—"Creed, I think you're right on the edge this time. I don't know what's going on with that Basie thing you're doing with all those singers." I'd say, "Harry, don't worry about it. It's going to be unique." "Well, OK." So it went along very smoothly as long as I created sales.

Larry Newton acknowledges that Taylor's reputation afforded him an uncommon budgetary license: "He was a great talent, Creed, [but] I never got two figures from him. He'd tell me [a recording project] was going to cost forty thousand and it may wind up costing ninety. He would just put in bills later, and I never wanted to fight with him." It was a strategy Taylor's successor at Impulse would freely employ as well.

Sing a Song of Basie was a solid seller and a technological sensation upon its release in mid-'58 in both monaural and stereo versions (ABC-Paramount, one of the first major labels to venture into the stereo frontier, had just begun issuing albums in that format). "It just came out of nowhere; it made Lambert, Hendricks and Ross," Taylor recalls. As well, it marked another rung in the producer's ascending reputation in both the demanding jazz arena and the numbers-driven side of the business.

But to Taylor, a marked incongruity remained. "Here they were pretty much on the same label that had [pop stars like] Paul Anka or Danny and the Juniors, or—you name it—the rock 'n' roll bands of the time." In an attempt to set his productions apart from such mainstream offerings as

TV's Wyatt Earp Sings or *Eydie in Love,* the producer took the audacious step of not only crediting himself on each album he produced, but affixing an image of his signature.

"I arranged for that in the typeface," Attaway admits. "It may have been my idea to put the signature. It seemed sensible to me, because frankly, I didn't see [that] ABC was going to be a long-range business as it was set up then, with that teenybopper music."

Taylor had his own motivation. "Why does a painter sign a painting? I realize the question is not necessarily parallel, but as far as I was concerned, I was producing records and I wanted the people, the fans or whoever, to know who did it. I wanted to make sure that if people didn't like it they could blame me for it, or if they did like it . . . well, I was shooting to go on line [with] the responsibility of making a really great-sounding and great-looking package."

A bold sound-on-sound breakthrough: Taylor's most successful production for ABC-Paramount set the stage for Impulse.

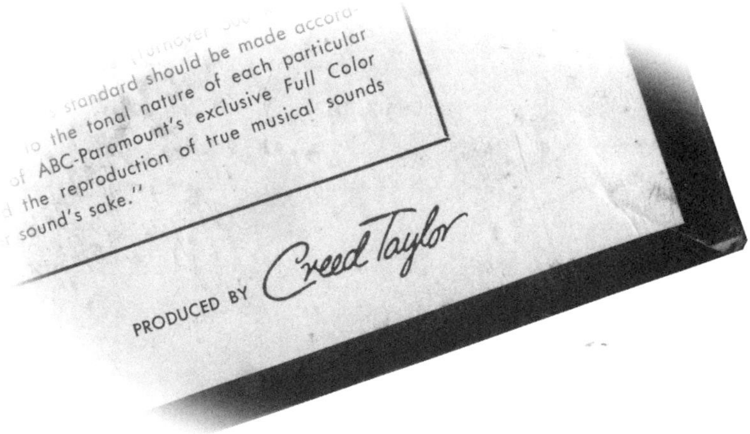

Taylor's distinctive inscription helped bring the producer together with a fledgling photographer whose talent would soon grace many album covers. "When I was just starting out [in photography], record covers seemed like fun because almost anything could be a subject matter for a record cover,"

says Pete Turner, later to earn international renown for his bold use of color. "The records that I liked the best always had a signature on it—and it was Creed Taylor. I was still in the army, and I made an appointment with him."

Turner remembers his first album cover assignment.

> Creed was exceptional about being open-minded to anything. The first thing that Creed and I worked on—he said, "I'm working on an album called *The Sound of New York,* would you be interested in maybe doing something like that?" I had done some photography. . . . It was kind of speculative. It was a picture of a traffic light and I had double exposed the red and the green and then the blue of dusk and the Empire State Building behind it, looking up. It was a nice, moody New York City shot. He loved it. It was the beginning of a real long, productive relationship.

Released in 1958, *The Sound of New York* [ABCS-2269] featured the music of composer Kenyon Hopkins (best known for his film soundtracks) performed by the "Creed Taylor Orchestra," with alto saxophonist Phil Woods its most noted member. The album musically rendered the Big Apple in its variegated sonic glory: "Taxi Ride," for instance,

employed sound effects and a horn-heavy arrangement, to capture the stop-start, staccato rhythm suggested by its title. The cover was a gatefold that opened up to a veritable mini-booklet inside—pages of liner notes attached to the inner spine—that explained the album's theme in detail and humor.

The Sound of New York naturally bore Taylor's signature and serves as a blueprint for a future formula: high concept, high quality, and in no sense low budget. Coincidentally, tucked away on an inner sleeve is a small black-and-white photograph of a Times Square movie marquee with the name of an adult movie in bold letters: IMPULSE.

It had been only five years since Taylor had walked into his first music industry job. He had come far, sharing office space and on a par with veteran producers and arrangers—Feller, Costa, others—who had been in the game a lot longer. Yet he aspired to more than a mere staff position. Soon enough, circumstances would deliver Taylor the chance to establish a label that regularly produced the intelligently conceived recordings he had envisioned as far back as high school.

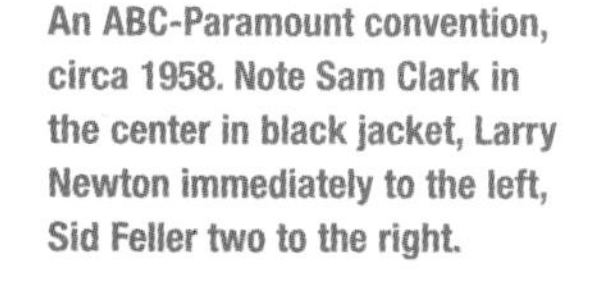

An ABC-Paramount convention, circa 1958. Note Sam Clark in the center in black jacket, Larry Newton immediately to the left, Sid Feller two to the right.

ABC EXPANDS ITS REACH

In 1959, the recording industry had settled comfortably into a multiplicity of formats. The 33⅓ rpm long-playing record, pioneered by Columbia Records, was ten years old. "The long-playing record . . . today accounts for 61 percent of the total industry volume. Album sales in fact now represent two-thirds of all popular music sales," reported *Billboard* magazine.

Yet it was the single—the 45 rpm format that locked in so well to radio airplay—that drove a substantial portion of those album sales. The LP, when not merely offering hit singles by a pop artist, was perceived as the format of more adult, and therefore less commercial, taste. Easy listening, spoken word, classical, and jazz recordings were deemed appropriate album material. In 1959, the Kingston Trio, Mantovani, Henry Mancini, and Johnny Mathis vied for the top-selling LP honor. Though instrumental music made the charts (two of the year's top fifteen singles—Dave Cortez's "The Happy Organ" and Santo and Johnny's "Sleep Walk"—were lyric-free), it still would be a stretch to consider jazz as commercially significant in the singles market.

That year, as *Billboard*'s singles charts reveal, ABC-Paramount officially arrived. Between Paul Anka, Frankie Avalon, and Lloyd Price, the label commanded the top-selling position for fourteen weeks. It was the only label to have four no. 1's—twice as many as RCA or Columbia. *The Music Reporter* saluted ABC-Paramount's first five years with a cover story listing its seven-strong "honor roll of million-dollar smashes." The seven million-earning hits: "A Rose and a Baby Ruth" by George Hamilton IV; "Diana" and "Lonely Boy" by Paul Anka; "At the Hop" by Danny and the Juniors; "Stagger Lee" and "Personality" by Lloyd Price; and "Venus" by Frankie Avalon.

With coffers bulging, ABC-Paramount expanded its focus beyond the singles market. In October 1959, it purchased the stereo-friendly, LP-oriented labels founded by orchestra leader Enoch Light, Command and Grand Award—labels that, interestingly, had established a reputation for high-quality packaging with gatefold covers. ABC's buyout kept Light in charge of the New Jersey–based labels and expanded their easy-listening audience. Looking to break into the rhythm and blues market—though Lloyd Price is black, his music fell in line with ABC's pop strategy—the company began scouting for a star who would appeal to a black audience. What they got was an unqualified mainstream triumph.

GAMBLING ON A GENIUS

It is now a permanent part of the Ray Charles legend—how the R&B pioneer, whose 1959 hit "What'd I Say" stood as a crowning achievement of seven years of groundbreaking music on Atlantic Records, chose to leave the much-loved independent label for ABC-Paramount that same year. And it still offers alternate interpretations: questioning personal motivation (how could Charles betray Atlantic's commitment?) while celebrating a stroke for artistic independence (did Charles himself come up with the idea of retaining ownership of his music?).

The details of the deal lay at ABC in a thick bound book. On its cover was the word "Tangerine," the name Charles chose for the record label he established as part of his agreement in coming to ABC-Paramount that summer. The significant points were generally known: a generous advance and a contract allowing Charles to maintain ownership of all his recordings. The man who knew it best was ABC's first in-house counsel, Bill Kaplan.

Am-Par Signs Ray Charles

NEW YORK — Ray Charles has signed a long term contract with ABC-Paramount Records, thus ending an association of several years with Atlantic Records.

Charles' deal with Am-Par reportedly calls for a guarantee of about $50,000 a year. Sid Feller, Am-Par's artist and repertoire chief, is working with Charles to select material for his first recording session for the label.

The artist currently has an up-and-coming pop hit, "I'm Moving On" on Atlantic — No. 45 on The Billboard's "Hot 100" this week.

The headline on December 7, 1959.

> I'm sure part of it came from his [booking] agency, the Shaw Agency, and part of it from our own imaginative people. They came up with a deal that was extraordinary: a sort of a partnership where the company paid for the costs of recording and the manufacturing, promotion, and advertising of the records, and royalties.

The Ray Charles deal was complete before Kaplan joined ABC, but he oversaw its implementation: wholesale revenue from all Ray Charles titles was isolated, ABC received a distribution fee and reimbursement for all out-of-pocket expenses, and the full net figure was divided between Charles and ABC.

In effect, it was a licensing deal—the record company paying a fee to release music owned by an independent producer, then sharing the profits—an approach ABC had employed with other producers and labels. It was a gamble that paid off handsomely.

"After Ray Charles came in 1959," according to Sid Feller, who arranged many of Charles's hits in the 1960s, "everything went major from then on."

Charles returned ABC's investment many times over, eclipsing the label's past teen-pop successes with a steady series of best-selling singles and classic albums, including one that specifically would help launch a new project—a jazz label.

CREATING A JAZZ BRAND

Taylor cannot pinpoint when the first spark of the idea came to him in late 1959 or early '60, only that it began with a name.

> I had thought about this name "Pulse" and looked into it. It had good connotations—I had thought of the motto "Feeling the Pulse," or "The Pulse of the music world," or whatever.

With a name to go on, Taylor let the idea gestate as his usual workload for ABC continued. Into 1960, he oversaw the release of numerous recordings he had ready in the can: a few flamenco guitar collections, various "Creed Taylor Orchestra" theme albums (horror music, tunes of loneliness), yet another LP devoted to bawdy drinking songs. Behind the scenes, though, he pondered a far different type of music for his ideal label, music that did not require marketing concepts, music for its own sake. "Very serious music, performed at the absolute top level of musicianship."

Taylor's habitual club-hopping took on a deeper purpose. He had the same favorites as many other fans—Miles Davis, J.J. Johnson, Stan Getz, John Coltrane—but, with a penchant for arrangers and composers, he was also sure to catch special engagements by the likes of Gil Evans and Quincy Jones.

"I sensed that Creed must have gone to a lot of clubs at night and really listened," recalls Attaway. "He always seemed to know exactly what he wanted—what he was looking for. That surprised me."

One thing Taylor knew he had to find was a look for his new label, and he still recalls his thinking when it came to LP covers. "I always thought there were two ways to look at an album. One is when it's on a coffee table and the other is on the bookshelf. So either way there should be no problem finding the label." Requiring little more than a head turn, he shared his idea with Attaway.

"We shared an office," Attaway says. "I mean, I was in his office. When I first came to ABC they were going to put me in a room filled with boxes. I said, 'I can't fit a drawing table in here!' Creed sort of motioned to me quietly. We went into his office, which was large, and closed the door, and he pointed to the corner."

Proximity fueled a creative dialogue resulting in the birth of the Impulse look. Taylor recalls: "I believe the colors—the orange and black—and the exclamation point was Fran. That wasn't me. 'The New Wave of Jazz is on Impulse,' that was mine." The orange and black (a color combination most associated with the recently departed New York Giants baseball team) was chosen for its brightness, and for the fact that no other record company employed it.

Taylor also credits Attaway for establishing the tradition of employing cutting-edge photographers, whose portraits and images would be reproduced on slick paper that would "bleed" to the edge of the covers. "She had great taste. She brought in famous [and] famous-to-be photographers like Roy DeCarava and worked with others who were already there like Pete Turner."

When Tony Scott accepted an Asian tour sponsored by the State Department, Attaway departed with her husband, leaving her job and home for years of travel. Almost immediately after, ABC hired Margo Guryan, a music student from Boston, to be Taylor's secretary. She moved into his office and recalls him saying that jazz was back in the picture and that he was starting a new label. "I remember he was getting a logo together. Originally it was 'Pulse!' with an exclamation point. Then they found that there was another label called Pulse. We were all terribly disappointed because the artwork was absolutely terrific." Guryan also recalls Taylor's solution.

> Creed took that logo home and came up with what I thought was an absolutely ingenious idea. He took Pulse, put I-M in front of it and dotted the "I" so it reflected the exclamation point, an exact design reversal at the end of it.

With a punchy logo, eye-catching design, and witty motto in place by the late spring of 1960, Taylor added the notion of high-quality packaging and an A-list of artists. Only then did he feel the time was ripe to present his full conception to the man who could help him realize his plan—and who would appreciate it best.

> It all started to come into focus—I had the first four albums in mind and I just talked to Harry about it: "Hey, look, I think that a gatefold with laminated packages would be the way to introduce the Impulse line in a dynamic way."

Levine was convinced, almost assuring a green light from Clark and Newton. He acted as a needed buffer as Taylor plowed ahead, finalizing design plans, scheduling sessions, shooting for a label launch in early 1961.

> Harry was an invaluable kind of conduit, knew how to handle Larry and Sam so I didn't have to come to them directly. Harry knew I was very much sales oriented, not just about the music. But I certainly wouldn't change the music in order to get the sales if the music didn't fit at the time.

JAZZ AT THE END OF THE FIFTIES

Jazz, in fact, did fit the time. The late fifties was proving to be a culturally transitional era. By then, the literature of the Beats, the canvases of the Abstract Expressionists, smoldering method actors like James Dean and Marlon Brando on movie screens were established signs of a culture preparing to leave behind a prim, buttoned-down past, to relax and embrace the adventurous, hip, and young. Jazz, the music that had matured from a functional, dance-oriented past to become a serious art form with its own smoldering sensibility, came across as the soundtrack of the age.

Billboard nailed the phenomenon in a headline article in early '59, "Late '50s Bid for Posterity, Fame as Real 'Jazz Age'": "The late '50s—rather than the '20s—may yet go down in musical history as the real 'Jazz Age.' Jazz is moving into the pop market in every arena—records, TV, radio, films singing commercials, etc.—and next Monday will even make the White House, via a 'Jazz Jubilee' concert sponsored by Mrs. Dwight D. Eisenhower." "Jazz is now big business, and its new friends include some of the most distinguished squares alive," echoed a Columbia Records producer in *Down Beat* that same year.

Playboy, the new gentleman's magazine sensation, described its ideal reader as a jazz fan. Hollywood had begun to infuse hard-hitting films like

The Man with the Golden Arm and *Sweet Smell of Success,* and such television shows as *Peter Gunn* with jazz—or at least "jazz-ish"—scores. The likes of Dave Brubeck and Erroll Garner had led a wave of jazz musicians onto campuses around the country. Blue Note, Prestige, Verve, and newer independent labels like Riverside and World Pacific were doing well, selling beyond a niche market of just-jazz collectors to a more mainstream demographic. Meanwhile, majors like RCA, Columbia, Decca, and Capitol made sure they had records by a number of jazz (or jazz-ish) artists.

Whether the definition of jazz was strict or loose, it was enough to create a general perception within the music business that the music was popular enough to warrant the type of investment Taylor was asking the ABC brass to make. And the move dovetailed with the general cover-all-bases strategy of the company, as Newton admits.

> We had a big company, and I believed that diversification was the way to go. Command Records didn't have anything to do with jazz—it was easy listening. There's a certain following who loves jazz [and] jazz was about seven or eight percent [of the market]. I got offered a few jazz labels. Bobby Weinstock [of Prestige Records] tried to sell his label to me. But I didn't want to just buy a jazz label.

Another motivating factor for the ABC decision-makers Bill Kaplan distills to one word: "Catalog. One thing that we used to discuss is that jazz is a catalog item. It's like classical [music.] You're not going to make a lot of money in any one year out of jazz, but it's something that will always be there."

What his higher-ups strategized and discussed, Taylor pursued by instinct. He knew that he wanted to kick off with a spread of music styles, with each album different from the other ones, and that each should be somehow timely—artists or projects that were new and unusual—yet timeless as well, carrying historic weight that might play out in long-term sales. In short order, Impulse's first groundbreaking wave—four albums that would bear catalog numbers A-1 through A-4 (with an added "S" for the stereo editions)—came together: J.J. Johnson and Kai Winding's *The Great Kai & J.J.,* Ray Charles's *Genius + Soul = Jazz, The Incredible Kai Winding Trombones,* and Gil Evans's *Out of the Cool*.

THE FIRST WAVE

Calling on two friends from his Bethlehem days, Taylor convinced J.J. Johnson and Kai Winding to revive their mid-fifties twin-trombone quintet concept, adding a sympathetic rhythm section that accented melodic grace: pianist Bill Evans, bassist Paul Chambers (or Billy Williams), and drummer Roy Haynes (or Art Taylor). The album title, as per Taylor's habit, preceded the actual recording: *The Great Kai & J.J.* [A(S)-1]. Guryan recalls that, despite Taylor's experience with and respect for Johnson, not all went smoothly at the outset.

She remembers one situation with J.J. Johnson, who did not want to record at Rudy Van Gelder's. "Creed was an enormous fan of Rudy as an engineer, his studio, and he recorded just about everything there. J.J. felt it was too live—it was all redwood [in the ceiling] and he felt the sound bounced off the wall. One day he stormed out of Creed's office. There was kind of some kind of internal signal and I went running out of the building and onto Seventh [Avenue] after J.J. I finally caught up to him, and I felt just great at being able to talk him back into Creed's office. Creed said he would do what J.J. wanted, which was to put baffles up—a lot of baffles. The situation did get ironed out and he finally did record at Rudy's."

The name of the person who first proposed the idea of a Ray Charles title as part of Impulse's debut now seems lost in time, but Taylor clearly recalls that with ABC heavily invested in the R&B star and equally committed to the idea of a jazz label, joining the two was logical and inevitable, even to the head of sales. "That's when Larry Newton became involved. He arranged for Ray Charles to do this package, and with Ray, I got Quincy [to arrange half the album] because Quincy was a very good friend of Ray from childhood. Ralph Burns arranged the other half of the album, and the Basie band was available." Taylor's memorable title for the album played off Charles's familiar sobriquet: *Genius + Soul = Jazz*.

Certainly, all involved were aware of Charles's last major project for Atlantic Records, the 1959 album *The Genius of Ray Charles*. Half the album presented Charles fronting a big band peopled by well-known Basie and Ellington sidemen, with Quincy Jones providing the charts. The other half featured him with a string section, arranged by Ralph Burns, who first came to Charles's attention through a singer Taylor had produced.

GENIUS + SOUL = JAZZ

Ray Charles / *Genius + Soul = Jazz* / Impulse A(S)-3

DATE RECORDED: December 26 and 27, 1960

DATE RELEASED: February 1961

PRODUCER: Creed Taylor

"If you want to tell the truth about it, when I first went over there, I started doing things that was really abnormal."

Ray Charles was speaking of his initial projects for ABC-Paramount. The label had invested heavily in Charles, who, up till his departure from Atlantic Records, was exclusively known as an R&B star. "ABC got me because they wanted a rhythm-and-blues artist on their label, but then when I got over there I started doing things like 'Georgia on My Mind,' which nobody thought was gonna work," he said.

Charles looked back on *Genius + Soul* as one more liberating step that his sweetheart deal with ABC-Paramount afforded him: the chance to expand beyond one specific musical genre and prove his mettle in a number of styles. His first two ABC albums were thematic, covering tunes that spoke of specific locales and specific ladies, respectively.

"Then I did this *Genius + Soul = Jazz.* I must say I didn't have any problem. Sometimes they said to me, 'Ray, we think you're screwing up your career. You want to do this, you want to do that. You're going to lose a lot of fans.' My attitude was, 'I may lose a lot of fans, but I think I'll gain more fans than I'll lose.'"

The challenge, stressed in pianist Dick Katz's liner notes, was to convincingly present Charles as a jazz instrumentalist (read: improviser) and composer (in big-band form). "'Ray can do jazz as well,'" Charles recalls the notes saying. "Yeah. That's what it was all about." To achieve this, he switched from his usual Fender Rhodes electric piano to the more churchy Hammond organ, accompanied by the Count Basie band. He chose to perform originals and a few covers powered by the hard-blowing arrangements of Quincy Jones and Ralph Burns, with ample room for improvisation by Charles and a few noted jazz soloists.

"You've got Clark Terry, Phil Woods, and whoever else with the solos, Ray's vocals, Quincy *and* the Basie band." To the normally sedate Creed Taylor, it was a formula that was bound to succeed and still excites. "What was I worried about? It was time for some magic, but not constricted [to a] 45 rpm format to get a hit."

In fact, the session did yield a charting single, a romping instrumental cover of a well-known vocal-group song, "One Mint Julep." In 1952 it had been a no. 2 R&B hit for the Clovers on the young Atlantic label; almost ten years later, as Impulse 800, it made no. 8 on the pop singles chart. A vocal fill in the song, it turns out, was Taylor's idea.

"Do you know that little vocal break in 'One Mint Julep'? White boy that I was, I said, 'Ray, when it comes at whatever bar it was, why don't you put in, "Just a little bit of soda" with the mint julep?' He did, but it came out, 'Just a little bit of soul, now.' It was almost soda!"

"Ray was very cool. No hard time. No artistic behavior at any point. And of course, he did the whole thing on the Hammond B-3. I'm sure he had played it at some point, but I don't recall too many recordings where he was. But if you listen to his Hammond B-3 sound, it's not like that organ which was so popular in jazz at the time. Rudy [Van Gelder] got inside the Hammond and did some very special things to it so that the attack was different. It didn't sound the same way in other studios."

Charles agrees, remembering that the Hammond had a problem that day. "But the public didn't know that the thing had a distortion in it. If you listen to my playing you can hear it, you'll know. But that's not the point. It's the magic in the music, man, which causes you not to even pay that no attention." And Charles still credits Van Gelder for his help.

"One of the things I feel that made that album so great was the sound of that studio. It had a great sound. It took me three hours to find that damn studio. We drove all around everywhere because it's way up in the woods, you know."

Quincy Jones recalls flying in to make the session. "It was in the snow. I had just been stranded in Europe for ten months with my band and I was working in the Birdhouse in Chicago and I came in and went out to Jersey [the Van Gelder studio in Englewood Cliffs, New Jersey], writing an arrangement on 'Mint Julep' in the station wagon [laughs]. That was the [song] that made all the noise. I'll never forget it because that's when Ray first got me into eighth notes, really. We took a jazz arrangement and put it in eighth notes."

Was it a true jazz album?

"I mean, an eighth-note feel is, well, not the antithesis of swing. But it is in a way because it's a different concept from doing just a straight four [4/4 time]. [The album] was really based on the rhythm and blues of the time, all that was coming in right after the big bands and bebop."

Besides the hit single, *Genius + Soul* sported a variety of material: Basie blues ("I'm Gonna Move to the Outskirts of Town"), hard-bop gospel (Bobby Timmons's "Moanin'"), big-band vocals ("I've Got News for You," a blues based on a Charlie Parker solo popularized by Woody Herman), and a number of Charles's own compositions, including the raucous flag-waver "Let's Go!" (replete with a frenzied Frank Foster saxophone solo and a quote of the NBC chimes—G-E-C—at the close).

Ultimately, *Genius + Soul* afforded a healthy boon to the nascent Impulse, proved the fourth-highest-charting album in Charles's career, and provided the R&B star the confidence necessary to attempt an unheard-of crossover on his next album for ABC-Paramount.

"Then I did a country and western album [*Modern Sounds in Country & Western Music,* 1962] nobody thought was gonna work. Did I know [*Genius + Soul*] was going to be a hit? I never thought about music that way. I never have, man. I've always wanted to do one thing: to make the music, in itself, as good as I can make it. Now, if it was fortunate enough to turn out to be a hit, fine. You must remember I've done a lot of music that was not a hit—quote, unquote—but it was damn good music and I can listen to it today."

"Atlantic sent me material they were recording of their other artists and that's how I got a certain Chris Connor release," Charles recalled. "I was particularly struck by the strings. So next time I talked to my friends at Atlantic in New York I asked them: Who wrote the strings for the Chris Connor record? Ralph Burns, they said."

Both albums sported liner notes presenting the same case: Ray Charles can play jazz. The writers—journalist Nat Hentoff on the Atlantic LP and pianist Dick Katz on the Impulse—based the weight of their argument on the fact that Charles was so respected in the jazz community. As Charles wrote in his autobiography, his passion for and understanding of jazz were unquestionable.

> To my mind, the average listener doesn't appreciate the technical feats of most jazz artists. I've heard people say what a bitch Mozart was, and yet in the same breath they'll tell me they can't hear what Charlie Parker was doing . . . Classical music is already written, it's a matter of interpretation. But with jazz—oh yes—with jazz you got to compose as you go . . . I suppose that's why I'm always proud that I can play jazz and why it isn't any accident that I've always wanted to make jazz records and have a true-to-life jazz band.

Taylor remembers that Charles's name and reputation as a radio star lent an added boon. "If you didn't have radio, you were just kidding yourself. The way to let people know about what you had was to get it on the radio, whether it was jazz, pop, R&B, or whatever. [Without radio airplay] Impulse would've really been just a hobby kind of thing." Thinking back on the state of jazz radio in 1961, Taylor remarks:

"There were certain jazz radio stations that were like bridge stations to the pop world—for instance, WMCA [in New York] had a jazz program on late. They had leverage that would get the attention of some of the bigger non-jazz stations. You'd build [a single] at the jazz level and then you'd get it pushed up to the big stations who had somebody on at midnight or an odd hour of the day that would play something that really had pop potential. That's the way we worked it." What ABC prepared to "work" was the single "One Mint Julep" from Charles's one and only Impulse album. "It was a pretty heavy single. It just had all the elements to launch a new line."

Not to ignore Kai Winding's then-current working group, Taylor was happy to commit Impulse's third title to the four-trombone septet—Winding called it a "trombone choir"—he had led since breaking up with Johnson in '56. "Kai Winding was a personal favorite of mine," Taylor says. "I loved that brash, kind of raucous approach that he had to playing. I could pick his sound out of Stan Kenton at any point. The idea of recording his choir was Kai's." Taylor's choice for title: *The Incredible Kai Winding Trombones*.

Taylor call his final choice "the most unique. I think I can say that he was the most unique arranger out there then—composer, colorizer, whatever you want to call him—Gil Evans." Being a longtime fan of the proto-cool, classically influenced Claude Thornhill big band of the forties, the producer had long sought the chance to work with Evans, one of the group's former arrangers. "Both Thornhill and Evans knew that less is more—that concept didn't start with Miles."

By 1960, Evans had earned renown through his association with Miles Davis on the legendary *Birth of the Cool* sessions in 1949 and 1950, and with a trio of collaborative successes the two created for Columbia Records: *Miles Ahead, Porgy and Bess,* and *Sketches of Spain* (the last released in early 1961). The arranger's perfectionist, even exhaustive studio approach dovetailed with the Impulse template for high-quality, carefully crafted productions.

> I liked arrangers. I first heard Gil Evans's arrangements at a dance at Duke that the Claude Thornhill band played—I just got goose bumps. Then to come to New York and actually meet Gil Evans, I couldn't believe it. He picked his bands man for man, very carefully. What he had done for the Thornhill band, with Gerry Mulligan and Lee Konitz and those French horns, I knew he would do for Impulse. Now we could work together.

Through November and well into December, Impulse's first recording sessions took place, all at Taylor's favorite studio: Rudy Van Gelder's in Englewood Cliffs, New Jersey, which also offered high-quality mastering. Guryan still marvels at Taylor's focus on the sonic quality of those sessions.

> The first four records were enormously different from anything that happened before. Creed came back with test pressings and for the first time he had me listening to a *record,* not the music, listening for surface noise—the pops and

clicks—and then to the imbalances in the recording. Is this too high? Is this centered? It was a totally new experience for me when Creed came back with the Ray Charles and the Gil Evans pressings.

Impulse's birth announcement was made on December 5, when enough of the plans were ready to allow for feature coverage in *Billboard* ("ABC-Paramount Bows Jazz Label—Impulse"), and included the label's *raison d'être*:

> Impulse was set up as a separate label because Am-Par prexy Sam Clark thinks a jazz line should be sold to the public as a separate entity (a la Am-Par's best-selling Command and Grand Award labels) rather than associated in a jazz fan's mind with ABC-Paramount's pop artist roster—Paul Anka, etc.

Clark promised "a totally coordinated merchandising effort," pointing to one more benefit that would boost Impulse out of the starting gate: though a "separate entity," it was serviced by the same promotion and sales force that all ABC-Paramount releases enjoyed.

"We only had one promotion man for all our labels—Irwin Garr," remembers Sid Feller. "And he handled whatever promotion people were on the road." As head of promotion for the entire company, Garr marshaled his forces and, as Taylor tells it, did not hesitate to use the label's pop prowess to deliver its new jazz child into the marketplace. "ABC-Paramount Records was getting stronger and stronger. To have a solid merchandising machinery in place, and then to put this Impulse thing into that, helped immensely."

The *Billboard* story first revealed another aspect of Impulse's grand design: evocative titles that—with wit and hip, poetic lingo—delivered an underlying conceit. *Genius + Soul = Jazz* referenced Ray Charles by popular alias and delivered the album's goal algebraically; *Out of the Cool* suggested a new, musically bolder phase for Gil Evans.

ABC-Paramount Bows Jazz Label—Impulse

NEW YORK—ABC-Paramount Records is bringing out a new label, Impulse, a de luxe double-fold LP series, featuring only modern jazz artists. Creed Taylor will head up the new label, which debuts next month with releases by Ray Charles, Kai Winding, J. J. Johnson, and the Gil Evans ork.

The advent of the new label—which will retail at $4.98 monaural and $5.98 stereo—is interesting in that ABC-Paramount was quite active in the jazz LP field some time ago, but more or less retired from the field in recent years.

Taylor, who has handled Am-Par jazz activities since its inception, said the firm's re-entry into the jazz market was sparked by the current upswing in jazz sales—both albums and singles. In line with this, Impulse will issue a single from every LP release, and will make 33⅓ stereo singles available to juke box operators.

Impulse will concentrate on modern jazz artists exclusively. There will be no reissues or traditional jazz packages in its catalog. Taylor believes the current jazz market is so competitive that only by maintaining a small roster of top jazz names can a new label break thru in a big way.

Impulse was set up as a separate label because Am-Par prexy Sam Clark thinks a jazz line should be sold to the public as a separate

(Continued on page 14)

> I tried to juxtapose the visual on the album cover with the title itself. A title like *Out of the Cool* . . . I chose because they're combinations of words that grab you and make you think, "What is it?"

One month into 1961, jazz-friendly consumers, wandering into stores and picking up the deluxe, highly visible albums with Creed Taylor's signature intact, began asking the same question.

FIRST IMPRESSIONS

> They were slick and they had that Saran Wrap around them. So you didn't know much because they didn't give you any information on the back except the names of the tunes—the liner notes were inside.

So says Gary Giddins, still in junior high school in New York City but already a jazz fan with a critical eye when he witnessed the label's arrival in early 1961. "When you first started going through the racks and looking at Impulse, you just felt like you were walking into this very hip world, because they didn't look like other records. Not Blue Note, Prestige—any of them."

In Gulfport, Mississippi, John Lee Johnson—later known as Jaimoe with the Allman Brothers—was a teenage drummer well under the influence of jazz.

> I can remember going in this store and there were all these new colorful-looking albums, man. All of these were like the finest album covers on the market! Even over rock 'n' roll records and stuff. I don't know what the first Impulse record was that I bought, though—*Ray + Soul = Genius + Soul,* or something.

There is little doubt that Ray Charles's contribution at the outset was invaluable. "I don't think it would have had the springboard without Ray, of course," notes Taylor. "He had the acceptance at all levels—pop, jazz, whatever." Charles's own reaction to the idea that he helped launch an important jazz label was more humble: "I'm not gonna blow no horns, man. That's nice if they think that way." In fact, the single from the album—an instrumental version of "One Mint Julep" with Charles's memorable aside

OUT OF THE COOL

Gil Evans / *Out of the Cool* / Impulse A(S)-4

DATE RECORDED: November 18, 30, and December 10, 15, 1960

DATE RELEASED: February 1961

PRODUCER: Creed Taylor

Though a familiar name in the jazz world through most of his career, arranger Gil Evans's recorded output was always limited; 1961 was a marked exception.

In October 1960, the Jazz Gallery, a new theater-sized venue in Manhattan, was the site of an unusually generous six-week engagement for Evans. It was his longest gig as a leader up to that point, enabling him to assemble a working group featuring such rising and risen stars as trumpeter Johnny Coles, saxophonist Budd Johnson, trombonist Jimmy Knepper, guitarist Ray Crawford, bassist Ron Carter, and drummer Charlie Persip. The extended gig also served as the launch point for Evans's debut on Impulse.

With the addition of drummer Elvin Jones on

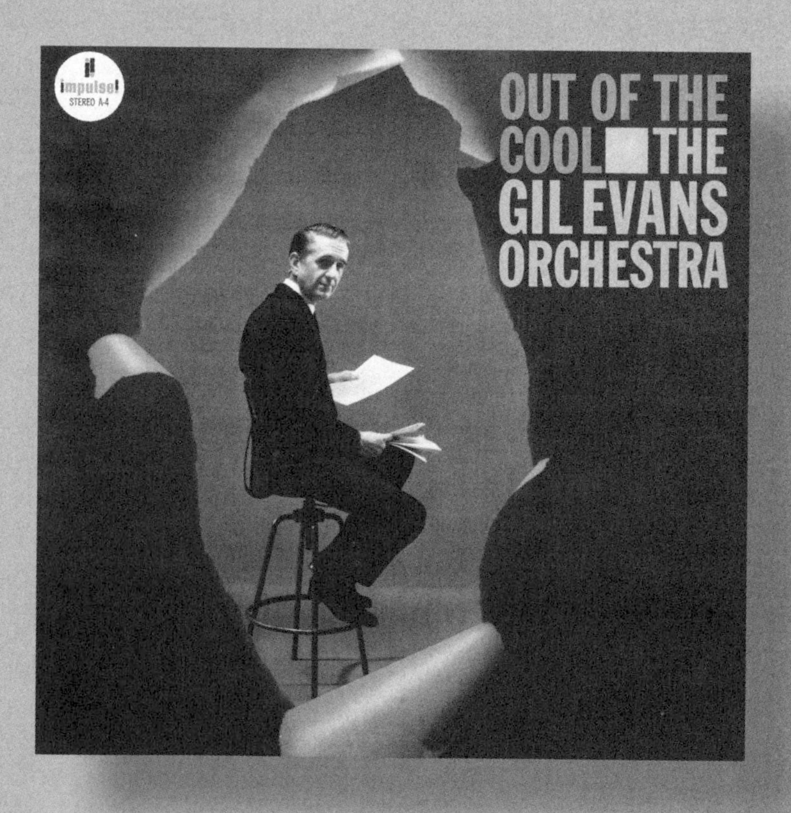

loan from John Coltrane's quartet, Evans took his fifteen-piece lineup into the studio and, as he later reported, "made the album in an afternoon." As Evans biographer Stephanie Stein-Crease writes, the album actually resulted from four visits to Rudy Van Gelder's studio; the three previous sessions were essentially rehearsals.

That Taylor had the insight and patience (and budget!) to allow Evans such license says much of the producer's confidence in the arranger's ability to eventually find his mark. Taylor recalls the album's fifteen-minute-plus centerpiece:

" 'La Nevada' was not only original but was totally spontaneous. . . . Gil started noodling at the piano for a while, and he started this thing, and the rhythm section started doing something and then something sparked in Gil. . . . The other pieces were a little more arranged. But we didn't get any of them down until he got whatever it was on 'La Nevada' out of his system."

They had found their groove. In rapid succession, Evans and the group nailed the rest of the album—the haunting ballad "Where Flamingoes Fly," with an evocative Knepper solo; the tension-filled bass vs. horn section duel of "Bilbao," featuring Carter; George Russell's blues-based "Stratusphunk"; and Evans's own "Sunken Treasure," highlighted by the Spanish feel in Coles's pained phrasing.

Upon its release in early 1961, *Out of the Cool* (a title chosen by Taylor, slyly referencing Evans's involvement with Miles Davis's historic *Birth of the Cool* sessions), with a cover photo of Evans throwing a cool glance over the shoulder (shot by noted portraitist Arnold Newman), peeled away layers of obscurity and pushed the arranger into the mainstream. Before the year was out, Miles Davis's hugely successful *Sketches of Spain,* arranged by Evans, elevated Evans's reputation to a career high point.

"When he is not concerned with the requirements of a specific soloist (and sometimes even when he is)," enthused John S. Wilson in the *New York Times,* speaking of *Out of the Cool,* "Mr. Evans can weave patterns of colors, rhythms and dynamics with an individuality of approach and sureness of touch that have been matched in jazz only by Duke Ellington."

Beyond that, Wilson added, "*Out of the Cool* must set some sort of high standard for an introductory disk from a new label."

Gil Evans, 1958.

"Just a little bit of soul, yeah!"—was a Top Ten hit on the pop charts and stands as Impulse's lone charting single. "One Mint Julep"—Impulse 200—would prove Charles's fourth Top Forty hit out of a staggering twenty-five over an eleven-year period (1960–71) for ABC-related labels. It also hit no. 1 on the R&B countdown, reaching another goal for Taylor.

> In the sixties, black consumers formed a solid base of support for new jazz product, number one. Whether it be Ray Charles, Gil Evans, or later Oliver Nelson. I mean, if you think about it, who were the usual jazz people at that point anyway? In addition, it was easier back then to break into black radio with a jazz record—if it proved popular late at night [when most jazz was broadcast] they would then move it to more prime-time slots.

Recalling his efforts, the normally soft-spoken producer is still enthused by Impulse's out-of-the-box success. The label, he says, was "a landslide on all fronts! Radio airplay, distributors running out of stock. *Genius + Soul = Jazz* sold 150,000 LPs within a couple of months! There was nothing else out there like that."

Music professionals of the day agree. Eliot Tiegel, who was *Billboard*'s West Coast bureau chief at the time, says the Impulse albums "knocked me out. They were spectacularly done and I found the music challenging and exciting. And you knew Impulse was spending a lot of cash to package this stuff. They took it one step beyond what Blue Note had done, what Savoy and the smaller independents had done." Bruce Lundvall, in mid-'61 a recent recruit in Columbia Records' marketing department, recalls Impulse almost creating a new jazz standard.

> It was overwhelming. In those days there was a whole aura about making the LP more sexy with gatefold jackets and extensive notes and extra stuff. I remember we had meetings about packaging and making [the albums] look more rich and more handsome, for jazz in particular. We had rigid standards in terms of costs and so we didn't go in that direction. But for a label like Impulse with that independent view, it was possible [and] it made a big impression.

George Avakian, who had been in charge of jazz and album sales at Columbia Records, was at Warner Bros. when Impulse first hit. He offers his take on how the upstart label fit into the 1961 business landscape.

> They were priced at $5.98, which was $2 more than the usual price for regular twelve-inch pop LPs that we had established some years earlier at Columbia. Knowing Newton as I did, I have to assume that the loss of volume was made up by the additional profit margin. The advertising and promotion was tastefully conservative. Impulse was not major competition to Columbia, which remained the leader in jazz recording for years after I left. Atlantic was definitely no. 2. After that it was a mixed bag which included such very different companies as Impulse and the various Norman Granz labels [like Verve]. Among the labels right behind these was Pacific Jazz/World Pacific, whose regular-style LPs—like Atlantic's—had high quality standards. They also had a "look"—even more unified from one LP to the next than Columbia's—which gave those companies quick identification, something which Impulse achieved better than anyone else.

Phil Kurnit points to another measure of ABC-Paramount's commitment to the deluxe look of Impulse, recalling that in the early sixties the cost of gatefolds and artwork pushed the cost of packaging to nearly a dollar per LP, almost double what a standard LP cover cost: fifty-five cents.

Impulse's sensational start was another feather in the cap—and lucre in the till—for ABC-Paramount. "Impulse made an immediate profit," notes Sid Feller, "so it became an important label for ABC." In a few short months the label was rooted in the minds of jazz fans, deejays, and record retailers, with the momentum carrying over to the next wave of Impulse releases, as Taylor relates:

> A real pattern began to develop with the onset of Impulse. Retail was really excited about those first four albums, and as a result got really excited about the next releases. Remember the record store [E.J.] Korvette? I remember the buyer there saying, "My customers come in and don't ask me what I have new, they ask what I have new on Impulse." Then *Blues and the Abstract Truth*—Oliver Nelson—did pretty well.

ANOTHER ARRANGER

Taylor had already approached Oliver Nelson to record an Impulse title during the label's long gestation period in 1960. In mid-February 1961, as Impulse's four-title debut made it to market, the producer focused on

THE BLUES AND THE ABSTRACT TRUTH

Oliver Nelson / *The Blues and the Abstract Truth* / Impulse A(S)-5

DATE RECORDED: February 23, 1961

DATE RELEASED: August 1961

PRODUCER: Creed Taylor

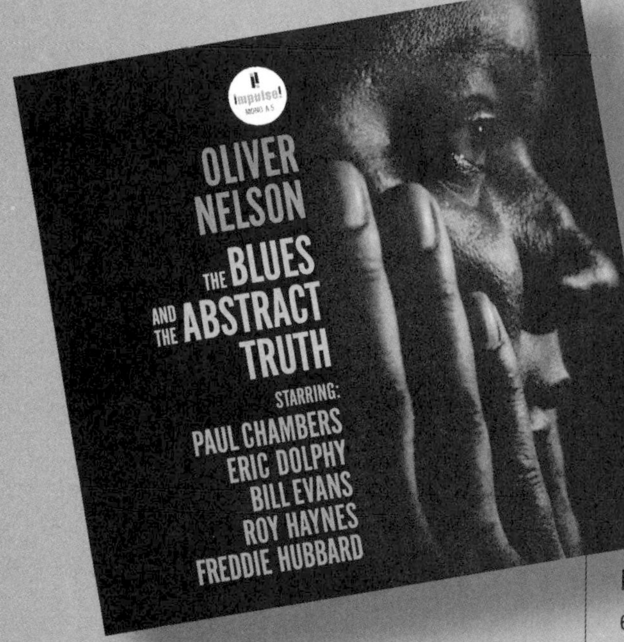

"That's my title. . . . If the blues is a truth, why not then add 'the abstract truth'? The word 'the' was supposed to be there—'*The* Blues,' you know? It was like, pardon the term, our white brothers dropped the 'the.' Still—it just worked."

Creed Taylor, familiar with Oliver Nelson's recordings as a leader on Prestige, was attracted by an unusual aspect of the saxophonist's personality.

"Oliver was so articulate, personally, that we could talk about a lot of things. He had a background in the history of music—classical or whatever. We both had the same hobby, by the way: H.O. trains. Oliver built a logging camp in his basement and I built the Norfolk & Western railroad, which went from Norfolk to Columbus, Ohio, in mine. Coal trains—not Coltrane. Oliver and I had a lot in common, so it enabled us to talk about music in a comfortable way."

Contracted to a one-record deal while he continued to record for Prestige, Nelson brought a band of young scene-makers—some established, some very new—to Rudy Van Gelder's studio for his Impulse debut: saxophonist and flutist Eric Dolphy, pianist Bill Evans, baritone saxophonist George Barrow, bassist Paul Chambers, drummer Roy Haynes, and trumpeter Freddie Hubbard.

"Me, Phil Woods, Oliver—all those guys were playing with Quincy," remembers Hubbard. "So I had a chance to hang with them, and then Oliver asked me to do the date with him. Oliver liked me because at the time I was practicing with Coltrane. He would be writing even while he was with Quincy . . . and he had a way of writing for saxophones, close notes among the reeds.

"He got some voicings, man, that were out of this world! Like when he did [sings "Stolen Moments"], he had the baritone up above the tenor; to have a baritone voiced that high is unusual. And he had the alto below the tenor, and he had me playing the lead."

In fact, Hubbard received the honor of the first solo on the album, though the trumpeter recalls a few misgivings as the tapes rolled.

"I didn't know it would sound that good because he didn't turn me up as loud as I thought I should have been. But he wanted me to blend with the horns instead of being out front. I remember the fact that I said, 'How is this rhythm section going to gel?' I mean, Roy Haynes doesn't play heavy and it seems like Paul Chambers was always on top with a big sound. So Roy would just lay back behind him, and I didn't hear Bill Evans until the playback because he played so quiet."

Taylor was as enthused by Nelson's sidemen choices as he was by the arranger's enthusiasm. "Everything Freddie Hubbard played knocked me out. And what can you say about Bill Evans? He was in great shape playing-wise. And Oliver was very animated. He wouldn't just give a downbeat or count the band off, he would leave the floor! Jump up in the air and come down right on the downbeat. I'm sure his blood pressure went through the ceiling every time he conducted or played. I don't mean out of control, but he just felt every ounce of what was happening."

And the tunes?

" 'Stolen Moments' was a given—just, whew!" Taylor enthuses. " 'Cascades' was the most unusual piece and 'Yearnin'' was just fantastic. I had never heard anything like it before, but I understood it. 'Hoe-Down' was kind of weird, I felt. . . ."

"He had this song on there, 'Hoe-Down,' that I'll never forget," says Hubbard. "I said, 'Man, what is this song?' [Sings melody.] To me it was kind of out of context, but he took a lick that I had stole from Trane and he put that on the bridge. [Sings.] He built it off of that line. Oliver wasn't so much of a soloist as he was a writer, so he would take bits and parts of people's stuff."

Released in the spring of 1961, *The Blues and the Abstract Truth* proved career-defining for Nelson, an instant hit on jazz and even non-jazz radio, and eventually led the in-demand arranger to move to Los Angeles in 1967. Taylor:

"I don't think the word 'crossover' had become part of the language at that point, but I know all the jazz stations at the time really went for it, and other pop stations, which are not around anymore, went full steam ahead on it too. Oliver was such a unique talent and I hated to see him go to Hollywood, where he kind of evaporated."

Partners in modern jazz (and model trains): Oliver Nelson and Creed Taylor, February 23, 1961.

Nelson, a multi-reedman, composer, and arranger whom he had come to know as a dependable saxophonist with a sense of balance.

> Oliver was another story. He was very special—melodic. He understood voicing like nobody else. He had done some dates with me before at Webster Hall [studio], as part of a sax section—he, Al Cohn, and Zoot Sims. There was something different about him at that point. He could blend in with a section, but at the same time he had a sound that was so strident. When he played a solo he was unmistakably Oliver Nelson.

With a handful of unusually angular compositions requiring a septet, Nelson recorded an album that received the full Impulse treatment: state-of-the-art sound (thanks to Rudy Van Gelder,) mood-setting cover portrait (courtesy of Pete Turner), and a cryptic title the producer himself concocted. *The Blues and the Abstract Truth* [A(S)-5] became Impulse's first title after the label's explosive debut, and yielded a second substantial jazz radio hit with the mood-setting "Stolen Moments."

Nelson himself wrote the album's liner notes, explaining the motivation and structure behind his tunes, praising his sidemen, and confessing that when he had first arrived in New York City, "I believed I had my own musical identity" until falling under the spell of two tenor saxophonists he "could not deny"—Sonny Rollins and the man Taylor had already pegged as Impulse's next project: John Coltrane.

ANOTHER LEAP FROM ATLANTIC TO ABC

By 1961, Coltrane's sound was one of the most influential in modern jazz, his brooding, vibrato-free tone and startling, searching style on tenor saxophone making his sound one of the music's most recognizable.

Coltrane's role as an innovator was respected and revered, but the persistent flux in his style could be divisive and controversial. It was process, rather than polish, that defined his sound. He constantly strove for original expression, juggling a tireless intellectual curiosity, pushing the limits of harmony, melody, and even his instrument itself, with a deep, church-inspired instinct that grew from his earliest years in North Carolina. He adopted a vocabulary of bluesy slurs and register-hopping screams—biting down on the reed, overblowing certain passages—that he had learned during his bar-walking R&B days in early-fifties Philadelphia. He repeated phrases as if wringing every possibility out of scales and note combinations, pushing his solos to unusual lengths. He was determined to avoid familiar melodic patterns and instead cut through the structures of tunes with unusual flourishes and oddly balanced fanfares, as if determined to out-bop the bebop heroes of his youth.

"He had that eruptive feeling that [Charlie] Parker had—of exploding into chords—but wasn't playing Parker's clichés," says his fellow saxophonist Jimmy Heath, who blew and grew up alongside Coltrane from the time they both were teenagers.

Coltrane first arrived on the national jazz scene in 1955, handpicked by Miles Davis to replace Sonny Rollins in the quintet that became the trumpeter's first great band. In five short years, he vaulted from a sideman role—with Davis, Thelonious Monk, then Davis again—to the status of leading bandleader, composer, and recording artist. In the spring of 1960, signed exclusively to Atlantic Records, he released a best-selling album that retooled a familiar Broadway show tune *and* resurrected an almost forgotten instrument. His version of "My Favorite Things," a waltz number from the musical *The Sound of Music,* proved a radio and retail sensation and reintroduced the reedy sound of the soprano saxophone to the world. And to one producer, it laid bare the saxophonist's commercial potential.

"I first met Coltrane at Rudy Van Gelder's [studio] in the fifties," recalls Creed Taylor. "He was just mind-boggling. A poet, but not a verbal poet. He really spoke through his horn, and what a lot of things he had to say." After catching a late-December show at the Village Vanguard, Taylor was inspired to pick up the phone. "I just called John, asked him if he'd like to record with Impulse."

At this point—had business proceeded as usual, had Coltrane simply asked for and received Atlantic's permission to record a "one-off" project for a competing label—this tale would almost certainly have been different: no singular artist-label relationship, no House That Trane Built.

Until Coltrane, two of Impulse's headlining artists (J.J. Johnson and Oliver Nelson) and three significant sidemen (Bill Evans, Eric Dolphy, and Freddie Hubbard) remained exclusive to other record companies while, per long-standing tradition in the music community, temporarily "on loan" to Impulse at Taylor's request. Coltrane himself struck such a one-album deal back in 1957, recording the classic *Blue Train* for Blue Note Records while still under contract to Prestige. For a jazz label needing to deliver new albums, "one-offs" had become a common way of doing business. The cost of doing a single album was simply more affordable than a multiple-album deal and limited the hassle of deal-making and career management, according to Phil Kurnit.

> The financial aspects of the deal were much easier with the one-shot deals: "OK, we're gonna pay you three, four, or five thousand dollars to do this album." We could put together artists for far less than it would have cost to keep the artist to an exclusive deal and we weren't involved with their careers . . . That's how you remain the good guy. Once they depend upon you to do this that, that, and the other thing—and then you're not doing the things that an artist wants you to and it's "I'm not making enough money!" I guess it still applies now.

Taylor agrees, suggesting that a good working relationship was more secure than a well-written agreement: "I felt more secure if musicians were available, to be perfectly blunt about it. If you had a meeting of the minds and it resulted in an artistic and commercial success, then they were going to stick with you. If I had a good relationship with them, I didn't need a contract."

But as Impulse looked to its sixth title, Coltrane would not be loaned out. This time, the artist was looking for a commitment. Why? Primarily, according to Bill Kaplan, because he could demand it.

> The Shaw Agency, which represented John Coltrane, felt that after having done some great records for Atlantic, he needed special treatment. He was not in the class of Ray Charles in the way of sales and popularity, but they felt something similar to Ray's deal should be used.

The Shaw Agency, a booking agency that offered management support in addition to securing appearances for its clients, was well aware of Charles's sweetheart deal with ABC-Paramount: the agency represented Charles as well. In addition, Coltrane was assisted by Harold Lovett, a savvy and respected attorney who also represented Miles Davis. He was "a smart businessman, as I recall," reports Taylor. "He got along with Harry Levine very nicely." Adds Kaplan:

> So John came in and we knew the kind of contract that he wanted. He didn't command the same kinds of advances as Ray would and there was no question about the fact that the company owned all the masters. But to a great extent the deal was based on the bare bones of Ray's.

With Impulse's track record, Taylor easily persuaded Levine to tell his superiors they should pony up the necessary funds to secure Impulse's first exclusively contracted artist. "They worked out the Coltrane deals and the contract," Taylor says. "I just wanted Coltrane with the label." The generous deal that lured Coltrane from Atlantic included a $10,000 advance for the first year, with two-year options that rose to $20,000 annually thereafter.

Kaplan is quick to point out that Coltrane was an aware and active participant in following Charles's footsteps from Atlantic to ABC. "It wasn't as if we stole John from Atlantic. He walked in! But then, most artists wanted to move on up. Get bigger money and bigger exposure, more distribution. They wanted to better themselves."

COLTRANE THINKS BIG (BAND)

In mid-'61, Coltrane revealed an awareness of his new contractual commitment and a desire to follow up his triumph at Atlantic.

"I know that I've got to make three records a year, and I'm always walking around trying to keep my ear open for another 'Favorite Things,' or something," Coltrane told journalist Ralph Gleason with a laugh in 1962. "Commercial, man! I used to go in the woodshed all day and practice and that was all there was to it, and I didn't have to worry about it."

Whatever pressure the saxophonist was feeling, Taylor maintains that the approach and context of Coltrane's debut on Impulse were not predetermined or dictated. "I didn't say anything—I just told him when the date was going to be. We would talk about whether it was a big band record or a live record or whatever it was going to be."

Since his first recordings as a leader in 1957, Coltrane had grown accustomed to choosing the shape and scope of his recordings, within limits. He was not used to the resources Impulse was able to offer him: extended studio time if necessary. In the small circle that was the New

York City jazz community, he would have been as conscious of the label's willingness to back up an expanded project as Taylor was of Coltrane's musical focus at the time.

> It was a pretty tight little clique there—the real jazz, "get out and make a living doing this stuff." I knew that John was intensely interested, along with George Russell, in the modal, African kind of music, just from talking to Bill Evans and Oliver [Nelson]. And I of course knew that he hadn't recorded anything with an ensemble like that.

Coltrane was familiar enough playing charts and unison parts, having spent his earliest professional years in the saxophone section of large bands led by trumpeter Dizzy Gillespie and alto saxophonists Earl Bostic and Johnny Hodges. The ensemble Coltrane chose to assemble was slightly different from those in his past, a brass-heavy big band built around the core of his quartet: pianist McCoy Tyner, bassist Reggie Workman, and drummer Elvin Jones. Taylor scheduled two separate sessions in early June at Rudy Van Gelder's—a happy return for the saxophonist, who had not recorded with Van Gelder since joining Atlantic in '59, and still preferred him to other engineers. From his conversations with Coltrane, the producer had a name ready for the project: "*Africa/Brass*—it sounds like a big band, a whole tribe, or whatever. And the music was that way: just drums at times and almost like sound effects that Eric [Dolphy] created with the arrangements." Though enough material was recorded to later fill a double-CD reissue package, only three tracks made it onto the original *Africa/Brass* package: "Africa," "Greensleeves," and "Blues Minor."

By reputation alone, Coltrane was able to attract the cream of New York City talent to participate—but the true VIP of the sessions was reedman Eric Dolphy, who pinch-hit for an absent Oliver Nelson as arranger, basing his charts on Tyner's rich, modern voicings. The material—some composed on the spot—often held rhythm as a priority, while Tyner's take on the age-old ballad "Greensleeves" was the follow-up to a recent hit. "We play 'Greensleeves,'" admitted Coltrane, "sort of like 'Favorite Things.' It doesn't have as much contrast because we're not going from a major vamp to a minor, but it does have a good mood if it's in the right tempo."

As one door closes, so another opens. *Africa/Brass* [Impulse A(S)-6] marks the beginning of the consequential and fruitful relationship between Coltrane and Impulse, and stands as the first of only two big-band projects by the label star during his career (*Ascension* in 1965 would be his far-reaching return to a large ensemble). But *Africa/Brass* also serves as a sad bookend: the last project Creed Taylor would complete for the label that he had brought down the long road from concept to reality.

THE CALL FROM VERVE

It seemed almost inevitable. As Impulse's star continued to rise and shine brightly, so its creator brought attention on himself. Before the summer of 1961 was half over, before Impulse itself was even a year old, Creed Taylor was approached by Metro-Goldwyn-Mayer to take over Verve Records. Just six months before, the Hollywood-based entertainment conglomerate had purchased the label from its founder, Norman Granz, for $2.5 million, and the company wanted the right person to oversee its investment.

> I got the call from Arnold Maxin, who was running Verve and was actually a former trombone player. He called and talked to Sam [Clark] and Sam said, "You need him worse than I do, I guess, so OK." At that time, they had just bought Verve from Norman Granz [the previous December], and what are they going to do with it? Well, they said, "Get this guy because that's what he did across the street." So I came across the street with Verve.

Verve also happened to be the label that Taylor associated with a production style he would rather avoid. "I thought I could do something Norman Granz certainly didn't do, because he was obviously very set in his ways about freedom in the studio. The musicians loved him because all they had to do was go in and play a lot of swinging stuff, just solo after solo without any particular form to it."

To be fair, since its days recording music associated with the jam-oriented *Jazz at the Philharmonic* series, Verve had developed a reputation in the late fifties based more on lush, articulate productions (the Ella Fitzgerald songbooks, Fitzgerald's landmark collaboration with Louis Armstrong on *Porgy and Bess*). Taylor's feelings about the label's roots notwithstanding, the unique opportunity and generous offer to follow in Granz's footsteps were not lost on him.

AFRICA/BRASS

John Coltrane / *Africa/Brass* / Impulse A(S)-6
DATE RECORDED: May 23 and June 4, 1961
DATE RELEASED: November 1961
PRODUCER: Creed Taylor

To Creed Taylor, Coltrane's debut for Impulse was an inspired plan: "I certainly thought that the big-band idea was good. because of all of the colors they could put together with the subject matter."

To Freddie Hubbard, it seemed more about rhythm than anything else: "All I remember was the groove. He wasn't so much interested in the songs on that record. 'Greensleeves' was the one everybody started listening to, but it was just the groove. He wanted the African sound."

To Coltrane himself, it all began at home: "I have an African record—they're singing these rhythms, some of the native rhythm, so I took part of it and gave it to the bass and Elvin [Jones]. . . . McCoy [Tyner] managed to find some kind of chords. . . . I had to make the melody as I went along."

The two-day *Africa/Brass* sessions in mid-1961 were a reunion, Coltrane's happy return to working with Rudy Van Gelder, in his new Englewood Cliffs, New Jersey, studio, and—as Taylor points out—an unusual extravagance. Coltrane was provided the chance to expand his lineup (he employed up to seventeen pieces on some tracks) and use the studio as a workshop and rehearsal space.

"There were no restrictions," Tyner remembers. "Rehearsal time was in the studio. Most things on that album happened in the studio setting."

But on the day of recording, an important element was missing. "Oliver Nelson would've been involved, but something happened," Taylor recalls. Though trumpeter-bandleader Cal Massey, Coltrane's old friend from Philadelphia, brought in a few tunes (notably "The Damned Don't Cry," which was recorded but left off the original LP) and Tyner did too, charts and

arrangements were woefully lacking. Enter Eric Dolphy.

"Eric Dolphy was immensely original and talented, at peace with himself and the world, but he didn't talk very much," Taylor remembers, commenting on how the reedman, soon to be a Coltrane sideman, orchestrated the music on site.

"I'm a little ashamed, in retrospect, that I didn't instantly light up and say, 'Wow!' I'd listen to Eric and I thought, 'This was going to be some really out-there recording, but I'll go for it anyway.' Eric was so advanced that it took me a while to kind of get the feeling of what that was all about at that time. You've got to remember how far back that was. Advanced harmonically, melodically jagged. What the hell's he doing? It's Stravinsky all over again in jazz music! Or Bartok string quartets. A lot of critics and insiders knew about Eric Dolphy; I never got to know him that well, except just at these sessions."

Tyner still feels a need to define Dolphy's contribution to the album.

"They said that Eric had written the arrangements, and that's incorrect. I wrote the arrangement for 'Greensleeves' and Eric just looked at my voicings on the piano, what I was playing under the melody of 'Africa.' He said, 'Wow, what are you doing?' So I showed him what I was doing and he orchestrated that."

Hubbard, who sat alongside such fellow brass players as Booker Little (trumpet), Julius Watkins (French horn), and Bill Barber (tuba) during the sessions, provides further insight.

"I remember Eric did the arrangements and had us doing the African calls—with the horns. I was just playing backgrounds—and listening. I wasn't trying to solo or nothing. I remember he had two bass players, Richard Davis and Jimmy Garrison.

"Coltrane wasn't playing so far out then. But he had so much energy, man, because him and Eric used to drink honey out of the jar. They would eat those sunflower seeds and raisins. They were on an energy kick. I said, 'Man, you're going to get diabetes or something, man! You drinking raw honey?'"

Upon its release, *Africa/Brass* left jazz critics behind, as Coltrane's music often did. It was praised, but with qualification. "If one looks for melodic development or even for some sort of technical order or logic, he may find none here," Martin Williams complained in *Down Beat.*

But as the years progressed, an entirely new generation of fans found something more important in Coltrane's first Impulse album: a portal into the deep emotionality of his music.

"In 1965 we were on the road, somewhere out in the Midwest, supporting the *Mr. Tambourine Man* album," recalls Roger McGuinn, the Byrds' founding guitarist and singer. "[Guitarist-singer] David Crosby had a friend who invited us over to his house. He had the Coltrane album that contained 'Africa.' I was just blown away. I'd heard the more Dave Brubeck-y kind of stuff, but never anything that kind of pushed the envelope. I felt an actual pain in my chest. It wasn't a heart attack or gas pain, it was like some emotional pain, like it was opening up a new emotional area. It hurt at first, and then I liked it."

"We never heard Coltrane live after the band started, so it was the recordings we would lean on," remembers bassist Phil Lesh of the Grateful Dead. "Mainly it was *Africa/Brass.* [Drummer] Billy [Kreutzmann] really got off on Elvin's drum solo on 'Africa'; for the other guys, it was pretty much the whole composition and the way it all developed, the use of the horns and stuff like that. And then just for the quality of Trane's playing, 'Blues Minor' is one of my favorites."

> I mean, I *had* planned to come to New York and do something that Norman Granz hadn't been doing with *JATP* [*Jazz at the Philharmonic*]. They offered me a lot of money, but it was really the artistic challenge—Verve offered me a lot of talent: Ella, Dizzy, Basie. That was the real attraction. "Wow! Wait till I get across the street and get into some of that!" It was just unbelievably exciting anticipating what was going to happen. Of course, I signed a lot of artists, too: Stan Getz, Tom Jobim, Bill Evans, Cal Tjader, Jimmy Smith.

And, as Taylor recalls, one former Impulse artist as well: "Gil [Evans] came over to Verve and we did a lot of things together."

Taylor's switchover proceeded rapidly: June 4 was the second session of Coltrane's *Africa/Brass* album for Impulse at Van Gelder's studio. July 14 was the first session of Getz's sax-and-strings album *Focus* for Verve, recorded at Webster Hall. For the few weeks in between, the producer remembers closing up shop on one side of Broadway while starting up business on the other. "I was floating; the MGM offices were just across the street. John came over and we finished editing *Africa/Brass* at Verve!"

Taylor had initiated three other Impulse albums, which his new obligations at Verve prevented him from completing. Two survived the producer's departure to become five-star classics, both featuring drummers.

Art Blakey's emphatically titled *Art Blakey!!!!! Jazz Messengers!!!!!* [Impulse A(S)-7] was a small-group session powered by one of the Blakey group's most legendary lineups: saxophonist Wayne Shorter, trombonist Curtis Fuller, trumpeter Lee Morgan, pianist Bobby Timmons, and bassist Jymie Merritt. Max Roach's meticulously constructed and self-produced *Percussion Bitter Sweet* [Impulse A(S)-8] was the politically charged follow-up to his *Freedom Now Suite* from the year before, benefiting from a few of the same soloists (vocalist Abbey Lincoln, trumpeter Booker Little, trombonist Julian Priester) and new talent (Dolphy, tenor saxophonist Clifford Jordan, pianist Mal Waldron, bassist Art Davis). Margo Guryan, already at Verve with Taylor, wrote the liner notes at Roach's request.

"I was staggered!" Guryan recalls. "Max and I somehow became friends when I was at Lenox [School of Jazz]. I remember that the actual production credit was his. It was interesting in that the music was supposed to be programmatic and [at the session] Max would go around telling each instrument,'You're this and you're that and you are responding to this person in this way.' That sort of thing. He explained it to me very carefully."

Max Roach with choir: the *Percussion Bitter Suite* session, August 1961.

But the last of Taylor's final three projects for Impulse is arguably the strangest, and certainly hints at the lack of a firm hand on the wheel in the fall of 1961. With album covers already manufactured bearing the name and image of Gil Evans for the arranger's next album, Evans chose nonetheless to approach the project more as a contractual obligation than a follow-up to *Out of the Cool*—as the title *Into the Hot* suggested. During two recording sessions in September and October of 1961, Evans opted to sit in the producer's chair in the studio control room, having handed over his album to the music of—and performances by—trumpeter (and Thornhill alumnus) John Carisi and avant-garde pianist Cecil Taylor.

Interestingly, *Into the Hot* was eventually released as Impulse A-9 in early 1962, while Evans's first album for Verve, *The Individualism of Gil Evans,* would not be recorded until the fall of '63. What seemed another Evans album was anything but.

Evans "got ahold of Cecil Taylor and me," recalled Carisi. "He got his own group, I got up my own group, and Gil acted as an A&R man. He sat there in the booth, and asked for certain things to be played over again . . . he didn't write one note. If you read the liner notes, you see that everything was done by other people."

"We just kind of wound up with that *Into the Hot* thing," shrugs Creed Taylor today, equally matter-of-fact about his departure from the label that launched and defined his career. "I just don't look back. I was there and that was that."

EXIT CREED

Taylor's exit left ABC-Paramount with three significant things. First, there was the label that had just begun to flower, already boasting an established identity. "At first there was this 'Who in the heck is an Oliver Nelson and what is *Blues and the Abstract Truth*?' kind of thing," says Taylor, but "soon enough there was a thread of 'Well, what do you mean? It's on Impulse! It's good-looking, great-sounding stuff.' "

Second, Taylor left ABC with a dire need to find a jazz-savvy producer. And third, as would prove of increasing value, he left behind Impulse's contract with Coltrane. "Look—I'm being very careful. I don't want to use the wrong description of what Coltrane was [because] there's such a mystique surrounding this artist, this man, now. But in terms of mass acceptance, it didn't exist then—it took time."

After a moment's thought, the producer adds: "I don't think he was getting helped by Impulse as much as he was helping Impulse. He could have gone to 'No-pulse' and remained quite solidly, successfully Coltrane."

A-17
STEREO A-18 IMPULSE!
STEREO A-21 IMPULSE!
STEREO A-22 IMPULSE!
STEREO A-23 IMPULSE!
STEREO A-24 IMPULSE!
STEREO A-26 IMPULSE!
STEREO A-27 IMPULSE!
A NOVA & JAZZ SAMBA STEREO A-28 IMPULSE!
ILTON QUINTET STEREO A-29 IMPULSE!
STEREO A-30 IMPULSE!
MONO A-31 IMPULSE!
STEREO A-32 IMPULSE!
MONO A-33 IMPULSE!

CHAPTER 2 THE RE-EDUCATION OF BOB THIELE (1961–1962)

For me, there are three different types of producer. First, there's the documentarian . . . then there's the Phil Spector type, where the whole thing is conceived in his brain . . . and then the third type I have no name for, but I can define it as "serving the artist." Most of the producers in this last category are original jazz fans and record collectors: John Hammond, Chris Strachwitz, Ahmet and Nesuhi Ertegun, Bob Thiele . . .

—Jerry Wexler, 1998

Depending on whom one asks, Bob Thiele was inventive or manipulative, modest or self-aggrandizing, a connoisseur or a hustler. On one quality all agree: he had a knack for maximizing the circumstances of a long, checkered career. Creed Taylor had the foresight to plant the seeds of Impulse, and Thiele had the good fortune and drive to bring the label to full maturity, nurturing it from 1961 to 1969, through its most fruitful years.

Thiele's dedication to jazz was sincere, constant, and in line with Taylor's. Yet the differences between Taylor and his successor at Impulse could not have been more pronounced. Thiele, New York born and bred, was in no way soft-spoken or demure. "A New York street guy," Sid Feller remembers him with a chuckle, "a Broadway cowboy." "An ingenious A&R man" is Archie Shepp's take. "A wheeler-dealer."

"He had what [in Yiddish] is called *seichl*—good, common sense. Horse sense," says Dan Morgenstern, who helped Thiele launch *Jazz* magazine in 1961. He offers a thumbnail sketch of the man whose story kicks off the second chapter of the Impulse story.

> He was a veteran record producer, an old hand at dealing with the vagaries of the business. From the start, he was a rich man's son, had a little money to play with, had a few of his own labels but they never achieved any kind of commercial stability—they always went down the drain. But he was a good talent spotter. Creed Taylor brought Coltrane to Impulse, but Thiele was able to see that there was something there, and he established a rapport with Coltrane.

Thiele was born in 1922 into what he termed "Sheepshead Bay aristocracy," referring to a neighborhood in Brooklyn, New York, where his mother's family owned Lundy's, the popular restaurant that served as a local landmark. His father had amassed a small fortune as a bulk chocolate salesman. Thiele attended private schools and, growing up during the heyday of swing, took up the clarinet, formed a high school dance group, and deejayed on a series of local radio stations. He assiduously followed the big bands led by his heroes Duke Ellington and Benny Goodman. Before turning eighteen, the precocious teenager had added to his list of accomplishments a magazine called *Jazz* (a precursor to his later publication) and a record label called Signature.

In the years before and during World War II, drawn by Thiele's fresh-faced enthusiasm, a host of New York–based jazz greats recorded for Sig-

Starting early: Bob Thiele promotes one of his first releases on Signature, 1945.

First forays: two early Thiele productions from the 1940s.

nature: clarinetist Pee Wee Russell; guitarist Eddie Condon; pianists Art Hodes, James P. Johnson, and Erroll Garner. But it was Lester Young and Coleman Hawkins—the two most responsible for first defining how jazz should be played on the tenor saxophone—who helped raise the young label and its founder to national prominence.

Young's recordings of "I Got Rhythm," "Linger Awhile," and "I'm Fer It Too" and Hawkins's "Get Happy," "Crazy Rhythm," and "The Man I Love" have all grown to be considered rarefied small-group classics, prefiguring the solo-focused magic of the bebop era. The last tune, an extended version released in 1943 on the unusual twelve-inch (as opposed to ten-inch) 78 format, is especially noteworthy: it provided Signature its first financial flush, and Thiele one of his earliest in-studio anecdotes.

> The reason this "The Man I Love" turned out as one of the few twelve-inch 78s in commercial release was simply because Coleman Hawkins wouldn't quit. He'd take extra choruses. We were recording at radio station WOR on Broadway in the middle of the night, and right during the middle of that record a cleaning woman walked in with a mop, intent on cleaning the studio. I literally walked out into the studio, put my finger to my lips to be quiet, then held her arms. They played, and I'm holding a struggling cleaning woman while one of the most immortal solos in jazz history was being recorded.

As it happens, a mere two decades later, Thiele would again help create jazz immortality with another tenor player given to extra choruses and late-night sessions. But no charwoman interrupted any John Coltrane recordings; by all reports Rudy Van Gelder kept his studio perpetually, fastidiously clean.

Discharged from a tour of duty with the Coast Guard that kept him safely in the New York area, Thiele entered adulthood already in a tight community of seasoned, self-made record men. They were fueled by passions for jazz and rhythm and blues, for artists overlooked by the pop-driven major labels of the day. They fought the good fight to get their records onto the airwaves and into stores, and to get paid. Thiele experienced the same financing problems and distribution headaches as other collectors-turned-producers of the day, like Atlantic Records' Ahmet and Nesuhi Ertegun, Prestige's Bob Weinstock, and Blue Note's Alfred Lion and Francis Wolf.

But while labels like Atlantic slowly built themselves up, Thiele's lack of sound financial practices, plus a predilection for the good times, prevented Signature from ever taking hold. It's almost impossible to run a business while on spontaneous, party-filled road trips to New Orleans or Hollywood, but Thiele tried. Little surprise, then, that the enterprising label head eventually became an itinerant record producer, seeking a home for his talents and his catalog of jazz recordings.

Decca was the first major company to take in the young producer, placing him in charge of its secondary label, Coral. Home to more established hitmakers like Bing Crosby, the Mills Brothers, Guy Lombardo, and others, Decca had formed Coral to compete for a slice of the independent market Thiele once called home. "I suppose I was the logical 'anti-establishment' sort for the damage my job mandate required" is how the producer remembered it.

At Decca, Thiele followed in the footsteps of another jazz enthusiast hired into the pop world: Milt Gabler, whom Thiele dubbed the champion of his "budding record business career." Eleven years Thiele's senior, Gabler first gained fame as founder of Manhattan's retail jazz mecca of the thirties, the Commodore Record Shop, and its namesake jazz label, the country's first independent record company. Commodore Records specialized first in reissues and later in a catalog of its own making, including most famously Billie Holiday's anti-lynching lament, "Strange Fruit," as well as "hot jazz" (Eddie Condon, Bobby Hackett, Pee Wee Russell), traditional jazz (Jelly Roll Morton, Willie "The Lion" Smith), boogie-woogie (Albert Ammons), and noteworthy big-band soloists (Lester Young, Ben Webster).

A comparison of Gabler's and Thiele's respective careers shows them to be uncannily parallel. They both turned teenage passion into booking

Record men on the town, sometime in the mid-fifties. Note Milt Gabler (third from the right), and Bob Thiele (clowning, sixth from the right).

shows and founding jazz publications. With limited or no musical education, they established independent labels, recording their jazz heroes while still remarkably young, and ended up in the pop realm working for Decca, producing the likes of the Andrews or McGuire Sisters. Later, they orchestrated rare studio meetings of jazz legends (Armstrong and Fitzgerald by Gabler for Decca; Armstrong and Ellington by Thiele for Roulette).

Ironically, the two producers also both helped midwife the musical phenomenon that ultimately pushed their first love—jazz—off the popular radar. Gabler produced rock 'n' roll's popular birth cry, Bill Haley and the Comets' "Rock Around the Clock," for Decca, while Thiele signed one of the genre's first great singer-songwriters, Buddy Holly, to Brunswick, a Decca label.

In short order, Thiele confirmed Decca's confidence. Pushing a more jazz- and roots-oriented approach with pop stars like the McGuire Sisters, Pearl Bailey, former Signature artist Alan Dale, and Thiele's future wife Teresa Brewer, he created hit after hit. In 1957, as the pop charts began to give way to a new sound called rock 'n' roll, a music publisher delivered the producer a recording by a guitarist-singer from Clovis, New Mexico. Thiele jumped when he heard Buddy Holly's "That'll Be the Day" and immediately signed him.

Thiele proved prescient in grabbing the young songwriter, and wily in dealing with the in-house resistance to what he recalls was dismissed by many in the industry as "hillbilly garbage." Decca didn't mind taking a chance on Holly, but grew nervous that his R&B sound might taint the mainstream image Coral had developed, adversely affecting the label's other hitmakers of '57, Debbie Reynolds and Lawrence Welk. Ever the discophile, Thiele came up with a solution.

> Brunswick [Records had been] devoted to "race music"—a prior euphemism for rhythm and blues—so I went back in and said, "We have to release this record ['That'll Be the Day'], and if all of you are so concerned about the image of Coral, put it out on the Brunswick label."

A string of influential rock 'n' roll classics by Holly ensued—alternatively on Brunswick (as the Crickets) and Coral (as Buddy Holly). The reactivated Brunswick label soon became home to another best-selling singer, Jackie Wilson, and Thiele's golden touch seemed unassailable, his position at Decca secure. Nonetheless, after nine years of producing hits beyond expectations, Thiele felt less than adequately compensated by his higher-ups and departed in March 1958 for three years of label-hopping. His creative impulses still seemed destined to put him at odds with those above him, while his path was bent on returning the pop producer to his first love: jazz.

A few months after joining Dot Records (home to whitewashed teen crooner Pat Boone) and producing albums with Louis Armstrong, composer Manny Albam, and trumpeter Red Nichols, Thiele recorded Jack Kerouac reading his Beat poetry while TV host Steve Allen, a former Coral artist, played jazz piano. The resulting album drew critical praise and the contrasting ire of Dot's morally outraged president. Thiele stood his ground and was summarily fired; the producer joined forces with Allen, resurrecting his old label and releasing *Poetry for the Beat Generation* on the new Hanover-Signature imprint.

A less contentious stint at Roulette Records, run by music mogul Morris Levy (who also owned the famed jazz nightclub Birdland), afforded Thiele the chance in April 1961 to pull off the singular coup of uniting Armstrong and Ellington in the studio. The resulting albums, *Together for the First Time* and *The Great Reunion,* featured Ellington as the guest pianist in Armstrong's band, the All Stars, performing all Ellington material. The session established a "jazz summit" formula Thiele would reprise in future years at Impulse, as well as access to two important jazz legends he would call on repeatedly.

In addition, the successful pairing of two legendary jazz figures helped re-establish Thiele's presence on the music scene, and toward the end of that summer, an expanding ABC-Paramount approached Thiele to join the label as an in-house producer. Interestingly, the offer came not because of his jazz roots, according to Creed Taylor: "Sam Clark [the president of ABC Records] knew Thiele from his days as a Boston distributor—he would have been more impressed by Teresa Brewer's music than any jazz Thiele had done."

Years later, Thiele noted, "What a lot of people don't realize is that most of the recordings that I've made through the years have been pop records." He also admitted that his years on the commercial side of the business did little to prepare him for the modern jazz he would soon encounter.

> I must confess . . . there was a period, when I was working at Decca, Dot, and Hanover-Signature, when I was really not keeping up with the new jazz players and the new music. I think I heard one of the Ornette [Coleman] records on Atlantic, and I didn't hear [Eric] Dolphy until I worked with him at Impulse. . . . Basically I was a pop producer, the old-time type of pop producer, making a living and taking care of a family. I'd always try and do some jazz recordings, but the jazz thing was always really for pleasure, and I never could make too many records wherever I worked.

Thiele's recollection calls to mind Creed Taylor "sneaking" jazz in among his other projects at ABC-Paramount before the creation of Impulse. But Thiele espoused a production philosophy that differed from Taylor's hands-on approach—and separated pop from jazz. "Those [pop] records were made strictly with me in complete control, directing balances, the songs, the arrangers, the artists themselves. But in the jazz field my style has always been to let the guys play and let them know when I feel they have it right."

What was common to both jazz and pop production—and paramount in Thiele's mind—was personal satisfaction.

> The finished product was, I think, a reflection of what I was satisfied about, what I liked. And that was it. The same thing even applied with pop records. The pop

> recordings that I made were almost made for me. I wasn't thinking about the audience, the masses out there. I was making records that I could take home and enjoy.

No matter the style of music, the bottom line was the bottom line. This was nothing new to Thiele, a veteran producer and A&R man: "It was all left up to the A&R guy in those days as to who to record, when to record, how much to spend. Then you worked closely with the sales department. But the A&R guy was the important guy. Everyone relied on the A&R man to have the hit records. . . . If you don't have hits, you get your walking papers."

Creed Taylor had already crossed Broadway for his new home at Verve when Thiele arrived at ABC's offices above the Paramount Theater. More spontaneous than planned, the decision was made by ABC to replace Taylor with the newly arrived "resident 'jazz freak' record executive," as Thiele liked to describe himself. "I was already working for the ABC pop label, recording people like Frankie Laine and Della Reese. But once I knew that the Impulse thing had opened up, I said, 'Hey, let me take a shot at it.' "

It was November of 1961, and to Thiele it must have felt like waking up to all his Christmases at once. He had been handed a successful jazz label to run, with a significant degree of freedom to run things on his own—as long as Impulse remained profitable. And yet Thiele's enthusiasm was surely tempered by a dose of ambivalence. Within days of his arrival, he found himself in a cramped basement room, fifteen steps below Seventh Avenue South, getting a crash course in a new style of jazz.

> I don't think I was at Impulse more than a week when we decided to record Coltrane live at the Village Vanguard. . . . That first night, as I recall, I was pretty shook up; I was confused. But by staying involved, the music began to make sense to me.

For four straight nights, Thiele sat next to Rudy Van Gelder, another Impulse asset the producer was fortunate to inherit. Van Gelder laughs when recalling the less than studio-perfect conditions of a recording process he still describes as "evenings in hell."

> It was smoky and crowded and I'm sure the club wasn't too happy with me taking up two tables near the bandstand. We had no [recording] trucks back then—I had

> my mixing console and one tape deck right next to me. We didn't have a lot of the things that you can just run out and get today. I did my best to find headphones, like they use in airports, to keep out the sound of the club [to hear what was being recorded] and then the music itself! But that was the nature of Coltrane—very dense and intense.

As challenging as the situation was to the engineer, so the music was to the producer. Coltrane was in the midst of a rapid series of experiments—he seemed to shift into top gear every four years (the velocity of his progress and variety of his output in the years 1957, 1961, and 1965 suggests such a cycle). He eschewed his recent hit "My Favorite Things" to try out new material, both original ("Spiritual") and very traditional ("Greensleeves"). He was playing with different lineups—Eric Dolphy on some tunes, Ornette Coleman's bassist Jimmy Garrison in place of his regular sideman Reggie Workman on others. His signature saxophone sound—dark, at times desperate in its search—had left behind its bebop-born reliance on harmony and was pursuing a melodic course. The spontaneous charge of the impromptu blues-blowing on "Chasin' the Trane" was surely like nothing Thiele had heard before.

Thiele remained curious nonetheless, despite Coltrane's tight-lipped nature. He reported finding the saxophonist "at first extremely withdrawn and reticent to talk about anything," adding to the nervousness the producer felt at the outset of the week.

"Typical of most musicians who meet a record company executive for the first time, he warily eyed me like an off-the-rack empty suit to be most judiciously tried on before any possible purchase could be contemplated," he recalled. But "as the music progressed and Trane became comfortable with the surroundings and results," Thiele was happy to find that "his natural warmth and friendliness surfaced, and we hit it off."

> I'll never forget this as long as I live; he said, "You grew up in the swing era . . . so you always go like this [snapping his fingers with a regular beat]. You keep time that way." He said, "With our music, you got to flow back and forth so as the bars go past . . . you really go 1, 2, 3, 4 . . . 1, 2, 3, 4 . . . 1, 2, 3, 4 . . ."

Next to Creed Taylor's convincing ABC-Paramount to fund the establishment of a jazz label, it could well be argued that those conversations at

LIVE AT THE VILLAGE VANGUARD

John Coltrane / *Live at the Village Vanguard* / Impulse A(S)-10

DATE RECORDED: November 2–4, 1961

DATE RELEASED: March 1962

PRODUCER: Bob Thiele

Coltrane's set list in late '61 was a quixotic mix: popular originals ("Naima," but not "Africa"), recently recorded tunes ("Greensleeves," but oddly not "My Favorite Things"), and new compositions that drew inspiration from foreign sources ("India," "Brasilia"), modal jazz ("Miles' Mode," "Impressions"), and traditional folk songs ("Spiritual"). Engineer Rudy Van Gelder, with mixing console set atop a commandeered table near the Village Vanguard bandstand, captured it all on tape.

The eventual album, released in early 1962, distilled numerous reels of live music down to one disc with three tracks. "Spiritual" and the standard "Softly, as in a Morning Sunrise" constituted Side A, but it was Side B that first drew attention (and derision) and set ears atilt, and for which the album is now celebrated. Later generations revere "Chasin' the Trane" as the birth cry of sixties avant-garde jazz: an outpouring of stylistic tongues and melodic ideas that linked the bebop dexterity and daring of the past with a free, stripped-bare, spiritually charged future.

Van Gelder recalls "Chasin'" primarily as a challenge, with Coltrane swinging his saxophone and stalking the small stage of the basement club (hence the title, which the engineer himself suggested). To Coltrane himself it was merely an impromptu blues—no theme, no opening statement, pure solo—that featured his horn, Jimmy Garrison's bass, and Elvin Jones's drums. It was the first time the bassist had played with the group. And significantly, no piano. "The melody not only wasn't written out but it wasn't conceived before we played it. We set the tempo and in we went," Coltrane recalled.

The avant-garde firebrand Archie Shepp, a Coltrane acolyte: "I was living in a loft in [New York's] East Village in 1962. I heard my neighbor's record player booming and I knew it was Trane. But the piano never came in. As he began to develop the line it became clear that the structure wasn't so apparent and he was playing around with sounds: playing way above the normal scale of the horn, neutral and freak notes, overtones, and so on. I found it as shocking a piece of music as Stravinsky's 'Rite of Spring' was in his day."

A fifteen-minute solo on tenor saxophone—especially in the context of 1961—must have seemed at least indulgent. What was Coltrane up to?

"It's basically a blues," Shepp explains. "But where the song's form is much less important than the melody itself, and the relation between the melody and the rhythm. Sonny Rollins had worked without piano before, but his playing was primarily harmonically oriented—and Ornette Coleman too, who was totally aharmonic. Coltrane was able to integrate the two, to put everything in context, in such a sophisticated way that it influenced everybody. [Without the piano] it's the point where the Coltrane Quartet became an avant-garde trio."

Rather than simply a zero hour for free jazz, Shepp sees the tune more as "a synthesis of what came before. You could say that it's free jazz, but it's not totally free because there are still very strong structural indications: chords, harmony. Trane said that *Giant Steps* [1959] was sort of the end of one phase where he had exhausted all of the permutations of chords. 'Chasin' the Trane' was another door that opened: the use of sound for sound itself.

"I think it's one of the most innovative pieces in the history of African-American improvised music, as important as Charlie Parker's 'Ko-Ko' [1945] or Coleman Hawkins' 'Body and Soul' [1939]. That's the greatness of Trane, that he always kept the feeling of dance and the spiritual elements so important to what they used to call 'hot jazz.' That's why his peers all respected him so much, because he didn't throw the baby out with the bathwater."

Critics of the day often diverged in their opinions on Coltrane. But in "Double View of Coltrane 'Live,'" twin reviews in *Down Beat* in April 1962, Ira Gitler and Pete Welding seemed to agree on "Chasin' the Trane." "More like waitin' for a train—a 100-car freight train—to pass," judged the former. "Sputtering inconclusiveness" and "a frenzied sort of soul-baring," wrote the latter.

Present-day judgment has been more generous. To producer Bob Thiele, it was a "musical mega-nova": "Physicists have long debated about the existence of a 'big bang.' Without any question the jazz equivalent occurred during that seismic quarter-hour." Gary Giddins sees in "Chasin'" "one of those crucial performances in which we can hear the subversion of a sensibility and a yearning for new worlds."

Indeed, if it can be said that there was one moment when Impulse took a leap of faith and yoked its fortune to that drive for the new—sharing Coltrane's path—it is here.

the Vanguard, Coltrane explaining his music to Thiele, stand as the most important event in the Impulse story. Out of those discussions came a fruitful, label-shaping relationship, and a most unusual level of trust.

To put it in perspective, the moments of epiphany that mark the history of the music industry are few but significant: The legendary talent scout and producer John Hammond catching Count Basie's band on a late-night radio broadcast. Sun Records' founder, Sam Phillips, hearing the voice of Howlin' Wolf, or Elvis Presley, for the first time. George Martin discerning a certain potential in a Liverpool quartet, then agreeing to produce the Beatles.

Rarer, however, is the occasion when a veteran pop producer sets years of experience aside and allows a sincere shift in his own musical values to take place. Thiele was almost forty years old when he listened to Coltrane and realized what he had to do. "Once I was at Impulse, I made up for lost time. I think that I was exposed to, and digested, about eight years of music."

It wasn't just about one groundbreaking saxophonist. For Thiele, Coltrane proved the door-opener to a whole new world—the first step on a learning curve that continued through the remainder of the producer's career as music progressed through the free, the amplified, and other changes of the late twentieth century.

"The best thing that happened to me was meeting Coltrane and working with him," Thiele later stated. "That association lasted for about five years, and we did an awful lot of work together."

THIELE HITS THE GROUND RUNNING

Thiele followed in Taylor's footsteps—and did it running. Before the end of 1961, he recorded a number of sessions that added a variety of popular titles to the Impulse catalog (Coltrane's *Live at the Village Vanguard* [A(S)-10], Curtis Fuller's *Soul Trombone* [A(S)-13]) and introduced a few more established artists: Quincy Jones's *The Quintessence* [A(S)-11], Benny Carter's *Further Definitions* [A(S)-12], and Milt Jackson's *Statements* [A(S)-14].

More impressive is the fact that through 1962, Thiele produced a wide-ranging list of stellar albums that have become career high points for three successive generations of jazzmen, such as *Count Basie and the Kansas City 7* [A(S)-15]; Jackie Paris's *The Song Is Paris,* Impulse's first excursion into vocals [A(S)-17]; Max Roach's *It's Time,* an ambitious fusion of choir and small group [A(S)-16] ; Roy Haynes's *Out of the Afternoon,* featuring the young reedmaster Roland Kirk [A(S)-23]; and *The Artistry of Freddie Hubbard* [A(S)-27]. To fully appreciate his workload, consider that between 1959 and mid-'61, Creed Taylor completed approximately eight Impulse and fifteen ABC albums. Even today, an in-house jazz producer who delivers, say, ten titles of new music a year is considered in-demand and extremely busy. In the last two months of 1961 and through the end of '62, Thiele recorded music for *twenty-five* Impulse albums—an annual pace he would maintain through his eight-year run at Impulse.

Though difficult to pinpoint exact release dates with available resources, an accurate charting of Impulse's increased productivity is possible through session dates. The label recorded music for four new albums in 1960, then ten in '61, twenty in '62, twenty-five in '63, twenty-one in '64, twenty-six in '65, thirty-two in '66, and approximately twenty-five in '67—Thiele's last full year at Impulse. Note that these numbers do not include Thiele's more pop-focused productions for ABC itself (Frankie Laine, Della Reese, Louis Armstrong) nor his second label after 1967, BluesWay! In addition to reviving *Jazz* magazine with editor Dan Morgenstern (eventually replaced by Thiele's then-girlfriend, Pauline Rivelli), the producer easily re-established his stature in the jazz world by the end of 1962.

"You want to record with a big band? You got a big band!" is how ABC counsel Alan Bergman recalls Thiele's generous approach, trickle-down largess from ABC's pop successes that helped Impulse stand out from the competition. "The [Impulse] budget was certainly way above the norm for any company making jazz records," stated Thiele.

Adds Bergman: "Bob did certainly provide that entree. How many big-band albums did you have on Blue Note or Prestige, right? The artists didn't get huge advances, but he treated them with tremendous respect. He allowed them financial freedom." Part of that respect lay in the packaging, according to Bergman: "those double-fold albums with the wonderful Chuck Stewart photos on them, and lots of liner notes."

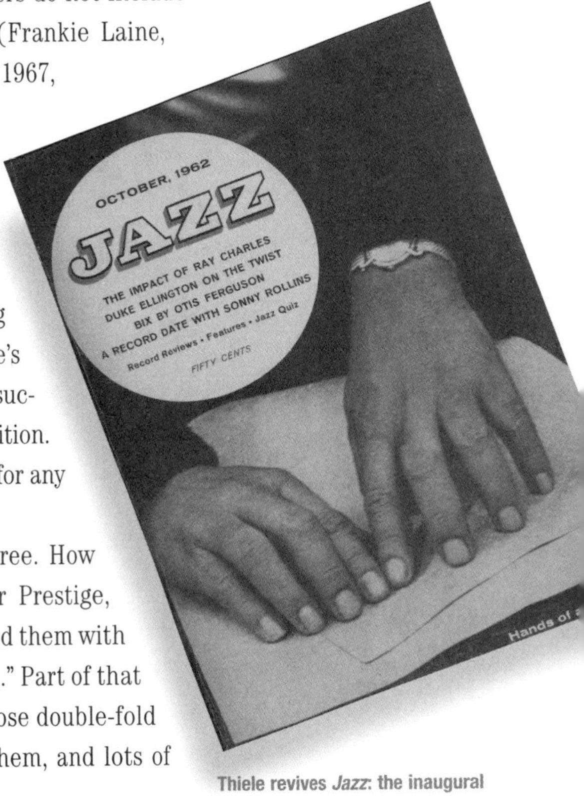

Thiele wisely maintained the attention and budgets devoted to

Thiele revives *Jazz*: the inaugural issue of the producer/publisher's new magazine.

FURTHER DEFINITIONS

Benny Carter / *Further Definitions* / Impulse A(S)-12

DATE RECORDED: November 15, 1961

DATE RELEASED: March 1962

PRODUCER: Bob Thiele

In the mid- to late thirties in pre-war Europe, Coleman Hawkins and Benny Carter blazed a lucrative cross-Atlantic path that generations of jazz musicians would follow. Basing themselves intermittently in London, Paris, and Amsterdam, the two performed in dance-hall orchestras and jammed with local musicians, traveled at will, and enjoyed time away from Jim Crow, and a degree of adulation greater than they had ever received at home. To two French jazz enthusiasts—producer Charles Delaunay and critic Hugues Panassié (author of the world's first jazz reference book, *Hot Jazz: The Guide to Swing Music,* in 1936)—Carter and Hawkins were modern-day cultural giants. When the two musicians crossed paths in their hometown, the two devotees decided to take advantage of the unique opportunity.

Paris—April 28, 1937: Delaunay and Panassié organize a recording session featuring the two with the city's hottest sidemen, pairing Carter with another alto player and Hawkins with another tenor and adding Stephane Grappelli on piano, Django Reinhardt on guitar, and a bassist and drummer. It proves a historic meeting of great American and European swing talent. Carter, famed for his fluid solo style and arranging prowess, brings along fresh arrangements of two pop tunes of the day.

A pair of tracks featuring Carter on his original instrument, the trumpet, were also recorded, but it was those first two performances, "Crazy Rhythm" and "Honeysuckle Rose," that caught the ear of a growing international jazz community. They are still universally revered as being among both Carter's and Hawkins's most important recordings, and, as significantly, were featured on the first release from the French record company Swing—the first jazz-dedicated label ever, anywhere. (Swing preceded the debut of Milt Gabler's Commodore Records in the United States by only a few months.)

When copies of the disc with the Art Deco label crossed the Atlantic, they were immediately embraced by Delaunay and Panassié's American counterparts—a tight cadre of jazz buffs destined for music-focused careers, including Gabler, Jerry Wexler, and a teenage Bob Thiele.

New York—November 15, 1961: In Capitol Records' 46th Street studio in Manhattan, Thiele, only weeks into his tenure at Impulse, decided to reprise the Carter-Hawkins match-up with the same instrumentation. Two altos (no trumpet), two tenors, guitar, piano, bass, and drums performed a hurriedly yet expertly arranged set list prepared by Carter, including "Crazy Rhythm" and "Honeysuckle Rose." Because Thiele regarded the 1937 date as a defining session, he titled the 1961 album *Further Definitions.* As a long-playing statement, Carter's Impulse debut is, according to his biographer Ed Berger, "considered by many not only Carter's finest overall album, but one of the all-time great jazz records."

Nearly twenty-four years had passed since Carter's European sojourn, and in that time his arranging and bandleading talents had become his primary source of income, and Los Angeles his home and workplace. A rare East Coast jaunt caught Thiele's attention and led to the session, as Carter remembered years later.

"I was in New York conducting Peggy Lee [at Basin Street East]. Bob came into the club one night, wanted to know if I wanted to make a session, and I didn't even have a horn with me. I had to borrow one! We had a few days to get it together and I wrote some stuff. [We] did that 'Blue Star' and things like that. And we had fun, it was a very pleasurable date—John Collins on guitar, and that pianist that I love so much. [Long pause, laughs.] My memory isn't what it used to be!"

Dick Katz was the name Carter was striving to remember, and he joined an unusual match of swing veterans and younger musicians that also included bassist Jimmy Garrison, drummer Jo Jones, tenor saxophonist Charlie Rouse, and alto saxophonist Phil Woods, known more for his bebop leanings.

"At that time I was straddling the fence between being a bop guy and doing studio work," says Woods. "I was doing everybody's sessions: Quincy [Jones]'s, [Bob] Brookmeyer's, Ralph Burns's, and Manny Albam's. But the call for Benny Carter—I had to sit and regroup on that one. Alto players make it their business to know other alto players. He was my hero!

"I learned later that any Benny Carter session is totally smooth. He was totally prepared, and exhibited control without being a control freak, and Bob knew well enough to leave Benny and the musicians alone. I remember the charts were for 'old friends': common-denominator material like 'Honeysuckle,' a few Benny originals. Nothin untoward—just the beauty of the ballads.

"As to the mix of musicians—chemistry would be the word. The ingredients Benny chose for the recipe I think were perfect, but I didn't think so at the time. 'This is a strange potpourri of types of musicians,' I thought. But it worked. I had to overcome my initial trepidation, especially with Coleman Hawkins. Everybody else I could handle, but Bean was an intimidator."

"Hawk's entrance on 'Honeysuckle Rose' right after my solo was awesome!" Woods later wrote in the liner notes to *Another Time, Another Place*—another Carter album on which he was featured. "To me it sounds like 'Get out of the way, kid. Let a real man play.'"

Pressed to recall any other memorable moments, Woods replied: "I remember when I arrived, I was very, very nervous, and I used to have a slight drinking problem—not to excess—but I saw that Coleman Hawkins had a pint of Scotch in his case, and man, I can't *believe* I actually asked him to have a taste. So he gave me a little sip to just cool me down, but the look on his face said, 'Hey, why don't you get your own?'"

It had been a date at which life lessons were learned, and lifetime friendships were forged. "I never did that again!" Woods assures, adding that "Benny and I got to be great friends—we made two albums together later, but I think that's a high-water mark. I wasn't aware of why we were doing the tunes we did. I became aware of that when Benny said the session was a remake of the Paris dates. But I was very proud to have been there—that was some glorious history. That was when giants walked the earth, and I was happy to be amongst them, trying not to get my toes stepped on—or other appendages!"

Impulse's distinctive gatefold covers, the label's trademark orange-and-black faithfully preserved to lasting effect. He continued to use many of the photographers Taylor had, including Pete Turner, Chuck Stewart, and Arnold Newman, while discontinuing Taylor's penchant for affixing a signature to each album (though a producer credit remained).

Avoiding the common music industry pitfall of reinventing a winning formula, Thiele built onto the Impulse model—in a number of ways. In 1962, the label briefly tested a folk music identity: "The New Wave of Folk Music" read the altered motto on the back covers of *Alarums and Excursions* [A(S)-24] by Michael Brown (best known as a Broadway lyricist) and *Morality* [A(S)-25] by Oscar Brand, a folk singer who had previously recorded for ABC-Paramount.

But Thiele's initial work at Impulse remained focused on, and most successful with, jazz. Under his stewardship, his predecessor's preference for carefully prepared one-of-a-kind projects became a more general series of one-shots—single-album deals that found favor among those keeping a wary eye on the financial habits of Impulse's new chief.

"I had conversations with Thiele about that," remembers Phil Kurnit. "On the one-shot deals he'd call the [artists] in and say, 'OK, we're gonna pay you three or four thousand dollars to do this album.' He could put together artists for far less than it would have cost to keep the artist as to an exclusive deal [usually $10,000 to $25,000 for a two-album contract]. That was by design. He could get albums very fast and the financial aspects of the deal were much easier."

"I always level in front," Thiele said, describing his one-step-at-a-time approach. "I say look, we'll make an album; if it doesn't happen, we're not going to hold you. But if it does happen, let us all enjoy the fruits of our efforts. So the musician really is not getting himself into a three- or four-year association unless the record is successful."

Thiele's reasoning also protected Impulse, according to Kurnit.

> Thiele really envisioned the label as being his chance to put together all-star groups, and to do that militated against having exclusive artists and their bands. His argument was not to get into that bag of having, say, [Art] Blakey and the Jazz Messengers who have a number of albums out [already]. We'd be competing with those same albums from his previous label, or from a subsequent label as they moved on. But if we weren't involved with their careers, that's how you remain the good guy.

Thiele's good-guy reputation among musicians was one he carefully, sincerely sought to maintain. "I love musicians," he once professed. "I've always felt they have a certain warmth and openness; it's friendliness." It was an affection the producer carried into the studio: "Jazz recording was really letting the guys play and sort of moving them along and using my own judgment as to when I felt we finally had the proper take."

OLD HABITS

Even so, there were hiccups at first at Impulse, especially when the pop producer lingering inside the jazz enthusiast surfaced. Pianist Dick Katz, who played on Benny Carter's *Further Definitions,* recalls: "My first major contact with Bob was when he called me to come to the studio to do an album with Benny. So there's Coleman Hawkins, Jo Jones, Charlie Rouse, Phil Woods, Nat 'King' Cole's guitar player Johnny Collins. There's Jimmy Garrison—he was sort of fish out of water in a way, playing with Ornette [Coleman] then—and me. And Bob is in the booth. So I'm very honored to be there, and I had a solo on the last bridge of 'Honeysuckle Rose.' So we made the take and Bob says, 'Dick, we're going to do this over. Would you mind playing a little Count Basie in that spot?' Whereupon Benny Carter took the mike and said, 'Bob, if you don't mind, I'd like to hear a little Dick Katz in that spot.' "

Hawk meets the Duke: Coleman Hawkins solos, August 18, 1963.

Carter's album—a re-creation of a legendary 1937 session in Paris that featured Carter with Coleman Hawkins—was but one of Impulse's stellar 1962 titles benefiting from the one-shot approach. Some revealed Thiele reaching out to old friends on both coasts, like jazz impresario and pianist George Wein (*George Wein & the Newport All-Stars* [A(S)-31]) and drummer Shelly Manne (*2–3–4* [A(S)-20]). Some featured legends (the aforementioned Count Basie) and veterans

Four old friends: from left, Johnny Hodges, Coleman Hawkins, Duke Ellington, and Harry Carney.

(Roy Haynes), while others reflected popular trends of the day, such as jazz treatments of Hollywood themes (Manny Albam's *Jazz Goes to the Movies* [A(S)-19]) and bossa nova (Coleman Hawkins's *Desafinado* [A(S)-28]).

Hawkins, whose second Impulse album as leader was the satisfying small-group session *Today and Now* [A(S)-34], was one of two personal heroes Thiele called on in 1962. The other was Duke Ellington, whose two landmark collaborations, *Duke Ellington Meets Coleman Hawkins* [A(S)-26] and *Duke Ellington & John Coltrane* [A(S)-30], resonate to this day with understated elegance and a bittersweet, only-this-once aura. Together, the two serve as symbols of Thiele's initial aspiration at Impulse: to span the jazz extremes of tradition and experimentation. But in the case of the Coltrane collaboration, as it turns out, the motivation had been more bitter than sweet.

THE SOUND AND THE CRITICAL FURY

In early 1962, *Down Beat* magazine's pages had bristled with a series of tirades against the edgier, more experimental reaches of jazz, with Coltrane and his sideman Eric Dolphy caught in the critical crosshairs. The two were then asked to answer their detractors and explain their music, which they did under the headline "John Coltrane and Eric Dolphy Answer the Jazz Critics."

Battle lines were drawn that would define critical confrontations through the rest of the decade. Thiele himself chose to pen the liner notes to *Coltrane* [A(S)-21], the first of three albums the saxophonist recorded that year for Impulse. In his essay, the producer predicted that "there will be plenty of accolades given in newspapers and magazines about the virtues of this album." Over the next few years, he would often speak out and pick up the pen in defense of Coltrane and the jazz avant-garde. He would also attract a younger, more strident circle of writers like Frank Kofsky and John Sinclair, whose words often found their way into the pages of *Jazz* magazine and onto the inside covers of Impulse albums.

But in 1962, Thiele gave much weight to any negative reviews of Impulse's releases. "Both *Ballads* [A(S)-32] and even [*sic*] *John Coltrane with Johnny Hartman* [A(S)-40; more on this album later] came about because of the jazz critics," he wrote. "We decided to straighten these guys

THE ELLINGTON SAXOPHONE ENCOUNTERS

Duke Ellington Meets Coleman Hawkins / Impulse A(S)-26
Duke Ellington & John Coltrane / Impulse A(S)-30
DATE RECORDED: August 18 and September 26, 1963, respectively
DATE RELEASED: March 1964
PRODUCER: Bob Thiele

Bob Thiele must have been smiling at the poetry of this two-record plan when he conceived it: uniting the jazz world's premier composer with the two men who, in 1963, represented the alpha and omega of jazz saxophone. Ellington—known for his sparse, pointillistic piano style—working it out with Hawkins, who had been the first to push the tenor saxophone into its prominent role as a solo instrument; then with Coltrane, the man who was pushing its creative possibilities further than anyone else at the time.

Of the two sessions, the Hawkins meeting was the first and more traditional, fine-tuning gems from the Ellington songbook for a seven-man lineup that featured such notable members of Duke's band as Harry Carney on baritone and Johnny Hodges on alto. The guiding principle was to blend the legendary Hawkins tone into Ellington's signature sixties sound: relaxed, open-spaced arrangements and generous solo room.

In the book that day: recent compositions (the soulful "Ray Charles' Place," the Latin-flavored "Limbo Jazz" and "The Ricitic"), old favorites ("Mood Indigo," "Solitude"), lesser-known compositions ("Wanderlust," "You Dirty Dog"), and musical profiles of Hodges and Hawkins ("The Jeep Is Jumping" and the tune that first planted the seed for the encounter, "Self-Portrait [of the Bean]").

"Duke Ellington came to me," Hawkins told Stanley Dance for the album's liner notes, "twenty years ago—or perhaps it was nineteen, eighteen or even seventeen—and he said, 'You know I want you to make a record with me, and I'm going to write a number specially for you.' 'Fine,' I said. 'I'm for it!' . . . But we never did make it, although we sometimes spoke of it when we ran into one another." Not until Thiele provided the chance at Impulse.

In the music business, joining legends together in the studio is as instinctual a gambit as breathing; making it happen—juggling schedules, bending budgets, getting managers happy—is the art. In his autobiography, Thiele credits his friendship with Ellington and the power of Roulette Records boss Morris Levy equally for enabling the famed Ellington-Armstrong session in 1961. Two years later at Impulse, Thiele was doing it all on his own, again playing matchmaker for Ellington.

A palpable feeling of respect and polite restraint—as opposed to the easy familiarity and swing on the Hawkins date—marks Ellington's summit with Coltrane. It's there when the pianist courteously lays out during the loquacious saxophone solos on upbeat tunes like Trane's "Big Nick" and Duke's "Take the Coltrane." Or when Coltrane blows with reserved and heart-tugging emotion on the tender melodies of "In a Sentimental Mood" and "My Little Brown Book." It's there in Coltrane's own humble words, as he told Stanley Dance:

"I was really honored to have the opportunity of working with Duke. . . . I once worked with Johnny Hodges [in 1954] and that was the closest I'd been to Duke before this date." The experimentalist confessed: "He has set standards I haven't caught up with yet."

In the explorative space the two stars provide each other, pleasant surprises abound. Hearing Coltrane improvising against the steady pulse of swing rhythm (Ellington sidemen Aaron Bell and Sam Woodyard played bass and drums, respectively, on three tracks) is its own reward. Another is his tenor solo on "The Feeling of Jazz." To enjoy Ellington's minimalist approach buoyed by Coltrane's distinctive rhythm team (Jimmy Garrison and Elvin Jones on four tunes) is to intuit the push and power of a much larger group, especially on "Angelica."

For Thiele, the session marked a turning point for Coltrane. "Up until the Ellington album, [he] had always spent what I would consider really too much time on his recordings. . . . The first tune we did with Ellington was 'In a Sentimental Mood.' We did that in one take . . . and I said, 'John, do you think we should do it again?,' giving him the opportunity to say something. Duke immediately interrupted and said, 'Well, what for? You can't say it again that way. This is it.' John said, 'Yes Duke, you're right.'"

Coltrane agreed in the album's liner notes: "I would have liked to have worked over all those numbers again, but then I guess the performances wouldn't have had the same spontaneity. And they mightn't have been any better!"

"From then on, John's recordings were based on one or two takes," Thiele added.

A historic footnote, and a question: between Ellington's saxophone encounters for Impulse, he recorded a one-off for the United Artists label with two virtuosi, Charles Mingus and Max Roach. It was a tension-filled and energetic session that yielded the singular album *Money Jungle*. On it, a charged facet of Ellington, not heard on either Impulse date, is revealed. The three albums he made in the fall of 1962 represent a spirit of collaboration and experimentation that seems nothing less than remarkable for any jazz veteran at sixty-four.

At the Ellington-Coltrane session, a photo was taken of the two men's drummers, Sam Woodyard and Elvin Jones. Jones would eventually leave Coltrane to join Ellington's band in January 1966—a gig that lasted all of three shows. Was the seed for that all-star trade planted at the Ellington-Coltrane session?

out once and for all by showing them that John was as great and complete a jazz artist as we already knew, and it was one of the few times he accepted a producer's concept."

Coltrane himself had been unmoved by the critical imbroglio, and the suggestion to record more accessible material or to collaborate with a jazz legend like Ellington or a singer of his own choice was easy to swallow. In fact, as he later admitted to Frank Kofsky, he had taken an active part. "Impulse was interested in having what they might call a balanced sort of thing—a diversified sort of catalog, and I find nothing wrong with this myself. [The] ballads that came out were definitely ones which I felt at the time I chose them."

In the long run, the issue of the motivation behind the much-loved *Ballads*—featuring such Coltrane favorites as "What's New," "Nancy," and "All or Nothing at All"—seems far less significant than the ultimate effect of the band that played them. The albums with Ellington and Hartman were critical favorites and strong sellers, while *Coltrane* and *Ballads* served to introduce the world to the saxophonist's so-called Classic Quartet: bassist Jimmy Garrison, pianist McCoy Tyner, and drummer Elvin Jones. Together, the four began to forge a collective sound that would become as identifiable and influential as Coltrane's individual sound.

Years later, Thiele looked back on his initial projects with Coltrane and admitted, "I think that [Coltrane] was less affected by the reviews than I was. . . . In those days, what *Down Beat* said with respect to sales of records wrongly affected record people, and now I find that most of the things they said at the time, and even the things they say now, amount to nothing."

THE FEW, THE CONTRACTED

Sadly, no sales records survive that might help gauge the relative impact of Thiele's variety of approaches in his first years at Impulse—of how, say, Hawkins's *Desafinado,* with its carefully arranged guitars and percussion, performed versus the relatively stark, modally based originals on *Coltrane*. But across such a range of styles, Thiele certainly generated enough overall sales to warrant taking the step of inviting a few jazzmen to join Coltrane as exclusive Impulse artists.

Not that Thiele took too much of a chance. The few who accepted the offer to commit themselves to Impulse in 1961 and '62 for the standard two-albums, one-year plan (with the option to extend) were all proven to a degree. They included two of Art Blakey's Jazz Messengers—trombonist Curtis Fuller and trumpeter Freddie Hubbard—plus Coltrane's pianist, McCoy Tyner, and the well-known drummer Chico Hamilton, whose 1962 quintet offered a stylistic parallel of a sort to Coltrane's sound of the day.

From the same Los Angeles scene (and even high school) that produced the likes of Dexter Gordon and Charles Mingus, Hamilton had first hit nationally as the drummer with Gerry Mulligan's pianoless quartet in 1952. In 1955, he formed his own group. He soon earned a reputation, similar to his fellow drummer Art Blakey's, for hiring younger talent-in-training—cellist Fred Katz; guitarists Jim Hall and Gabor Szabo; saxophonists Paul Horn, Eric Dolphy, and Charles Lloyd—ensuring that their

Chico chooses Impulse: Hamilton in the studio with Thiele, 1962.

CABIN IN THE SKY

Curtis Fuller / *Cabin in the Sky* / Impulse A(S)-22

DATE RECORDED: April 24, 1962

DATE RELEASED: October 1962

PRODUCER: Bob Thiele

Not all of Impulse's big-budget efforts achieved commercial success; and at least one proved a deal-ender.

Curtis Fuller recalls the initial inspiration for his second album for the label, a soloists-and-strings treatment of *Cabin in the Sky.*

"Thiele said, 'Why don't you do a musical?' because he wanted to do something with strings. I said, 'Well, why not do a black musical?' I mentioned *Cabin in the Sky*—I saw the movie three or four times as a kid, and the music was beautiful, with 'Taking a Chance on Love' and all those songs, and Thiele agreed."

Manny Albam, an arranger familiar with the jazz scene, was recruited for the project, with Fuller's OK. "I heard around the circuit, if you want to do strings, Manny's the guy.

"I didn't have a great knowledge of strings—but I wanted Quincy [Jones], that kind of jazz element in there. I said, 'I've got to have some jazz people in there, I want a jazz feeling. I agreed to [the orchestra] if he'd promise to let me choose the brass section. I wanted Kai Winding, Bob Brookmeyer, Wayne Andre, and we got them."

The trombonist remembers that for a session requiring intricate coordination with large ensembles, all went surprisingly well—until extra studio time was requested.

"They allowed me three hours with the strings and three hours with the brass. The strings, obviously, went perfect; we got that done, boom, with time to spare. But we needed time to fuse the thing, to connect the strings with the brass: not on every song, but decide whether we're gonna have [sings entrance melody], then the brass [sings main theme]. And you'd hear the mesh! I said, 'No that's kind of harsh, can we have another hour?' They raised hell for about a week."

The album was completed, released with an evocative double male-female profile by photographer Pete Turner, and received positive notice in the jazz press. Yet what ultimately transpired, from Fuller's perspective, was a bitter lesson in record company accounting that can leave an unwary musician with little chance of recouping expenditures, some of which were hidden.

"Thiele said, 'If we're going to have strings, we're going to go all out.' We went from a six-string ensemble to the New York Philharmonic. Well, now, whose budget is it anyway? Then I found out that they would charge me for the ashtrays and the music stands and everything else—you know, this is a big business. I learned that at a time when there was no one there to advise me, or those that knew, wouldn't say, 'Well now, let's think about this one.' I think Creed [Taylor] would have run that over with me, but Bob Thiele was 'Let's just do this and let's let it be done.'

"But once the album came out, I just don't think that the company was prepared to put the kind of [marketing and promotional] money into it. I just happened to be in the [ABC-Paramount] office and heard a conversation that I shouldn't have heard. 'Why we spending this kind of money on this cat?' It was somebody talking to Larry Newton. 'You didn't spend that kind of money on [trombonists] J.J. Johnson or Bob Brookmeyer.' They were kicking things around, and to my displeasure I heard it. But I took that in stride."

Fuller walked away from his deal with Impulse rather than try to climb out of a financial hole with future releases. But that did not prevent the trombonist from continuing his sideman role on other projects with the label.

"I think they sold a few thousand [copies of *Cabin in the Sky*] and then I got my first royalty check, and it was 'You owe us $67,000,' that type of thing. I was never gonna pay this bill off! I did my two [albums for Impulse] as a leader and that was the end of that. But I worked with several other ensembles in the Impulse family, and they used me on both of Freddie Hubbard's albums."

performances reflected new and experimental sounds in the air at the time. By the early sixties, his music had absorbed the freedoms of the avant-garde and the flavor of foreign folk songs while maintaining a solid hard-bop drive.

For an established artist like Hamilton, familiar with the variety of labels purveying jazz, the decision to join Impulse was easy to make. "During that time, Impulse in a sense was [the] number one label for pure jazz. Blue Note had their thing. Columbia had their thing going. But Impulse had Trane and Max [Roach]. All the artists that came out on Impulse were hot artists. And they had Bob Thiele, who was to me the perfect producer, 'cause all he would do was be in the booth smoking his pipe."

Not that Hamilton required direction at that point. He was leading one of his greatest lineups, boasting strong soloists, composers, and future bandleaders. "It was a dynamite group, with [tenor saxophonist–flutist] Charles Lloyd, [guitarist] Gabor Szabo, [bassist] Albert Stinson, and [trombonist] George Bohanon all in the band. A lot of people don't realize that we were doing things before Miles was doing that particular style of playing, where we would change tempos and stretch out—you know, things like that."

Recorded in 1962, *Passin' Thru* [A(S)-29] was Hamilton's initial title on Impulse, powered by the drummer's powerfully diverse range of Latin and world influences, Lloyd's distinctive, trance-like excursions, and Gabor's Gypsy-flavored licks, reflecting his Hungarian roots. *Passin' Thru* proved the first of a half-dozen strong sellers Hamilton created for Impulse that helped define an alternative edge to sixties jazz, with Lloyd's contributions heavily influenced by Coltrane's searching sound—and earned both critical applause and Thiele's focus. "If [Thiele] liked what you did, dynamite. If he didn't like what you did, forget it, you'd never find him [chuckles]."

Fuller and Hubbard were both working steadily in '62 and had recorded solid albums for Blue Note, and yet—unlike Hamilton—they were not fronting consistent groups when they signed to Impulse. For Hubbard, it was a conscious decision, allowing him a project-by-project freedom. "I didn't ever keep a group. I used top all-stars on all my records. I always thought of that because certain guys . . . have their own way of what they want to play and it's hard to get them to [change]. Now, I knew that Tommy Flanagan played soft, but I knew by him being from Detroit and

Louis [Hayes] being from Detroit that they could keep that bebop going, because it was mainly a bebop-type record."

"It" turned out to be *The Artistry of Freddie Hubbard* [A(S)-27], an Impulse album that remained true to the trumpeter's experience with Art Blakey: a tough-swinging hard-bop effort recorded on a midsummer's day, with Thiele in the background. "He wasn't a producer like Creed was. You know, [Taylor] wanted to be in on every little thing. Bob would get the guys to do the job [and] he'd let you be free."

Fuller, who played on *The Artistry,* recalls Thiele taking a more proactive role with his own label debut, pushing an idea he repeated with other Impulse artists. "He wanted me to do an Ellington thing, he liked everything Ellington, and it wasn't like I wasn't versed in it." The trombonist declined that idea, but opted for another of the producer's suggestions.

> When I asked could I have Freddie Hubbard and [tenor saxophonist] Jimmy Heath [on the album], that was OK, but then Bob Thiele wanted some of the material to have sort of a funk thing in it. He kept emphasizing funk, you know, like we were just going to market it funk, like black spiritual shout and stuff. It didn't go with my lyrical nature, but I had written one of those songs like that—it was called "Down Home" [recorded for Blue Note in 1957]. But I was asked to do something like that.

The album *Soul Trombone and the Jazz Clan* [A(S)-18] did indeed veer down a funk-driven path, with Hubbard and Heath joined by pianist Cedar Walton, bassist Jymie Merritt, and, alternately, drummers Jimmy Cobb and Herbert Logan.

> It was just a small-group session, a sextet thing. We did "[Dear Old] Stockholm," "[In the] Wee Small Hours of the Morning"—Jimmy Heath helped me with that arrangement. I did the arrangement for "The Clan" and "Ladies' Night." I chose "The Breeze and I," because it's not an overdone song.

Soul Trombone also featured a Fuller original titled in gratitude. "Larry Newton—he said 'name one for me and my family' at the signing of this large contract. They signed me for a big contract in those days—ten thousand [dollars]. That was money, you know—I went to New Jersey and put a down payment on a home. So I called it 'Newdles.' "

THE ARTISTRY OF FREDDIE HUBBARD

Freddie Hubbard / *The Artistry of Freddie Hubbard* / Impulse A(S)-27

DATE RECORDED: July 2, 1962

DATE RELEASED: March 1963

PRODUCER: Bob Thiele

For trumpeter Freddie Hubbard, his Impulse debut still marks a personal breakthrough: his first fully composed and arranged album, an accomplishment that earned it its title.

"[Bob Thiele] called it *The Artistry* because of the writing. I would say that that was a pivotal time in my career because I was writing and a lot of times you write music and you've heard somebody else do it. I had done some arrangements on my Blue Note [albums]—*Ready for Freddie, Hub-Tones.* I had help from [tenor saxophonist] Tina Brooks on the Blue Note stuff, but on *The Artistry* I felt as though these arrangements really sounded like me."

Of his originals, Hubbard recalls that one track

might seem to have referred to the album's producer but didn't—"Bob [of 'Bob's Place'] was a boy I knew in Brooklyn"—while another carried a personal resonance. " 'The 7th Day' is very meaningful—a holy day for me. I did a lot of research on that: I keep it holy. It's a rhythmic thing with the congas, and I wrote some pretty heavy arrangements for that small-group style."

The other memorable aspect of the album for Hubbard was his complete choice of sidemen, combining the familiar and the unexpected. "I felt as though I had the guys that I finally wanted. I had [drummer] Louis Hayes, who's my man; I had [pianist] Tommy Flanagan, and I had [tenor saxophonist] John Gilmore.

"Louis and I were living together in Brooklyn for about eleven years. He did some of his best playing on [*The Artistry*]. Tommy Flanagan? Whew. Man, he's got the touch at piano. I was happy. [Bassist] Art Davis surprised me too, man. He's got a good sound on records and made some good records with Max [Roach]."

If one choice is a sore-thumb standout, it would be Gilmore, who is featured throughout the album. Better known as an avant-gardist than a hard-bopper like the others on the session, he had come to prominence playing with the bandleader and avant-garde pioneer Sun Ra. Hubbard explains that his inclination to use Gilmore was confirmed by another saxophonist's taste.

"Coltrane loved him. I used to go from Indianapolis to Chicago every Sunday, [where] I heard John Gilmore and Sun Ra. You ever meet Sun Ra? I used to go over to his house. He had a harem of guys—like a commune, more or less. He took care of them. I don't know if he made any money, but he taught them a lot of music. A lot of people wanted John Gilmore, you know, but he would not leave. His sound and his notes made him fit the part with [Sun Ra].

"On this session? Well he didn't play like Wayne Shorter or Joe Henderson, but he played the type of sound that I heard for the album. When he played that solo on 'Caravan,' I said, 'Man, what is this?' [Chuckles.] . . . It was kind of a Coltrane sound, and I liked that because he didn't play like anybody else. When I wrote those arrangements, I didn't really know what they were going to sound like. But I had an idea that by getting Art and Louis and Tommy and John that they would, some kind of way, gel. See, if you get certain combinations of guys, they can get a sound."

Though *The Artistry of Freddie Hubbard* will always be associated with a painful memory for the trumpeter ("I was going through some changes then, man. I was getting ready to break up with my wife. I had a son that I had to leave"), he admits to a measure of satisfaction with it. "I've listened to that one a lot over the years," he says. "I did some of my best playing on that."

That Newton's request was made directly to the trombonist reveals that contracted Impulse artists did not deal with Thiele alone. McCoy Tyner recalls the same type of office meeting with ABC's head of sales.

> The contract was basically [for] two albums a year. If anything else needed to be recorded, that would be negotiable—we'd talk about it. After I signed with the label I met with the head of [sales for] ABC, Larry Newton. He was sitting there very casually. He said, "Listen, we're proud to have you on the label. We're going to work with you." I was welcomed by one of the head execs there at ABC; with that initial greeting I felt very comfortable.

But it was Thiele, according to Tyner, who "was spearheading the whole thing. When Bob approached me I was so happy because he was very encouraging, you know. I liked the way he dealt with musicians. It was very casual, not demanding." For Tyner at least, the trust was well placed. As Thiele later explained, he was willing to have Impulse invest in potential, if not immediate, earnings.

> For example, when we started recording McCoy Tyner for Impulse, I think the first album [*Inception,* A(S)-18] sold eight hundred [copies]. But we stayed with him for four years, and at the end . . . his initial orders [from retail] were seventy-five hundred, ten thousand albums.

In 1962, there was little ensuring Tyner's eventual worth, nor a guarantee that he would be asked to record a half-dozen albums for Impulse. For the pianist, there was simply one overriding factor that influenced his decision to sign with the label: "John [Coltrane] was there and I said, 'Why not?' "

Tyner's sentiment, that Coltrane's easygoing association with Impulse was a thumbs-up reference for the label, was soon shared by an expanding number of musicians. The pianist had felt it when Coltrane first informed his band of his decision to sign with the label: "It was kind of informal [how] we found out that he had a new home—that he was going over to Impulse. We definitely were welcomed there with open arms."

Inception soon led to *Reaching Fourth* [A(S)-33], Tyner's second album for the label, recorded in late '62. Its title punned on the pianist's penchant for voicings that leaned on fourths, a harmonic interval that allowed a flexibility that worked well with Coltrane's extended solos. The two albums not only stand as Tyner's first efforts as a leader, but signify a debut for Coltrane too—as a de facto talent scout for Impulse. The pianist recalls Coltrane's happy reaction.

> He was glad that I signed [with Impulse]. As a matter of fact he came over to my house when I would do a recording to look over stuff, because we didn't live far from each other in Queens [at the time]. He sort of watched my development. He was my teacher. He really was.

INCEPTION

McCoy Tyner / *Inception* / Impulse A(S)-18

DATE RECORDED: January 10 and 11, 1962

DATE RELEASED: June 1962

PRODUCER: Bob Thiele

Any musician's debut recording as a leader can be a daunting step forward, especially when he has served behind a high-profile powerhouse like John Coltrane. But given his own musical leanings, McCoy Tyner saw his in a welcoming light.

"What really motivated me in a lot of ways was that I didn't want to do the same thing I was doing with the [Coltrane] quartet. I was recording on the-label with John doing the modal thing, [and] I loved doing things with John. It was definitely an integral part of my musical character. But I wanted to do something that was more indicative of me—more characteristic of things I wanted to do. That's why I did standards, a lot of those songs—and the

trio's a bit different from the quartet."

As Tyner recalls, the idea first came from his producer.

"Bob Thiele came to me and said, 'Listen, your piano is a pretty accessible instrument.' I don't know if he said those exact words, but in essence that's what he meant. 'I think you ought to start your own recording career.'"

Whether Thiele was referring to Tyner's melodic style or the general nature of the instrument, it works both ways. In the opening weeks of 1962, McCoy Tyner was already a young veteran, of various bands and recording situations.

"I had been doing some recording early on with different labels and different people. I did an album with Curtis Fuller. Then, of course, the record *Meet the Jazztet* [with trumpeter Art Farmer and saxophonist Benny Golson]. I was kind of glad [Thiele] came to me because I was kind of thinking about that: 'Why don't I just do something on my own?' I wouldn't say it surprised me, but it got me excited."

Tyner admits Thiele helped steer the focus of later Impulse albums—like, unsurprisingly, *McCoy Tyner Plays Ellington*. "He's the one that came up with that: Why don't I do something with Duke Ellington's music?" But the pianist's debut featured tunes largely of his own choosing—and writing.

"*Inception*—I wrote a lot of the songs on that record. 'Sunset,' I think, is a good one. It's a ballad. And, of course, 'Blues for Gwen'—that's a song I wrote for my sister. So the [material on my] first record was not necessarily a suggestion of Bob's."

The album offered six tunes bristling with the lyrical brilliance and maturing style of a youthful improviser: two standards ("Speak Low" and "There Is No Greater Love") and four originals (the title track, "Sunset," "Blues for Gwen," and "Effendi"—the last most indicative of his modal experience with Coltrane)

Tyner with Bob Thiele, 1965.

Tyner also recruited support familiar to him through his current boss: Art Davis, one of Coltrane's favorite bassists, and drummer Elvin Jones, his fellow sideman in the saxophonist's quartet. "Playing with Elvin spoils you for other drummers," Tyner confessed to Nat Hentoff in the album's liner notes. Hentoff also quoted Coltrane ticking off the pianist's praiseworthy qualities like a proud parent.

"Melodic inventiveness . . . clarity of his ideas . . . personal sound . . . well developed sense of form . . . and finally McCoy has taste. He can take anything, no matter how weird, and make it sound beautiful."

NT AND THE SINNER LADY STEREO A-35 IMPULSE!
S McCOY TYNER STEREO A-39 IMPULSE!
Y HARTMAN STEREO A-40 IMPULSE!
Y • PAUL GONSALVES IMPULSE!
ANE STEREO A-42 IMPULSE!
STEREO A-43 IMPULSE!
AN QUARTET STEREO A-47 IMPULSE!
W and much more!!! FREDA PAYNE A-53 IMPULSE!
NGUS MINGUS MINGUS SMAS 90218 IMPULSE!
GONSALVES A-55 IMPULSE!
YUSEF LATEEF STEREO A-56 IMPULSE!
O JOHNNY HARTMAN STEREO A-57 IMPULSE!
ERRY MONO A-64 IMPULSE!
EBSTER STEREO A-65 IMPULSE!
STEREO A-68 IMPULSE!
N STEREO A-69 IMPULSE!
IMPULSE!

CHAPTER 3

INTUITION AND IMPULSE (1963–1964)

At Impulse, he had this license to do whatever was in his field of vicion, and I know it didn't serve him well financially. My dad didn't cash out of the music business like other guys did. He made unbelievable mistakes. But they were due to his need to immediately satisfy what was going on inside of him. That's what music was to him—it was beyond the intellect. You could call it this extrasensory compulsion.

—Bob Thiele Jr.

From 1963 through '64, such was the diversity of the music on Impulse that the question is inevitable: Was it the product of planning or personality? Intention or, well, impulse?

From swing and bebop stalwarts to more modern explorers, from blues singers to cabaret stylists to John Coltrane himself, telling the tale of Impulse during these years offers a somewhat rambling course, as the label itself defied the notion of a distinct musical identity. Yet, even if Thiele's initial years at Impulse placed his own restless nature in the foreground, his continuing education at the hands of Coltrane and the rising fortune of ABC-Paramount played in the background. Still, one could argue that Impulse was entering its first golden period. Starting in 1963, a still-impressive majority of the label's new releases were instant classics. The "i!" logo served as a jazz-production seal of approval, guaranteeing a well-recorded, well-packaged recording well worth the price of (roughly) $1.69 per album.

"There was this period from, I guess, about '63 to '67, maybe '68, where there was a tremendous consistency," remembers Gary Giddins. "Every once in a while there would be some record by a singer and you'd say, 'How did that get in here?'

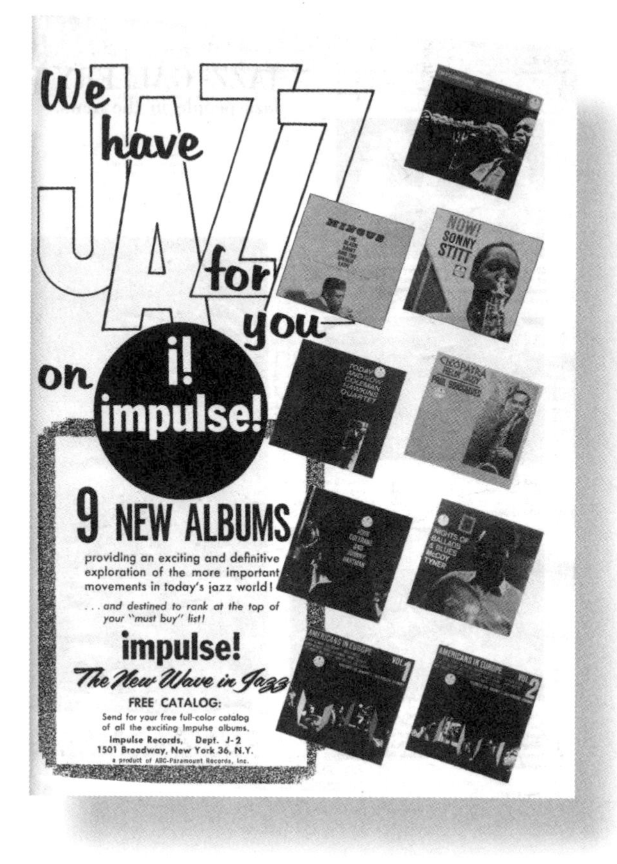

Coltrane on top: an Impulse advertisement, 1963.

Lorez Alexandria or somebody like that. But there was something about Impulse for a very few years there that you were willing to try it out."

"Thiele knew each album had to be special, and the conceptual thought and care that went into these albums was evident to all, including the jazz record buyer," echoes veteran record producer Michael Cuscuna. "The opulent, gorgeous packaging was an incredible draw in the competitive jazz industry of the early sixties, but the music usually lived up to what the packaging promised."

"Thiele was an old-timer in the sense that his real love was not so much with Coltrane but with the swing guys," adds Giddins. "But because they were putting it all out in the same orange jackets—Coltrane's *Live at Birdland* and Lionel Hampton's *You Better Know It*—the [swing musicians] became, by association, hip. There was this trusting thing. 'Duke Ellington we know is hip—he recorded with Coltrane.' Impulse brought a lot of people to music that they might not otherwise have reached."

By 1963, as Thiele began to notice, Impulse was attracting younger listeners new to jazz who had chosen a particular doorway in.

> In the early days of recording Coltrane [at Impulse], it was impossible to hear a Coltrane record on the air and yet his records were selling. And we were always trying to figure out who was buying them. Then I went on a tour, with Stan Kenton. . . . When I arrived on a campus and was with student musicians, all they wanted to talk about was John Coltrane. And they had all his records.

"Coltrane Leads the Way," declared a full-page ad that year, proclaiming his primacy in a varied list that included Freddie Hubbard, McCoy Tyner, and veterans like Coleman Hawkins, Sonny Stitt, Charles Mingus, and Coltrane's first musical hero, Johnny Hodges. In 1963, even as ABC-Paramount's top executives were pushing singles by the Impressions and Ray Charles into the Top Forty and topping the LP chart with comedian-vocalist Frank Fontaine, they did not overlook the sax star's consistent sales.

"We had Max Roach, Chico Hamilton. We had some other good players, but nothing like Trane," says Larry Newton. "Leading jazz artist for us? Absolutely, far and away."

COLTRANE IN THE LEAD

The pattern of Coltrane's recording schedule at the time reveals his privileged status. In a day when a typical jazz session was expected to neatly yield one album, allowing for easy accounting of cost against revenue, Thiele was content to leave the studio door open for the saxophonist to improvise his own ratio. In '62, eight visits to Van Gelder's yielded three albums (*Coltrane, Ellington,* and *Ballads*). The next year saw Coltrane utilize the studio only three times, but from those sessions and two live performances also recorded that year—the Newport Jazz Festival on July 7, Birdland on October 8—Impulse eventually released four titles: *John Coltrane and Johnny Hartman, Impressions, Live at Birdland,* and—in 1993—*Newport '63*.

Things got a bit confusing. Two of Coltrane's 1962 albums were cobbled together from live and studio recordings. His *Impressions* album featured a track from the '61 Vanguard recordings, while *Live at Birdland* included two studio tracks, and then there were other recordings not released until years later. Thiele blamed it on Coltrane's prolificacy.

> People like Coltrane, or Duke Ellington, record so much they almost forget about what was recorded, and it literally piles up. And in most instances, you release the latest recording when a new release is needed. [Coltrane] was selecting the things that he wanted to record.

If Coltrane required an entire session to focus primarily on the tune "Alabama"—as he did on November 18, 1963—Thiele willingly stood between his artist and those who were used to a more standard way of doing business.

> I was sneaking studios at night so the top brass would not know we were making so many records. He was prolific, he wanted to record, and I tried to record him as often as possible. The only problem was that struggle with the brass; it was a continuous fight over the amount of recordings we were making.

Thiele and Coltrane started on friendly footing and grew closer over time. It made sense that the saxophonist would be open to considering (though not always accepting) the producer's suggestions of more mainstream projects; when Thiele floated the idea in early '63 to match his label star with a singer, Coltrane suggested a deserving vocalist.

John Coltrane and Johnny Hartman [A(S)-40] is one of the crown jewels of the Impulse catalog, boosted by celebrated—some argue definitive—interpretations of "My One and Only Love," "Lush Life," and "They Say It's Wonderful." The combination of the singer's comfortable insouciance with Coltrane's unhurried solos proved a critical and commercial success, despite a track list of only six tunes. The deep-voiced singer would record two more albums for Impulse, but neither with Coltrane: *I Just Dropped By to Say Hello* [A(S)-57] later in 1963 (with the inspired choice of Illinois Jacquet on tenor sax) and *The Voice That Is!* [A(S)-74] in 1964.

Was Thiele hoping to do as he had done on past labels and establish more singers at Impulse? Three other projects with female vocalists in '63 strongly suggest it. Singers then—as now—were seen as the most likely candidates to cross over from jazz into pop territory, and accordingly received generous production support: noted sidemen and, at times, full orchestral backing.

The first left the smallest mark. Beverly Jenkins, wife of the noted bandleader and arranger Gordon, delivered a laid-back set of blues on *Gordon Jenkins Presents My Wife the Blues Singer* [A(S)-44], with a title that begged the question: just how many album titles that year played off Allan Sherman's wildly popular comedy LP *My Son, the Folk Singer*?

By the time Freda Payne came to Thiele's attention, she was still a teenager but had already been discovered in Detroit and performed with Duke Ellington and Quincy Jones. *After the Lights Go Down Low and Much More!!!* [A(S)-53] balanced big-band numbers (arranged by Manny Albam, with a tune contributed by Ellington) and small-group support (including a credible take on Ornette Coleman's "Lonely Woman," with a lyric by Margo Guryan). The influence of Sarah Vaughan and Dinah Washington is noticeable throughout. A promising debut, leagues from the soulful sound she would take to the Top Ten in 1970 with her pop hit "Band of Gold."

But it was Lorez Alexandria who carried Thiele's crossover hope into 1964. At thirty-five, she had a light, impeccable sense of swing and wide dynamic range (coming out of Chicago's demanding gospel scene) that had fully matured, commending her to a role straddling Broadway and blues, jazz standards and recent pop material. On *Alexandria the Great* [A(S)-62], she covered it all with ease and style, playfully half-speaking the lyric to "Get Me to the Church on Time," snapping her fingers on "My One and Only Love," lingering behind the beat on "The Best Is Yet to Come." And what support: the Wynton Kelly Trio (pianist Kelly, bassist Paul Chambers, and drummer Jimmy Cobb, formerly Miles Davis's rhythm section) on most tunes, with vibraphonist Victor Feldman added on a few, and a big band on "I've Grown Accustomed to His Face" and "Show Me."

For Alexandria, Impulse was to be her jump to a national career, after seven years on independent labels like Cincinnati's King and Chicago's Argo. Her follow-up, *More of the Great Lorez Alexandria* [A(S)-76], was culled from the same sessions that produced her debut and appeared at the end of the year, but her stay at Impulse ended there. With no further vocal albums appearing on the label (save for Hartman's) after '64, it's easy to intuit the red light Thiele must have been given. To hear it from Newton, ABC ultimately held to a hard rule that any vocal music—even jazz-flavored—should be the responsibility of the pop side of the company.

JOHN COLTRANE AND JOHNNY HARTMAN

John Coltrane and Johnny Hartman / Impulse A(S)-40
DATE RECORDED: March 7, 1963
DATE RELEASED: August 1963
PRODUCER: Bob Thiele

What worked for Jimi Hendrix in the sixties was not exactly a wise career move for a jazz singer in the previous decade. Johnny Hartman, Chicago-born and schooled in big bands led by Earl Hines and Dizzy Gillespie, made the move to England at the start of the fifties. A two-week run in a London club grew to a two-year stay, a television series, recordings, and a variety of appearances.

"Then the English labor department complained that I was doing too many things," Hartman told jazz critic John S. Wilson in 1982. "I came back to the United States and found that I'd been forgotten."

Fast-forward to 1963. Hartman, a self-described "all-around singer" who never felt comfortable with the jazz designation ("I studied classical, I go back to heavy spirituals"), had been rebuilding his career and was on tour in Japan when a producer telephoned with a proposition. "I was a Coltrane fan and, although I'd never met him, I'd been listening to him for years. I told Bob Thiele that I didn't think we'd fit too well."

Nonetheless, Thiele was insistent. "I had the idea of the vocal; *he* chose Hartman," Thiele explained later. "He," of course, was Coltrane. Though their respective stints with the Gillespie band never overlapped

(Hartman was there in 1948 and 1949; Coltrane joined two years later), the singer's voice left a mark, wherever or however Coltrane heard it. "Johnny Hartman—a man that I had stuck up in my mind somewhere . . . I liked his sound," Coltrane recalled of the smooth, unmannered baritone. "So I looked him up and did that album."

Listening to a playback: Coltrane, Johnny Hartman, Elvin Jones.

Upon his return from overseas, Hartman sat in with the Coltrane quartet at Birdland in late February 1963. "After the show, when the place had closed . . . just me, Coltrane and his pianist," Hartman recalled. "A week later we went out to Rudy Van Gelder's studio. . . . We had lined up ten songs to do. But as we were driving out, listening to the car radio, we heard that Nat Cole song 'Lush Life.' I said, 'That is a fantastic song,' and I started singing it in the car, although I didn't know all the words."

The meeting of Hartman and the Coltrane quartet was momentous and momentary: six tracks only, with the hint of only one alternate version. "We did everything in the album in one take except 'You Are So Beautiful,'" Hartman added. "We had to do two takes on that one because Elvin [Jones] dropped a drumstick."

Interestingly, Bob Thiele recalled another number as the session's sole re-take. "I remember Johnny Hartman being so transfixed by Coltrane's elevatingly radiant solo during the recording of 'My One and Only Love' that he completely forgot to come back for his vocal close. A second take would be necessary, and, as tape-splicing was still a prehistoric craft, all of us in the sound booth were heartsick that a classic performance would be lost. For the next take however, a buoyantly unworried John Coltrane then created [another] timeless solo."

In his notes for the CD version of the album, reissue producer Michael Cuscuna pointed out two interesting facts. "At a later date," he wrote, "Coltrane decided to overdub additional obbligato saxophone phrases behind Hartman's vocals on 'My One and Only Love,' 'Lush Life,' and 'You Are Too Beautiful.'" He also noted that "a version of 'Afro Blue' was recorded at this session" but had been lost. It eventually proved to be an unissuable take of Hartman repeatedly intoning the title—but no lyric—over the group's performance. The master tape of the session turned up in a lot of thirty-three Coltrane recordings collected for a much-publicized jazz auction in February 2005 that originally belonged to Impulse, and were subsequently pulled from the block. It's intriguing to note that Coltrane would later employ the overdubbing technique on his album *A Love Supreme,* and that he adopted "Afro Blue" as part of his regular instrumental repertoire.

Though one writer has opined that *John Coltrane and Johnny Hartman* "revitalized the careers of both men," there is no doubt that Coltrane deserves credit for rescuing an overlooked talent from undeserved obscurity, so that "at the time of his death in 1983, Hartman had become, with Mel Tormé and Joe Williams, one of the most highly regarded male singers in jazz."

> You talk to the average layperson, they'll say that there's two different versions of jazz. Trane was an out-and-out jazz player; I mean, his licks were really jazz. The average person couldn't understand that kind of music. But you could call Sarah [Vaughan] a great jazz singer, and yet she could sing a good ballad, right?

Accordingly, through the sixties, when jazz singers—Shirley Horn, Louis Armstrong—joined the ABC family, Thiele handled the production but the results were issued on the ABC imprint. After 1964, Impulse was exclusively an instrumentalist's label, with an odd vocal track popping up now and again. The sole exception would be a reissue of Lambert, Hendricks and Ross's vocalese landmark *Sing a Song of Basie* [A(S)-83] in early '65.

THREE LEADING WOMEN

In the jazz world, most female headliners are (and were) vocalists, and as Impulse never became a home to singers, the label might appear to have been gender biased. But given the overall paucity of woman bandleaders on the scene then (and now), perhaps Impulse was more of a leader. The label ultimately boasted three female headliners. Interestingly, all were married to tenor saxophonists, and all focused on the jazz organ. While Alice Coltrane recorded on piano and harp as well, Gloria Coleman and Shirley Scott were exclusively organ players when they signed with Impulse in 1963.

Hard-swinging organ combos were then the rage, holding sway in black urban centers. The trend began with the popularity of Jimmy Smith, and was essentially a groove-driven extension of hard bop's return to gospel- and blues-based harmonies, initiated by the likes of Horace Silver, Art Blakey, and others in the fifties. By the early sixties, the entire wave was operating under the rubric of "soul jazz" and included small groups led by saxophonists Lou Donaldson, Willis "Gator Tail" Jackson, Gene Ammons, and Eddie "Lockjaw" Davis, and organists Brother Jack McDuff, Jimmy McGriff, and Shirley Scott. Jazz labels like Prestige and Blue Note, once geared to a more focused definition of the music, were finding that their profit leaders were musicians like those above, and that a larger chunk of their revenue came from single sales—spurred by inner-city jukeboxes where

STEREO
impulse!
COLTRANE
COLTRANE
THE JOHN COLTRANE QUARTETTE
EP AS-21
Side 1
CHICO HAMILTON
QUINTET
EXTENDED PLAY
STEREO 33⅓
EP AS-29
Side 1
1. THE SECOND TIME AROUND
2. EL TORO
COLTRANE
THE JOHN COLTRANE QUARTETTE
STEREO
33⅓ R.P.M.
EP AS-21
Side 2
1. MILES' MODE
QUINTET
EP AS-29
Side 2

jazz 45s by Jimmy Smith, Gene Ammons, and Cannonball Adderley sat alongside those by the R&B groups of the day.

Impulse wanted in on the action: album and single sales *and* jukebox play. In addition to the infrequent 45 rpm single like Charles's "One Mint Julep" or Coltrane's "Greensleeves," the label began releasing a series of 33⅓ rpm extended play (EP) discs that packed four tunes apiece by the likes of Coleman Hawkins, Chico Hamilton, Shirley Scott, and John Coltrane. They served a double purpose: promotional when spinning on a new generation of jukeboxes that could play EPs, and commercial when sitting on retail shelves.

The label's search for new soul-jazz talent began only a few subway stops uptown. In 1963, Gloria Coleman was holding down a regular gig in a Harlem bar while husband George was on the road with Miles Davis. The Chicago-born organist's quartet featured guitarist Grant Green, alto saxophonist Leo Wright, and drummer Pola Roberts. The novelty of two female players in a small group suggested the title of Coleman's sole Impulse recording: *Soul Sisters* [A(S)-47], an unabashedly hard-swinging set of down-home and upbeat tracks, mostly composed by Coleman.

Coleman and her group kept to a narrower interpretation of soul jazz than Shirley Scott, the Philadelphia-born organist who had played alongside Eddie "Lockjaw" Davis in the late fifties, then recorded for Prestige after breaking out on her own in 1960. With a wide emotional palette that compromised none of the idiom's sharply rhythmic drive, Scott stood out from Jimmy Smith, Jack McDuff, and other organists.

All things happily converged for Scott after she joined Impulse and released *For Members Only* [A(S)-51], her first album with big-band support. She married tenor saxophonist Stanley Turrentine, with whom she co-led a band and recorded some of her best work. Her fourth Impulse album benefited from the union, as she swiftly became the label's bestseller in the soul-jazz market. Scott's career rose to a high point in '64, when she appeared in the Bette Davis thriller *Dead Ringer,* her music swelling on the soundtrack behind the pivotal murder scene.

That same year, Scott recorded three popular discs for Impulse. *Great Scott!!* [A(S)-67] was another half-and-half balance of big-band numbers arranged by Nelson, featuring a funky take of his "Hoe Down," and trio performances that included Scott singing a blues. *Everybody Loves a Lover* [A(S)-73] saw Scott working mostly with a quartet—Turrentine, bassist Bob Cranshaw, and drummer Otis Finch—with two Latin-tinged tracks featuring twin guitars and congas.

But *Queen of the Organ* [A(S)-81] was the live set that finally caught her in top gear, in a neighborhood bar (Newark's Front Room) with Turrentine at her side. As Turrentine recalled, "We called it the 'chitlins circuit.' A lot of small places, with bad sound systems, small audiences. . . . We'd go in that night and we'd blow our hearts out." The album captures the spark to which many soul-jazz fans were drawn.

GETTING IMPULSE ON, THEN OFF, THE RACKS

As popular as the music itself proved, Impulse's success in marketing Scott, Coltrane, or any of its other artists would never have notched the sales numbers it did, nor kept the ABC hierarchy as satisfied, if it were not for ABC's marketing and promotional clout—of the early-sixties variety. "There was no science about it—there was no such thing as marketing!" laughs ABC counsel Phil Kurnit of the lack of in-store push received by Impulse, or any ABC product. "Marketing was the sleeves on the record showing the catalog of records. And there weren't Impulse sleeves. It all went on an ABC-Paramount sleeve."

For the first four years of Impulse, jazz consumers found Max Roach, Benny Carter, and John Coltrane discs in paper sleeves that promoted polka and Hawaiian music collections, comedy by Marty Allen and Steve Rossi, and Ray Charles's catalog. As well, Impulse's well-designed, high-quality, glossy covers served as its own effective marketing tool in the days before in-store displays.

"They talk now of point-of-purchase materials, etc.," adds Kurnit. "Back then there weren't posters. There weren't things done in the stores like now. I can't tell you that that's what Columbia or RCA did, but I don't think that Kapp or Mercury Records did it. ABC was still thinking like a small company in reality, using independent distribution."

Record marketing may have been in a primary development stage in the first half of the sixties, but record promotion was not. Thiele, like many jazz executives, relied on a few independent, jazz-savvy promotion men around the country to get Impulse tracks on the radio.

"It was up to each label to decide on who they used to plug their music," recalls Sid Feller. "We [ABC-Paramount] had our choices, and Bob [Thiele] had his. Of course, if there were over a hundred deejays in the country at

The range of their releases: the inner sleeve worn by all ABC-Paramount LPs, early sixties.

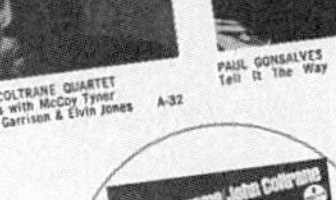

A sleeve of their own: Impulse markets its catalog, 1963 on.

that time, only ten would have been playing jazz." One of those deejays was Joel Dorn, today a veteran jazz producer and in the early sixties an on-air host on Philadelphia's WHAT-FM. Dorn recalls that "the promotion guy for Impulse was Matt 'Humdinger' Singer. . . . He would bring you a record, like Chico Hamilton's *Man from Two Worlds* on Impulse [1962]. But for some reason, I didn't listen to it. He called me up, and he always called everybody 'Mr.,' though I was like twelve years old, and he was fifty. 'Mr. Dorn, how come you're not playing the Chico Hamilton record? "Forest Flower"!' 'I listened to it, Matty, I don't know . . .' 'Play it! PLAY IT!' "

Matt Singer cajoled even the reclusive Coltrane into a promotional role, according to Dorn.

> Coltrane didn't do interviews, man, Coltrane didn't do any of the stuff that everybody else did. He was really above all the nonsense. Trane agreed to do one interview, and I think it was for the Johnny Hartman album.

When the white-label deejay copies of Impulse albums were delivered, Singer's work was already done. "He didn't have to do anything," Dorn recalls. "He just brought it and said, 'Here's the new Coltrane.' "

The end result of a good marketing and distribution scheme—as anyone with business experience will attest—is an increased demand for product. Coltrane's new releases added to an expanding awareness of Impulse's releases in general, and kept ABC's distribution pipeline flowing and Thiele's bosses happy. Happy meant busy, and the producer was constantly in the recording studio, jumping from one production to the next.

THE IMPULSE PIPELINE

"I don't know how I made so many albums, but I did," Thiele would later comment. "I even slept in the studio. I'd record maybe Freddie Hubbard in the afternoon, Shirley Scott in the evening, go to sleep on a couch, and then record Roland Kirk. It seemed endless."

Saxophonist and flutist Roland Kirk's lone appearance on an Impulse title was actually not as a leader but as a sideman, on drummer Roy Haynes's 1962 quartet outing *Out of the Afternoon,* featuring the standout, self-referential tune "Snap Crackle." Thiele can easily be forgiven for the confusion: the forty-six titles he brought to market in '63 and '64 must have passed by like a blur.

To fully appreciate the producer's juggling of sessions and schedules during this period, while avoiding a numbing list of album titles, dates, and sidemen, the more memorable high points of Thiele's productions follow, while expanded title-by-title discussion and details are in the book's Source Notes section.

Some titles derived from contracted artists like Freddie Hubbard, whose *The Body & the Soul* stretched from small-group tracks to music with a full string section [A(S)-38]. There were also one-offs like Chico Hamilton's *Man from Two Worlds* [A(S)-59]. Highlighted by the original version of Charles Lloyd's popular "Forest Flower," it proved a strong enough seller to induce ABC to extend Hamilton's multi-album deal, recalls Phil Kurnit. "It was actually the single that was making some noise on jazz stations in California. ABC jumped on that. So we made [another] exclusive recording deal with Chico, which was quite profitable for Impulse."

The one-offs continued: Thiele delivered four albums from four leading vibraphonists of the day (Gary McFarland, Terry Gibbs, Milt Jackson, and Lionel Hampton); four swing-era stalwarts (saxophonists Ben Webster, Johnny Hodges, and Paul Gonsalves, and trumpeter Clark Terry); three bebop/hard-bop veterans (J.J. Johnson, Art Blakey, and saxophonist Sonny Stitt); one big-band arranger (Oliver Nelson); and another of Thiele's style-hopping summits (Stitt and Gonsalves).

A cursory cross-check of the albums above reveals Thiele's plan to squeeze a maximum number of titles from Impulse's recording dates and deals. In a musical round-robin, he was able to record Sonny Stitt as a leader, as a featured soloist on the Art Blakey recording, and as a co-leader on a Paul Gonsalves title. In turn, Gonsalves himself recorded two titles as a leader and proved invaluable on Johnny Hodges's Ellington-flavored album, while Hodges returned the favor on Gonsalves's second. Ben Webster—yet another Ellington alumnus—was a surprise guest on both Oliver Nelson's sophomore effort and Clark Terry's debut for Impulse, in addition to recording his own title for the label.

Among all these Impulse dates, an inevitable circle of support developed, as the names of alto saxophonist Phil Woods, guitarist Kenny Burrell, and pianists Roger Kellaway and Hank Jones (Elvin's older brother) popped up repeatedly on a number of Thiele-produced sessions. "They were relaxed dates, there was never any pressure," Jones recalls. "Well, it starts from the top, doesn't it? From Bob Thiele himself. He created the atmosphere. He left you to your own devices. We did all the dates at Van Gelder's in New Jersey. Bob would have an idea of what he wanted, but when you got into the studio it was up to you."

The pianist's memory of those sessions suggests another jazz producer of note.

> At most of those dates with Sonny Stitt, Webster—Ben was the consummate artist—Paul Gonsalves, there was really no written charts. Maybe there were lead sheets, but the arrangements were sort of built as you went along. "Arrangements while you wait" [laughs]. Those Verve sessions of the fifties with Norman Granz were the same.
>
> The thing I most remember about those dates [was that] the personnel was always correct for the date. That takes a little advance planning. I'm sure Bob must have had some input as to the personnel.

WORKING THE JAZZ HUSTLE

Thiele's fingerprints—and image—were indeed all over Impulse's albums at the time. What Creed Taylor established with a simple signature, his successor maintained with numerous photos of himself on the inside of the gatefold covers. His most common pose: jacketless in the studio, cigarette dangling from lip, at a musician's side. Chatting with Ellington. Laughing with McCoy Tyner. Listening to Coltrane, relaxed and, yes, determined.

What might seem shameless self-promotion is as easily interpreted as self-preservation in a business where allegiances to musicians last only a breath longer than those afforded in-house staff. Any public display that might bind the producer to his label consciously came, to some degree, from a survival strategy. "You never knew what the hell was going to happen in the record business," Thiele once said. "A guy could say, 'Listen, you're fired.' It was as simple as that."

Over the years, Thiele had certainly learned a trick or two about staying alive, and a few about keeping well. "It was still an era of innocence and probity when music publishers could give A&R executives checks 'in appreciation' throughout the year ('appreciation' all of us would declare on our tax returns)," Thiele wrote in his autobiography. "And producers were actually encouraged to write and publish the songs they recorded."

Such encouragement had a tendency to come from the producers themselves, and a few Impulse artists were swayed to record tunes that yielded publishing revenue to Thiele. Elvin Jones's "Dear John C." and Chico Hamilton's "Conquistadores" listed partial composer credit to the producer, while Coleman Hawkins's "Don't Love Me" was co-credited to Thiele's girlfriend at the time, Pauline Rivelli, editor in chief of *Jazz* magazine.

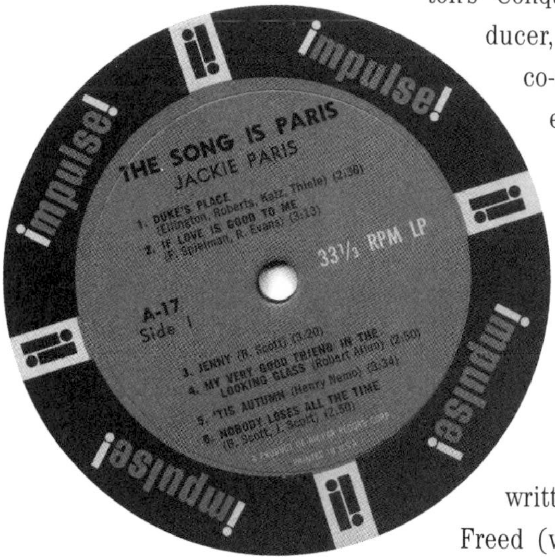

The most telling example made it onto four different albums. "Duke's Place," basically a renaming of Ellington's "C Jam Blues" with a lyric added by Thiele, first appeared on the famed studio summit of Ellington and Louis Armstrong, and was later covered by Gonsalves, Jackie Paris, *and* McCoy Tyner for Impulse.

Note Thiele's inclusion as one of the songwriters of an Ellington composition.

As a rule, Thiele did not force his name onto already written compositions. Unlike the influential deejay Alan Freed (who traded songwriting credit for airplay of Chuck Berry's "Maybellene") or Roulette Records chief Morris Levy (who legally defended his claim to have co-written "Why Do Fools Fall in Love?"), Thiele had basic musical training and extensive experience crafting music. His input could relate to song structure or be merely suggestive. And most wisely and profitably, he collaborated with other, more musically adept songsmiths. There are 126 tunes in the ASCAP database credited to Robert Thiele, most in part and a few solely. The songs date from a thirty-year period, including some obviously penned for his heroes ("Ballad for Pee Wee," "Zoot's Toot," "EKE," "We Love You Fats"), some obvious trend-chasers ("Beatle Jazz," "Here Comes Sergeant Pepper"), and some reaching for perennial popularity ("Merry Christmas Polka," "Happy Birthday My Sweetheart").

In addition to his songwriting efforts, Thiele established in the mid-fifties a music publishing company called Vernon Music for his own compositions and other musicians'. "At that time," he explained, a producer's "ownership of a publishing company and/or writing songs was considered entirely appropriate and without ethical conflicts."

Thiele was acutely aware that one hit song could provide a steady income for years, and though many of his songs were never even recorded, he managed to hit serious pay dirt at least four times: in 1954, as publisher of Erroll Garner's perennial favorite "Misty"; in 1958, as co-composer of Buddy Holly's "Mailman, Bring Me No More Blues," later performed by the Beatles; in 1961, as lyricist of "Duke's Place," recorded eventually by a wide range of musicians, including Oliver Nelson, Red Garland, David Murray, and Thiele's wife, the singer Teresa Brewer; and—most profitably—in 1968, as co-composer of Louis Armstrong's enduring classic "What a Wonderful World."

Various Impulse musicians are alternately bemused and perturbed by Thiele's hustling tendencies. Alice Coltrane remembers that "Bob wrote this piece ["What a Wonderful World"] and he sent it to John. Once I said, 'You like it?' and he said, 'It's nice, it's fine, and I like it.' But that was the end of it, and not much more. [Bob] really wanted John to record it."

Chico Hamilton recalls that the title for his album *The Dealer* "came out of a conversation I had with Bob. He said, 'Hey, man, you're a dealer, you get the business done,' which is cool. But if there was a melodic line, or some bars [of composed music] and no one claimed them, he would [laughs]. I was really shocked one time on one of my albums, when I read that one of the things was composed by Bob Thiele ["Conquistadores"]. It came as a total surprise to me."

The stakes were still small in Thiele's "small community," while pressures grew during his first years at Impulse, both in the office (maintaining a steady stream of new, profitable recordings) and outside (dealing with the lingering demands from three failed marriages). For Thiele, the personal and professional could not help but overlap. "I had a son, Bobby Jr., a house in New Rochelle [New York], and a particularly nasty divorce that totaled me!" he wrote in his autobiography. "I started to sell off everything I could . . . [including] my Vernon Music stock," which featured his valuable stake in "Misty."

ABC counsel Alan Bergman recalls, "I was kind of caretaker of his own fragile financial situation up there [at Impulse]. Bob had a lot of financial troubles. Wives and children and things like that. His personal life was not terribly tidy." "My salary was at the level comparable with that of all other A&R men at the time," Thiele himself later confessed. "Whatever monies came our way were always a matter of survival rather than influence."

Whether Thiele's priorities at Impulse were personal or professional, there's little doubt that bubbling below that cool and calculating exterior ran a current of passion for the music he produced, and for his label. On the rare occasion when he permitted unbridled sentiment to show, it was in anger over an affront to a favorite musician or his own role. In the opening months of 1964 a verbal skirmish raged between Thiele, a reporter, and readers of the jazz magazine *Coda*.

"Impulse appears to be pinning their faith on Coltrane. He is featured in every release," wrote Fred Norsworthy in a roundup of the 1963 jazz scene, adding: "Other than Coltrane, McCoy Tyner and Charles Mingus they seem to have a one-shot policy with no firm commitments." The writer ended his assessment predicting, "Unless they take some gambles or chances don't expect much from Impulse this year."

Thiele blasted a letter to the editor that was printed in its entirety. He

Second of three: Mingus leads a session for Impulse, September 20, 1963.

attacked "Norsworthy's ramblings," writing that "under exclusive contract as Impulse artists are John Coltrane, Charlie Mingus, McCoy Tyner, Yusef Lateef, Johnny Hartman, Lorez Alexandria, Elvin Jones and Paul Gonsalves . . . Impulse *gambles* [his emphasis] continuously with people like Shirley Scott, Sonny Stitt, Milt Jackson, Coleman Hawkins, Art Blakey, Gary McFarland, Roy Haynes, Chico Hamilton . . ."

Thiele wasn't done: "jerko writer" . . . "insane statements" . . . "I think I met him once and remember him as the fool-type." In closing, the man whose self-identity had become more closely linked than ever with the label he ran revealed his true vitriol:

> Norsworthy's last statement—"don't expect too much from Impulse this year"—is a gasser. I feel like Mingus now—I'd like to punch this idiot right in the mouth.

OF SAINTS AND SINNERS

Through the early sixties, bassist, composer, and bandleader Charles Mingus had become increasingly well known among jazz fans for his music, and outside the jazz circle—through interviews in *Time* and *Newsweek*, for example—for outspoken remarks on race relations, the music business, and himself. Though an ambitious 1962 Town Hall concert ended in confusion, the fiasco could not dissuade Thiele. He was clear he wanted Mingus, and he was clear why.

> I was initially more impressed with his arranging capabilities as opposed to his bass playing. Not that he wasn't one of the great bass players! But I was always amazed at how he could come up with these arrangements. That was really my reason for wanting to record him.

Mingus arrived at Impulse in 1963 with a reputation that warned he could be as volatile as he was creative. Thiele had firsthand experience.

> [Mingus] was a real character. Once, I went into the office at ABC-Paramount . . . I was always in the office, certainly no later than nine o'clock—and on the back of my chair was a note with a knife through it, stuck into the chair. It was addressed to me from Mingus, saying that he hadn't been paid for his last recording date. He said he wanted to be paid as soon as possible or else. Which, of course, I had nothing to do with. I would merely do the necessary paperwork. That would go to the accounting department, and they would send out checks. It was scary at the time but funny now.

According to Mingus biographer Gene Santoro, the incident occurred at the close of 1963, when an advance due from Impulse was supposed to be raised $5,000 from the bassist's initial $10,000 deal. But his sales had not reached beyond the label's investment, and the label had been reluctant to pay. Thiele put in the call, Mingus was eventually paid, and over a brief period he delivered albums that today are praised as a career-high trifecta, on a par with his best projects for Atlantic and Columbia. Of the three, the most significant arrived first.

The Black Saint and the Sinner Lady [A(S)-35] was an artfully arranged self-portrait presenting the various facets of a complex, fiery soul in suite form. The album was conceived for an eleven-piece band, exhibited an appreciation for the colors and textures of Ellington, and, most famously, included liner notes written by Mingus's psychiatrist.

Mingus himself also wrote liners for *The Black Saint,* demanding: "Throw all other records of mine away except maybe one other. I intend to record it all over again on this label the way it was intended to sound." True to his word, his next album, *Mingus, Mingus, Mingus, Mingus, Mingus* [A(S)-54], featured re-recordings of a few of his better-known tunes: "Haitian Fight Song" was renamed "II B.S."; "Goodbye Pork Pie Hat" became "Theme for Lester Young"; and "Better Git Hit in Your Soul" was recorded for the third time (after versions on Columbia and Atlantic). The album also included an expressive take of "Mood Indigo," yet another nod to Ellington. The solo effort that followed, *Mingus Plays Piano* [A(S)-60], captured him at his most pensive, playing his primary compositional instrument.

Mingus's run with Impulse was brief, over by late 1964, and he would not return to the studio for any label until 1970. He left behind three classic recordings and, on one, a written sentiment for his producer and label acknowledging his appreciation:

> Impulse went to great expense and patience to give me complete freedom, [and] there is Bob Thiele. Thanks, man for coming to my Town Hall open recording session, hearing the music, liking it, and hiring my band to record for your company when the critics scared the pants off the people for whom I wrote the music.

FUNKY BOB AND BROTHER JOHN

Mingus was not the only Impulse musician who singled out Thiele by name, nor was the producer alone in earning a written or musical salute from members of the label's expanding family in '63.

"Funky Bob" is the title of a laid-back blues on Gloria Coleman's album, written by Grant Green with Thiele in mind. "Brother John" is a track penned by multi-reed player and flutist Yusef Lateef that appeared on his second album for Impulse, indicating Coltrane's growing impact at Impulse and a mounting level of respect from his peers.

Coltrane's primacy at Impulse was also measurable by the number of releases one could connect to him by his sidemen or his stylistic influence.

THE BLACK SAINT AND THE SINNER LADY

Charles Mingus / *The Black Saint and the Sinner Lady* / Impulse A(S)-35

DATE RECORDED: January 30, 1963

DATE RELEASED: Fall 1963

PRODUCER: Bob Thiele

"You haven't been told before that you're phonies!"

It was 1959 at the Five Spot in Manhattan's East Village. Charles Mingus was mid-tirade, berating a chatty audience. "A blind man can go to an exhibition of Picasso and Kline and not even see their works, and comment behind dark glasses, 'Wow! They're the swingingest painters ever, crazy!' Well, so can you. You've got your dark glasses and clogged-up ears."

Calling listeners inattentive dilettantes may not seem the most advisable public relations move for a jazz musician trying to make it, but being diplomatic was never a Mingus priority. In fact, as the innovative bassist and band-leader's star grew in the early sixties and the mainstream press took notice of him, his eruptive personality became part of the story. In 1962, *Time* magazine described him as "talented, successful and angry." "Volatile," John S. Wilson wrote in the *New York Times* in 1963, "on and off the bandstand." "A Volcano Named Mingus," read the headline of a 1964 *HiFi/Stereo Review* profile.

Small surprise that Mingus would choose to initiate his Impulse association with an ambitious recording to explain himself in his preferred fashion: a musical self-portrait. He initially imagined the work as an extended non-stop performance with dance accompaniment, then settled for a flowing, suite-like structure that would travel an emotional range—from sentimental and elegant to bold and, yes, *angry*—flavored with strong hints of Ellingtonia and flourishes from a flamenco guitar.

The work would employ the colors and textural variety of a tight eleven-piece ensemble including relative unknowns, a group Mingus intermittently referred to as the

"New Folk Band." Trombonist Quentin Jackson; reed players Jerome Richardson, Dick Hafer, and Charlie Mariano; pianist Jaki Byard; guitarist Jay Berliner, and drummer Dannie Richmond were among Mingus's hand-picked lineup. Editing technology of the day, like tape splicing and overdubbing, would help suture together what Mingus called "my living epitaph from birth til the day I first heard Bird and Diz"—approximately the first twenty years of his life.

The session went well, and Mingus was satisfied beyond his normal expectations. "I'm doing what I want to do on the *Saint and Sinner* album, with people trying to get the best balance possible," he noted soon after. Thiele recalled the date as one requiring a constant check on the studio clock: "The sessions for *Black Saint* stretched out a bit. He had a lot of basic stuff written down but a lot of his arranging was actually almost improvised on the session. There were things that weren't written down but they sound as though they were written down."

"I write compositions on mental score paper," Mingus explained to Nat Hentoff later. "Then I lay out the composition part by part to the musicians. I play them the 'framework' on the piano so that they are all familiar with my interpretation and feeling, and with the scale and chord progressions to be used."

Mingus's reliance on the musical signatures of his sidemen brings to mind Ellington's approach to his own orchestra. "Each man's particular style is taken into consideration. They are given different rows of notes to use against each chord, but they choose their own notes and play them in their own style, from scales as well as chords, except where a particular mood is indicated. In this way I can keep my own compositional flavor in the pieces and yet allow the musicians more individual freedom in the creation of their group line and solos."

Their names may have been unfamiliar to most jazz fans, but under Mingus's tutelage they had become a compelling force, in Hentoff's opinion:

"When a Mingus unit begins to achieve its potential, the music is among the most mesmeric experiences in contemporary jazz. Mingus' presence acts as a stimulus to his colleagues, and the result is an impassioned, mutual testing of wills and ideas that—when the collective spirit takes fire—spirals into a remarkable organic unity."

True to form, Mingus came up with an enigmatic title for his opus, one suggesting a balance of opposites. But who are they, the Saint and the Sinner?

Mingus himself did not clarify it in his self-penned liner notes, but as the titles of other autobiographical compositions suggested—"Myself When I Am Real," "Self Portrait in Three Colors"—the two figures could easily be seen as parts of a fractured self. One biographer sees the Saint and Sinner as Mingus's parents. Dr. Edmund Pollack, the bassist's psychiatrist, hired for $200 to write a second set of liner notes for the album, interpreted Mingus himself as the "Black Saint who suffers for his sins and those of mankind."

"From every experience such as a conviction for assault or as an inmate of a Bellevue locked ward, Mr. Mingus has learned something and has stated it will not happen again to him," Pollack continued. "He also is cognizant of a power-dominated and segregated society's impact upon the underdog, the underprivileged and the minority."

Mingus was all too familiar with the martyr's role when it came to his art: he was an underdog and a victim, as well as the towering talent vanquishing all detractors and reaching the disinterested with the power of his music. In terms more poetic than his onstage tirades, he implied as much in a line of poetry printed on the album's cover:

Touch my beloved's thought while her world's affluence crumbles at my feet.

In 1963 and 1964, Coltrane's own recordings and those by his sidemen and by labelmates whose playing fell under the spell of his innovations—namely Yusef Lateef and Archie Shepp—amounted to 25 percent of Impulse's total output.

Lateef had been a part of Cannonball Adderley's pioneering soul-jazz outfit, but when he joined Impulse in 1963, his own music expanded beyond any one style. "The late [trumpeter] Don Cherry said that style is the death of creativity," says Lateef today. "What people call style is actually I think a person's persona, if you will, [his] inner expression."

Lateef's persona—his spiritual bent and expansive musical curiosity—placed him in line with a growing number of jazz artists, especially Coltrane, and led to a label contract. His unusual adeptness with other-land instruments (like the nasal-sounding shanai and argol) shaped his label debut, *Jazz 'Round the World* [A(S)-56], a musical travelogue that suggested European, African, and Asian traditions in sound and title.

Like Shirley Scott, Lateef and his group at the time, one of his best—trumpeter Richard Williams, pianist Mike Nock, bassist Ernie Farrow (Alice Coltrane's brother), and drummer James Black—shone brightest with lights low and air smoky. *Live at Pep's* [A(S)-69] caught the quintet in a famed Philadelphia nightclub in June 1964, swinging but still experimental and exotic. Even eerie, as on the finger-snapping Middle Eastern feel of "Sister Mamie." And the band could boogie: "Slippin' and Slidin'" exploited Black's New Orleans–born shuffle to full rocking effect. *Live* was a seven-song set that inspired various repackagings years later, with further recordings added from that evening.

Lateef remained with Impulse through 1966 and recorded four more albums, including another live set, with a title inspired by its catalog number: *1984* [A(S)-84]. The association stands out for him for a reason shared by others: "I was free to record what I chose to: that was a strong point to me. When you give a person freedom, they give you their utmost. I think Bob Thiele realized that."

McCoy Tyner certainly was giving it his all. In a two-year period for Impulse, he recorded with Coltrane and with other Impulse leaders, including Johnny Hartman, J.J. Johnson, and Elvin Jones, and completed four stellar albums as a leader. *Nights of Ballads and Blues* [A(S)-39] was a collection of wee-hour tunes by the likes of Monk, Ellington, and Henry Mancini. "Bob came up with that concept," recalls Tyner. *Live at Newport*

[A(S)-48] was a giddy, impromptu set, the pianist's first live recording as a leader, while *Today and Tomorrow* [A(S)-63] featured an unusual lineup that included Sun Ra's tenor saxophonist John Gilmore in a key role.

Tyner's final Impulse album (he would not return to the studio under his own name until 1967 for Blue Note) was *McCoy Tyner Plays Ellington* [A(S)-79], a trio-plus-percussion session, again suggested by Thiele. "I was so young. He gave me some of Duke's sheet music I had never heard of—like 'Mr. Gentle and Mr. Cool.' I came up with 'Caravan' and some of the other songs. I had some of my own ideas of some of the things that Duke had written, so it worked out well."

Tyner's work in 1963 and '64 ("There was no disillusionment," he said of his departure from the label. "It just ran its course") left behind much of the intensity and experimental charge of his work with Coltrane. Collectively, his albums suggest that the pianist's abiding affection for a more familiar approach to chordal structure—well-known standards, melodies of his own making—was a point of distinction from his bandleader, and a point to which he would return after departing Coltrane's employ in late 1965. "A lot of things I was doing with John was—well, I wouldn't say far out, but it was moving out. More of a spiritual, intellectual approach to the music."

Elvin Jones, on the other hand, teamed up with bandmate Jimmy Garrison to record a sextet session in the tumultuous Classic Quartet mold. *Illumination!* [A(S)-49] was the drummer's first album for Impulse (and his second as a leader for any label) and drew on the talents of Tyner and a trio of Coltrane acolytes: clarinetist-flutist Prince Lasha, alto saxophonist–English horn player Sonny Simmons, and baritone saxophonist Charles Davis. It wasn't Coltrane himself, but the material and setting were engaging and familiar to those wanting more of what Impulse was becoming the home for, which Thiele was happy to accommodate.

Illumination! was recorded on August 8, 1964, at Van Gelder's studio, but the album Thiele produced two evenings later found him at his most hesitant. *Four for Trane* [A(S)-71], Archie Shepp's debut album for Impulse, was a direct result of Coltrane's intervention, and his faith in the young tenor saxophonist from Philadelphia. Shepp reports that even though Coltrane had Thiele's ear, the producer insisted that the *avant-gardista* record only tunes composed by Coltrane.

Shepp was more than happy to agree. In title and material, the album is a salute to his mentor: a reworking of four better-known Coltrane tunes

Passing the torch: Archie Shepp, John Coltrane, and Bob Thiele, December 10, 1964.

from his Atlantic years, three from *Giant Steps,* plus the Shepp original "Rufus." At the session, Thiele himself was smiling by the third tune, content he had bowed to his star's urging. Coltrane received a late-night call with the good news, and drove to the studio to hear the results. Thiele recalled a few years later that the Shepp session was only the first of many inspired by suggestions from Coltrane.

> It was certainly through Coltrane that I became aware of Archie Shepp and many of the younger players. When John heard any good player, he would call me and ask that I please give him some consideration. He was very much concerned about the young musicians. I think that if we [had] signed everyone that John recommended we'd have four hundred musicians on the label.

OF SUITES AND SPIRITUALITY: TRANE IN '64

In 1964, Coltrane himself seemed to be putting on the brakes—for a minute, anyway. He visited Van Gelder's four times, twice in late spring and twice in early December, delivering only two albums.

But what titles! Both were of lasting, iconic stature. Both sounded a tranquil departure from his frenetic path of development, a stylistic resting point that seemed to reflect a calming satisfaction with his personal life (he had fallen in love with keyboardist Alice McLeod and had fathered his first son with her), and with his career. Both came across as complete musical statements, reflecting Coltrane's long-standing affection for suite-like extended compositions.

"I like extended jazz works," Coltrane told a British jazz journal in 1961. "I'm studying and learning about longer constructions. If I become strong enough I might try something along those lines."

Crescent [A(S)-66] was structured in a manner that saluted each of Coltrane's sidemen and gave ample room for them to showcase their talents. Of special note was the tune "Wise One." In both title and prayer-like mood, it predicted much of Coltrane's spiritually inspired future work. It also proved the model for Coltrane's follow-up, the fully conceived musical self-portrait *A Love Supreme* [A(S)-77].

The four-part suite that was Coltrane's "gift to God," according to his liner notes, would eventually sound a call to prayer for an entire generation poised for spiritual exploration. For Coltrane, the shape and arrangement of *A Love Supreme* were the result of a five-day homebound hiatus at the end of a season of non-stop touring. Originally intended to be performed by a nine-piece group augmented by Latin-flavored percussion, Coltrane's opus was instead recorded by his Classic Quartet. The album was a sensation upon its release, becoming a double Grammy nominee, receiving a Record of the Year award from *Down Beat*, and listed by Thiele as his second-favorite production of his career (Armstrong-Ellington ranked first.)

Yet, according to producer George Avakian, Thiele may well have first resisted Coltrane's suite-focused intentions. "In early 1964, John became disillusioned about his situation at Impulse Records," reports Avakian, who had been in charge of album production at Columbia Records when he first worked with Coltrane on the sessions for the Miles Davis album *'Round Midnight*. "We had become good friends when I first signed Miles to Columbia, and he knew I had recorded several of Duke Ellington's long suites and had continued to do so even when sales were modest."

Avakian adds that Coltrane made a note to call him in late spring of '64—evidenced by a handwritten reminder the saxophonist scrawled on an envelope postmarked that month—and that the gist of the call was that "Trane was frustrated because he wanted to record some long compositions, but Thiele wanted more standards and shorter tracks. Knowing something of the contract I had worked out with Prestige Records in 1954 that had enabled me to record Miles for Columbia eighteen months before his contract with Prestige expired, Trane suggested that I try to get Impulse to agree to let him record long original works for another label, even if he were kept under contract at Impulse."

Avakian reports that, as a freelance producer at the time but with active contracts at the labels where he had recently worked (Columbia, Warner Bros., and RCA), he did follow up on the idea, but to no avail. "The best bet

FOUR FOR TRANE

Archie Shepp / *Four for Trane* / Impulse A(S)-71

DATE RECORDED: August 10, 1964

DATE RELEASED: November 1964

PRODUCER: Bob Thiele

Archie Shepp: Let me explain it this way: When I did that recording, Bob Thiele had made the stipulation that all the songs had to be written by John. I had to use Trane's music. That was the deal. . . . In a way, he made those stipulations because he was hoping that my ego would make me say, "Well, I only want to do my own thing, Bob, so let's forget it," because he really didn't want to record me.

Ashley Kahn: Was that a feeling you got or did you really know that?

AS: I knew that! I had spent months trying to get Bob on the phone and he never answered the phone. Every time I'd call, his secretary, Lillian, whom I got to know very well, but at that point I hated her because she said, "Well he's gone out to lunch," or "He's gone home and he's not coming back." I was living in a fifth-floor walk-up and I'd save a dollar a day just to make ten calls. I'd run down and put a dime in the phone in the drugstore. This went on for months.

So this one night I sat in with Trane at the Half Note. I got up enough courage to ask if he would intercede. So John gave me a look—the first time he really sort of looked at me in a very critical way, very questioning. He said, "You know, a lot of people think I'm easy." Then he took a very hard look at me. I said, "Well, John, you can be sure I'm not trying to take advantage. I need this." He knew I loved him. It wasn't about just trying to get off easy. So he looked at me and he says, "Well, I'll see what I can do."

The next day I called Thiele's office and lo and behold the secretary says, "Well, he's not in now but he will be back at three o'clock and he's waiting for your call." So when I did talk to him, the first thing he said is, "You guys are avant-garde. I know you're into your own thing. If you do this recording you're going to have to record all of John's music." I had just been waiting for the chance to do that. I loved Trane's music and I had my own ideas about how to work with it. That became the *Four for Trane* date.

When we did the *Four for Trane* date, it went down almost take by take, because we had rehearsed nightly for months. After the third song, Bob, who had been really terribly rude at the beginning, smoking his pipe like a chimney, he brightened up a bit, sat down and said, "I've got to call John and tell him this stuff is great." He said, "John, you got to come out and hear this!" Well, Coltrane already knew. He had been listening to this stuff for the last couple of years because the avant-garde was all around New York.

John was very gracious. He drove out from his home in Long Island to Englewood, at about eleven o'clock at night. I assumed he got out of his bed, because when we took that photo they put on the album cover [he was] with no socks, you know.

AK: So the next time you two were together in the studio was for the second *Love Supreme* session, when you were on Trane's ground?

AS: You're telling me [laughs]. . . . But after *Four for Trane* I was given a lot more leeway to write my own music, and in fact that's all I did. Practically all the stuff I did was original. The company was very accessible to me when I needed composers, or if I wanted special guest artists like Roy Haynes, Ron Carter, or Woody Shaw.

Scenes from a groundbreaking session: [*Below*] Drummer Charles Moffett, Thiele, and Shepp.

[*Bottom*] Shepp, trumpeter Alan Shorter, trombonist Roswell Rudd, and alto saxophonist John Tchicai.

was my old colleague, Ken Glancy, head of pop A&R at Columbia. Ken indicated mild interest but thought that my proposal for an advance was much too high—I think I asked for $50,000. As for the idea of recording only Trane's long compositions, Glancy was echoed by Thiele's lack of enthusiasm, 'How many times do you want to hear "Greensleeves" for half an hour?'"

Avakian and Coltrane left it at that; if ABC did not renew the next option on his contract, they would revisit the idea. The popular reception of *A Love Supreme* the next spring made the point moot. In Thiele's autobiography, he described the album's success as "both a musical and marketing event," exaggerating slightly the duration of the album's tracks:

> Its length was practically unprecedented in that era. Jazz musicians were ever mindful that jazz radio stations, which were essential to record sales, demanded each song be an absolute maximum of five to six minutes long; and made albums that usually contained ten selections. Now Coltrane makes an album with just four tracks, none less than ten minutes each (you can imagine how my bosses screamed about this!), that so moved and magnetized people that it began to be uninterruptedly played on all the jazz as well as the classical stations. John's sales were around 25,000 to 50,000 over a year's time-tremendous for a jazz album-and *A Love Supreme* became his best seller, going into six figures.

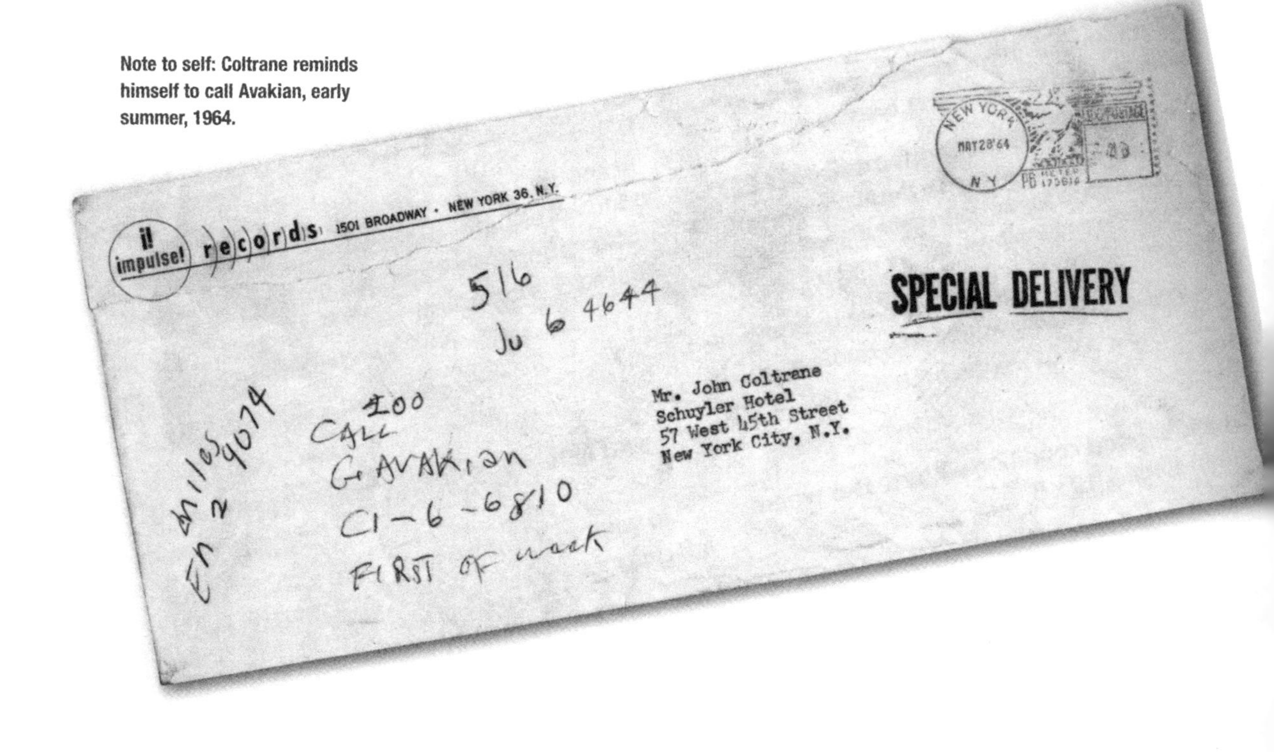

Note to self: Coltrane reminds himself to call Avakian, early summer, 1964.

IMPULSE WORLDWIDE

In 1964, Impulse was not alone in proving jazz to be a profitable commodity: both Blue Note (with Lee Morgan's album *The Sidewinder* riding the boogaloo craze) and Verve (with *Getz/Gilberto* cresting the bossa nova wave) successfully pushed jazz into the pop charts that year. Even Louis Armstrong managed to briefly unseat the Beatles, topping the singles charts with the Broadway tune "Hello, Dolly!" for the Kapp label.

What Impulse lacked in pop charters, it made up for with consistently solid sellers bubbling under the charts. What it lacked in sales in the United States, it made up for with lucrative deals overseas. "We not only sold a lot of Impulse records in the United States," Thiele said. "It was a worldwide thing. We were selling in Japan and France and England—all over."

ABC attorney Alan Bergman explains further: "See, ABC was not a big enough company like Sony or Warner Bros. [today] to have its own companies abroad, so they had independent companies they did business with."

Phil Kurnit recalls the list of ABC's foreign licensees: "Phonogram was in Germany and in Holland. Sparton in Canada. Hispavox in Spain. England was EMI. I think it was RCA in Japan, Barclay in France. I forget the name of the one in Mexico. ABC made a lot of money from their foreign licensees—the deals usually were that the foreign licensee would pay a dollar per record plus the shipping and then pay the royalty on top of that."

Impulse benefited, in different countries *and* with various formats, Bergman adds. "There were no separate Impulse deals, it was all included within the ABC umbrella—for foreign, for tapes, for whatever. In those days you had the reel-to-reel format; jazz sold pretty well on that stuff. Of course, ABC had a lot of worldwide hit product, so they made a lot of money from their foreign record licensees and from their tape licensees."

Though the numbers (of sales, of listeners, even of general population) in each separate country could not match the sheer size of the United States, Coltrane's sales figures—relative to the size of each market—easily matched his popularity in America. Coltrane and many of the newer artists helped to establish Impulse on foreign soil.

Now and again the doorway swung in the opposite direction, and Thiele licensed foreign jazz productions. The two-volume *Americans in Europe* [A(S)-36 and 37] featured music from a January 1963 concert in Koblenz, Germany, with three bands led by legends (pianist Bud Powell, tenor saxo-

A LOVE SUPREME

John Coltrane / *A Love Supreme* / Impulse A(S)-77
DATE RECORDED: December 9 and 10, 1964
DATE RELEASED: February 1965
PRODUCER: Bob Thiele

Alice Coltrane reports that though her husband worked out his four-part gift-to-God suite in a five-day fever in the late summer of 1964, the original idea went as far back as 1946, when he was still in uniform.

"When he was in the navy, he had a vision that he couldn't interpret at that time. It was just beyond him, and he didn't know who to turn to who could provide any clarity to it. He said that's when [the idea for] *A Love Supreme* started to blow into his consciousness. So [in 1964] he remembered the vision he had in the navy, and then he could see everything clearly: the sound. 'Resolution.' 'Acknowledgement.' The prayer . . . I should have a copy of his notes, the original. I'll double-check, I'm certain that it's still in our family."

[*Opposite*] The first page (of six) of John Coltrane's blueprint for *A Love Supreme*. Interestingly, it seems that the suite was originally conceived for a nine-piece group, with Latin percussion. Also note that many of the suite's defining moments were quite consciously planned, including: playing the four-note motif through all keys in "Acknowledgement"; the "recitation of prayer [his poem] by horn" in "Psalm"; and the suite's closing, invoking "bliss-ful stability" and "sound like [the] final chord of [his recording] 'Alabama.'"

COMPOSITION A Love Supreme A

Tenor Saxophone (one other Horn) Horns

2 Bass 2 Conga 1 Tymbal

PAGE I

Horn opening

E♭ — BASS & Piano in E♭ mi — melody Horn

TO Drums 4/4 Primary Rythmmic motif

I

SOLO 4/4 — Quartet Accompaniment

into all Drums multiple meters and

Voices chanting motif in E♭mi "A Love Supreme" this male

motif played in all keys together — to Pause

— Voices concert key

II

Quartet Horn melody Bbmi Blues Form moving Harmonies

Piano solo lead

Horn solo

melody

III Bass solo

Ending Bass move into solo Pause

IV Cmi

musical Recitation of Prayer* by Horn in

Bass

Cmi Bass accompaniment only

To Ending

(make ending) attempt to reach transcendent level with or chanting

Final notes by Bass Viol

Horn ends on — Thank you God —

& Amen these final notes by Bass say Amen — symbolically

Rising harmonies to a level of blissful stability at end.

All paths lead to God.

Last chord to sound like final chord of Alabama —

* Prayer entitled "A Love Supreme"

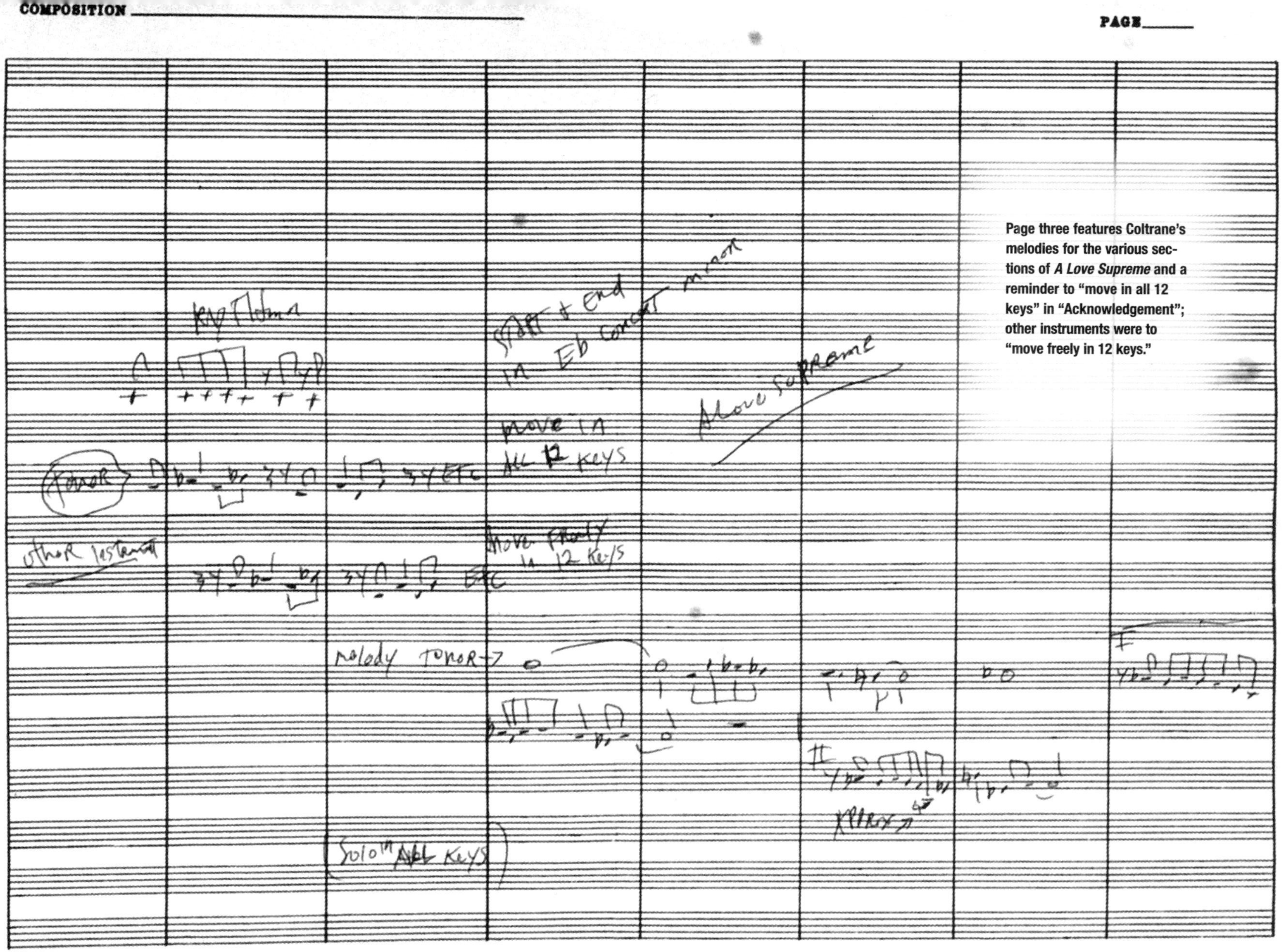

COMPOSITION ____________

PAGE ______

Rhythm

Start & End in Eb concert minor

A Love Supreme

move in all 12 keys

Tenor ... ETC

other instrument

move freely in 12 keys

... ETC

melody Tenor

Solo in all keys

Page three features Coltrane's melodies for the various sections of *A Love Supreme* and a reminder to "move in all 12 keys" in "Acknowledgement"; other instruments were to "move freely in 12 keys."

I will do all I can
To do worthy of Thee Oh Lord

(Buy Reeds in S.F.)

Avenues of Awareness
& God's index file
Dimensions
No. Containing
ALL

It ALL Has To Do with It.

Thank You God

Peace There is none other

God IS It is so Beautiful

Thank You God God IS ALL

Help us to Resolve
Our Fears & weaknesses

We are nothing without You O God
Everything with You

In You ALL Things are Possible

Thank God!

We know! God made us so.

Keep your Eye on God

God is He Always was He always will Be.

No matter what...
...It is God

It is most important That I know Thee

Words sounds speech
men, memory, thoughts, fears & emotions
& time all related, all made
from one all made in one
Blessed Be His name

Thought waves
Heat "
ALL vibrations

All Paths Lead to God

His way -- It is Lovely
It is Gracious - It is merciful

Thank you God.

Page four includes most of the Coltrane poem printed on the inside cover of the album, which acted as the structure of the last section of the suite, "Psalm" (through his saxophone, Coltrane followed the cadence and phrasing of the text). The apparent random order of the phrases suggests that he first joined the music and words, and later ordered the poem to match the musical flow of the piece. Note also certain phrases that did not appear in the final draft of the poem ("Avenues of awareness," "God's index file") and a reminder to buy saxophone reeds in San Francisco.

phonist Don Byas, drummer Kenny Clarke), two New Orleans traditionalists (clarinetist Albert Nicholas and pianist Champion Jack Dupree), and two leaders-come-lately (trumpeter Idrees Sulieman and clarinetist Bill Smith).

Happiness [A(S)-80] was *perestroika* twenty-five years too soon: an album by the Russian Jazz Quartet, formed by two recent U.S.S.R. defectors (alto saxophonist–clarinetist Boris Midney and bassist Igor Berukshtis) and two New York stalwarts (pianist Roger Kellaway and drummer Grady Tate). Taking the Modern Jazz Quartet as a point of inspiration, the foursome locked into a mix of originals and a pair of standards. "Jazz music is truly the Voice of America," said the promotional paragraph on the cover, reflecting the mid–cold war context in which the album was delivered.

ABC AT TEN

In late 1964, ABC-Paramount Records was ten years old and had been expanding consistently. "It wasn't a magical comet," says ABC counsel Bill Kaplan. "It was a steady kind of a thing with some very good executives doing it and artists who contributed. I don't recall that many no. 1's that we had, outside of Ray [Charles] and Paul [Anka]. And the Impressions—they were big."

ABC had pop stars and catalog, a profitable classical arm, and a jazz label of burgeoning reputation and sales. The company owned manufacturing plants and boasted a branch distribution system delivering its product to stores nationwide, with a minimal reliance on the independent distributors that smaller labels—particularly the jazz-focused—depended on. All of ABC was hale, and so was Impulse.

In a pre-echo of today's push to bypass conventional retail outlets and sell music online, ABC was even attempting to create its own alternative distribution network. "If you made it easy for people to buy, like they buy a greeting card, then they pick it up," states Larry Newton.

> I saw that the future of the record business was that music would be sold wherever people could see it, not just going into music stores. The record business was turning to the rack-jobbing business—which means they could sell records on a rack like they did with magazines in drugstores, and in supermarkets too. I said, "I think I'm going to go into business and buy these companies up." And that's what I did—went out and bought those companies that had racking contracts with big, big [retail] chains. I started a company called ABC Record and Tape Sales, and the first rack jobber I bought was in Seattle.

The result? Phil Kurnit recalls an after-work huddle at ABC.

> This was still at 1501 Broadway, so it was '64. I remember one night sitting in Harry [Levine]'s office and Sam was there and Newton and Alan Parker, who was the sales manager. You have to understand the picture: when five-thirty would come, Harry would open up his bottle of J&B and it'd be cocktail time. He hated to drink anything better than J&B—you couldn't give him Chivas [laughs]! But that night we were talking about what we had grossed, and I think the record division had grossed eleven million dollars. Sam said, "Hey, that's not bad. Our entire recording budget is $255,000. I defy any other company to have that kind of a ratio of recording costs to total sales." It wasn't done in those days on a scientific basis. Everybody had come up from the street, stocking records, etc., including Newton.

And they would climb higher. In the final weeks of 1964, the music trades carried an announcement telling of an executive shuffle at ABC-Paramount. "By '65, Sam Clark moves upstairs to corporate and Larry Newton took over," recalls Kaplan. For Impulse, it was a move with positive consequences, as the former V.P. of sales continued to build the ABC empire; for Thiele, Kurnit remembers, it put in motion an unfortunate clash of personality styles.

> Thiele became less important particularly because—from my observation from afar—of the friction between Newton and Thiele. Thiele was a very free spirit and Newton didn't have any regard for Thiele at all.

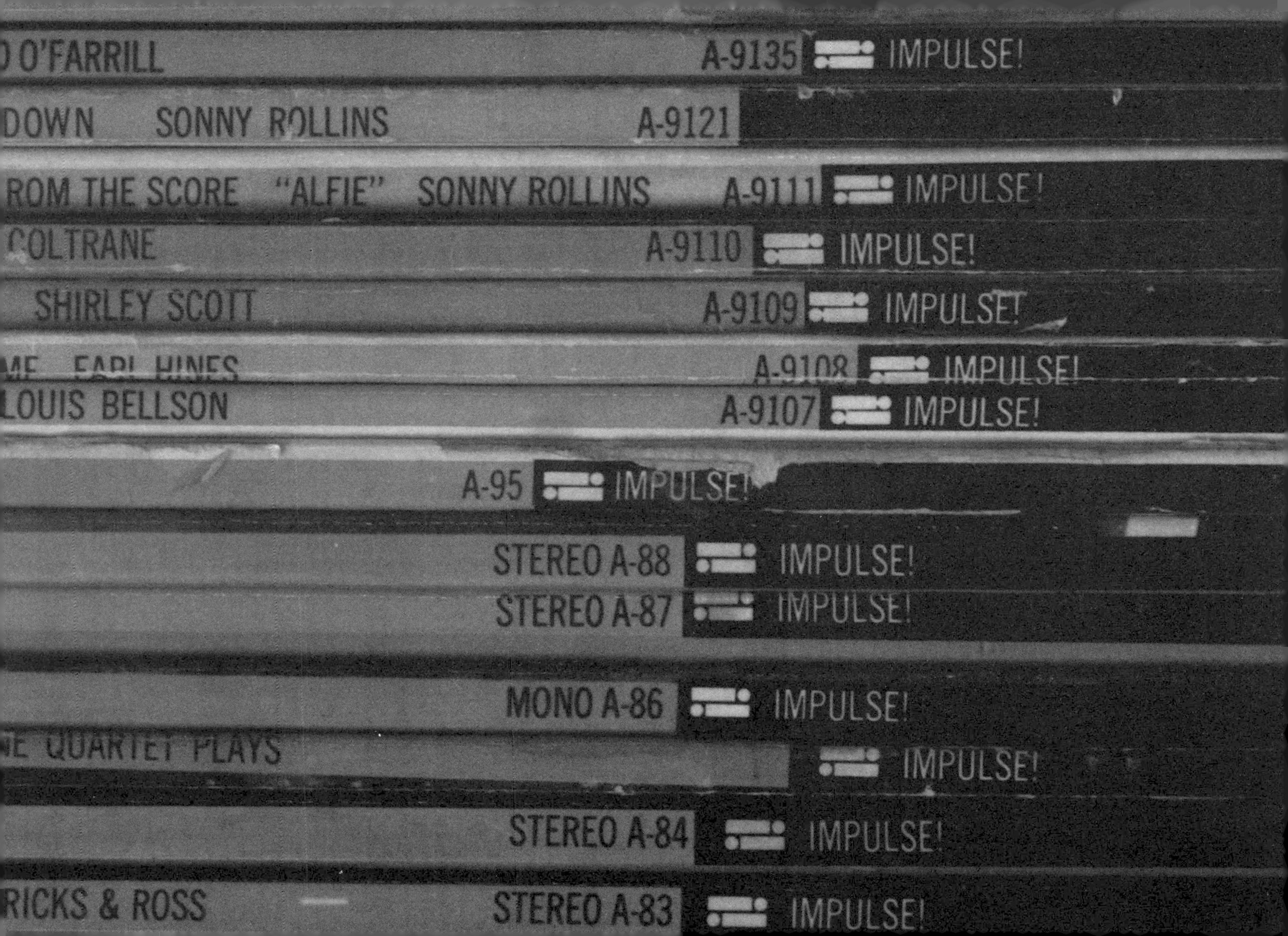
O'FARRILL A-9135 IMPULSE!
DOWN SONNY ROLLINS A-9121
ROM THE SCORE "ALFIE" SONNY ROLLINS A-9111 IMPULSE!
COLTRANE A-9110 IMPULSE!
SHIRLEY SCOTT A-9109 IMPULSE!
A-9108 IMPULSE!
LOUIS BELLSON A-9107 IMPULSE!
A-95 IMPULSE!
STEREO A-88 IMPULSE!
STEREO A-87 IMPULSE!
MONO A-86 IMPULSE!
QUARTET PLAYS IMPULSE!
STEREO A-84 IMPULSE!
RICKS & ROSS STEREO A-83 IMPULSE!

CHAPTER 4

THE NEW THING AND IMPULSE (1965–1967)

By comparison, the Ornette Coleman controversy [of 1959] was an argument carried on by physicists on the blackboard at the Princeton Institute for Advanced Study; discussions about Coltrane can take on some of the truculent, hysterical aspects of political arguments in neighborhood bars.

—Joe Goldberg, 1965

If an era can be defined by a primary emotion, then by mid-decade, the sixties were about anger. From 1965 through 1967, civil rights, black militancy, and the American presence in Vietnam fast became the wedge issues feeding passions, causing upheaval and division. The civil rights movement seemed to have stalled, and race riots in various urban centers were commonplace as frustration mounted. A distrust in the slow pace at which the Establishment was handling the issues at hand—and in the established patterns of thinking (political, social, spiritual, and musical)—was spreading, especially among the generation coming of age.

On both sides of the racial divide, ears began to search out music charged with the outrage and outcry of the day. In 1965, five years before rock would get heavy, fifteen before rap would appear, no widely distributed music was louder, angrier, or more aggressive than the avant-garde jazz on Impulse—especially with Coltrane in lead position.

"I heard many things in what Trane was doing," says Max Roach. "I heard the cry and wail of the pain that this society imposes on people, and especially black folks." "Some of his solos have exactly the rage that was being expressed in the streets, by the Muslims and the Panthers, and many people thought Trane's music was very angry," avers Archie Shepp. "It *was* assertive, it was strong, and it did have an anger to it," stresses Roger McGuinn, then leader of the rock group the Byrds. "It sounded like he was going, 'I'm not going to take this anymore. I'm just going to do what I want to do, and that's it.'"

Tenor saxophonist Frank Lowe, representative of a generation of black musicians who inherited the energy and much of the style of Coltrane, intuited a deep bond to the politics of the day.

> The Black Panthers and Malcolm X—what these cats were saying and what we were listening to were all of the same mind; it's in the body, it's in the walk, it's in the air. But you couldn't help but pick up on it, being a black kid in America and being in the generation I was in, and I was right up into that.

Coltrane's own followers were cognizant of the import of their music. Whenever Archie Shepp shared his opinions in print (as he often did), he linked his music to an overdue need for societal change. Albert Ayler, Coltrane's heir apparent and eventual Impulse labelmate, saw his music as sounding the spirit of black America: "I'm playing their suffering whether they know it or not. I lived their suffering."

It wasn't that Impulse had a lock on music that called for change. Other labels purveying jazz or folk, the preferred genres for protest at the time, released much music tied to message. But a heated buildup of emotion—and energy and volume—through the sixties seemed unique to the sounds that came off records with the bright orange and deep black spine—colors that were also finding their way into the pan-African palette of dashikis and skullcaps.

From the outset, Impulse releases had contained an element of protest, with tune titles implying black pride and a call to political action, like "Praise for a Martyr" and "Man from South Africa" on Max Roach's 1961 album *Percussion Bitter Sweet* and the title track from Roach's *It's Time,* a year later. In 1963, Coltrane recorded "Alabama," which referenced a murderous firebombing in Birmingham, and "Up 'Gainst the Wall," a term easily interpreted as the situation facing all black America. The same year, Charles Mingus recorded his half-spoken, half-sung poem "Freedom."

Various Impulse tracks in the mid-sixties maintained that outspoken spirit—particularly those including or suggesting the spoken word. "The voice becomes more and more relevant to contemporary jazz," noted political firebrand LeRoi Jones, soon to adopt the name Amiri Baraka. "From the vocal quality of the most impressive horns to *A Love Supreme* or Archie Shepp's spoken "Malcolm ["Malcolm, Malcolm, Semper Malcolm" on *Fire Music*] or Albert Ayler . . ."

Critic Gary Giddins goes further: "I think *Fire Music* is one of the really courageous albums of the sixties. God, I love that record! And it's a surprising record. You listen to it now and except for the 'Malcolm' poem, which I like a lot, it's full of melody and fun and dance rhythms. What the hell was everybody so frightened of? They were frightened of the verbiage!"

"In those days, things were pretty hot and heavy," recalled Thiele. "What happened was that for a literary fraternity, the music of Coltrane and others, like Mingus and all of the modern group, really represented black militancy. Most of the musicians, including Coltrane, really weren't thinking the way their militant brothers were. I mean, LeRoi Jones could feel the music was militant, but Coltrane didn't feel that it was. But he didn't go out of his way to tell LeRoi Jones that."

TRANE IN THE FAST LANE

When asked his political stance, Coltrane consistently maintained he was a pacifist—"I dislike war, period"—and focused more on musical process than protest: "Maybe it sounds angry. I'm trying so many things at one time, I haven't sorted them out." Music was of primary concern, but he had a growing family to worry about by then. As 1965 began, he was living in a recently purchased house on Long Island with Alice and their two children, with another on the way. His ongoing business relationship with Impulse accordingly received much of his attention.

Coltrane had learned that, at least for him, popular (and royalty-earning) success swung in 3/4 time, and through his soprano sax. His conscious search for another hit in the meter and feel of "My Favorite Things" led him to record "Greensleeves" in 1961 and "The Inchworm" in '62. In 1965, Coltrane tried it one last time with "Chim Chim Cheree" on *The John Coltrane Quartet Plays* [A(S)-85], an album culled from various sessions that spring, which now stands as his farewell to the familiar.

The album in fact represents a number of lasts for Coltrane: it was the last released during Coltrane's lifetime to focus on his Classic Quartet, though it includes a haunting two-bass version of "Nature Boy," the last jazz standard he would record in the studio. He recorded versions of "Nature Boy" on February 17 and 18, 1965. On May 17, he recorded the last non-original song other than a standard "Chim Chim Cheree."

By mid-1965, the days of Broadway tunes and ballads were over; Coltrane's preference was simply not to record the compositions of others. Rather, Alice Coltrane explains, "What he became aware of is that as long as you're expressing someone else's music, you are either trying to re-create their moments, you know, their happiness, joy, pain. You're involved in a *re-creation*, you're not involved in a creation—because that would come from you, principally."

On September 2 that year Coltrane entered the studio one last time alone with his quartet, to record his *Meditations* suite, the results from which would eventually be released in the seventies as *First Meditations*, having been pre-empted by Coltrane's quintet version with Pharoah Sanders, recorded in late November 1965 and issued in early 1966.

At the age of thirty-eight, when most musicians have settled into a signature groove, Impulse's star was experimenting with the reckless vigor of a rookie. Looking back a year later, Coltrane described his efforts: "I figured I could do *two* things: I could have a band that played the way I used to play, and a band that was going in the direction that the one I have now is going in—I could combine these two, with these two concepts going."

Through 1965, Coltrane logged thirteen studio sessions, including dates in San Francisco, Los Angeles, and near Seattle. He was recorded live in New York, Newport, Seattle, and in Paris and Antibes, France. He bounced between his quartet and a quintet of looser design. Despite the road-honed efficiency of the former—and the gold copy of *A Love Supreme* hanging in ABC's main lobby—the Classic Quartet would eventually morph into the latter, and his two most identifiable sidemen, McCoy Tyner and Elvin Jones, would depart. Of his post–*Love Supreme* releases, *Ascension* [A(S)-94] rang with the undeniable sound of change—and expanded well beyond a quartet or quintet.

On a warm afternoon in late June, Coltrane assembled a diverse lineup of eleven musicians: his regular quartet plus six horn players and an extra bassist. He proceeded to conduct a forty-minute non-stop exercise in free energy and spontaneous form. Twice. When released, the frenetic sound of that large a band pushing persistently at the extreme ranges of their instruments was frenetic and frightening to many listeners, even to some of Coltrane's strongest supporters in the music community.

"That was the turning point for some musicians who had been Coltrane enthusiasts up to that time, but after that they turned off on it," remembers saxophonist Frank Foster. "I thought it was a little extreme, but he was always my man. Some of us were thinking, 'Well, it's not even about the tenor sax anymore. It's about exploration, just trying to find oneself spiritually.'"

"*Ascension* blew everybody out of the water," saxophonist Dave Liebman recalls. "That was like monumental. That was the torch that lit the free jazz thing. It put the proclamation of 'this is valid' on top of what had been going on for the last four or five years in New York with Albert Ayler and others."

Coltrane had been reluctant in 1964 to accept a leading role in any musical movement, but *Ascension* roared like a cacophonous acceptance speech. As welcoming as he was to new talent on that album, so his club and concert gigs in 1965 opened the door to a retinue of young improvisers who joined him onstage, including two future bandmembers, drummer Rashied Ali and saxophonist Pharoah Sanders. On a West Coast tour, Coltrane entered a Los Angeles studio with members of his quartet and an expanded guest list: Sanders, poet-percussionist Juno Lewis, bassist-clarinetist Donald Rafael Garrett, and drummer Frank Butler.

Part of that session became *Kulu Se Mama* [AS-9106—Impulse's catalog numbers had grown to four digits after A(S)-100], which furthered Impulse's commitment to spoken-word/music collaborations and a growing African sensibility in black America.

THE WAKE OF TRANE

Through 1965, Archie Shepp continued to be the primary beneficiary of Impulse's warming to the avant-garde. That year, he recorded two albums that revealed an impassioned awareness of the jazz tradition far beyond his Coltrane-focused debut—as well as the far-ranging applications possible with his emotionally driven approach.

ASCENSION

John Coltrane / *Ascension* / Impulse A(S)-95
DATE RECORDED: June 28, 1965
DATE RELEASED: March 1966
PRODUCER: Bob Thiele

Before *Ascension* was released in late 1965, Coltrane himself, in a radio piece produced by the deejay Alan Grant, seemed proud and slightly bemused by the results of what was essentially a large-band experiment.

Coltrane: I made a thing recently with Archie, and also another young tenor man named Pharoah Sanders, and Freddie Hubbard, and [trumpeter] Dewey Johnson, and [saxophonists] Marion Brown, John Tchicai. A big-band thing, you know.

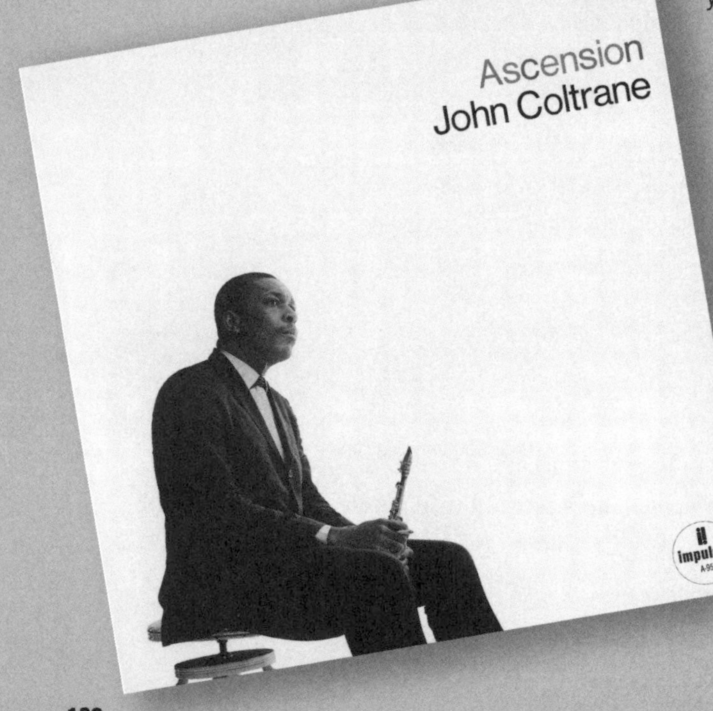

Grant: The way you smile . . .
Coltrane: Well, there's something, there's something in it I like.

It had been a tumultuous session, with players of varying degrees of experience and styles: his regular quartet plus two trumpeters, four saxophonists, and an additional bassist, Davis. Taking a huge leap of faith, the saxophonist invested as much confidence in his impromptu aggregation as he afforded his sidemen of three and a half years. They all met in the studio without rehearsal and were given loose instructions (such as order of solos) and lead sheets that described an even looser sense of structure.

"The ensemble passages were based on chords, but these chords were optional," remembered Shepp. "In those descending chords there is a definite tonal center, like a B-flat minor. But there are different roads to that center."

If any album tested the allegiance Coltrane had earned at Impulse—and inside his own quartet—it was *Ascension.* Mid-session, he looked at his tired, shirtless drummer, Elvin Jones, and requested another try at the forty-minute effort; Jones grudgingly agreed. But at the end of the second take, he flung his snare at the studio wall, signaling his decision that for him, the date was over.

Even at Impulse, where the sounds of avant-garde jazz had become commonplace, the album raised many eyebrows.

"We used to get these test pressings: an LP with a white label on it and nothing written on it," says ABC counsel Alan Bergman. "You'd have no idea whether it was Sabicas, the flamenco guitarist, or B.B. King or Ray Charles or what. So I put this thing on. I listened to about five minutes. It was *Ascension*. I walked into Bob Thiele's office and I can see myself holding this thing up with my mouth open. He says, 'I know, I know.' I mean, twelve records came out that day and he knew which one I'm bringing in to him! He says, 'It's going to be a classic!'"

Ascension was released to immediate controversy and head-shaking, even among Coltrane's supporters. What was Coltrane thinking? It wasn't just the intensity of the performance (Coltrane himself reached those levels nightly) or that the intensity was prolonged (again, nightly), but that it was *so* dense, layered, and free of familiar—to some, any—structure. To more flexible ears, it was enervating, intriguing—yet still sphinx-like.

Gary Giddins recalls that *Ascension* benefited from the focused attention that albums received in college dorm rooms in that era.

"We used to listen to albums in college and talk about [them as] 'main courses' or 'chasers.' The night we listened to *Ascension*, the first version, we were wired. We were young and impressionable, and because we didn't give a shit what the critics said, we all thought that *Ascension* was wonderful. We had to think very carefully about the chaser, and we chose Dexter Gordon's *A Swingin' Affair*. Perfect! It brought us right back home again. Those two albums were a total of eighty minutes' listening with a lot of dope going around. That kind of deeper listening experience has disappeared."

Adding to the haze and hagiography surrounding the album was Thiele's too-late realization that Impulse had initially pressed *Ascension* with the wrong take.

"I [had] sent both takes to Coltrane to listen to. I don't remember which take he chose, but by accident I put out the other one. I then decided, with Trane's approval, to play a little game on the jazz community. After we went through the initial press run, I switched the masters to the other take, the one John had originally picked, and inscribed 'Edition Two' on the inside of the runout circle on the lacquer . . . so really there are two versions of *Ascension* out there."

When Giddins and his friends discovered this, the search was on.

"When we found out about the second take that Coltrane preferred and that they were secretly manufacturing it, a bunch of us went to Chicago on our spring term with razor blades in our hands. We went to every record store slitting the [shrink wrap], sliding the disc out, looking for the [take] number on the vinyl. 'Got one!' So I have always had the LPs of both the number one and number two."

Both *Fire Music* [A(S)-86] and the follow-up, *On This Night* [A(S)-97], featured Shepp's deep, vibrato-heavy tenor in a sextet setting, bouncing from R&B-flavored riff tunes ("Hambone," "The Original Mr. Sonny Boy Williamson") to Ellington ("Prelude to a Kiss," "In a Sentimental Mood") and even bossa nova ("The Girl from Ipanema"). Shepp's penchant for the literary surfaced with tributes to Malcolm X ("Malcolm, Malcolm, Semper Malcolm") and W. E. B. DuBois ("On This Night," with Shepp on piano and Christine Spencer on vocals).

To be sure, Thiele proceeded with a degree of caution. He preferred to add Coltrane's name to a project whenever possible, as he did on a trio of albums in 1965. Elvin Jones's *Dear John C.* [A(S)-88] was a hard-swinging quartet effort more straight-ahead than the drummer's previous title, declaring its fealty in title if not in avant-garde style. *The New Wave in Jazz* [A(S)-90] served as a five-track sampler of some of the most adventurous jazz of the day, recorded at a Sunday afternoon benefit for the Black Arts Repertory Theater School, organized in part by LeRoi Jones. Coltrane's performance of "Nature Boy" was featured, preceding tracks by Archie Shepp, Albert Ayler, trumpeter Charles Tolliver, and trombonist (and former ABC employee) Grachan Moncur III. Jones had been hoping that the album would have an even stronger African-American identity, and that it would include all the performers. "The Impulse record called *The New Wave in Jazz* was supposed to be called *New Black Music* [and] two other groups were supposed to be recorded: singer Betty Carter, who turned the place out, and Sun Ra's huge band." But, he added, "This is the record to get." *New Thing at Newport* [A(S)-94] paired live tracks from Coltrane and Archie Shepp, recorded at the 1965 Newport Jazz Festival.

On *New Thing,* Impulse's measured approach to the avant-garde can be intuited in a now somewhat amusing introduction delivered by jazz booster Father Norman O'Connor, which now can be heard on the CD reissue of the album.

> One of the things that must become obvious to anyone listening to the new music is that in order to, literally, to hear what's going on, the audience has to be very aware in terms of musical lines—and rhythmic lines. It's not easy listening but we're glad you're out to make the effort.

WHAT TO CALL IT

"[Coltrane] brought me to what, in that period, was the 'new jazz' or the 'new black jazz,'" stated Bob Thiele. "The critics were giving it all sorts of names. Another classification at the time was 'avant-garde.' . . . At that stage I had actually joined in the movement. It was invigorating."

From a purely business standpoint, Impulse's warming to the New Thing made sense; there was little competition out there. Blue Note had welcomed a few newcomers with avant-garde leanings—tenor saxophonist Sam Rivers and trombonist Grachan Moncur III, for instance—but none of the major labels or jazz independents were courting the wild side of the avant-garde. In fact, save for a by-the-bootstraps operation called ESP-Disk begun in 1963, and two albums on the Savoy label in 1964 featuring Archie Shepp and trumpeter Bill Dixon, Impulse stood alone when recording players like Shepp, Pharoah Sanders, Albert Ayler, Marion Brown, Roswell Rudd, and others.

Thiele was convinced the so-called New Thing was worth the investment. He responded to an article that ran in the trade weekly *Variety* lambasting the avant-garde—the headline was "Jazz Mugged by 'New Thing'"—by submitting his primary artist as evidence to the contrary.

> Schoenfeld [the writer of the article] is on thin ice when he states that records by "new thing" artists do not sell. Briefly, John Coltrane sells a fantastic quantity of albums in the United States and in many countries around the world. . . . A Coltrane, Mingus, Monk, etc. [album] sells better than a Goodman, Ellington, Basie, etc. These are the hard facts of record sales today.

In the same letter, he defended the art behind the commerce.

> These young people (today's generation) are extremely proficient and technically advanced musicians who are looking towards new roads for musical expression. . . . Today's college students, young writers and critics all recognize the new jazz as a sincere means of expression.

In no way blind to the value of controversy, Thiele was happy to position himself, Impulse, and his magazine, *Jazz,* on the side of the underdog (small surprise the letter cited above was published in *Jazz*). Through editorial policy, he was even willing to fuel it: in the summer of '65, scattered skirmishes over the New Thing grew into a war of words in the publication's letters column. While Thiele remained on the sidelines, younger champions of the avant-garde—activist John Sinclair and hot-blooded writers Frank Kofsky and LeRoi Jones—took on the established jazz front: critic Ira Gitler, *Voice of America* deejay Willis Connover, even contemporaries like Michael Cuscuna.

Jazz magazine was not alone. *Down Beat* printed essays and arguments—by critics, academics, and musicians alike—over the musical and cultural merits of the latest wave of jazz experimentation, and the role of political discourse in improvisational music. All was interwoven with comments on black nationalism and anti-Establishment rhetoric.

By 1966, major publications like *Esquire* and *Newsweek* had weighed in as well, the former complaining of "the rankling racket of Coltrane" while the latter quoted Nat Hentoff calming the waters:

> The jazz revolution is not a programmatic black-power movement. It believes in soul and law and freedom. There's almost a touching belief in music as a cleansing, purifying, liberating force, as if jazzmen were unacknowledged legislators of the world. They all want to change the social system through their music.

At the heart of it all was the pacifist himself, John Coltrane—and, by association, Impulse Records. As the year drew to an end, even the harshest critics had to admit that the New Thing was here to stay. Don Heckman, a supporter, summed up the jazz world's recent leap forward in his year-end view in *Down Beat*:

> Impulse, Blue Note and ESP-Disk continued their activity; there were stirrings from the two giants, Columbia and RCA Victor. All this makes a promising picture. The jazz avant-garde has not yet "arrived," but its breakthrough in 1966 has confirmed its growing eminence as the jazz of the decade.

[*Opposite*] Controversy by headlines: the "New Thing" rallies rancor and support, 1965.

A FINAL SWING FLING

From 1965 on, Impulse affected a symmetric cross-fade: as one jazz style was welcomed to the label, so another slowly found its way out, leaving an

DOWN WHER
WE A
LIVE

Today's Avant-Garde R
As Seen In Light Of Ja
History Of Internal St
By Gus Matzorkis

sters in northern ghet
ning to learn, as a re
ence, that the problem
and complex than
and involve more than

HERETICS' BREW

lowing page is a 41-page section dealing with
from several points of view.
section 10 *Down Beat* critics review the same

An Artist Speaks Bluntly

By ARCHIE SHEPP

GILBERT ERSKINE

I address myself to bigots—those who are so inadvertently, those who are cold and premeditated with it. I address myself to those "in" white hipsters who think niggers never had it so good (Crow Jim) and that it's time something was done about restoring the traditional privileges that have always accrued to

tragedy. I am the
Bird, Billie, Ernie, S
white America, murde
tematic and unloving d
nigger shooting heroin
at 35 with hog's head
and horse for blood.

But I am more tha
superimpose on me, th
inflict. I am the persis
the human heart to be
regain that cherished
always mine. My esthet
lies about me is a sim
no longer defer my
sing it. Dance it. Screa
be, I'll steal it from thi

Get down with me,
where I go. But think
rife. Fear of the tru
murder of James Pow
of 30 Negroes in W
are crimes

A Few Notes On The Avant-Garde

Apple Cores

being.
Do he swing?
Do anything?
The titles, *PG1*
record, along wi
Milford's album Y
Sounds in Your
spirit of sensing
involved in each
different bits of a
These two playe
are making som
anywhere. It wa

THE NEW JAZZ

A MATT

DO

By DON HECKM

A complete examination ments will hav begins to clear spective of its by the music Despite this tion can be made, sarily subject to the potentia ing influences of time and perspective.

John Coltrane and The Jazz Revolution:
THE CASE OF ALBERT AYLER

Jazz and Revolutionary Black Na

• The following is the first installment of a panel discu which took place on December 29, 1965 at St. Pa School Hall, New York, N. Y.

• The panelists were Frank Kofsky, St George Wein, LeRoi Jones, Robert Fe Hentoff; Father Norman J. O'Connor ac and statements from membe

The Life Perspectives Of The New Jazz

By NAT HENTOFF

TO *Down Beat*, I get letters, and musicians by listeners: "Why mix politics and with music? Let music

THE AVANT-GARDE REVOLUTION:
Origins And Directions

Wednesday, April 14, 1965 VARIETY MUSIC 49

JAZZ MUGGED BY 'NEW THING'

Another Tidal Wave of Brit. Rockers Hit U.S. Shores; Brace for Beatles

The tidal wave of British rocking combos, set off by the click of The Beatles early in 1964, is still beating on U. S. shores. This least three groups have

Top Alltime Recordings

N.Y. Daily News' Charles McHarry, rebutting

LATEST IDIOM POISON AT B.O.

By HERM SCHOENFELD

Whatever its future as an art form may be, contemporary

Disneyland Tunes Up Record 330G Music Budget for Upcoming Season

By W. A. SCHARPER

Disneyland's R&R

Anaheim, Calif., April 13.
"Disneyland Digs"

Anaheim, Calif., April 13.
Disneyland, which over the past five years annually upped its

enduring swath of recordings by swing-era musicians. The torch Thiele still carried for the big-band and traditional jazz of his youth sparked a series of lasting one-offs from this period.

Clarinetist Pee Wee Russell was an alumnus of New York City's famed 52nd Street scene, in its earliest, pre-bop days. Russell and colleagues like guitarist Eddie Condon were still easy enough to catch, but to some modern jazz listeners they were playing outdated music on antique instruments. With the help of trombonist Marshall Brown, Russell set to prove otherwise. On *Ask Me Now!* [A(S)-96], an album independently produced by Brown with producer George Avakian, Russell and Brown co-led a quartet that convincingly recast melodies conceived by Monk, Coleman, and Coltrane in a traditional setting. Thiele kept the clarinet star in the Impulse catalog for two more titles: in 1966, a live recording with a swing colleague, *The College Concert of Pee Wee Russell and Henry Red Allen* [AS-9137], and a year later, a big-band performance, *The Spirit of '67* [AS-9147], with arrangements by Oliver Nelson, who was fast becoming the label's go-to arranger for big-band projects.

The idea of bringing jazzmen of yore into the modern era—through a mix of songs, styles, and better fidelity—was not limited to Russell's albums.

Old friends, new arrangements: Oliver Nelson, Thiele, and Pee Wee Russell at Russell's last session, February 15, 1967.

Other swing-era headliners similarly modernized on Impulse (further titles and details in the Source Notes section) included Coleman Hawkins, Clark Terry, Benny Carter (reprising his *Further Definitions* triumph), trombonist Lawrence Brown and drummer Louis Bellson (both former Ellington sidemen), and the recently rediscovered piano pioneer Earl Hines.

On his sole album for Impulse, Hank Jones went the contemporary route by plugging in. Today, the notion of the electric harpsichord serves as a switched-on metaphor for the mid-sixties. But as Jones saw it, it was simply a matter of economics: Baldwin, manufacturer of the instrument, covered certain production costs, or at least provided the keyboard.

> As a matter of fact I was loaned an electric harpsichord to record on by the company that makes them—out of Boston, someplace in that area. There were only one or two instruments like that in New York at that time.

Happenings [AS-9132] was the title of Jones's one-time foray into electric land (on seven of eleven tracks). The album's strongest elements were arrangements by Oliver Nelson, as well as a few funky blues Nelson composed.

"It fit right in, I suppose, with the new musical thinking of the time," adds Jones. "I think that was Bob Thiele's thinking—maybe this was the time to make a change in the musical approach. I wasn't particularly attracted to that."

Jones's first and last title for Impulse represents the last time the label would acknowledge the early, pre-bebop part of the jazz timeline. But the impact had been made. As 1965 ended, Nat Hentoff noted in *Down Beat*: "Thiele has taken a chance on swing-era music—one of the very few A&R men to fill at least partially the huge vacuum left in this area by the departure from recording of Norman Granz. One can hear Johnny Hodges, Ben Webster, Lawrence Brown, and Lionel Hampton (in optimum context) on Impulse."

NEW LABELS, MORE WORK

A loose-leaf binder filled with handwritten pages listing the label's recording activities, session by session, year by year, is one of the label's few surviving written records. As sparse as the details therein may be, much can

ASK ME NOW!

Pee Wee Russell / *Ask Me Now!* / Impulse A(S)-96
DATE RECORDED: April 9 and 10, 1963
DATE RELEASED: March 1966
PRODUCER: George Avakian

Take one revered swing-era clarinetist. Place in a cool-style pianoless quartet. Mix well with ballads and blues, and spice with more modern, angular melodies from the books of Monk and Coltrane. Rehearse three times a week, until tight and swinging.

Such was the recipe the trombonist and educator Marshall Brown had successfully concocted for Pee Wee Russell in 1962 on the Columbia album *New Groove*. "It was highly acclaimed. Our album got five stars in *Down Beat* and they began to give it away with a subscription," bassist Russell George recalls.

Free to shop their next project to any label, Brown decided to take charge of the entire project himself, paying the band (drummer Ronnie Bedford rounded out the quartet), renting the studio, and choosing the music. Brown "was a great catalyst for putting things together," Bedford states. "All the charts, all the arrangements were Marshall's—and doing Monk and Coltrane was his idea." "We had done John [Coltrane]'s 'Red Planet' on the first album," says George. "It got such acclaim that we decided to continue with that sort of thematic material. We added a Monk and Ornette [Coleman] tune for the second album."

The *Ask Me Now!* session itself was preceded by ample run-throughs for the quartet, as the bassist tells it.

"We rehearsed on 72nd Street—Marshall had a soundproof studio on the first floor, mostly for Pee Wee's benefit. His brain was a little fried on alcohol by then and, especially to play something in exactly the same way, it took a while for Pee Wee to absorb it. Believe me, that isn't even slightly a put-down. Pee Wee was the star and the lead. I just loved him to death. But it took a lot of rehearsal to get it to Marshall's satisfaction."

Bedford also remembers the need to repeatedly practice new tunes, and the clarinetist's reaction.

"It was very well rehearsed, but Pee Wee didn't care too much for rehearsing at all. He wasn't very interested in reading either, so this music had to be rehearsed and rehearsed and rehearsed. He would make some strange faces about having to go over one piece at a time to get the parts straightened out. You really couldn't tell what he was saying, but he used to do a lot of mumbling to himself. You know, [mumbles] 'I can't get with this.'"

Despite his grumbling, Bedford noticed that Russell proved adept at handling both vintage compositions ("Angel Eyes," "Prelude to a Kiss") and newer compositions like Coltrane's "Some Other Blues," Coleman's "Turnaround," and Monk's "Hackensack" and "Ask Me Now."

"He didn't change his playing at all from how we were doing the gig with Condon [guitarist Eddie Condon, a mainstay of the traditional-jazz movement]! He played the way he played. There were some changes for him with this type of group. First of all there was no piano, no guitar—no chordal instrument. He was fine as long as he could hear those bass notes. Also, there was a lot of strolling. In other words, just Pee Wee or Marshall with bass. That was a new thing for him."

Bedford and George remain fond of another aspect of the session.

"As far as anything I can remember about the session or the rehearsals, they were full of laughs and constant humor," notes the bassist. "If there's not some love in the band you really can't reach a common theme."

"Pee Wee was a very entertaining individual," adds the drummer. "He would tell stories about the thirties, about the clubs he worked in Chicago and the mobsters who ran them. He had one story where he was playing with some band, I forget who was the leader. He said that they were rehearsing something and the [club] owner came up with a six-shooter, shot that gun off in the air, and said, 'Youse ain't together!' That cracked everybody up. In other words, 'Boy, you better get it together because I'm not fooling around here!'"

The recording session itself was relatively brief. "It was in Plaza Sound, on one of the upper floors of Radio City," recalls Bedford. "But George wasn't even mentioned on the original LP as producer. He was in the booth the whole time."

"George" is George Avakian, the veteran producer who by 1963 could boast of fruitful years at Columbia Records (where he spearheaded the signing of Miles Davis), RCA (where he did the same with Sonny Rollins), and Warner Bros. (where he brought the label its first best-sellers with the Everly Brothers and the button-down humor of Bob Newhart) The Pee Wee Russell session, Avakian says, "wasn't a side job, it was a friendship gesture. I refused to take payment for it because I knew that Marshall was sinking a certain amount of money in it. Pee Wee had been on the first date I ever produced, on August 11, 1939, with Eddie Condon."

In the end, the session masters went unreleased for almost two years. "It was in the can for quite a while," says Bedford. "Then Marshall finally played it for Bob Thiele and he bought it." Thiele insisted on a flat-fee purchase—which put the album permanently in the Impulse catalog—and on not listing another producer in the credits.

"What happened is that Thiele said he would accept the tapes," Avakian recalls. "And Marshall said, 'You know, they were produced by George and I can't pay him, so George has asked me to ask for a modest fee.' Thiele said, 'No, I don't have any money for that. You'll have to pay him.' I told Marshall, 'Look, give him the tapes. That's more important.' The only thing that I wanted out of it at the end was a credit for having produced it. I didn't even get that."

Avakian did eventually receive credit on the CD reissue of *Ask Me Now!,* while Russell received positive reviews upon the album's release in 1965. His Impulse tenure would prove to be the last label association of his career.

be gleaned simply from the number of recording dates. Not including the sessions he produced for ABC itself, Thiele spent forty-one days in the studio for Impulse in 1965. The next year, he spent almost two weeks more overseeing jazz sessions that progressively found his infatuation with avant-garde jazz proceeding to the foreground of his activities, with little abatement in his dedication to more traditional styles.

In addition, Thiele found the time to add not one but two new labels to his portfolio. One was sanctioned by his ABC higher-ups and dubbed BluesWay. The other he initiated on the sly and named Contact.

It was an old idea in the jazz world, stretching back to 1932 when Milt Gabler had first offered reissued 78s through the mail from his Com-

The label on the side: an advertisement for Thiele's "connoisseur" label, 1966.

modore Record Shop: create a specialty label producing higher-priced, high-fidelity reissues and limited-edition releases for the cognoscenti. By 1966, the old concept seemed to be timely again: "It may be that one main answer for the future is specialized labels sold mainly by mail, something like the Connoisseur Society in classical music," wrote Nat Hentoff.

A series of coincidences—Earl Hines's rediscovery, Duke Ellington's theatrical production *My People*—gave Thiele the idea to create Contact, a short-lived label that he owned outright, and molded in the top-shelf style of Impulse.

"I first became aware of Bob's 'secret' label in the pages of his 'secret' magazine, *Jazz*," chuckles Michael Cuscuna, who today runs Mosaic, the premier mail-order jazz reissue label. "If you subscribed, you'd get a copy of an Earl Hines LP that looked very much like Impulse—gatefold cover, photos by Chuck Stewart. I remember seeing them in stores too, but it was basically a connoisseur-y, mail-order kind of thing."

In a few months, the Contact catalog included two Earl Hines discs (a solo album and a trio album with Richard Davis and Elvin Jones); Ellington's *My People*; a trio performance by pianist Steve Kuhn; and, from the forties, reissues of Thiele's recordings with Lester Young and Coleman Hawkins and of a Shelly Manne session. Perhaps Thiele intended Contact to be a new home for swing-era musicians, while Impulse focused on newer jazz styles, but the label soon disappeared.

"I don't know if Newton or ABC knew anything about Contact," Cuscuna says. "Maybe they did, because the label wasn't around that long. I would say the idea of Thiele running another jazz label while at Impulse was highly unusual by any standards—but typical for Bob."

It's difficult to know whether or not ABC knew or cared about Thiele's side label, as Contact never made an impact large enough to be seen as possible Impulse competition. One can surmise that the label's relatively low profile—for example, it never benefited from retail presence or distribution—was part of Thiele's design.

Contact Records may have only survived from 1965 into 1966, but its demise coincided closely with a headline that ran on December 17, 1966, on *Billboard*'s front page, "ABC to Bow a Blues Label," under which Thiele explained the motivation behind BluesWay Records. "Blues is perhaps the most important American song form today; it is the bedrock of much of jazz. . . . It is a major factor in the contemporary pop scene."

ONCE UPON A TIME

Earl Hines / *Once Upon a Time* / Impulse AS-9108

DATE RECORDED: January 10 and 11, 1966

DATE RELEASED: April 1966

PRODUCER: Bob Thiele

"Rediscovered," when filtered through the music business, is a term that usually translates to "ignored until now."

In late 1964, the toast of the East Coast jazz scene was Earl "Fatha" Hines, the pianist who had accompanied Louis Armstrong as a member of the Hot Five in 1928 (that's him on "West End Blues"), then led a big band through the thirties and well into the forties (Charlie Parker, Dizzy Gillespie, Billy Eckstine, and Sarah Vaughan were all in the band at one point). In 1947 he was back with Armstrong, but he slowly fell of the map through the fifties.

In 1964, reports circulated of Hines living in San Francisco, ignominiously playing to tourists with a Dixieland revival group. Journalist Dan Morgenstern found him and invited him back east, co-producing a trio of concerts in New York City that clinched his rediscovery. "There are a few undiluted moments of joy and pride in anyone's life, but I will never forget Hines's Little Theater concert on that March night," Morgenstern wrote. "A triumph," agreed Whitney Balliett in *The New Yorker*.

Pittsburgh-born and Chicago-adopted, Hines had invented a modern style that took unprecedented license with the left hand—a jump ahead of the stride kings of his day.

Then there was the Hines attack: playing octaves allowed him to amp up his instrument, so the piano's effective volume matched the horn soloists', with single-note runs that mirrored their solos as well. (McCoy Tyner is another whose distinctive approach was in part shaped by a search for volume.)

Hines's rediscovery led to a spate of recordings over the next few years. The most often recalled, and for reasons beyond just the music, is *Once*

Upon a Time, his lone effort for Impulse. In early 1966, Thiele opted not to record him with a quartet, the context of his return, or within a Dixieland setup. Recalling Hines's glory days fronting a big band, the producer chose to equip him with the best swing survivors out there. The full Ellington lineup (Duke must have appreciated the work his men were getting while off the road) was joined by clarinetist Pee Wee Russell, while drummer Sonny Greer was replaced by Elvin Jones on four tracks.

Hines and a few old friends, January 1966: Hines (behind baffle on left), Lawrence Brown, Sonny Greer, Clark Terry, amd Buster Cooper.

Among the highlights on the seven-track album is Ray Nance's rich, jump-blues vocal (echoes of Louis Jordan) on the session opener, "The Blues in My Flat," with Russell and Hines soloing strongly. There's the title track, and "Hash Brown," both written by Johnny Hodges and both tailor-made for Jones's thunderous rolls and skip-swing rhythm, favoring the drum work of Gene Krupa.

And there's Ellington's mini-suite "Black and Tan Fantasy," first recorded in 1927. The only member still with Duke in 1966 was Greer, who navigates the sections of the piece with familiarity, pushing the rhythm through into the funereal Chopin quote at the end. Centered in a string of pearl-like solos, Hines's improvisation is restrained yet clearly articulated—blues power with grace.

One of Impulse's most creative packages, the cover of *Once Upon a Time* shows a behatted Hines, mouth joyously agape, the lenses of his shades reflecting piano keys. The remaining 80 percent of the cover is text in the color and font of "olde English" manuscripts. In language a prep school alumnus like Thiele could easily conceive, it told the somewhat self-congratulatory tale of The Visionary (read: Thiele) who "decided to summon the most famous of those [players] to make plans for a Musical Celebration [as a] great player of the piano had come to the East. . . ." The notes also spoke of overcoming challenges like darkness and transportation hardships in "Fun City," an obvious reference to the labor strikes and power blackout that engulfed New York City that year ("Fun City" being a term coined by Mayor John V. Lindsay for his constituency at the time).

For reasons of budget and contract, Duke Ellington never recorded with his own group for Impulse. But *Once Upon a Time* is a playful, satisfying proxy. Hines brought the right balance of spirited elegance and blues economy to the party—a party that marked a late-career high point.

According to ABC counsel Alan Bergman, one artist in particular inspired the creation of a blues-focused label at ABC. "The whole blues effort just came from B.B. King, who had signed there a few years before. An important dimension of ABC was already the R&B area: Curtis Mayfield and the Impressions, Ray Charles. B.B. was blues. He wasn't that big, but there was a potpourri of different kinds of stuff happening in the pop area then."

In fact, a greater range of musical styles were crossing over onto the popular charts in the mid-sixties. It was also a time when fading R&B and jump-blues stars of the forties and fifties (T-Bone Walker, Roy Brown, Eddie "Cleanhead" Vinson, Big Joe Turner) were still around, and through staff producer Johnny Pate, ABC had a toehold in the active Chicago blues scene with Jimmy Reed and Otis Spann. Add in a blues resurgence triggered by rock bands like the Paul Butterfield Blues Band, the Yardbirds, and Cream, and creating BluesWay was an easy decision for the ABC brass.

For Thiele, BluesWay was a chance to recruit some old friends and some recent discoveries who did not fit the Impulse brand, from John Lee Hooker and veteran Basie vocalist Jimmy Rushing to the electric Dirty Blues band. From '66 through '68, Thiele personally handled the lion's share of BluesWay titles beyond his recording dates for Impulse and ABC.

Jimmy Rushing with Bob Thiele, 1965.

THE DEFINITIVE LABEL

In late 1965, Impulse neared its hundredth release. Thiele took stock and smiled: little by little, what had been accomplished at Impulse in five short years merited recognition. Even the inner sleeves protecting all Impulse LPs were by then label-specific, promoting only jazz titles. In addition, as many an Impulse artist noticed, Thiele had a knack for delivering a new twist with each successive album by the label's established artists.

"Impulse was a special label: it was slick, it was dynamite," says Chico Hamilton. "Everything they put out was good: good productions, good covers, and the notes were good, the overall package. I think the biggest mistake that a player makes when he's going to record [is to] record his same group over and over and over and over. One thing Bob Thiele made sure of is that he would add another instrument or do something different each time around."

Thiele assembled *The Definitive Jazz Scene* [A(S)-99, 100, and 9101], a three-volume series that marked the milestone and celebrated Impulse's range of talent—Ray Charles to Lionel Hampton, Oliver Nelson to John Coltrane—with a self-congratulatory dive into the catalog that featured many tracks previously left off Impulse releases.

Simultaneously, Thiele continued to record significant albums (titles and further details in the Source Notes section) by contract artists like Yusef Lateef, Chico Hamilton, and Shirley Scott, all of whom ended their relationship with Impulse by the close of 1966. The producer also oversaw a variety of quirky, one-of-a-kind one-offs—with saxophonists Zoot Sims, Phil Woods, and Stanley Turrentine and drummer Dannie Richmond—during this time, including a memorable date with trumpeter Dizzy Gillespie, a pioneer of bebop.

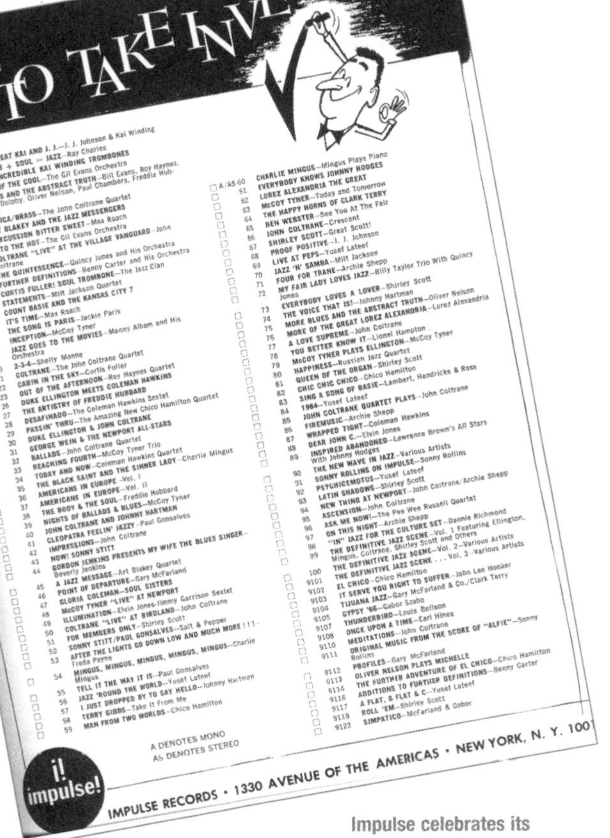

Impulse celebrates its numbers, 1966.

Swing Low, Sweet Cadillac [AS-9149] is essentially a snapshot of Gillespie's quintet of the day, showcasing the talents of saxophonist-flutist James Moody and pianist Mike Longo along with Gillespie's signature high-register solos. Recorded as a live-in-the-studio performance, it also featured humorous stage banter and an odd lot of material: a Brazilian samba, a movie tune, the faux-gospel title track, and a lengthy mini-suite dedicated to Mother Africa ("Kush"). One attendee recalls the session fondly.

"I was newly married in the sixties," says Alan Bergman. "I worked with Bob a lot and he kind of befriended me. He had a few sessions which were in the studio, like Dizzy Gillespie, but he invited an audience so there would be some sort of crowd participation there.

"Those were heady times. We had Dizzy *and* Coltrane *and* Archie Shepp *and* Yusef Lateef. But Bob was not an avant-gardist by any means, he had no doctrinaire philosophy or anything. He was just allowing some space for that stuff." This was certainly the case when Thiele approached another legendary giant of the saxophone, of John Coltrane's stature and generation, to record for Impulse.

SONNY ON IMPULSE

As the tenor saxophone grew to prominence in jazz from the thirties on, Coleman Hawkins and Lester Young were the first to stand out as the yin and yang of the instrument. By the mid-sixties, a new pair was in place, each exerting a stylistic pull on younger players and each with a strong avant-garde flavor.

John Coltrane was clearly one pole of influence. The other was a Harlem-born musician who, like Trane, had developed a penchant for extended

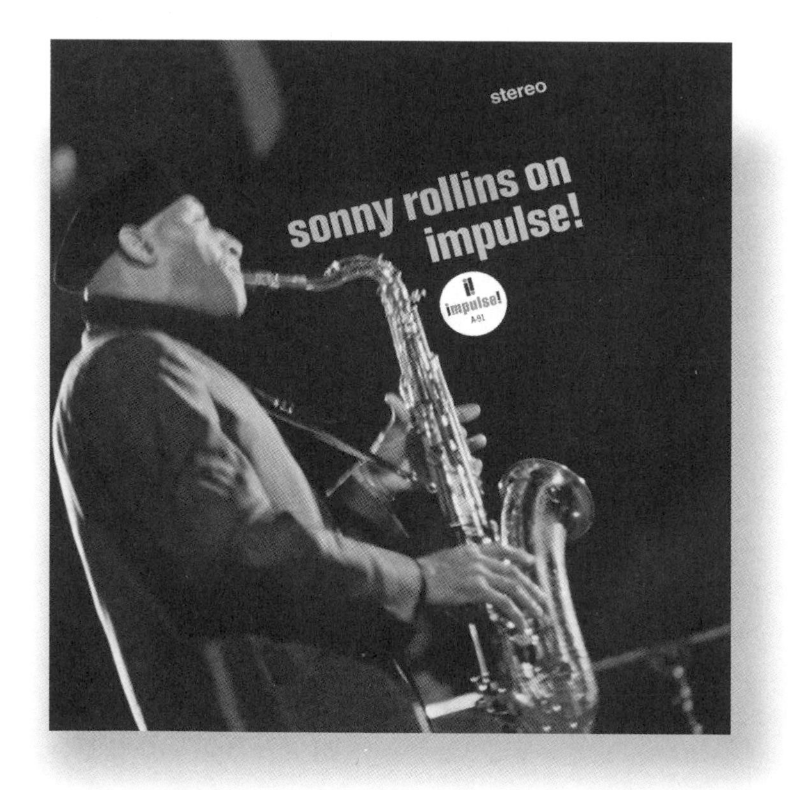

improvisation through arduous searching and exercise. Like Trane, he boasted technique and power and was drawn to spiritual paths from the East. And like Trane, he had broken through as sideman with Miles Davis.

Though Sonny Rollins's midlife career echoed his colleague's (Rollins turned thirty-five in 1965), he was still flirting with a variety of styles and contexts at a time when Coltrane had thrown in his lot with the avant-garde. In 1959, Rollins had effectively disappeared from the scene to rethink his musical approach. His return two years later had been met with warm acclaim, a multiple-album deal with RCA Victor, and a quartet that became renowned for Rollins's intuitive dialogues with guitarist Jim Hall. Proving that Impulse did not have a lock on cross-generational summits, RCA paired Thiele's tenor hero, Coleman Hawkins, with Rollins on *Sonny Meets Hawk* in 1963, to positive reviews and sales.

By 1964, Rollins was nearing the end of his six-album RCA contract. Though he had no complaints, he stated that he wanted "to go with a company which is a little more oriented to the jazz idiom, if you know what I mean." Years after, he explained why Impulse was a likely candidate, and why that *other* saxophonist held part of the charm.

> Everybody sort of knew each other in those days, so I knew they were interested in signing major jazz musicians. Coltrane never tried to convince me to sign with Impulse. I think I just realized that they were doing a good job with him, and so I thought that maybe it would be good for me too.

For a brief period, the two pillars of modern jazz tenor were labelmates. Rollins's association with Impulse lasted only one year (1965–66), but it produced three studio albums.

On Impulse! [A(S)-91] started the association, with Rollins drawing ideas from recent recordings as well as personnel—bassist Bob Cranshaw and drummer Mickey Roker had recorded with him on recent RCA sessions. He favored texture over clearly pronounced melodies on a West Indian dance tune, "Hold 'Em Joe," and standards like "On Green Dolphin Street" and "Three Little Words," which had the album's standout saxophone solo. *Alfie* [AS-9111] features music written for the 1966 film, with Rollins's writing and playing in a hard-bop mold. Of note is the memorable "Alfie's Theme," as well as the sharp, well-rehearsed arrangements, partially the handiwork of Oliver Nelson.

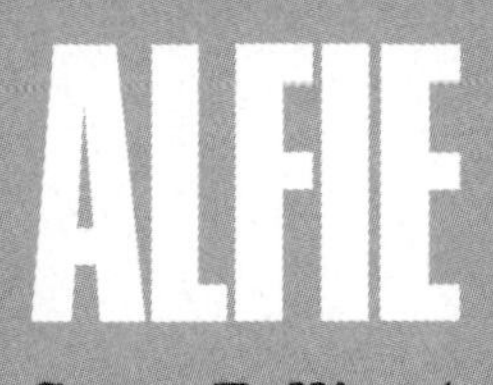

Sonny Rollins / *Alfie* / Impulse AS-9111

DATE RECORDED: January 26, 1966

DATE RELEASED: October 1966

PRODUCER: Bob Thiele

Is it not the phone call every musician hopes for at some point? "We want *your* sound in our movie." A generous payday can be counted on—usually. Better yet, it holds the possibility of providing an entrée into the profitable and exclusive circle of music-makers in the film world.

In 1966, two American jazz musicians leapt at the chance to compose and record an original soundtrack for British productions. Herbie Hancock created music for Michelangelo Antonioni's *Blow Up,* and Sonny Rollins did the same for the movie *Alfie,* starring a screen newcomer named Michael Caine.

Actually, Rollins was first approached with the idea during a week-long stand at Ronnie Scott's nightclub in London in January 1965. *Down Beat* reported on the ensuing project in August.

"The method is unusual. When the film is completed (it is in production now), Rollins will fly to London to see it and talk with the director. Then he will return to New York to write the score. Then back to London again, to record the music with himself and English musicians."

Rollins arrived with five hip and breezy melodies, including the waltz-time "On Impulse" (unrelated to his album of the same name), which matched the lifestyle and tempo of the film's modern-day Lothario. Rollins had high praise for director Lewis Gilbert: "a very good understanding of music without knowing all the technical aspects. . . . If the score is a success, he deserves a large share of the credit."

Back in New York City, Rollins proceeded to re-record the music so that Impulse could coordinate its release with the film's. He assembled a nine-piece group, including such A-list jazzmen as trombonists J.J. Johnson and Jimmy Cleveland, guitarist Kenny Burrell, pianist Roger Kellaway, and alto saxophonist Phil Woods. Oliver Nelson stepped in as the group's second tenor saxophonist and arranger, tweaking the music—but not too much. "Nelson's arrangements for this recording of the score are based on Sonny's original charts," Nat Hentoff wrote in the liner notes to the LP. "Oliver kept pretty close to those," agreed Rollins, "adding a little here and there and editing. But this is basically the sound we got in the picture."

The experience left Rollins looking forward to similar work. "I hope to compose for more films, because I've been wanting to work in explicitly dramatic areas for a long time. Not only motion pictures, but theater too. After all, it's all part of the same thing—finding and expressing yourself through music and finding links to yourself in the experiences of others."

The year 1966 ultimately proved more a door-opener to film (and TV) work for Herbie Hancock and Oliver Nelson than for Rollins. After *Blow Up,* Hancock continued to be called on by Hollywood, scoring such films as *Death Wish* (1974), *A Soldier's Story* (1984), and *Harlem Nights* (1989). Nelson, who had composed the theme for the TV series *The Virginian* in 1962, pursued the same track through the sixties and seventies, moving to Los Angeles and creating memorable themes for *Ironside, Night Gallery, The Six Million Dollar Man,* and other top TV programs.

Despite *Alfie*'s popular and critical success, the film also proved more a boon to its star (in fact, it launched Caine's career) than to Rollins, partially due to the fact that his music, used infrequently in the film, was eclipsed by the theme song, written by the renowned songwriting team of Hal David and Burt Bacharach. Nonetheless, Rollins's involvement helped raise his profile. Yet after *Alfie,* no consistent film work materialized for Rollins. Not until *The Talented Mr. Ripley* in 1999 would his sound figure prominently on another soundtrack, with excerpts from his old Prestige recordings "Tenor Madness" and "Pent-Up House."

Years later, Rollins admitted that the experience, and the years since, had schooled him to be more limiting in his choice of projects.

"I enjoyed writing and playing the score for *Alfie* very much. However, if I were offered another opportunity such as this, I would only do it if the film highlighted the music rather than the story itself."

East Broadway Run Down [AS-9121] continued Rollins's flirtation with the avant-garde. He had recorded with trumpeter Don Cherry and drummer Billy Higgins—both alumni of Ornette Coleman's quartet—for RCA, and had experimented on *Sonny Meets Hawk,* removing the mouthpiece from his saxophone and blowing into it alone. He repeated the unorthodox maneuver on *East Broadway,* a mostly quartet record (Freddie Hubbard plays on the twenty-minute title track) that left ample room for two members of Coltrane's rhythm section, Jimmy Garrison and Elvin Jones. A fourth album had been recorded live at the Museum of Modern Art's sculpture garden in 1965 and then scrapped because the saxophonist was often out of range of the microphones. Released in 1978 as *There Will Never Be Another You* (and quickly removed from the market as Rollins claimed that it was unauthorized), it defined a willful range of styles and experimentation that briefly matched Coltrane's own.

Many years later, Rollins does not view his Impulse experience in a positive light, but bears no grudge against Thiele. "It turned out they were a rough group of people, and they really screwed me out of stuff. . . . Their lawyers were really tough. I never had any problems with Bob Thiele. Bob was a very accommodating fellow." Yet some of the fault, Rollins admits, was his own.

> I was kind of naïve and didn't have anybody representing me at the time when I was doing contracts and working out a royalty agreement and all that kind of thing. I really got used.

TRANE LEARNS THE GAME

"Early in the game, [jazz] musicians didn't even have lawyers," recalls Bill Kaplan, ABC-Paramount's head counsel. "They would just sign the contract and send it back. I can still remember—although I can't remember the name of the artist—that we had sent a contract out to the West Coast and we got a letter from a lawyer! Can you imagine?"

Coltrane was an exception. In retaining Harold Lovett, Miles Davis's attorney, from the start of his Impulse deal, the saxophonist proved himself avant-garde in how he proceeded in the music business. Kaplan dealt personally with Coltrane and Lovett for a specific reason: "John's contract provided for an advance each year and provided for the monies—his share of the net—to be held, not paid out. It was for tax reasons: they didn't want to build up too much in the way of taxes in any year."

Yet when Coltrane wanted to tap into his income, Kaplan hipped him to a more tax-friendly solution.

> This is what John was encountering—he found that he wanted to borrow against his money. I said, "John, Harold, you're going to hate us. But for your own protection, we're going to have to charge you interest on money that isn't yours. If you want to say it's your money, then you may have to face the I.R.S. about the whole thing." So they agreed. It was very low interest.

During his days with Atlantic, with Lovett's help, Coltrane had established Jowcol Music to collect publishing royalties on all his original compositions. It was another way in which Coltrane proved a role model for many of his peers. At that time, most musicians were compelled to use the recording company's publishing division for their compositions. Before the sixties, artist-owned publishing companies had been few; Ellington was a notable pioneer in this respect. But as the avant-garde scene matured, Ornette Coleman, Archie Shepp, and Pharoah Sanders, like Coltrane, were all recording music that they composed *and* published.

Alan Bergman recalls Jowcol business being the reason he often spoke with Coltrane, and he also remembers his own deference to the saxophonist. "If John called with a question, I would probably take it, especially if it concerned publishing. He'd call usually on publishing matters that related to his albums. I guess I was a little guarded because he was a legendary figure and I was a young lawyer, so I didn't want to say anything wrong."

As the sixties brought change, as recording artists in general secured more artistic control and commercial participation, so jazz players benefited as well—with Coltrane setting an example. But it was often more than just business. According to Thiele, "During the period I was at ABC, the musicians started to look to the record company not only to record them, but to help them in every area—see that they get a proper place to live, and whenever they needed, they could pick up the phone and call and say, 'Hey, I need some money.' But you know there can only be a handful that can conceivably record on the same basis as Coltrane."

THE MARK OF AVANT-GARDE DISTINCTION

"It's a lot easier to yell than to make good music," complained Ornette Coleman in late '66. "Today, every black guy with a horn says he's avant-garde. That's a lot of crap." "The term 'free' was often a euphemism for, in my estimation, people who were total novices in some cases," agrees Archie Shepp today, although he points out that many players fell victim to a baby-with-the-bathwater syndrome. "At the time guys like Miles [Davis] dismissed it all as bullshitters, motherfuckers who couldn't play."

As 1966 ended, Impulse served as a mark of avant-garde approval, helping to distinguish the innovators of the day when many of the new *avant-gardistas* sounded similar to untrained ears. That year, Shepp himself recorded *Live in San Francisco* [AS-9118] and *Mama Too Tight* [AS-9134], unafraid to mix his experimental approach with gutbucket blues and Ellington covers that showed off his raspy tenor.

Meanwhile, Thiele's one-offs with New Thing artists kept to a tight circle (those albums are detailed in the Source Notes section). He produced titles by trombonist Roswell Rudd, a Shepp sideman, by alto saxophonist Marion Brown, and by Pharoah Sanders, Coltrane's second tenor man. Sanders recalls: "Bob Thiele approached me about doing something with them. *Tauhid* was the first record I did, and it had about the best sound. I played alto and tenor saxophone on that, but they [listed] just tenor."

A measure of the difference a year can make: in an end-of-the-year summary in *Down Beat* in 1965, Nat Hentoff hailed Blue Note Records for recording "new jazz," which he defined as the music of drummer Tony Williams, saxophonist Sam Rivers, vibraphonist Bobby Hutcherson, pianist Andrew Hill, and others. At Impulse, he noted, "Thiele has not yet taken as many chances with advanced jazz as has [Blue Note's Alfred] Lion, but he has recorded Archie Shepp and given John Coltrane the fullest scope."

Ten months later, Hentoff focused on Impulse exclusively. "I keep wondering about the lack of acumen on the part of the regular record producers. Thiele has proved through Impulse that a diversified catalog, conscientiously produced and astutely packaged, can profitably encompass Johnny Hodges and Archie Shepp, [guitarist] Gabor Szabo and John Coltrane."

Hentoff was not alone in his praise. "One can just about count the number of independent, full-time jazz record companies on the index finger of his right hand," wrote Martin Williams in the final week of 1966, surveying the jazz recording scene. "Prestige is still there, still on its own and still recording new music. Blue Note has been bought by Liberty, and Verve has been a part of MGM long since . . . Atlantic has been sold to Warner Bros."

Williams closed with the kicker: "We can be grateful that Impulse, although a subsidiary of ABC, does apparently go its own way, and does record younger avant-garde musicians."

At the start of 1967, through its own efforts and the circumstances of the music business, Impulse was widely considered *the* leading jazz label. Among journalists keeping pace with the music, the label was being congratulated for diversity, profitability, and dedication to a new generation of improvisers who were busy inventing the "New Thing." At the point position of this musical charge was Impulse's best-selling artist, the ever-active, ever-searching John Coltrane.

Little could anyone have known that within a few months Coltrane would be gone, and that in the vacuum of his absence, Impulse would be pulled to the avant-garde side almost exclusively. Nor could anyone have gauged the full power of another singular musical force that had been building steam for a few years at that point—a force that would soon sway Impulse, ABC-Paramount, and the entire recording industry.

What Impulse means, 1966.

ODDS & TRENDS—PART 1

Various Titles / Impulse

DATE RECORDED: various sessions, 1966

DATE RELEASED: 1966–67

PRODUCER: Bob Thiele

Bob Thiele was the first to admit he was a commercial creature at heart, one of habit. Years in the business had made him quick to follow trends or leap to promotional schemes. Mickey Mantle? Yes, Thiele produced the Yankee legend's lone stab at musical stardom while working for Decca, sort of singing with Thiele's future wife, Teresa Brewer: "I love you, Mickey! *Who*? The fella with the celebrated swing . . ."

When inspired, Thiele widened Impulse's focus on jazz, enough to allow the unexpected. Take for instance, Oliver Nelson's *The Kennedy Dream* [AS-9144]. A six-part suite composed in tribute to the fallen president, it included snippets of his spoken sentiments on peace, human rights, and religious tolerance; featured a pastoral tune titled "Jacqueline"; and sported an original portrait painted by graphic artist and jazz fan Vic Kalin on the cover. Upon its release, a copy of the album was sent to Rose Kennedy, mother of the deceased president, who wrote a personal note back.

HYANNIS PORT
MASSACHUSETTS

June 9, 1967

Dear Mr. Thiele:

I just listened to the record "The Kennedy Dream" which is a musical tribute to the memory of my son, John Fitzgerald Kennedy, the late President.

My heart is full of pride and joy that he could so inspire young Americans with a desire to preserve on record some quotations expressive of his ideals and further highlight them by the profoundly moving music of the composer, Oliver Nelson.

It is a tribute to the emotional and dramatic qualities of your endeavor that my eyes are so misty and my heart is so full, I can write no more.

Gratefully,
Rose Kennedy
Mrs. Joseph P. Kennedy

Mr. Robert Thiele
ABC-Paramount Records
1330 Avenue of Americas
New York, New York

The Kennedy Dream stands as an example of Thiele's more elegant stretches for Impulse. There were occasions, however, when he allowed the commercial to take priority.

"There was just some oddball, carny kind of cross-promoting things and gimmicky things that were coming out at the same time that he was doing people like John Coltrane," remembers jazz producer Michael Cuscuna, who has been involved in reissuing Impulse material for many years. "There were these bizarre tie-ins, like one with Nine Flags cologne. Thiele got Chico O'Farrill to arrange an album with nine pieces based on the nine country flags [laughs]. I guess it was his favorite cologne, and they told him they'd give him a lifetime supply."

Nine Flags [AS-9135] was O'Farrill's lone Impulse album, and while offering an intriguing musical travelogue of nine countries, it also betrayed the same cross-promotional strain Thiele exerted in 1964 with Milt Jackson's "The Oo-Oo Bossa Noova" (off his *Jazz 'N' Samba* album) when he paired the vibraphonist with Joe E. Ross, one of the stars of the sitcom *Car 54, Where Are You?*, who punctuated

the music with his trademark "Oo-oo." In 1966, Thiele provided titular credit to the manufacturer of a new line of motorcycles on the psychedelic jazz tune "Yamaha Mama" on Gabor Szabo's *Simpático* album, the guitarist and arranger Gary McFarland sitting astride the bikes on the cover.

"It could go from the idiotic to the sublime on some Impulse releases," Cuscuna adds. "Some of the Gary MacFarland–Gabor Szabo stuff was blatantly trying to get a commercial record. I thought it didn't hold up then and it doesn't hold up now. Then there were odd things, like Clark Terry playing a Varitone [electric trumpet], which is, to me, the worst thing."

Terry's *It's What's Happenin'* [AS-9157] might be easily construed as a lapse in judgment. Yet, as music history has shown time and again, had any one of those titles proved to be a popular or critical phenomenon, Thiele would be lauded for his creative bravery. The odds and ends of the label's catalog, in the years 1966 and 1967, included:

- John Lee Hooker's *It Serves You Right to Suffer* [AS-9103], which tied in to the blues revival of the mid-sixties and prefigured Thiele's establishment of ABC's all-blues label, BluesWay. It also stands as an excellent example of the producer's musical instinct, providing the deep-throated bluesman with understated and unobtrusive backup from jazz stalwarts Milt Hinton on bass, Panama Francis on drums, and Barry Galbraith on second guitar.
- *Sweet Love, Bitter* [AS-9142], the original soundtrack to an undeservedly lost movie starring Dick Gregory in the lead role of a jazz saxophonist modeled on Charlie Parker. Pianist Mal Waldron's alternately brooding and bopping score to the 1967 film is a small masterpiece, with expressive support from saxophonists George Coleman (on alto rather than his customary tenor) and Charles Davis and bassist Richard Davis, among others.
- *Intercollegiate Music Festival—Vol. 1* [AS-9145], an album covering the top college-level big bands at a festival in Florida. The music is predictably young and derivative, and not surprisingly, a Volume 2 never transpired.
- *A Lovely Bunch of Jazzbo Collins and the Bandidos* [AS-9150], which featured the well-known jazz deejay Al Collins (along with Steve Allen and a few L.A. session men) fracturing and then recasting children's fairy tales with bebop characters and hip, streetwise lingo. Small surprise that Collins's collaborator was Allen; was there a label Thiele ran that did not release at least one album with the name of the TV host and pianist on the cover? What indeed are friends for?

Terry goes electric, July 24, 1967: note Varitone trumpet attachment around neck.

THE VARITONE SOUND OF CLARK TERRY A-9157 IMPULSE!
STEREO A-9156 impulse!
AS-9155 IMPULSE!
RCHIE SHEPP A-9154 impulse!
BROWN A SE!
RACK A-9142 IMPULSE!
RD DAVIS STEREO A-9160 impulse!
AL JAZZBO COLLINS & THE BANDIDOS A-9150 IMPULSE!
LLAC DIZZY GILLESPIE A-9149 IMPULSE!
LICE COLTRANE
OLIVER NELSON AND HIS ORCHESTRA A-9144 IMPULSE!
WOODS A-9143 IMPULSE!
A-9140 impulse!

CHAPTER 5

BETWEEN JAZZ AND A HARD PLACE (1965–1967)

Jazz has had a peculiar history. . . . At just the moment when it assumed the mantle of the most creative music in this society, the whole electronic world erupted, rock and radio gave birth to an amazing amalgam of poetry and music with which we have been blessed these past few years, and jazz seemed to diminish somehow. . . .

What was really happening was . . . the very purpose of jazz's existence was being redefined.

—Ralph J. Gleason, 1971

As America passed the midpoint of the sixties, an exciting and very loud musical phenomenon occurred. A variety of musical styles—electric blues, folk music, and an outgrowth of guitar-based rock 'n' roll—converged and, riding a tidal wave of popularity, threatened to drown all other musical styles. It was a far cry from the rock 'n' roll of the fifties, with its basic three-chord roots. It was wrapped up in a huge change—a maturing—of youth culture. With musicians like the Beatles and Bob Dylan in the lead, popular songs had become more poetic and socially relevant. The music itself was growing in sophistication as well, influenced by classical and jazz forms, while the sound of the electric guitar became the most instantly recognizable imprint of the musical revolution that eventually restructured the recording industry.

Critics initially called it "underground rock" or the "new rock"—later shortened to simply "rock"—and its effect on Impulse, Bob Thiele, and ABC was like its effect on most of the music business: slow at first, then inevitable. Before the decade ended, much of jazz would change as never before: how it was recorded, packaged, and promoted. How it sounded and, ultimately, how it sold.

FOOT-DRAGGING

In mostly musical ways, jazz would ignore the rock explosion, but it was impossible to ask the same of any label. No part of the industry could resist the pull of a new, expanding market. By 1967, many record companies—even the more entrenched majors like Columbia—were ready to invest heavily. "Checkbook A&R" was the new term for it, as Columbia's president, Clive Davis, agreed to an unheard-of advance of $250,000 to secure Big Brother & the Holding Company and their star singer, Janis Joplin, after catching them at the Monterey Pop Music Festival.

At ABC, Thiele and his higher-ups were tuned in to the same frequency but picking up different messages. Like Clive Davis, Thiele had been scouting bands in San Francisco, but found, as he recalled, that he "had a difficult time convincing the company of the validity of the new rock." "I wanted the company to sign Big Brother, Quicksilver, Steve Miller, and Blue Cheer."

"I remember going to San Francisco with him that summer," Bob Thiele Jr. says. "I think a couple of the bands were signed, Big Brother had a record deal with Mainstream, the [Jefferson] Airplane was on RCA, and the [Grateful] Dead were on Warners. But there were all these other bands and Dad was very close with Steve Miller and his band, and he had a handshake deal with Steve for what I believe was $25,000."

> I remember they made this deal in a strip bar in North Beach, and I had to sit outside in the vestibule behind the curtain because I couldn't go in. He had gone back to New York within the week. Miller's people had called and said, "Look, Capitol has offered us $100,000 but we want to go with you, can you add a van and some equipment to the deal?" So the 25,000 was going to cost 40,000, but they were still going to do the deal with my dad. And Newton was like, "A deal is a deal. We aren't doing this shit!" And he blew Steve Miller out.

"They turned these artists down," Thiele said with incredulity, noting that ABC did permit him "to record the Free Spirits with Larry Coryell and a San Francisco group, Salvation. They OK'd these two because they were less expensive to record."

That both groups ended up on the pop-oriented ABC label, rather than Impulse, furthered Thiele's lack of patience with what seemed an old-

The brass and the band: top ABC executives—including Larry Newton (far left) and Thiele, listening to their new signing, the Free Spirits, 1966.

school way of thinking about styles, genres, and audiences. At Columbia there was no separate jazz label and Miles Davis was another artist handled by the pop music department, enjoying the same promotional and publicity support that a wide stylistic range of artists—Dylan, the Byrds, Johnny Cash, Barbra Streisand—all enjoyed. By 1967, the trumpeter had also begun to engage in a musical dialogue with the "new rock," inserting amplified instruments and rock-powered rhythms into his music, with Columbia's full backing. ABC's heterogeneous approach was, in Thiele's view, as out of date as its understanding of avant-garde jazz.

> Some large companies are run by men who are insensitive to creative people. . . . They are usually followers rather than creators. While I was at ABC, there were three main problems as far as I personally was concerned. Number one: I had a terrible time obtaining approval to record the new young black players. Number two: I had a difficult time convincing the company of the new rock. . . . Lastly, I just couldn't stomach sales people's views controlling the acceptance or rejection of recordings.

ROCK-JAZZ, POP-JAZZ, AND THE GUITAR LINK

If Thiele had been the compliant type, perhaps he would have been content to sit back and allow other labels to continue the exploration of the new rock or the cross-fertilization of jazz and popular music.

But Thiele wasn't, and he didn't. In July 1967, he appended "Pop" to the title of his magazine, *Jazz*; a month later, *Jazz & Pop* had a photo of Archie Shepp and Frank Zappa in conversation on its cover and a joint interview inside. Besides producing the Free Spirits and Salvation for ABC, he steered a number of blues-rock bands—the Outlaw Blues Band, the Dirty Blues Band—onto BluesWay. On Impulse, he developed a number of musicians and projects that though of varying approaches and quality were all trying to make the jazz-rock or jazz-pop overlap work. And if there was a way of selling Impulse to a rock audience, while spending no more than before, all the better.

> What I tried to do at Impulse was to record new, young players [and] put them under contract, such as [guitarist] Gabor Szabo. But then, I was trying to make the label a successful *jazz* label, so I would try and record name musicians such as Sonny Rollins, Dizzy [Gillespie] on a one-shot basis. So there was a design to it.

Gabor Szabo on sitar, 1966.

Nearing his thirtieth birthday, Szabo broke from Chico Hamilton to pursue a solo career at the close of 1965; *El Chico,* that August, was their last session together. By November, the guitarist, whose single-note patterns played with microtonal accuracy—seemingly in and out of tune—began recording his first album for Impulse, *Gypsy '66* [AS-9105]. True to the title, Szabor's playing betrayed the flavor of his Hungarian roots. Yet even with the unusual makeup of the recording unit—multiple guitars, Sadao Watanabe on flute, and Gary McFarland on bass, drums, and vibes—Szabo's debut stands out most for being the label's first title to lean heavily on rock or pop material of the day, featuring two covers each of tunes by the Beatles and Burt Bacharach. (Shirley Scott had been the first Impulse artist to record a Beatles song, covering "Can't Buy Me Love" on *Queen of the Organ* in '64.)

"Playing pop songs can only prove you're a better musician by being able to do something with them," Szabo reasoned. "I'm all for it. Original material in jazz is so limited . . . and people in jazz are writing and playing for each other and they're only listening to each other. Consequently, the circle becomes tighter and tighter."

"Gabor called me up [around that time] and he said, 'Do you think there is such a style as pop-jazz?'" recalls Larry Coryell, the young guitarist who replaced Szabo at Chico Hamilton's final Impulse session. "I said 'No,' [laughs] because at that point, I wanted to stay faithful to the jazz thing, whatever that was, even though we were doing fusion."

"We" was the Free Spirits, a short-lived New York–based group formed in 1965 and considered one of the first attempts at fusing rock instrumentation and jazz improvisation. Including Coryell, second guitarist Columbus Baker, bassist Chris Hill, drummer Bob Moses, and saxophonist Jim Pepper, the band was among a slew of young pop-oriented groups contracted to ABC in 1965 and 1966, such as less-remembered groups like the Fraternity of Man, the Bubblegum Machine, and Bagatelle.

The Free Spirits were assigned to Thiele because of their jazz credentials: "Jim Pepper was one of the reasons that ABC signed us because he was a great tenor player," says Coryell. But they ended up on the larger ABC label "because they were trying to market us as a pop act—because we were doing all this horrible singing! We were totally experimental; we were a bunch of jazz musicians doing folk-rock."

Whatever the classification, the first and only Free Spirits album, *Out of Sight & Sound,* reflects its time ("The only real solos were taken by the tenor player on the record. It had one awful sitar solo") but sadly lived up to its title. But Coryell sees it as an important step toward the development of jazz-rock.

> That record is good, too, to see what we were trying to do. I was really trying to go as far away from the jazz thing as possible in order to bring something back, and it took many years to bring something back.

The entire menagerie of sounds, looks, and leanings of the sixties became integrated into the Impulse mystique—for most young musicians, the label provided the soundtrack to a variety of sixties activities. "We all thought the Coltrane stuff was the pinnacle," Coryell states. "We'd listen to *A Love Supreme* over and over again. I remember every time I'd hear it, I would hear something different—of course I was on acid. Jim was a big fan of Albert Ayler, and could have been the next Coltrane.

> I was into Chico, of course, because I loved Gabor. I was around when Gabor was doing his transition into what he would like to call "pop-jazz." . . . When he first started playing, he was playing like Tal Farlow [a jazz guitarist known for his light and rapid touch], and then he started using more open strings—more influenced by Ravi Shankar. He wanted to be the first pop-jazz guitarist to record "California Dreaming," and Wes [Montgomery] beat him to it!

Over the next few years, Szabo brought forth a series of albums—*Spellbinder* [AS-9123] and *Jazz Raga* [AS-9128] in mid-'66; *The Sorcerer* [AS-9146] and *Wind, Sky and Diamonds* [AS-9151] in '67—paralleling the rock experimentation of the day. The guitarist introduced sitars, hard-driving rhythms, and Indian raga structures into his music. He experimented with controlled feedback and other electric effects. He layered multiple guitar parts, often overdubbing his own guitar or sitar playing, and covered pop and rock tunes.

One cannot reference Szabo without mentioning Gary McFarland. If there was one other Impulse artist whom Thiele was consciously grooming as a crossover to a young, rock-focused audience, it was McFarland, a vibraphonist and arranger who had entered the Impulse fold in 1963 with his one-off album *Point of Departure,* left to record for Verve, then resigned with Thiele in 1965. When he returned to Impulse, the label championed him as the next great jazz arranger-composer, making sure never to hide his movie-idol looks.

McFarland shared Szabo's enthusiasm for a wide range of musical forms like rock, pop, Brazilian and Latin sounds. "I'd get bored stiff if I could only write one kind of music," he told an interviewer. "There are even times when I like to do rock 'n' roll arrangements. . . . Life is tension and release, and rock 'n' roll is a kind of release."

Thiele utilized McFarland for five projects at Impulse (titles and details in the Source Notes), though they never achieved substantial sales. Sadly, McFarland's name has been largely forgotten for the most part today (an early death in 1971 did not help), but he had his moment in the sun. In his heyday, he earned critical respect, with some writers putting him on a par with Duke Ellington and Antonio Carlos Jobim. He was also one of a brotherhood of jazz arrangers at Impulse—Lalo Schifrin, Chico O'Farrill, and Oliver Nelson were the others—whose sound reached its largest audience through their work for TV or film.

Thiele's work with Coryell, Szabo, and McFarland never achieved the style-shifting influence or popular success of other late-sixties artists who are today credited as pioneers of the fusion of jazz and rock, like Blood, Sweat & Tears, Santana, and Miles Davis. But these albums serve as worthy examples of a groundswell, and of the visionary possibilities still inherent at Impulse, at a time when its parent company was distracted by bigger, more industrywide concerns.

DUNHILL ARRIVES

Ultimately, Bob Thiele and ABC-Paramount president Larry Newton wanted the same thing: a big piece of the (new) rock. Essentially, the dif-

THE OCTOBER SUITE

Steve Kuhn / *The October Suite: Steve Kuhn Plays the Compositions of Gary McFarland* / Impulse AS-9136

DATE RECORDED: October 14 and November 1, 1966

DATE RELEASED: January 1967

PRODUCER: Bob Thiele

"I'm looking at it right here. It says 'The Virtuoso Series' on the cover."

So says pianist Steve Kuhn, adding: "*The October Suite* was going to be the first in a series of recordings that sort of went beyond the traditional jazz format. I think this might have been the first and only; I don't recall anything else coming in the series.

"There was a gentleman named Norman Schwartz who was managing both Gary [McFarland] and me at the time. Norman was very friendly with Bob Thiele and suggested a new series on Impulse—trying to get in what you would call the Third Stream. I hate that term. I think the album succeeded because Gary *wasn't* trying to synthesize the two musics, European [classical] music and jazz, at all. He kept everyone in their own arena, so to speak.

"Gary and I had a very close relationship. He played vibraphone and composed. He came from a small town in Oregon, really unsophisticated in a way, but he learned fast. We were both students at the Lenox School of Jazz in 1959, up in Lenox, Massachusetts. Ornette [Coleman] was a student that year, and Don Cherry and David Baker. The faculty was Gunther Schuller, George Russell, Bill Evans, the Modern Jazz Quartet, Kenny Dorham, and so on.

"Gary was really a very natural writer. He had an idea in his head of the mood he wanted, all figured out before he started writing. He didn't obsess over certain things that other

The October Suite Steve Kuhn PIANO
COMPOSED AND CONDUCTED BY Gary McFarland
THE VIRTUOSO SERIES impulse! A-9136
MONAURAL

writers who had more training would have. He really had a unique voice considering the number of years he was on the scene, which wasn't that many. Still to this day, I think about him a lot. Him and [bassist] Scott LaFaro—in those early years those were the two main people that left. That really impacted me greatly.

"For *The October Suite*—I don't recall why it was called that —Gary wrote six pieces. One of them was the theme for a movie he did the music for called *13*. The other five were written specifically for me, three of them with a string quartet and the others with a woodwind quintet and a harp.

"We had a great rhythm section, [drummer] Marty Morell and [bassist] Ron Carter, and Phil Ramone was the engineer. Gary had talked about what to do, and basically he let me alone. He wrote what he wrote and there was a lot of freedom for improvising.

"That Third Stream thing, if there was any crossover between classical and jazz, it succeeded because he wrote for the strings and the woodwinds naturally, in the way that they would normally play. There was no improvising there.

"What resonated for me more were the string pieces; there was a certain atmosphere and elegiac quality to the string writing that he did. The woodwind section pieces were more upbeat in a way, and the strings were a little more melancholy. My favorite was 'Remember When,' which is the last song on the side with the strings.

"Bob [Thiele], as I recall, was just sort of invisible. I don't recall any kind of presence, in terms of him giving direction or anything like that. He was like that with two other Impulse albums I did: a live concert at the Kresge Auditorium at M.I.T., with Charlie Haden, Marty Morell, and myself with Henry Red Allen and Pee Wee Russell. Thiele was trying to consolidate the two eras there. I also was on *Sound Pieces* with Oliver Nelson.

"Impulse was one of the few labels where they were taking chances, they weren't going with formulaic stuff. It was a prestigious label *and* they had good distribution.

"I was invited to play the music from *The October Suite* in California [in March 2003]. That was the first time the album had been performed live, and the first time it had been played since we recorded it in the late sixties. That's almost forty years that went by. The music sounded to me as fresh as it did back then. That for me speaks volumes—it didn't sound dated at all."

Interpreted and interpreter: Gary McFarland (left) and Steve Kuhn, 1966.

ference in their approaches can be summed up as "Do we buy the bands?" versus "Do we buy the companies that have signed the bands?" What made fiscal sense to Newton, and what was in tune with ABC's ongoing strategy, was to think big.

Under Newton's leadership, ABC had been thinking bigger and bigger for a while, searching to expand its musical holdings in the area of recording, manufacturing, and distribution. It began by buying a distributorship in Seattle and then one in Salt Lake City, enabling the company to capture distribution profit on both its own releases and those of other labels requiring distribution. Acquiring other labels was still part of the plan as well, as ABC's Alan Bergman recalls.

> You know we almost bought Atlantic [Records]. . . . We were at loggerheads with them and we wanted the owners of Atlantic to make certain warranties and representations, which really revolved around the integrity of no payola. Finally we walked away from the deal, which was a terrible thing to do. Not too long after that they were snapped up.

Within the ABC corporate structure, the music division took on a higher and higher profile.

> ABC Records was doing very nicely for Leonard [Goldenson, the chairman of ABC]—it had become a favored part of his empire. At that point, ABC included a film division, which was turning out some pretty good films and TV series; then we had the radio and TV networks, and an arm called ABC Syndication. It was pretty far-flung.

Indicative of the music arm's growing importance, ABC's Phil Kurnit notes, was the move that placed it in the same offices as the ABC television network.

"The Paramount Theater building was a dinky building," Kurnit remembers. "It had been there a long time. There was nothing posh about it. But in July of '65, we moved into the ABC building on Sixth Avenue [just north of Radio City Music Hall]. That was pretty ritzy. That was the first time where we really had the feeling that we were together with the big entity of the network. When we moved we became just ABC Records—we dropped the 'Paramount.' Soon after, ABC made the deal with Dunhill

Records, which would bring us the Mamas and the Papas, Barry McGuire, and others. That would really launch ABC Records."

Dunhill Records was the Los Angeles–based brainchild of a trio of music industry veterans. Lou Adler, a songwriter and producer who had worked with the likes of Sam Cooke and Johnny Rivers, joined forces with producer and engineer Bobby Roberts (formerly of a group called the Dunhills), while Jay Lasker handled the business side. What was first a distribution deal grew into a much tighter subsidiary relationship as Dunhill proved its worth with McGuire's chart-topping single "Eve of Destruction" in August 1965 and a wave of Top Ten hits through '66 and into '67 from California-based folk-rockers like the Mamas and the Papas and the tight-harmony pop of the Grass Roots.

No deal signed into effect by Newton would have a greater impact on the future of ABC Records—and by association, Impulse—than the deal with Dunhill. "Ray Charles was slightly on the wane then, never mind jazz," recalls Alan Bergman. "So the focus of excitement and activity was Dunhill and L.A.—no question about it."

A metaphor for how the Impulse cache rose in value as its profits were dwarfed by ABC's pop triumphs hung on the walls at the new Sixth Avenue offices of ABC Records. Bill Kaplan commented:

> Those, quote, gold albums, unquote, were displayed in everyone's office. They didn't come from the R.I.A.A. [the Recording Industry Association of America, which certifies records gold and platinum]. We had them made: they were simply copper covered with a gold color. *A Love Supreme* and other albums weren't selling *that* big. Yes, we knew that Coltrane was getting well known, that he was getting awards from *Down Beat* and so forth, but it didn't show in the coffers. At that time, when he was alive and on Impulse, nobody made a big thing out of John Coltrane.

COLTRANE'S WAY

Maybe his sales weren't big, but for one whose music had grown exceedingly edgy and abstract, John Coltrane's substantial weight in the commercial marketplace of the time is still impressive. It was also more than enough to warrant ABC's decision to renew his Impulse contract in April 1967, as it had in '63 and '65.

Coltrane began 1967 celebrating the one-year anniversary of the new quintet that had replaced his celebrated quartet, featuring Pharoah Sanders, Jimmy Garrison, and Rashied Ali, with Coltrane's wife, Alice, on piano. Gone was the drama of McCoy Tyner's hammered chords; Alice's facile sweeps along the keyboard painted a more diffuse rhythmic background. Sanders favored Coltrane at his most forceful and vocal-like: his unabated energy could roar and exhilarate. Elvin Jones had always suggested a steady swing, but Ali, whom Coltrane praised for being multidirectional in his drumming, explored an intuitive, improvised drive.

Together, Coltrane's quintet produced a distinct shift from what went before, but arguably not as startling as the saxophonist's own sound. In their company, he came to rely on a vocabulary of vibrato, screeches, and cries: dissonance and atonality were now a regular part of his sonic palette.

Through 1966, Coltrane's group had toured the United States and then Japan, and had found time in their schedule to make ten studio dates back in Englewood, New Jersey. Impulse also recorded four live performances—at the Village Vanguard (again), at the Newport Jazz Festival (again), in Japan, and at a small Harlem community arts center run by the Nigerian percussionist Olatunji. Coltrane's sound and influence were expanding further and further into an orbit of their own, exceedingly modern at a time when music prided itself on being innovative and new.

On record, Coltrane never spoke out about, nor was he asked about, the subject of rock—old, new, or underground. Back in the day when rock 'n' roll was a seedling growing from the vibrant, pervasive rhythm-and-blues sound of the late forties, he served a stint as a sideman in the jump blues world, honking the saxophone and walking the bar. In 1965, he had been given an electric tenor saxophone by Varitone, the manufacturer, but he never played it publicly or on record. Alice Coltrane remembers that his listening preferences around that time were varied and vast: the music of Igor Stravinsky and Al Hirt, music from India and Africa, music heard in Japanese Shinto temples and on David Susskind's television program. But no pop or rock.

[*Opposite*] Trane's last band: Coltrane's quintet in Van Gelder's studio. From left: Rashied Ali (obscured), Pharoah Sanders, Jimmy Garrison, and John and Alice Coltrane, 1966.

Nonetheless, Coltrane's music had found a growing audience among younger, more rock-oriented listeners, even as his name and music spanned distinctions of generation and genre. The demand for new releases—answered by his older labels Prestige and Atlantic as well as

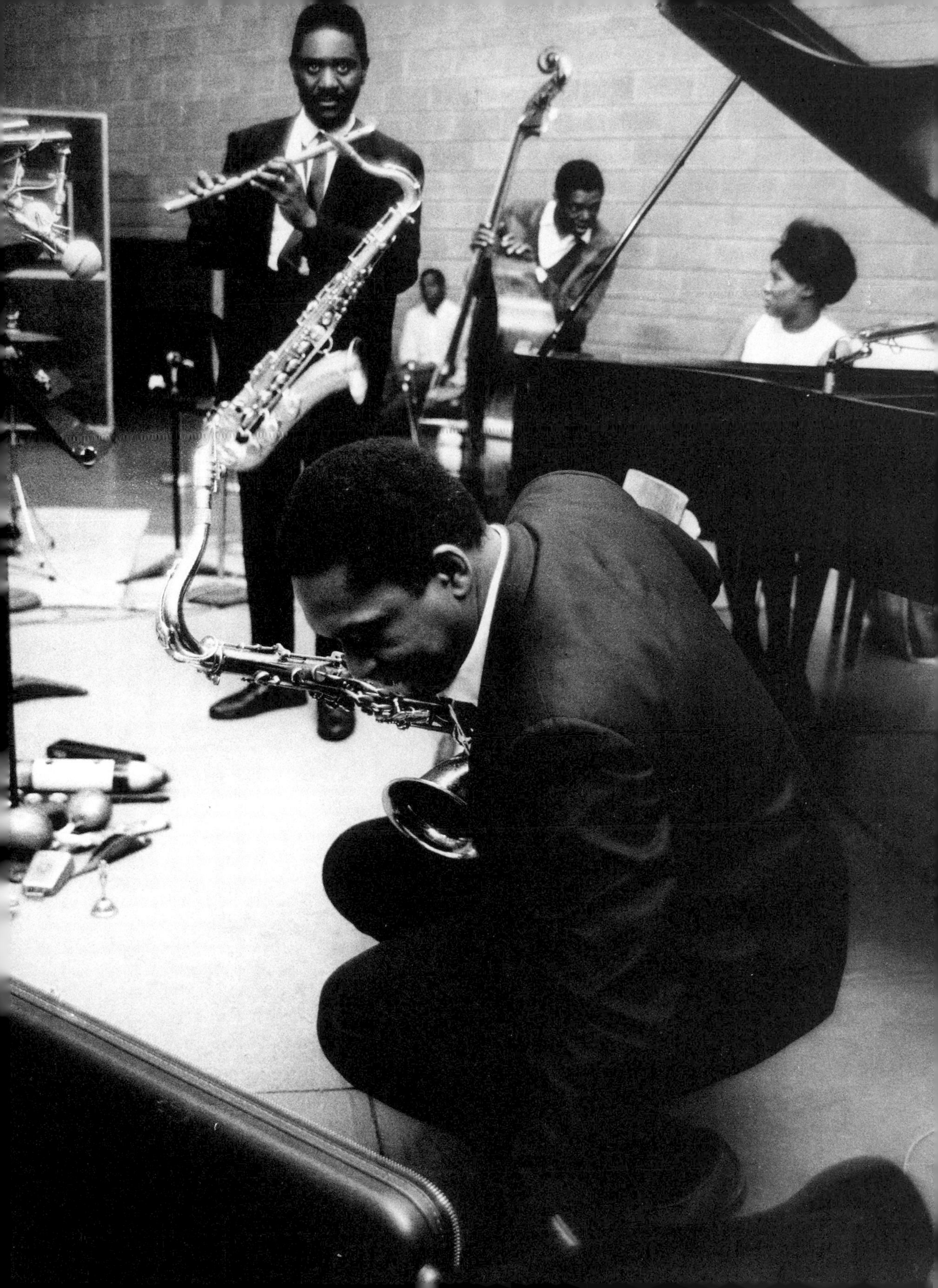

ODDS & TRENDS—PART II

Various Titles / Impulse
DATE RECORDED: 1967 and 1968
DATE RELEASED: 1968
PRODUCER: Bob Thiele

To a trend-friendly producer in 1967, no musical movement held more sway than the profitable sounds of the youth market: amplified guitars and sitars, long jams and hair. Thiele visited San Francisco's rock scene and made a valiant attempt to bring Janis Joplin and Steve Miller into the ABC fold. An immediate no from a superior was quickly followed by a "What else did you find?"

"I then half-heartedly told him about a group of beatnik characters named Salvation who offered to make an album for $5,000," Thiele reported, adding that "Salvation turned out to be just a name, not a prophecy."

Later that year, Thiele journeyed to Los Angeles and focused his efforts on projects for Impulse that fell in line with ABC's budget standards and resonated with the timely strains of psychedelia and exotica. With an exercised sense of bravado, he even recorded himself in the studio and briefly became an Impulse artist. Four results follow.

• Thiele dusted off his old clarinet, joined forces with Gabor Szabo, and assembled a rock orchestra that featured a cast of new Impulse hopefuls (percussionist Emil Richards, saxophonist Tom Scott, bassist-sitarist Bill Plummer) plus various session men and the California Dreamers, a pop choir. Inspired by the sudden resurgence of interest in the music of the twenties, he called the large and loose aggregation the New Happy Times Orchestra. For Impulse, the group recorded *Light My Fire* [AS-9159], an odd recasting of Dylan, Doors, Paul Simon, and Byrds songs with a Jazz Age feel. For ABC, Thiele recorded the same group with his name as prominent headliner, delivering two more albums: *Thoroughly Modern* and *Do the Love,* both featuring the Sunflower Singers.

• Tom Scott—nineteen years old in 1967 and already a veteran of Oliver Nelson's L.A. big band—was signed to a two-record Impulse deal that produced *Honeysuckle Breeze* [AS-9163], also with the California Dreamers, and *Rural Still Life* [AS-9171]. Both titles reveal a solid player tied to an unfortunate collection of mostly pop songs, uncomplimentary to song or saxophonist, save for the redeeming "With Respect to Coltrane," a Scott original on the second album.

• *Bill Plummer and His Cosmic Brotherhood* [AS-9164] featured a big band led by the bassist that reflected (or refracted) the many sounds of the day into a loose-limbed symphony: three sitars, two guitarists, multiple percussionists, a rock rhythm section, young Tom Scott on reeds and flute, and an electric harpsichordist trading lines with a sitar on "The Look of Love."

• Emil Richards was long established in the L.A. jazz scene by the late sixties, and had also worked in groups led by Charles Mingus, George Shearing, and Shorty Rogers. But it was his co-leadership of the Hindustani Jazz Sextet, a band exploring a jazz-Indian hybrid with trumpeter Don Ellis, that made him hip to the times. Richards and his Microtonal Blues Band were signed to a two-album Impulse deal in 1968, and *Journey to Bliss* [AS-9166] was the immediate result. Evoking the spiritual and cultural curiosity of the day, the album featured a six-part "Meditation Suite," with unusual time signatures (19/4, 12/4, 7/4) as well as a vast array of otherworldly instrumentation (Tibetan mouth organ, flapamba, 31-tone bells).

Impulse—meant that there was always a wide and somewhat confusing variety in most record bins. Then there was a backlog of master tapes in Impulse's vaults, which was becoming an issue.

So how to determine what to release next, and what to sit on? According to Thiele, Coltrane took a hands-on role in the decision-making. "If we were trying to make a certain release date, [Coltrane] had enough confidence in me to let me pick the takes and put the album together. If we had the time, we would try to do it together. Naturally I tried wherever possible to give him the time to listen to the things that we had done. . . . He would say, 'Let's hold up on what we've done [and not release it yet because] I've got something new.'"

After *Kulu Se Mama,* Coltrane's next Impulse release was a sextet recording, *Meditations* [AS-9110], a five-part suite that was clearly—as

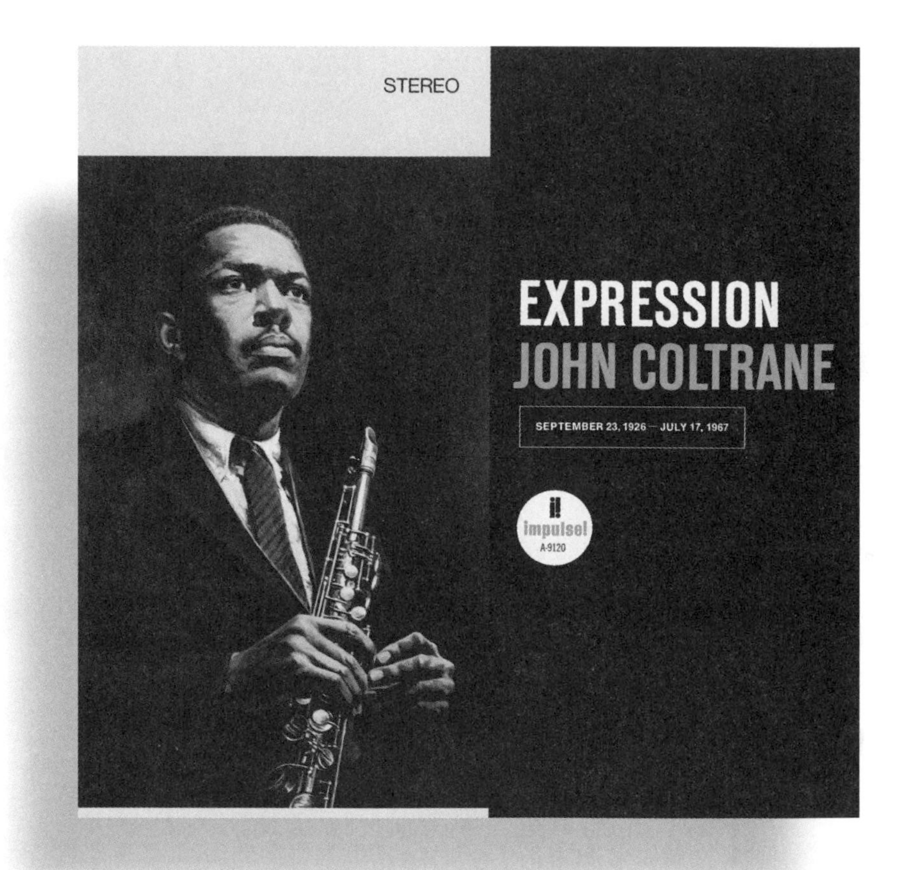

the liner notes and song titles confirmed—a spiritual follow-up to *A Love Supreme.*

By spring of '67, Coltrane had chosen the tracks for his next album, a collection that would be known for the extended workout "To Be," which featured both Coltrane and Sanders on flute, with Coltrane singing as well. He decided to title it *Expression*.

On May 17, with his quintet and an added percussionist, Coltrane taped two tracks for Impulse at Van Gelder's studio. It was to be his last studio recording.

THE BLACK BORDER

Released a few weeks after Coltrane's death on July 17, 1967, from liver cancer, *Expression* [AS-9120] serves as his memorial album on the Impulse label, the thick black border on its cover lending it a sense of bereavement. His demise was sudden and keenly felt by an extended circle of musicians, fans, and all associated with ABC-Paramount and Impulse. To some it came as a surprise, to others not.

"I had talked to John three days before he died—I had no idea he was that sick," says Alan Bergman. "Then I heard he died. I don't know what effect it had on Thiele."

"I don't know about the drugs he was using in the early days," Thiele remarked. "He confided that he went cold turkey . . . but I think the damage had been done over so many years that even though he stopped over the next ten years he was going downhill all the time. When he visited my office three days before he died, I went to the sales manager of the company, who was in the next office, and I said, 'I hate to tell you this, but he's going to die.'"

"We were all crushed," recalls Bill Kaplan.

The funeral was held on July 21 at St. Peter's Lutheran Church in midtown Manhattan. Among the thousand mourners crammed into the church was a Who's Who of jazz legends and avant-garde players, including many Impulse artists, as well as a number of ABC executives. "I do remember at John's funeral that Newton asked Chuck Stewart to bring a camera," Kaplan remembers. "Chuck said, 'Mr. Newton, I've never taken a camera to a funeral before and I don't intend to start now.'"

As Coltrane lay in state, the mourners were serenaded with music performed by Ornette Coleman, with whom Coltrane once took lessons, and by Albert Ayler, who had recently signed to Impulse (a recording of a Village Vanguard gig would become his first release on the label).

"He was our leader," recalls Archie Shepp. "He may have left town, but he remained so." Seated in the front row was Alice Coltrane, a widow at age thirty with four children. Today, she looks back on a spirit that had passed to another plane, and on a business relationship that was still to grow. "At that point, John was one of the musicians who had been at Impulse from the beginning to the end. He would have recorded on for many more years. It wasn't really over—not according to the contract."

In six short years, the Impulse-Coltrane association had yielded sixteen albums, far more than any other single artist's output and far beyond the standard two-albums-per-year arrangement. His widow could not have known how enduring that contract would remain. Though it might have been construed as a conflict of interest, Bill Kaplan decided to offer Coltrane's widow a word of advice.

> I had never spoken to Alice Coltrane, but I took it upon myself to call her and gave her my condolences. I said, "Alice, you're going to need an attorney to take care of the estate. I really would hope that you don't use Harold Lovett. I don't think he's the right man for it, and I do have a suggestion. He's in Long Island, not far from you. He's honest and all that." And she used him for the next several years while she lived there and he took care of them. Now in retrospect, should I have been doing that? I never even thought about it.

There certainly was much for Alice Coltrane to ponder: multiple recordings her husband had set aside for release, multiple recordings in the vaults that suddenly made Thiele's liberal habit of recording Coltrane seem incredibly prescient and wise. "I'm sure that Larry Newton said, 'Well, how much have we got in the can on him?' " remarks Alan Bergman. Thiele began to consolidate and plan ahead, working closely with Coltrane's widow.

"I've had some lengthy discussions with Alice Coltrane, who is a very, very beautiful woman," the producer stated in 1968, his last year with Impulse. "She is leading a life right now according to the wishes of John. The life she lives is based on the things that he said."

Then came the promise of more Coltrane music, and with it the future of Impulse.

> We have agreed, not because of any legal reasons, but because of John Coltrane, and because of my own feeling about the man, that we're going to try and work together on selecting material for the next three or four albums. . . .

D THE MICROTONAL BLUES BAND STEREO AS-9182 impulse!

STEREO A-9181 impulse!

STEREO A-9178 impulse!

A REVISITED STEREO A-9176 impulse!

S A-9175 impulse!

STEREO A-9171 impulse!

STEREO A-9170 impulse!

STEREO A-9169 impulse!

STEVE ALLEN STEREO A-9168 impulse!

STEREO A-9167 impulse!

E MICROTONAL BLUES BAND STEREO A-9166 impulse!

RT AYLER A-9165 impulse!

AND THE COSMIC BROTHERHOOD A-9164 impulse!

E FOR A QUARTER ONE FOR A DIME

GS JOHN COLTRANE STEREO AS-9161 impulse!

CHAPTER 6

IMPULSE AFTER TRANE (1967–1969)

The changes in his work, of course, may have been signs of growth, and if they were, perhaps no important jazz improviser ever grew and developed as much as Coltrane did in so short a time. . . . Perhaps a deeper frustration and tormented indecision are part of the unacknowledged truth of the temper of the times that it was Coltrane's destiny to articulate.

—Martin Williams, 1967

"Died" is not in Alice Coltrane's vocabulary.

"Once John had left, that was a very crucial year for our family," she says. "Everything was held in suspension. We had all of these plans for albums, for a [home] studio. He had ordered me a harp because I had no experience with it. He would let me know that if there's something you really want done, do it yourself. Not only have a studio, but also make your own recordings. Any of the companies could give you distribution. The whole production would be done by us."

The very idea! Artists controlling their own music, and productions, even designing their own album covers . . . but then, in the late sixties, the recording industry was getting used to the idea of sharing more control and profits with artists, such was the effect of rock on the business side of the industry.

Yet in the two years after Coltrane's passing, jazz itself slid into a relative decline—lower sales of albums, fewer nightclubs to play. Record labels were absorbed, retired, or altered forever. Thiele's issues with the ABC brass would be put to the test as never before, and the effect of the increasing friction is quantifiable: through 1968 and the producer's final months at Impulse in 1969, his productions yielded a mere fifteen albums for the label, and two of those were best-of's.

That the Impulse identity held true during this tumultuous phase speaks volumes of the momentum generated by the label during the Thiele-Coltrane relationship. Even after both had departed the label—in different ways—the force of their mutual drive helped the label survive an unstable corporate environment.

Coltrane's departure put his plans on hold for only a moment. Within a few months, the harp arrived and Alice began to master it. A studio was built in the garage of the Coltranes' Dix Hills home. Going through recordings of a session her husband had produced in California, she began assembling an album for release on their own label.

PICKING UP WHERE TRANE LEFT OFF

In late 1967, only a few months after the release of *Expression*, Impulse brought out *Om* [AS-9140], Coltrane's second posthumous album and the second title culled from the recordings he had instigated during his prolific summer two years before. In title and cover, it could not have been more timely, tying into the look and feel of the year that brought forth the Summer of Love. *Om* featured a single spiraling, epic composition that stretched over both sides of an album, and musically fused the spontaneous energy of *Ascension* with the spiritual resonance of *A Love Supreme*, featuring the quartet plus flutist Joe Brazil, second bassist Donald Garrett, and Pharoah Sanders.

Like, *psychedelic*: Impulse keeps up with the flavor of the day.

In early '68, not long after the release of *Om*, Thiele suddenly noticed that another Coltrane title had made it to market: *Cosmic Music*, catalog number CRC-5000 on the new Coltrane Records label, consisted of two John Coltrane recordings from 1966 and two quartet tracks led by Alice Coltrane. For a brief few weeks, the Coltrane family was in competition with the label John Coltrane had led.

Quick discussions took place among ABC executives, who realized that though music recorded by Coltrane while under contract to Impulse would remain so after his death, it would be a good idea to bypass legal action. They offered Coltrane Records a compromise: *Cosmic Music* would be released on Impulse, and Alice herself—who had already begun to actively record as a leader in her home studio—would become an Impulse artist. The second part of the compromise, she recalls, was an idea her husband had once suggested.

> I never really thought much about recording [as a leader] at all. But John would mention it occasionally. And I am sure that he spoke with Bob Thiele, because he said, "You know, they're very much interested, if you can put out some original music, some new music." And I said, "It would be nice to do."

A Monastic Trio [AS-9156] was Alice's first full album as a leader, and her first—and last—with Bob Thiele overseeing its release; Alice herself was credited as producer. "My experience with Bob Thiele was so short that all I can say is that he was a gentleman, and very professional," she says. "And I think that, in the memory of John, he wanted to just present everything in the best way possible."

A Monastic Trio is a peek at the signature style Alice had been developing while attending to a growing family (she had given birth to John's three sons—John Jr., Ravi, and Oranyan—between 1964 and 1966, and had a daughter, Michelle, born before she met Coltrane). Echoing the arpeggio-rich approach she eventually taught herself on the harp (she appeared on the cover of her first album playing the instrument), her piano playing had become filled with a loose, lyrical flow. It was an approach she credits to the suggestion of her husband.

> Now, you will not hear me play within a two-octave range, or a three. You're gonna hear the entire piano from one to eighty-eight. When I became a part of the group I only played through two or three octaves like we all did, chording for the soloists. But John said, "You have all those keys. Why don't you play all of them as completely as you can?"

Her husband's influence was pervasive. She favored using her former associates from Coltrane's final quintet: Pharoah Sanders, Jimmy Garrison,

COSMIC MUSIC

John and Alice Coltrane / *Cosmic Music* / Impulse AS-9148
John Coltrane with strings / *Infinity* / Impulse AS-9225
DATE RECORDED: February 2, 1966
LATER OVERDUBS: April 16 and 17, 1972
First released on Coltrane Records: 1968; later on Impulse: February 1969
With overdubs, as *Infinity*: 1972
PRODUCERS: John Coltrane, Alice Coltrane

OK, this was one of the ones we produced. I say "we" as if he was right there with me. . . .

—ALICE COLTRANE

Of all the posthumous John Coltrane releases initiated by his wife, Alice Coltrane, none has a more confusing tale than *Cosmic Music,* the first release on Alice's short-lived Coltrane Records label. It began as a San Francisco session produced and paid for by Coltrane in early 1966, with his quintet (Pharoah Sanders, Jimmy Garrison, Rashied Ali, and Alice) and an added percussionist (Ray Appleton). Four tracks, filled with intense solos and flowing, irregular rhythms, were recorded: "Manifestation," "Reverend King," "Peace on Earth," and "Leo."

For two years, the tapes sat in the Coltranes' Long Island house. In early 1968, Alice chose to pair "King" and "Manifestation" with two tracks she had recorded in the home studio that January with her first quartet: Sanders, Garrison, and drummer Ben Riley. The tracks were "Lord, Help Me to Be" and "The Sun," the latter opening with an invocation chanted by her husband and Sanders back in 1966.

When the album was released later that year, its cover featured John and Alice's name jointly in old English font, over a black-and-white rendering of a design attributed to the deceased saxophonist. As others had done previously in the jazz world (Dizzy Gillespie with his DeeGee Records, for one), it seemed the Coltrane family would be releasing their own recordings—old and new—through their label, effectively competing with Impulse.

ABC was caught unawares. Despite Coltrane's passing, their rights to release his music lived on by contract—especially recordings that were in the family's possession but had been produced under Impulse's auspices. ABC's Bill Kaplan recalls, "There were problems because [Alice] had a lot of the masters and she was going to start bringing out John Coltrane albums. Alan Bergman stepped in to stop it." Rather than simply halting the idea of Coltrane Records (and cognizant of how it would look to legally tangle with a recent widow), the label offered a compromise.

"Once [*Cosmic Music*] was available," reports Alice Coltrane, "the Impulse people said, 'Your ideas are fine, the music is good, but let us produce it. Let us have control of the artwork, and we'll put out a beautiful cover and music that's in your hands, and it'll be a very nice album and we also can get it out throughout the world.' There was no sense of someone coercing or whatever, or even trying to persuade me. It was just, 'If you would like, we can produce it very nicely for you.' And it was!"

Impulse released *Cosmic Music* [AS-9148] in 1969 with a cover that featured a Jim Marshall photograph of Coltrane against a moon-like circle, emphasizing the track dedicated to the Reverend Martin Luther King Jr., and with the co-credit "produced by Coltrane Records." It received favorable reviews, including one in *Rolling Stone* that warned: "The fervor on this album—from tapes his wife found posthumously—is frightening."

Fast-forward to 1972. Having moved her family to Southern California, Alice Coltrane took the two remaining tracks from the San Francisco session, "Leo" and "Peace on Earth," into the Village Recorders studio in Los Angeles and did what many jazz purists consider the unthinkable: overdubbing. She added bassist Charlie Haden, a string section, and herself (playing organ) onto the six-year-old recording. The tracks were released as half of John Coltrane's *Infinity* [AS-9225] by Impulse later that year.

"Some people didn't like the addition of strings," Alice told *Wire* magazine in 2002. "They said, 'We know that the original recording didn't have any strings, so why didn't you leave it as it was?' I replied, 'Were you there? Did you hear [John's] commentary and what he had to say?' . . . We had a conversation about every detail; [John] was showing me how the piece could include other sounds, blends, tonalities and resonances such as strings. He talked about cosmic sounds, higher dimensions, astral levels and other worlds, and realms of music and sound that I could feel."

[Right] All smiles, starting anew: Bob Thiele and Alice Coltrane.

[Below] DIY in Dix Hills: Alice Coltrane in her home studio, Long Island. From left: Pharoah Sanders and Alice Coltrane.

and Rashied Ali. The titles of her original tunes were as spiritually focused as her husband's had been, pointing to both American gospel and Eastern mysticism: "Gospel Trane," "Oceanic Beloved," "Atomic Peace." "John meditated a lot. I meditated. Sometimes we had meditations together," Alice recalls of their home life. "So you can see even that was an influence with the spiritual titles that we recorded back then."

THE NEW COLTRANE?

By 1968, it was becoming abundantly clear—as the Beatles traveled to India, as "transcendental meditation" became part of the general vocabulary—that *A Love Supreme* had been an accurate bellwether of a burgeoning, culture-wide spiritual adventurousness. "Before the sixties, you didn't hear about Hare Krishna and some of these gurus that had come from India," states Alice Coltrane. But as alto saxophonist Marion Brown stated, the new spiritual trend did not always look to foreign shores for inspiration:

> I think you'll find that the spirituality of the music during the sixties wasn't something exotic. It was coming directly out of the church, especially the Holiness Church. I know there was a whole tradition of saxophones in the church, and I don't know if Albert had been a part of that, but what he was doing was sure related to it.

Albert Ayler wore his spiritual roots on his sleeve. Like Coltrane, he had once donned a military uniform and marched, then later developed a musical vocabulary intertwined with a philosophy of universal understanding and supreme love. Ayler's song titles and gospel-intoned phrasing on alto and tenor saxophone testified as much. Like Coltrane, he had recorded for various small labels (in Ayler's case, very small, and often foreign) before coming to Impulse.

Unlike the music of Impulse's original star, Ayler's had bypassed bebop and other modern jazz styles, skipping over foreign scales and Eastern sounds to create a wild, emotionally expressive style from more down-home sources: spirituals, blues, even military marches.

On Coltrane's urging, Thiele first recorded Ayler live, issuing the track "Holy Ghost" on *The New Wave in Jazz* in '65. That Thiele hoped to nomi-

MUSIC IS THE HEALING FORCE OF THE UNIVERSE

Albert Ayler / *Music Is the Healing Force of the Universe* / Impulse AS-9191

DATE RECORDED: August 26 and 27, 1969

DATE RELEASED: April 1970

PRODUCER: Ed Michel

It had been one hell of a month. Hardly three weeks had gone by and August of 1969 was already reeling from a political and cultural cavalcade. Vietnam was embroiled in its most heated battles to date; the Woodstock nation was busy being born in upstate New York, days after the Manson family ran amok in southern California. In New York City, Miles Davis recruited what he called "the best damn rock 'n' roll band in the world," recording the first sessions that became *Bitches Brew*. The album's impact would only be fully appreciated in years to come; with an electric charge sparked by such talents as keyboardists Joe Zawinul and Chick Corea, guitarist John McLaughlin, bassists Dave Holland and Harvey Brooks, and drummers Lenny White and Jack DeJohnette, it bravely sounded the arrival of fusion jazz.

Davis was not alone in his pioneering efforts. Only a few city blocks away, Albert Ayler was forging his own rock-jazz hybrid the very same week. Over the past five years, the free-blowing saxophonist had become the darling of the avant-garde, but by August 1969 he had begun to integrate other music—primarily late-sixties rock and soul—into the mix. His 1968 recording *New Grass* first introduced his singular blend of free, funky, and electric sounds, and included Ayler's spoken explanation for his new direction. A year later he carried the idea further.

Over four days in Plaza Sound, seven stories above Rockefeller Center—the same generous space in which the Rockettes honed their high-kicking routines—Ayler assembled an unlikely group. Electric guitarist and Delta blues enthusiast Henry Vestine, of Canned Heat fame; journeyman bassist James Folwell; and singer and songwriter Mary Parks—Ayler's girlfriend—joined forces with a free-jazz quartet: pianist Bobby Few, bassist Stafford James, drummer Muhammad Ali (not the pugilist), and the saxophonist himself.

Ed Michel, on his first trip east as in-house producer and de facto label chief for Impulse, remembers the session.

"Suddenly here I was in New York, out from LA, to record Impulse's stars—Pharoah Sanders, Archie Shepp, and Ayler—knowing who they were and what they did. I had been around jazz recording for a while, and knew musicians pulled inspiration from wherever." But Ayler, he notes, was "reaching for everything, trying lots of stuff."

"He was definitely interested in a rock 'n' roll audience, and he thought that Mary Parks [credited as Mary Maria] was writing commercial songs. Because a lot of the tunes had lyrics, there was probably more organization in his head than other dates. But Albert talked a lot and didn't say much, if you know what I mean; he didn't lay out a deep philosophical road map. It was, 'This is what we're going to do,' and bam! Four afternoons of recording, August 26 to 29: almost three LPs' worth of material."

On tunes suggesting spiritual and mystical matters ("Masonic Inborn," "Oh! Love Is Life"), between spirited and often squealing saxophone solos, Parks preached and sang her lyrics while Vestine layered blues-flavored lead guitar runs. The session itself seemed rife with ritual—photographer Chuck Stewart recalls Ayler anointing himself with a salve that made his skin shiny and slick. Michel reports that Ayler's decision to sing and even blow the bagpipes held little surprise in context.

"I mean, that was the aura of the time: things were spacy, experimental. Albert played bagpipes on one track, but it didn't sound far out enough, so I said, 'Well, let's do something I've done on a rock 'n' roll record—let's turn the tape over. We can play the bagpipe backwards.' And we did."

The album resulting from the first two days of recording, *Music Is the Healing Force of the Universe*, is, to be generous, less than Ayler's best. Its historic importance as an attempt by one of the leaders of the avant-garde to move forward and find a new path, employing a palette of amplified and exotic instruments and adding lyrics, exceeds its musical impact. "Back then, I wouldn't have thought of Albert as a fusion guy, but now, looking back, that music with Vestine, it does seem like that's what he was doing," concedes Michel. "Just maybe a failed effort at fusion."

Spiritual healing: pianist Bobby Few and producer Ed Michel flank Ayler in lamé.

nate Ayler as an heir apparent to Coltrane was obvious once he was signed to the label at the start of 1967. "For Coltrane" was the opening track of Ayler's Impulse debut, *Live in Greenwich Village* [AS-9155], recorded at two venues closely associated with Coltrane: the Village Vanguard and the Village Theatre. Two tracks, "Our Prayer" and "Spirits Rejoice," can be seen as successors to Coltrane's tune "Spiritual."

Thiele's push to have Ayler fill Coltrane's shoes was more evident on *Love Cry* [AS-9165], Ayler's studio debut for Impulse. Frank Kofsky's liner notes open on Coltrane's funeral, offer *Love Cry* as another *A Love Supreme,* then quote Ayler himself describing the avant-garde trinity of the day: Coltrane as "The Father," Pharoah Sanders as "The Son," and himself as "The Holy Ghost." The album benefited from the fact that a more consistent band had settled in behind Ayler, including his brother Donald on trumpet, plus Call Cobbs on piano and harpsichord, bassist Alan Silva, and drummer Milford Graves.

Much has been written of the mutual admiration and influence between Ayler and Coltrane. "Albert Ayler had a different approach and was seeking his own identity, but respecting the contributions of John Coltrane and acknowledging it in his sound," says Alice Coltrane. "And I thought it was beautiful."

Ayler's path at Impulse took a significant turn with his next album, *New Grass* [AS-9175]. Dismissing most of his quintet, Ayler began to integrate rock and R&B forms into his music and plugged-in instruments into his band. He hung on to Cobbs and bassist Bill Folwell but added the R&B studio drummer Bernard Purdie. *New Grass* also featured a horn section and vocal chorus. It was a serious enough shift to warrant the spoken introduction to the opening track, "Message from Albert":

> The music I bring to you is in a different dimension of my life. I hope you will like this record. . . . The music I have played in the past I know I have played in another place at a different time.

Many writers have summarily dismissed *New Grass* and the Ayler recordings that followed, *Music Is the Healing Force of the Universe* [AS-9191] and *The Last Album* [AS-9208]—the latter released after his death in 1970—as examples of a jazzman increasingly persuaded by Thiele's commercial direction. But that seems unlikely. Ayler had for years pursued his own headstrong path, never mind the detractors, and would continue to do so after Thiele's departure from ABC. Perhaps replacing "commercial" with "accessible" would lend the argument credence, since by all accounts none of Ayler's albums sold in numbers equal to Alice Coltrane's or Pharoah Sanders's; certainly nowhere near John Coltrane's.

It seems Ayler was consciously finished with a five-year period of rapid growth by the time he joined Impulse: his *Live in Greenwich Village* album was a farewell look back to his more celebrated recordings for ESP and various European labels, while his next four discs experimented with shorter song forms, lyrics (supplied by Ayler's girlfriend, singer Mary Maria), and

The new hope: Albert Ayler, 1968.

HEAVY SOUNDS

Elvin Jones and Richard Davis / *Heavy Sounds* / Impulse AS-9160

DATE RECORDED: June 19 and 20, 1967

DATE RELEASED: May 1968

PRODUCER: Bob Thiele

It was a trio date—minus one.

"It was one of those things Bob Thiele was doing at the RCA studio on 22nd Street, and Larry Coryell was supposed to be there, but didn't show up," explained Elvin Jones. "He was sick or something, and so Richard and I were there."

Richard Davis picks up the thread: "Bob said, 'Why don't you guys just go ahead and start playing?' I had always thought that perhaps one day I would play 'Summertime' as a ballad with luscious strings, the harp, the flutes, and all the accessory instruments for flamboyancy—the harp strumming or something like that. And as it turned out I played it with just Elvin Jones [laughs]."

"So we just started fooling," Jones said, "Richard using his bow, warming up basically. I asked him, 'What's that you're playing?' and he said, 'Summertime.' So we kind of made a thing out of it, like a duet, tom-tom, mallets, and bow."

Davis: "No discussion, no editing, no plan, I just started playing the melody, and there he was. We played it for fifteen minutes [11:35, actually] . . . and I just thought there was some very brotherly thing about that particular piece."

Jones: "It was so good that they didn't want to discard it. I said, 'Look, Larry isn't here, I should call up my band and have them come in. . . .' "

Davis: "Bob said, 'OK, why don't you guys come back tomorrow and get somebody?' Elvin got [saxophonist] Frank Foster and [pianist] Billy Greene."

In the year and a half that had passed since leaving John Coltrane's group in January 1966, Jones had overcome depression, a failed marriage, and substance abuse issues. With the help of a new woman in his life, he assembled a working band in 1967 and began an extended run at Pookie's Pub in Manhattan's West Village. Richard Davis remembers: "We were working in these local joints around New York then. I remember [Pookie's]—that was a *funky* joint. All of a sudden Keiko came on the scene, and he started changing. He was always neat, and looking good, and taking care of business, and stuff like that. I always thought it was because he was with a woman of his choice."

By chance, the date of the second session was one day before Coltrane's funeral. The quartet performed two tunes brought by Foster, a veteran of the Basie band ("Raunchy Rita," "Shiny Stockings"); one by Greene ("M.E."); a standard ("Here's That Rainy Day"); and—tantalizingly—a version of "Take the A Train" that was somehow lost. The last tune of the day was a surprise to all: "Elvin's Guitar Blues," featuring the drummer singing and playing an acoustic guitar.

From sticks to strings: Jones (with guitar) and Thiele, June 20, 1967. Photographer Chuck Stewart identifies the mustachioed gentleman as Duke Ellington's cousin.

"They had heard me fooling around with guitar before," Jones said. "Freddy Greene [Count Basie's long-time guitarist] used to let me play his guitar. I'm not a real guitarist, but it's something that I love. It just so happened that Bob came in with a brand-new guitar, and I had to string it up, and the tips of my fingers were just burning up.

"It was one of these old blues tunes—something an old man, his name was Red, taught me when I was a kid in Pontiac [Michigan]. I've always liked to play that because it was one of the first pieces I learned how to play. And I like to listen to these old guitar players: Muddy Waters, John Lee Hooker . . ."

The cover of *Heavy Sounds* features a photo of Davis and Jones, shot by Chuck Stewart. As he had done with other Impulse covers (notably Johnny Hartman's *I Just Dropped By to Say Hello*), Stewart artfully backlit the pair puffing away on cigarettes. "I liked the cover, because it has Elvin and me, both looking in a profile, smoking cigarettes," Davis said. "But I haven't smoked since '77."

The drummer and bassist were separately asked, many years after their affiliation with Impulse, what that label brought to mind.

"I think about me and Elvin Jones doing *Heavy Sounds,*" said Davis. "That record is one of my all-time favorites," echoed Jones.

even bagpipes. "You have to make changes in life just like dying and being born again, artistically speaking," Ayler stated. "You become very young again through this process, then you grow up, and listen and grow young again."

Ayler's saxophone playing, it must be noted, remained as emotionally unbound as it had always been. At Impulse, he was not alone in choosing to absorb the soul, gospel, and rock resonances of the day and match them to his own wildly primitive vocabulary. Archie Shepp had already played free-jazz solos against soul backgrounds on his albums, while other recordings from the jazz and rock arenas—notably Miles Davis's *Bitches Brew* and Captain Beefheart's *Trout Mask Replica*, both in '69—can be considered close parallels to Ayler's integrationist approach.

"About the same time Miles was making his transition, I was trying to make mine, Albert was making his," recalls Shepp. "Miles, let's face it, as a leader, an innovator, a master of so-called jazz music, is *the* man. But as far as funk and this rock 'n' roll music, I didn't feel that he had any special stature over and above anybody else, because he himself was going into a new area like all of us. Miles was much more successful because of the support he had behind him. It's more than a notion that you want to suddenly play blues or pop music. Somebody has to want to get that music over to the public, no matter how good it is. It's money and marketing and having people who believe in what you're doing."

MARTIN OR MALCOLM

If Impulse did not take on a leading role in the overlap of jazz and rock, it did in the fusion of jazz and politics—particularly those associated with black identity and the fallen heroes of the black power struggle. In line with the sentiments behind Oliver Nelson's album *The Kennedy Dream*, Impulse saluted another fallen leader on the *Cosmic Music* cover, emphasizing the inclusion of the tune "Reverend King"—recorded prior to his assassination on April 4, 1968.

As the civil rights marches and linked arms of the early sixties had given way to Black Panther rallies and raised fists in 1968, the stances of two prominent black leaders, the Reverend Martin Luther King Jr. and Malcolm X, came to represent the fork in the road for black America. Passive, peaceful resistance or a more aggressive, militant push for change: it was a choice faced in many social and cultural arenas, and the jazz world was no exception.

"John was very interested in the civil rights movement; he appreciated both men from their different perspectives," remembers Alice Coltrane. "He knew that Dr. Martin Luther King was an intelligent man, and as a preacher could reach the heart of the people. As for Malcolm, I know he would go downtown and attend some of the talks that were in [New York City]. Once he came back and I asked him how was the lecture, and he said he thought it was superb."

> He did see the unity in what they were trying to achieve, taking different directions to reach that point of achievement, different approaches to the same goal: be wise, try to get some kind of economic freedom, be self-sufficient, stop lying, strengthen your family ties. Things like that, things not even involved with religion.
>
> Many people wanted John to take his music into a militant zone. They'd say, "Why don't you take your horn, use it as an instrument to rally people together, to awaken consciousness in these people to really stand and fight for their rights?" He would not be a part of it. He just said, "That's not the way for me to go with this music." I would imagine John's philosophy would be closer to Martin Luther King: "Let me try to reach your heart, your spirit, and your soul, and then we can move forward uniformly as a people, and we can accomplish great things."

Coltrane's pacific tendency proved one of the strongest forces he left behind at Impulse, as evidenced by a slew of avant-garde jazz titles released through Thiele's final year at the label by the likes of Ayler and Sanders. Shepp, on the other hand, retained a feared confrontational spark that influenced musical opinions.

"That's always been a problem," Shepp says. "My music tends to carry a message with it, usually a quasi-political message, which makes it more difficult for it to flourish in a market where people shun the mixture of politics and art."

For all the implied fire and critical fury, Shepp's music actually upstages any political message on most of his late-sixties recordings. *The Magic of Ju-Ju* [AS-9154], featuring a toothless skull on the cover made benign by Day-Glo daisies, comes across as more about pan-Africanism than politics—especially on its title track, on which five leading drummers join together behind Shepp's free-style solos. *Three for a Quarter, One for a Dime* [AS-9162] includes two extended live performances from San

Francisco in 1966, exposing Shepp's stream-of-conscious inventiveness and Coltrane-like endurance. *The Way Ahead* [AS-9170] introduced Walter Davis Jr. into the band, marking the first time Shepp used a pianist on one of his Impulse albums, emphasizing his group's soul-jazz possibilities and begging further Ben Webster comparisons.

Looking back on his first stint with Impulse (his contract would lapse in 1970 and he would re-sign two years later), Shepp is still struck by the freedom Impulse offered him to find his own balance of music and message—a balance that, despite his following in the footsteps of Mingus, Coltrane, and Roach, was ultimately his own.

> I was trying to find a way to bring art and my political message together. My ideas about music were sometimes, perhaps, more academically oriented than others at the label. Although we might have been doing similar things from an objective point of view, subjectively I don't think we were, really. Plus we came at different times: Mingus was not really at Impulse at that point [in the late sixties]. John was working in a very spiritual area. Max [was] as much political as spiritual in his area.
>
> It was just the way the company was set up. There were these big open spaces for guys to do what they wanted to, and with deep pockets, they were very generous in allowing certain artists to do things that might never have occurred with smaller record labels like Blue Note or Prestige or Riverside.
>
> For me, it's never been like that since those years with Impulse.

THE BOILING POINT

In Thiele's last two years at ABC, Impulse had come under the stewardship of Howard Stark, a marketing vice president (and son-in-law of former president Sam Clark) whose immediate responsibilities were the Impulse and BluesWay lines. But Thiele's ongoing struggle at ABC came down to one man—ABC-Paramount president Larry Newton—and one head-to-head encounter at a session with his greatest hero: Louis Armstrong.

The salient details are: In July '68, Thiele had successfully arranged a producer's Daily Double. Not only had he secured the legendary trumpeter to release his next performance on ABC, but he persuaded Armstrong to record a song that Thiele had helped create: "What a Wonderful World." A handsome payday for both label and producer was almost certain.

The purpose of Newton's appearance at the studio that day was ostensibly to meet Armstrong and shoot some publicity photos. But when the label head heard a ballad was to be recorded—rather than a more upbeat Dixieland number like "Hello, Dolly!"—a screaming match ensued. The session was completed, apparently with Newton physically barred from the studio, furiously banging on the door.

No one else present (among those in the studio were drummer Grady Tate, trumpeter Joe Wilder, and engineer Bob Simpson) seems to have witnessed the confrontation, but no matter. In the long view, whatever happened is now less important than the fact that Thiele viewed it as a defining point in his career, which he forcefully told in the opening chapter of his autobiography. Whatever his success at Impulse, Thiele began to look for a way out.

It had been a struggle of wills that had been threatening to erupt for years, and it's not difficult to see Newton's viewpoint (he was the head of ABC, and that was an ABC—not Impulse or BluesWay—session). But it's also easy to see Thiele and Newton's persistent head-butting as emblematic of a larger, society-wide storm that was blowing through cities and campuses and even into the ABC Records boardroom by 1968. The old way of doing things—record heads telling producers to tell artists what to do—was meeting resistance. In the realm of jazz, it was a defiance that carried racial overtones, as black America found a more defiant voice than ever before.

In Thiele's view, "I fought for the black musicians all my life. . . . What happened in the last few years with me at ABC, the musicians, when they couldn't get what they wanted, the only person they had contact with was me. And they would blame me, not knowing I was the only one fighting for them at the time."

"What a Wonderful World" was eventually released, but with minimal support from ABC's sales force, and the record never realized its full potential until 1988, when it became a Top Forty hit off the *Good Morning, Vietnam* soundtrack. "The unanimous reaction was, the lousiest Armstrong record ever made! Naturally, then, it didn't sell in the States but sold a million and half copies overseas," remarked Thiele.

"I could sense my days at ABC were at an increasingly inevitable end," he added. "Larry Newton and I would never respect each other."

At the close of 1968, *Billboard* reported on Thiele's attempts to loosen his links to ABC yet maintain his role at Impulse, morphing from employee to independent producer. "Flying Dutchman Productions, the independent production company set up recently by Bob Thiele, has been signed to produce exclusively for ABC's Impulse jazz line. Thiele was executive a&r producer for ABC for seven years before starting his own company. . . ."

FREELANCE AND FREE

One can intuit Thiele's departure from ABC in the trickle of jazz sessions he produced in the first six months of 1969, which stood in contrast to the sheer quantity of past years' Impulse releases. Gone was a sense of label strategy, balancing straight-ahead and avant-garde artists, one-off albums and career-building sessions from players under contract. He was now working project by project. The production credit "Bob Thiele, for Flying Dutchman Productions" began appearing on various Impulse titles, introducing his new independent identity.

"We are looking to go more funky with Impulse, while also starting to use outside producers," Howard Stark declared that March in *Billboard,* speaking up for the label that had enjoyed Thiele as its spokesperson to that point. Stark added that the label would continue to record and support avant-garde musicians.

Through the spring, Thiele was working out a way to grow his production company into his own label, while Impulse received less and less of his attention. He nonetheless produced three strong titles—Oliver Nelson's pop-driven *Soulful Brass* [AS-9168], with Thiele's old pal Steve Allen on electric harpsichord; guitarist Mel Brown's *Blues for We* [AS-9180]; and bassist Charlie Haden's first album as a leader, *Liberation Music Orchestra* [AS-9183], a title bound to cause consternation at ABC with its overt political leanings.

In addition, Thiele began discussions with veteran jazz pianist Ahmad Jamal to record for Impulse, even as Jamal himself established a trio of Chicago-based labels, then with saxophonist Ornette Coleman to lease self-produced masters in a deal patterned on Ray Charles's setup.

Ironically, with one foot out the door, Thiele notched one last commercial success—not with Coltrane but with Pharoah Sanders. *Karma* [AS-9181] was a one-off, two-track album that stood out—particularly on free-form rock radio—with the singular yodeling technique of vocalist Leon Thomas, and proved to be in tune with the spiritual uplift of the day. As underground and college deejays began to program the album's hit tune, "The Creator Has a Master Plan," *Karma* became the successor—in message, sales, and episodic length—to *A Love Supreme*.

For Thiele, it proved a point. "Despite the prolific sales, the endless bureaucratic assaults and inexplicable inanities [at ABC] remained constant," the producer bristled in his autobiography. "I also recall that . . . *Karma* was at the top of the *Billboard* jazz charts for 12 weeks."

Thiele had wanted to put Sanders under contract since 1965, but had met indecision and derision: "It was the same tired tune: 'What kind of crap is this? This isn't going to sell.'" *Karma*'s unexpected success proved both Sanders's value and the unbridgeable gap between Thiele and his higher-ups. "After the record [*Karma*] was released, I remember the president of the company saying, 'Hey, did we sign that Pharoah Sanders?' I replied, 'No, you didn't want to.' 'Oh,' he said, 'sign him up now; he's hot, let's get him.'"

Thiele did as instructed, signing Sanders to a multiple-album deal. It was among his last duties for ABC.

LOOKING WEST

In 1969, as Thiele was hastening for the exit, ABC itself was preparing for a major shift as well; Newton and his staff could not disregard the winds of change blowing in from the West, pungent with a heady rock flavor and emanating from the offices of Dunhill Records.

The explosive growth of Dunhill, initially a distributed label and later an all-out acquisition, had far outpaced any other imprint under the ABC umbrella. With Jay Lasker in charge—Lou Adler had departed two years previously to set up his own label, Ode, and produce the historic Monterey International Pop Music Festival in 1967—Dunhill had built on the success of the Mamas and the Papas with a steady stream of best-selling rock albums (Steppenwolf, Three Dog Night) and chart-topping pop singles (the Grass Roots, Mama Cass Elliot's solo efforts, actor Richard Harris's memorable "MacArthur Park"). By the end of '68, Dunhill was the West Coast tail wagging the East Coast dog.

In January 1969, ABC restructured to reflect the new balance, creating

LIBERATION MUSIC ORCHESTRA

Charlie Haden / *Liberation Music Orchestra* / Impulse AS-9183

DATE RECORDED: April 27, 28, and 29, 1969

DATE RELEASED: January 1970

PRODUCER: Bob Thiele

Making *Liberation Music*, 1969: Haden leads the troops.

From the outset, Charlie Haden intended his first recording as a leader to be strong and outspoken, if metaphorical (Vietnam protest by way of a history lesson). Next to albums by Max Roach and Archie Shepp, it remains at the core of Impulse's political consciousness. Yet, as arranger and composer Carla Bley—who crafted a large part of the album—sees it, "I wanted to be part of anything at all that was important and exciting and different. But none of the guys in the band shared Charlie's political viewpoints. It was just a gig."

Haden explains his motivation. "I was real concerned for a long time about what we were doing in Vietnam. That first [*Liberation Music Orchestra*] album was conceived when Nixon bombed Cambodia. I called Carla Bley and said, 'I want to do a record of political songs.'"

Bley was living in New York with trumpeter Michael Mantler at the time. "Charlie and I had known each other in Los Angeles since he was like sixteen years old. We had kept in touch. We liked the same kind of music; we always were exchanging tapes of Shostakovich or Satie." By 1967, when vibraphonist Gary Burton recorded her song cycle *A Genuine Tong Funeral*, Bley's abilities had begun to gain serious attention.

"I really loved her arranging," says Haden. "So I had a lot of songs from the Spanish Civil War in 1937, and some originals of mine, and I explained to her what I really wanted to do. Then I went over to see Bob Thiele, and he said, 'Great.'"

Bley got to work immediately. "He gave me these little tiny lead sheets with the melody and chord changes—'Song of the United Front,' 'El Quinto Regimiento,' 'Los Cuatro Generales,' 'Song for Che'—and I made them into something that ten, twelve, or thirteen people could play."

The ensemble featured such adventurous talents as saxophonists Dewey Redman and Gato

Barbieri, trombonist Roswell Rudd, clarinetist Perry Robinson, and drummer Paul Motian. "Great musicians," Haden remembers, adding that "Sam Brown was playing guitar, Carla played piano, Don Cherry and Mike Mantler played trumpet, Bob Northern played French horn, and Howard Johnson played tuba." "I probably chose most of the horns," adds Bley. "We wanted John McLaughlin to be the guitar player, but we couldn't get him."

For a variety of reasons, Bley remembers the three days of sessions well. "It was at Judson Hall, and Charlie even wore a tie. There was a table on the balcony and Bob Thiele was sitting up there, overlooking the situation, and Gil Evans was there in the front row, like it was a concert or something! I was just thrilled that he was there and went to talk to him."

There were other special guests as well—survivors of a legendary group of volunteers who fought in the Spanish Civil War against Generalissimo Franco. "Charlie had also invited actual members of the Lincoln Brigade that were still alive to be in the audience. There were at least six of them with their wives, sitting there sort of scratching their heads, wondering what kind of music this was. I said a polite hello to a couple of them."

To Haden, the volunteers' presence still holds deep meaning. "I had met some veterans of the Abraham Lincoln Brigade. Three thousand volunteered. Fifteen hundred came back, and they were all blacklisted and weren't able to keep jobs."

When it came time to think of the album cover, an impromptu photo session was held outside the studio. "I made that banner," recalls Bley. "I just got a big roll of red fabric and cut out the letters in felt."

Snippets from the 78s of Spanish folk songs that had initially inspired Haden were ultimately interspersed between the recorded performances of Haden's group, and Thiele took the master to ABC. But, the bassist soon learned, the conservative bent of certain higher-ups at the company—coupled with Thiele's having one foot already out the door to pursue his own label—did not help the project.

"They said, 'No, we're not gonna release this.' I had to try really, really hard to talk them into letting it come out. They finally let it out but didn't promote it at all, and it just got lost in the shuffle. Ed [Michel] helped put it back out [in 1971]. But the record still became an underground, cult kind of classic."

Bley attained a cult status of her own. Two years after *Liberation,* she would collaborate with poet Paul Haines on the magnum opus *Escalator Over the Hill,* a kaleidoscopic work of impressive emotional force and range. The longest jazz project of its day, it still impresses in its use of stars borrowed from the rock world (singer Linda Ronstadt, bassist-singer Jack Bruce) plus many *Liberation* alumni. So how does she look back on her groundbreaking work with Haden?

"I thought it was great. I would love to be thought of as an underground 'Weather Woman,' but I was just the composer. I mean, I still am thought of as a lot more political than I am. I remember I got paid $1,300 for doing that album, which was a lot of money in those days. . . . I used it as a down payment on some land up in Maine."

Despite Bley's apolitical claims, she has reunited with Haden whenever the bassist has revived the sound and left-wing spirit of the Liberation Music Orchestra: the three instances notably coinciding with a succession of Republican administrations.

"We did another record in '82 called *The Ballad of the Fallen* [with music] from El Salvador," says Haden. "That was when Reagan was president. Then we did another when Bush's father was president called *Dream Keeper,* which was nominated for a Grammy. And now we're going to do another: Carla is writing the arrangements as we speak and it's going to be phenomenal. We're going to make the record in Paris and tour in the summer."

Not in Our Name was released on August 30, 2005, in the final days of a summer that found American troops dying overseas in an apparently endless conflict. On the CD cover, Haden and Bley supported opposite ends of their red, handmade banner one more time.

Thiele, Haden, and Bley take a break.

four autonomous parts, and Howard Stark relocated to Los Angeles. Two divisions remained in New York (including ABC, Command, and the recently acquired distribution rights to Riverside Records) and two were stationed in L.A. (Dunhill, Impulse, BluesWay, and the revived teen-pop label Apt, the latter three under Stark's aegis). In June, ABC acquired a two-story headquarters for its West Coast divisions at 8247 Beverly Boulevard, indicative of the company's increasing confidence in a bicoastal future.

It had been a rapid shifting of priorities at ABC. Only two years before, Newton was hailed in the music trades for his ongoing mission to purchase smaller labels and establish a distribution network. By the fall of '69, his words suggested a change of strategy: "California means a fresh approach for ABC Records. We are no longer concerned with the great mass of records. We are concerned with individual records and individual projects." In the same *Billboard* article, Stark offered a comment that promised an even looser approach: "Impulse is no longer a jazz label and Apt is no longer a bubblegum label because music has become so universal and people of varied backgrounds are now listening."

All that was Impulse—its staff, its contracts, and, most importantly, its vaults—was packed and shipped to L.A. Yet, despite being overseen by Stark—who soon assumed a no. 2 position in the California office—the label lost stature in the shuffle. According to Phil Kurnit:

> Howard [Stark] became Jay Lasker's right-hand man. They were, like, inseparable, and they had a very good relationship. And Impulse was putting out a lot of records and the catalog was expanding fairly quickly. But I think Impulse lost a lot of its positioning at ABC partly because of Newton, who never had much of an appreciation for it, and because its sales never could expand the way the pop sales had and ABC was now making a lot of money [with pop and rock]. It became relatively less important.

Evolution of a logo: the Impulse insignia (from left to right) in 1962, 1966, 1973, and 1976.

Even Impulse's distinctive color scheme and logo slowly lost priority as a series of designers started to fiddle with the formula. The gatefold format and full-bleed glossy images were maintained, but Coltrane's *Selflessness* became the first title to lose the orange-and-black spine (other than *A Love Supreme,* which had first broken form in 1965 with a black-and-white treatment of the Impulse uniform). Mel Brown's *Blues for We* sported a solid purple spine, and purple and mauve graced the edge of Emil Richards's *Spirit of 1976* [AS-9147]. By the end of '69, on Milt Jackson's live set *That's the Way It Is* [AS-9189], the "i!" logo was replaced by the word "Impulse" written in a font with all the charm and memorability of limp spaghetti.

Meanwhile, as Thiele phased himself out, he left behind a number of albums awaiting release (including Ahmad Jamal's live *At the Top: Poinciana Revisited* [AS-9176] and Ornette Coleman's *Ornette at 12* [AS-9178]), contracted artists (Alice Coltrane, Albert Ayler, Pharoah Sanders, Mel Brown, and others), and a trove of recordings that had only begun to be exploited—a trove that would find its most lucrative gems in the recordings of John Coltrane.

FLYING DUTCH

There was no one day when Thiele finally severed his ties to ABC, but there were hints along the way. In the music business, reissues and best-of's tend to signal the end of a relationship; accordingly, among Thiele's final Impulse releases were the label's first greatest-hits collections: *The Best of Gabor Szabo* [AS-9173] and *The Best of Chico Hamilton* [AS-9174].

KARMA

Pharoah Sanders / *Karma* / Impulse AS-9181
DATE RECORDED: February 14 and 19, 1969
DATE RELEASED: May 1969
PRODUCER: Bob Thiele

I call what I do "egoless" because it goes into the unconscious. It can be a moan or a cry or a tear. It can be a great big sigh—but under control. The thing is, however, not to be limited to what you consciously think or feel—you have to let it all well up. . . . I guess there isn't a name yet for what it is.

—LEON THOMAS, 1970

There's a moment on "The Creator Has a Master Plan" (to be exact, 20:22 into the tune's thirty-two-minute run) where voice and saxophone meet and parry in a free-jazz pas de deux. To generations of ears familiar with it, it marks a career high for vocalist Leon Thomas. "We're into a new period," Thomas maintained in 1970. "So far the horns have been in the forefront in terms of exploring the new dimensions of sound and expression. But no one has been nearly adventurous enough—for *this* time—with the voice."

Adventurousness, like singing, had come naturally to Thomas (born in 1937 in East St. Louis, Illinois). But he felt he was without a peer until his brother heard a Coltrane album in the midst of his late-fifties sheets-of-sound period: "He said 'Hey, he's doing on the horn what you've been trying to do with your voice,'" recalls Thomas. "And he was right. Trane was running all those changes, as was I."

When Pharoah Sanders first heard Thomas in 1968, he had already sung with Count Basie, Randy Weston, Rahsaan Roland Kirk, and Tony Scott, developing his unique style.

"I met Leon at the Dom on St. Mark's Place," Sanders says. "It was some sort of a fund-raising event. . . . Elvin Jones was in the room so I got a chance to play with him in more of a bebop situation. And I heard Leon: he was doing some yodeling stuff. It was maybe a blues or something he was doing. I heard him sing a few tunes and after it was

Bob Thiele and Leon Thomas, 1971.

over I got his name and number and asked him if he would join my band, because at that time I was doing some things at Slugs."

In early 1969, a little more than two years after his first album for Impulse, Sanders was offered a chance to record another. He relied on the talents of a wide variety of musicians: flutist James Spaulding; French hornist Julius Watkins; pianist Lonnie Liston Smith; bassists Reggie Workman, Ron Carter, and Richard Davis; and percussionists Billy Hart, Freddie Waits, and Nathaniel Bettis. Vocals and lyrics were left to Thomas. "We recorded 'The Creator Has a Master Plan,' 'Colors,' and another tune called 'Light of Love,'" not included on the original LP, remembers Sanders.

"Leon came up with the words on that album. I had asked him to write some lyrics for it and he brought them by the house and I didn't like them. It was something way off limits. I just said, 'Naw man, this ain't happening.' It wasn't anything that would enlighten people—an inspiration kind of thing. I said, 'Leon, I want this to be more of a spiritual type of thing.' Then he understood me a little bit more clearly. So he went home and a couple of nights later he brought by 'The Creator Has a Master Plan.' I told him, 'That's what I want you to do!'

"It's funny [laughs], when he put the lyrics on *Karma,* he wrote the lyrics to the bass line; it wasn't the [melodic] line of the tune. I think he did put out an album [on which] he sang the line of the tune. . . ."

"The Creator . . ." stands as one of Impulse's most recognized tracks, helped by a lyric timeless in its message and memorable in a sing-song fashion. It's been covered by jazzmen from Louis Armstrong to Don Cherry; by a host of funk, ska, Latin, and African groups; and by various hyphenated hybrids.

Despite the tune's enduring popularity, Sanders harbors an unhappy memory of the session.

"You know it sold. People liked it. But I just couldn't be proud about the engineering part of it. *Karma* had me and the bass player on the same channel, so they couldn't turn me up [separately], so it was very horrible to me at the time, you know."

Yet, to a new generation of listeners who helped *Karma* outsell many rock albums, any production pitfalls were well hidden by the recording's positive message and the singer with the singular yodeling style. "All I need is a chance to get to the ears of the people," Thomas stated. "I feel [the voice] can be unusually therapeutic."

February 1969: Thiele and Sanders creating *Karma*.

The clearest mark of Thiele's departure from ABC appeared in the music trades on April 26, 1969: Flying Dutchman Productions, with international distribution and funding from the Dutch-based Philips record company, "has set up three labels . . . Flying Dutchman Records, BluesTime and Amsterdam. Thiele is negotiating for American distribution. . . ."

Thiele himself recalls: "I resigned [my relationship with ABC] and with an appropriated name from ancestral mythology . . . started my Flying Dutchman jazz label. Louis Armstrong and Johnny Hodges became Flying Dutchman artists, and both my friend Oliver Nelson and my discovery [Argentinean saxophonist] Gato Barbieri followed me from Impulse to join my new enterprise."

It still took a few months before Thiele found an American distributor and a half-year before the first Flying Dutchman releases appeared. When they did, it was a potpourri of jazz, rock, and politics obviously informed by Thiele's Impulse experience. In October, with much ballyhoo and expense (a fourteen-page insert in *Billboard* funded by Philips's generous advance), Thiele celebrated his new label and his career and spoke of his changing role with an enlightened tone.

Fly with the Flying Dutchman

"What is the Flying Dutchman?" The name belongs to a new record production company, headed by Bob Thiele.

As indicative of his long-standing involvement with avant-garde jazz as the producer of John Coltrane, Pharaoh Sanders, Albert Ayler and Ornette Coleman, Thiele has already signed and recorded a pair of Watts-based black music groups, the Horace Tapscott Quintet and the John Carter-Bobby Bradford Quartet. Tapscott has for several years been a key figure in Watts cultural organizations and self-help projects for Los Angeles underground musicians. Bobby Bradford spent a number of years with Ornette Coleman's group, and Carter has conducted for Coleman during his recent appearances with a symphony orchestra in Los Angeles.

Besides these burgeoning avant-garde jazzmen, Thiele has signed a number of other artists to Flying Dutchman, including the popular Steve Allen who has recorded a number of tunes arranged by Oliver Nelson; a Los Angeles jazz/rock group appropriately called Spontaneous Combustion; young multi-reedman genius Tom Scott, also of Southern California; Stanley Crouch, a Watts poet whose work has been anthologized in several recent collections of black poetry; and Jon Appleton, director of electronic music at Dartmouth College. Flying Dutchman has recorded a two-album set directed by Thiele himself, to be released as the Bob Thiele Emergency.

In addition to all of these, be sure to dig Esther Marrow from Newport News, Virginia. She is a black soul singer destined to become an international star! Dig guitarist Ron Anthony's **Oh! Calcutta!** and Rosko's **A Night at Santa Rita** which can't be played on the air, but as Nat Hentoff says, "I cannot conceive of a more important album than this being released this year." You'd better Fly with the Flying Dutchman!

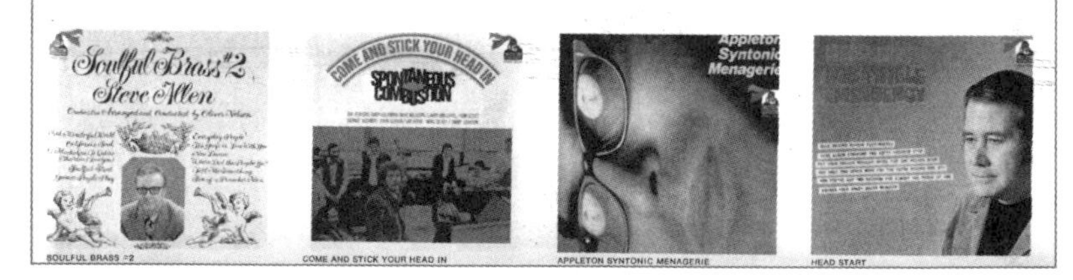

Breaking free: Bob Thiele launches his own label—again, 1969.

> In the last several years, the relationship between producer and artist has undergone a profound change. . . . The a&r executive, in the traditional sense of the term, is a thing of the past. . . . The relationship with the artist has become a much more sensitive one. The record act of today, be it an individual or a group, is very often a self-contained unit. . . . They are often skilled in production techniques. . . . They write their own material . . . and they relate, in a sociological way, to the climate of the times.

There is little doubt that the first artist to fit into Thiele's template of "record act of today," the individual responsible for reshaping his view of the music recording experience, was John Coltrane. Coltrane "was probably the greatest musician in the history of popular music, and I was lucky enough to be involved with his recordings. . . . Not to sound corny. I think he opened up a lot of things for me. I think that if I had never met Coltrane, I would be in serious trouble with respect to the real crappy economic aspects of my own career, and so I think I owe a lot to Coltrane."

Impulse entered the seventies healthy and vibrant. It boasted a number of established artists under contract who helped define its continuing role as the avatar of the avant-garde (Alice Coltrane, Pharoah Sanders, Albert Ayler, Archie Shepp, Marion Brown, Sam Rivers) with a taste of more mainstream jazz (Ahmad Jamal, Mel Brown). It would continue to grow along experimental lines, releasing licensed recordings by free jazz pioneers (Ornette Coleman, Sun Ra) and introducing new bandleaders (Keith Jarrett, Dewey Redman). And before the label was sold—along with the rest of ABC Records—to a larger entertainment conglomerate in 1977, it would benefit from three more A&R men, whose stories are collected hereafter: Ed Michel, Steve Backer, and Esmond Edwards.

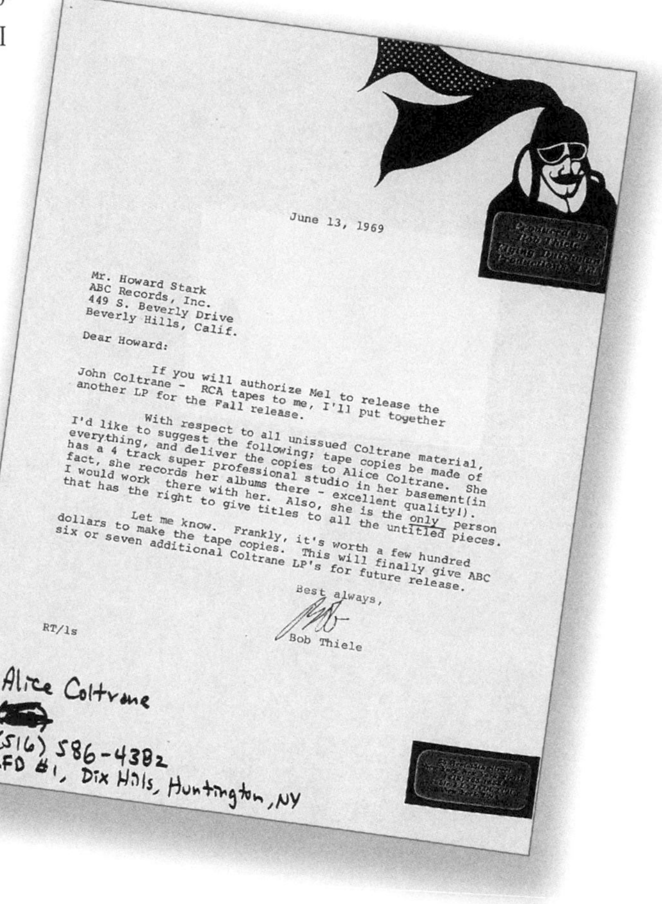

June 13, 1969

Mr. Howard Stark
ABC Records, Inc.
449 S. Beverly Drive
Beverly Hills, Calif.

Dear Howard:

If you will authorize Mel to release the John Coltrane - RCA tapes to me, I'll put together another LP for the Fall release.

With respect to all unissued Coltrane material, I'd like to suggest the following; tape copies be made of everything, and deliver the copies to Alice Coltrane. She has a 4 track super professional studio in her basement(in fact, she records her albums there - excellent quality!). I would work there with her. Also, she is the only person that has the right to give titles to all the untitled pieces.

Let me know. Frankly, it's worth a few hundred dollars to make the tape copies. This will finally give ABC six or seven additional Coltrane LP's for future release.

Best always,

Bob Thiele

RT/ls

Alice Coltrane
(516) 586-4382
RFD #1, Dix Hills, Huntington, NY

Still in touch: correspondence from Thiele to Howard Stark re ongoing Impulse business, 1969.

SAXOPHONE

LAGE OF THE PHAROAHS • PHAROAH SANDERS

ECHEE RECOLLECTIONS • MARION BROWN

(RECORDED IN PERFORMANCE AT THE MONTREUX JAZZ FESTIVAL)

TO CHAPTER I: LATIN AMERICA • GATO BARBIERI

RA • THE MAGIC CITY

THE LAND OF SPIRIT AND LIGHT IMPULSE RECORDS

FORT YAWUH IMPULSE RECORDS

TLANTIS IMPULSE RECORDS

222 ARCHIE SHEPP ATTICA BLUES

MICHAEL WHITE PNEUMA STEREO AS 9221 impulse!

HN KLEMMER WATERFALLS AS-9220

HEALING FORCE OF THE UNIVERSE STEREO AS-9191 impulse!

THOUGHT STEREO AS-9190 impulse!

STEREO AS-9187 impulse!

THUMB STEREO AS-9186 impulse

GTON ASHRAM MONASTERY STEREO AS-9185 impulse!

CHAPTER 7

IMPULSE OUT WEST (1969–1975)

Bob Thiele was leaving and setting up Flying Dutchman. I remember talking to [jazz producer] Orrin Keepnews: "Who's going to get that job?" He said, "It's going to be a friend of mine, Ed Michel. He doesn't like avant-garde music, so I don't think it will be *that* stuff." Of course, Ed got so deeply into the avant-garde that the Coltrane legacy stayed the prevalent aesthetic for the label.

—Michael Cuscuna

To quote a friend of a friend: "Going into the business because you love music is like going into the cattle business because you like animals." Emblaze that on an arch someplace.

—Ed Michel

Jazz entered the seventies willy-nilly. The distinctions of the recent past—swing, bebop, hard bop—became less relevant. All that had been labeled "progressive" and "modern" in the fifties, save for a few eternal avant-gardists like Cecil Taylor and Ornette Coleman, was considered mainstream by the seventies. Jazz saw an increasing hybridization with amplified musical styles—rock, pop, R&B—inspired in part by the unparalleled success of Miles Davis's *Bitches Brew*. As the decade progressed, a jazz album that could sell 100,000 copies—a number on a par with that of many rock bands—became less of a phenomenon, and more of a goal to reach for at major record labels.

From 1969 until well into the seventies, Impulse would operate from Los Angeles, where, tighter than ever, its fortunes would be lashed to ABC's triumphs and setbacks in the rock arena. Until 1975, Impulse would manage to produce its share of healthy-selling jazz recordings without compromising its avant-garde stance, or its unusual intra-corporate freedom.

Credit for the label's musical and commercial continuance is due in a large part to two young record men who stepped in after Thiele's departure, who both shared his commitment to artist over label, who eyed the music industry with even deeper distrust, and who sported the lengthy counterculture coifs of the day. (Of course, Thiele's own hair had reached below the collar of his flowered shirt by the time he exited ABC.)

In order of their arrival at Impulse, they were Ed Michel, a musician and jazz producer, and Steve Backer, a rock promotion man and jazz enthusiast. They brought to Impulse a certain rock-generation sensibility Thiele could not: An understanding of the new forces in youth culture like the rock press and FM radio. An appreciation of studio recording innovations and a willingness to employ them on jazz sessions. An outsider's devotion to the Impulse aesthetic that had begun when they were fans of the label. An intense jazz fan's appreciation of the man whose name and sound defined Impulse by 1969 and, as they found, accounted for a significant portion of its business.

"Something new on Impulse might do OK, but Trane *always* did well," Ed Michel recalls. "His records were the backbone of the catalog."

ENTER MICHEL

Ed Michel came to ABC in the late spring of '69 after years of both playing and recording music in the Los Angeles area. He had been bassist in the house band at the Ash Grove folk club, then was recruited by the Pacific Jazz label, where he learned all aspects of record production. Moving to New York City, he furthered his jazz studio experience as a production assistant for Orrin Keepnews at Riverside Records.

By 1969, he was thirty-three and securing music for "Madman" Muntz, creator and purveyor of the new four-track tape cartridge (soon to lose its format battle to the eight-track format). A chance remark from a contact at ABC led to a meeting with Howard Stark, who, lacking new BluesWay or Impulse product for the ABC distribution pipeline, was desperate to produce a new album. Michel, knowing the acoustic blues duo Sonny Terry

A new producer enters the picture: (from left) Cedar Walton, Archie Shepp, Ed Michel.

and Brownie McGhee were in town, assured Stark he could deliver a master for him—with cover art—in twenty-four hours.

Long Way from Home [BluesWay 6028] was recorded on March 1, 1969, and proved to be both Michel's audition and his first production for ABC. He was hired as an in-house producer for Impulse and BluesWay, reporting to Stark. Like Thiele, only a generation younger and on a different coast, he became the lone jazzman in a pop environment. Michel describes his new place of employment:

> Between Steppenwolf and Three Dog Night, Dunhill was thoroughly dominating sales of the ABC labels. Jay [Lasker, the president of Dunhill] was clearly the best record man they had, and Howard Stark was the vice president in charge of many things, and Impulse was one of his babies. The cigar and the duck: Jay was the cigar because he always smoked big cigars and had the most ferocious cigar lighter known to humanity sitting on his desk. Jay would pull a lever and this immense flame would come out to light his cigar. Howard was the duck because he wore tight pants, which accentuated his walk. We had an office in Beverly Hills, on South Beverly Drive, and that was the big revolution: suddenly this was not a New York–based label anymore.

Michel fell into a steady routine from the get-go.

> I was in the office about fifteen minutes [on my first day] and Mel Brown came in. I had heard him play but I'd never met him. Howard said, "Mel, this is your new producer," and Mel said, [low voice] "What do you want me to do?" I said, "Whatever you want to do." He says, "I want to record with this organ player," and pulled out a tape of a guy named Clifford Coulter. I said, "Great. What time do you want to hit?"

From the spring into the summer, Michel picked up where Thiele had left off, producing a number of artists who were based in L.A. or, in the case of Milt Jackson and bassist Ray Brown, visiting the city. Jackson and Brown's *That's the Way It Is* [AS-9192], a live quintet set from Shelly's Manne-Hole, is noteworthy as the first Impulse LP with a cover listing both the New York and L.A. addresses of ABC, as well as the ABC-Dunhill name. When Michel produced vibraphonist-pianist Buddy Montgomery's one-off for Impulse, *This Rather Than That* [AS-9192], it sported the label's last orange-and-black spine, much to Michel's chagrin.

> The [Impulse cover] design . . . I thought was wonderful. But somewhere in the shuffle it went away. Howard Stark once took me to task and said, "Why are you always screaming at art directors about things? They care as much about what they're doing as you care about what you're doing!" Art directors are their own world, and if an art director decides to change something it takes an act of Congress or a firing by the president of the company to change it back.

Michel's first wave of recordings for Impulse included a few names destined for obscurity. "I was recording people like [guitarist] Howard Roberts and [organist] Clifford Coulter and Mel [Brown] and [vibraphonist] Emil Richards and [the pianist-vocalist duo] Dave MacKay and Vicki Hamilton, who all went off the screen. They didn't fit the image [of an Impulse artist] so they didn't benefit from the association. There are a lot of Impulse albums like that that I did at the start."

Despite Michel's efforts to establish a local talent base in Los Angeles (see the Source Notes section for L.A.-derived album titles), the focus of Impulse remained in New York. The musicians who still defined the label remained there. Self-produced efforts by Alice Coltrane (like *Huntington Ashram Monastery* [AS-9185], with bassist Ron Carter, drummer Rashied Ali, and titles that revealed her burgeoning interest in Vedantic spirituality) and by Ornette Coleman (*Crisis* [AS-9187], a rare live performance that brought together many of his noted sidemen, including bassist Charlie Haden, trumpeter Don Cherry, saxophonist Dewey Redman, and Coleman's fourteen-year-old son, Denardo, on drums) continued in step with Impulse's avant-garde reputation.

"The Coltrane and post-Coltrane image, the guys who fit into that style of music are remembered and a lot of other things are forgotten," notes Michel. "Pharoah Sanders, Archie Shepp, Alice Coltrane, Albert Ayler, Ahmad Jamal—they were a given. They were who were there, and that's who I went out to record."

BACK EAST: AN AUSPICIOUS START

In August of 1969, as the country's cultural attention shifted to Woodstock and the Vietnam War was heating up, Michel began a series of regular trips to New York to oversee sessions. Impulse's leading stars were mostly impressed by Thiele's successor.

"A gentleman all the way, professional, knew the business very well," remarks Alice Coltrane. "Nice man. I worked very well with Ed. He had a good approach to producing—left you alone," notes Jamal. "A nice man but the kind of guy that didn't make any waves particularly, not confrontational or aggressive," recalls Shepp.

The results of Michel's first New York trip were diverse and largely successful. Shepp's *For Losers* [AS-9188] pointed back to the standard side of jazz—an artful, intriguing version of Ellington's "I Got It Bad"—and forward to new, funky frontiers, mixing electric bass and his rough tenor sound on "Stick 'Em Up." Ayler's *Music Is the Healing Force of the Universe* [AS-9191] and *The Last Album* [AS-9208], derived from the same recording dates, blended the sounds of rock guitar, jazz freedom, and spiritually focused poetry, a mixture that both soared and sank with its experimental weight. A bagpipe solo tracked backwards on an Ayler session was emblematic of Impulse's free-thinking approach at the time, according to Michel:

[Opposite] **Blowin' the bagpipes: Ayler at one of his final sessions, 1969.**

> The sessions were all typical that way. [The Impulse artists] were all finding different directions, many of which started with Coltrane, and which Coltrane made possible. Since Impulse was doing something that other people weren't particularly doing . . . I mean, Sam Rivers was doing it at Blue Note, Eric Dolphy did it everyplace he went, but Impulse was a place where this was an acceptable procedure. This kind of stretching was something we *looked* for.

Even Pharoah Sanders's recording-date-as-tribal-happening approach was somehow normal.

The *Jewels of Thought* session was "a sort of a traveling gypsy orchestra complete with cooks and camp followers. The room [Plaza Sound's studio] was huge, and they'd set up a table with lots of food, lots of incense. It was a party. This was the first time I'd recorded Pharoah. He was a guy who is not a talker [but] everybody knew what they were doing. Leon [Thomas] yodeled. There were two bass players: one of them was Richard Davis and there was this other young guy I didn't know. What an eye-opening experience that was: Cecil McBee! I was more stunned by Cecil McBee and Roy Haynes than anything else, and Pharoah was easy. The music would roll on."

"It was just a good band," Michel continues, "and the only problem was that Pharoah's tunes tended to run as long as they could run. I had to find a way to let him know when he had to bring it down and get out. We decided that just flashing the lights on and off would work fine, except that Pharoah frequently played with his eyes closed. But we worked it out."

Jewels of Thought [AS-9190] established the feel and flow of Sanders's releases of this period: lengthy jams filled with percussion and world-beat rhythms, spiritual titles referencing Eastern and Western religions ("Hum-Allah-Hum-Allah-Hum," "Let Us Go into the House of the Lord"). The saxophonist followed the pattern through *Summun Bukmun Umyun* [AS-9199] and *Thembi* [AS-9206].

Michel points out another factor of Sanders's extended studio recordings of that time. "I realized looking at the earlier albums Bob [Thiele] had produced, like *Karma,* that on the very long tunes Pharaoh was being paid a two-cent [mechanical royalty] rate for a track that ran the length of a side. So I said, 'On these side-long tunes, would it be OK with you if I broke it into four or five places? You'll at least get paid ten cents for the side instead of two cents.' I felt my responsibility was to the artist. My responsibility to the record company was to deliver a master and, if they're really lucky, a master they can sell. I didn't want my artist crippling himself by not getting the money that he should get for his compositions."

For two simple reasons, *Jewels of Thought* remains Sanders's personal favorite of his Impulse recordings: the sidemen and the sound. "They were just great musicians," he says, "and the engineer brought the horn up [in the mix] on that one."

NEW STUDIOS, NEW TECHNIQUES

If anything deserved Sanders's complaint, certain studio limitations in New York did. Impulse was no longer using Rudy Van Gelder's studio: its reliance on the New Jersey facility had been fading steadily as other labels began block-booking weeks at a time. Coltrane was the last Impulse artist consistently using Van Gelder's; after his passing, Thiele recorded in Manhattan studios exclusively—Sanders at RCA, Archie Shepp at National, Charlie Haden at Webster Hall—save for his out-of-town productions. The New York studios Michel chose at the start, RCA and Plaza Sound (above Radio City Music Hall), left him cold.

> This was during a time when [the business] was growing from two-track, occasionally three-track and even four-track to multi-track—to eight and sixteen [tracks.] Suddenly you weren't locked into one studio. You could take your multitracks and mix them someplace different than where you recorded them. I liked the mix facilities in L.A. better. I thought New York had a real attitude about how far ahead they are, but in fact they were three or four years behind California in terms of recording technology and skills.

Proximity can breed influence. Driven by a desire to stay up to date on rapid advancements in recording technology, Michel learned of—and was open to—employing the new studio techniques then coming out of the rock world. All he had to do was look to his office neighbor at ABC.

> I was running Impulse and the guy across the hall from me was Bill Szymczyk, who was a rock 'n' roll engineer starting out as a producer [at ABC]. He influenced me in a way that no jazz producer ever had. The substantial way that recording

changed in the mid-sixties, with the Beatles, really opened me up. You could hear parts better on rock 'n' roll records than you could on jazz records. Why? A lot more time was spent on the recording.

The "cross-production of acts for Impulse"—as *Billboard* described it under the headline "Impulse Producers Giving Acts Double-Edged Effect"—was implemented with ABC's blessing. Szymczyk arrived at ABC in early 1969, working first with B.B. King on the bluesman's popular BluesWay album *Completely Well* [BW-6037], which yielded the huge crossover hit "The Thrill Is Gone." When the rock trio the James Gang, featuring guitarist Joe Walsh, signed to ABC, Szymczyk took charge of its production. With Michel, he co-produced Pharoah Sanders's *Thembi* and Howard Roberts's *Antelope Freeway* [AS-9207], the latter an unusually modern context for the veteran L.A. session guitarist with a heady dose of psychedelia.

Close-miking, isolating certain instruments (placing the drummer or singer in his own booth, for instance), tape overdubbing, and even relying on effects like reverb, echo, and phasing became more commonplace at Impulse sessions. Yet it was all about striking the right balance between technology and the live interaction essential to group improvisation, Michel maintains:

I dislike recordings that show off technique. . . . That's basically not what the music is about as far as I'm concerned. For me, jazz and blues, which are the main things that I produced, are performance music. And it should feel like performance music.

You shouldn't be stunned by the special effects. [But] there have been circumstances where piano players have said, "Gee, it would really be nice if I had an electric piano on this," and I could say, "Turn around. There's one behind you miked and ready to go."

AHMAD AND ALICE

Michel might have been thinking of Ahmad Jamal. His use of electric piano was but one of the unusual steps taken by the pianist while signed to Impulse.

ANTELOPE FREEWAY

Howard Roberts / *Antelope Freeway* / Impulse AS-9207
DATE RECORDED: December 17, 1970; March 18 and 23, 1971
DATE RELEASED: August 1971
PRODUCERS: Ed Michel and Bill Szymczyk

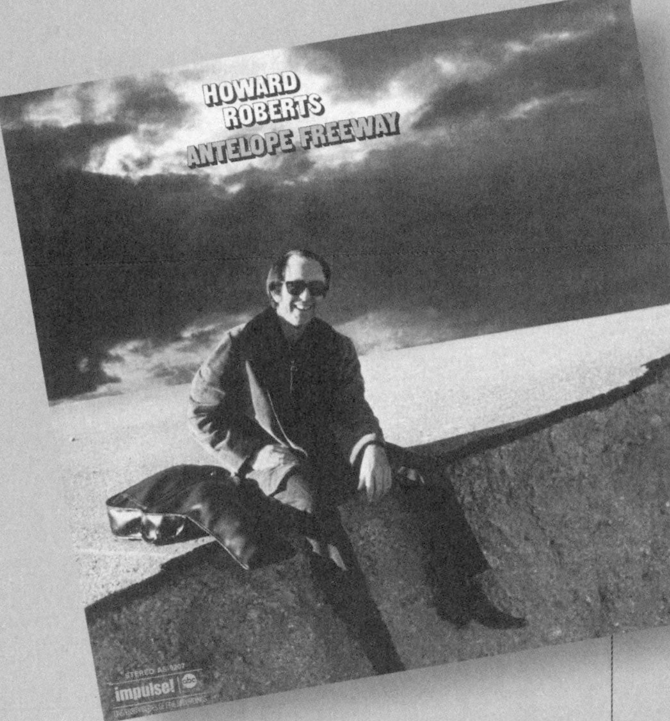

MADE LOUD TO BE PLAYED LOUD.

—INSTRUCTION ON THE INNER JACKET OF *ANTELOPE FREEWAY*

Bill Szymczyk—it's pronounced "Zimzick"—is a rock producer famed for his mega-selling successes in the seventies and eighties with heavy hitters like the Eagles, the J. Geils Band, and others. With no effort at all, he remembers more modest days, his brief overlap with Impulse, and producing an album of what was then referred to as "head music."

"At the end of '69, the power at ABC-Paramount had switched to L.A. with Jay Lasker and Dunhill. They let everybody in the New York office go except for the guy who hired me and myself and moved both of us to L.A. I was stuck in a back office, where my next-door neighbor happened to be Ed Michel. We were the black sheep of the entire deal: he was the jazzbo weirdo and I was the New York rock 'n' roll weirdo. So of course we immediately struck up a friendship [laughs]. That Howard Roberts record? To me that's the high point of our relationship."

In the hazy context of the early seventies, it made sense to take a jazz guitarist—a twenty-year veteran of the L.A. studio scene—add a variety of guitarists, keyboard and rhythm players, and blend it with newly developed electronic effects and studio wizardry. Of course, there was also a generous infusion of a certain herbal substance to help it all blend better. Such was the inspiration of *Antelope Freeway,* a still-modern-sounding disc that echoes (literally) with the irreverence and humor of the day.

"That was a blast—a big fun album to do," continues Szymczyk. "Howard was up for doing it and I brought a lot of rock 'n' roll ideas to it. So we hired players that were jazz *and* rock players. We turned them loose and, like a lot of jazz in those days, it was a jam session that took on a life of its own.

"Howard was willing to try anything that we brought up. One time I said, 'I want to put you outside on the curb and just play acoustic [guitar] to the city sounds, to the traffic, to the noise, to whatever's going on on the street.' This was like maybe ten o'clock at night. He went, 'OK!'

"So I set up two [Neumann] 67 mikes, about fifty yards apart. One of them was in front of a restaurant and you can hear the people coming out and talking, and then a couple of mikes on his guitar. We recorded this stereophonic street scene, as it were. Then I had a brilliant idea to jump in my car, go around the back way, and pull up in front of him. He thought I was in the control room and I'm pulling up in a car outside and start talking to him [laughs]."

"Antelope Freeway, Parts 1 and 2" was later joined on the album by tracks with humorous, counterculture-type titles: "The Ballad of Fazzio Needlepoint," "That's America fer Ya" and—featuring the voices of Szymczyk and Michel—"Five Gallons of Astral Flash Could Keep You Up for Thirteen Weeks."

"That was just a collage of stuff that Ed and I recorded, and we made a radio program out of it with station-changing in between and pretended we were truck drivers, trucking spinach. Howard wasn't even around for that. We played it for him and he was on the floor, he thought it was hysterical."

Szymczyk offers one further memory of the session's rock-jazz overlap:

"I brought over Joe Walsh, who was in the James Gang. I wanted him to show Howard an Echoplex, because Howard had never worked one. The two of them got along famously, within minutes, because they were both guitar players coming from the same head space. When Walsh was leaving, he turned and said, 'Well, Howard, always remember one thing: the smoker you drink the player you get.' And we just fell out! It wound up being the title of one of Walsh's solo albums. That's the day that phrase was invented."

The impact of the album?

"None! [Laughs.] Zero! Not much—I mean, there were a few folks that got it, but very, very few."

Years later, some still remember. One present-day writer claims it as a undeservedly forgotten favorite, "a fun recording [that] has all sorts of great blues-inflected jazz-guitar showcases, humorous tangents, and audiophile sound effects to recommend it—assuming your tastes run to concluding an acoustic guitar transition with a stereo-panned motorcycle zooming through your living room."

"I made like eighty-some albums in my life and that's still in my Top Ten," Szymczyk says. "I would play that for people and they would either die laughing or scratch their heads."

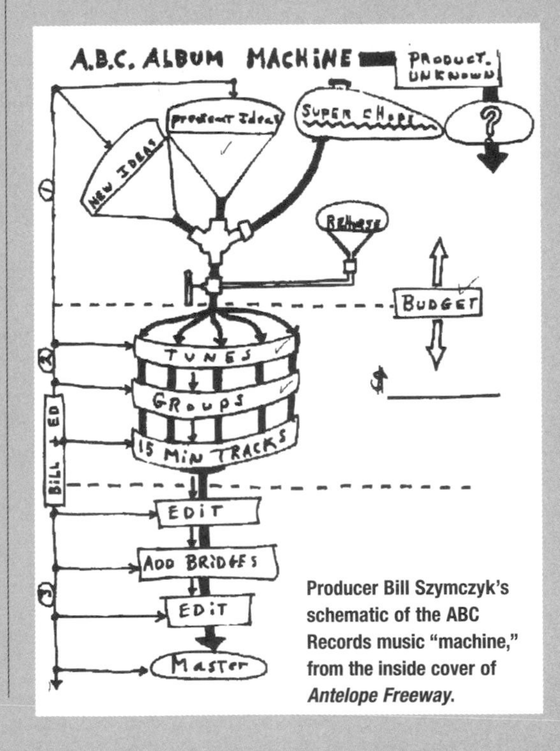

Producer Bill Szymczyk's schematic of the ABC Records music "machine," from the inside cover of *Antelope Freeway*.

The Pittsburgh-born piano prodigy rose to national prominence with his hit recording of "Poinciana" while living in Chicago in the fifties. By 1969, he was a New Yorker looking to break into another part of the business: running his own record label. "Jamal Plans All-Trade Expansion" read the headline in *Billboard* on May 24, 1969, announcing his new trio of labels—Cross, AJP, and Jamal—with executive staffing soon to follow at his 119 West 57th Street office.

"During that period with the ABC/Impulse business, I wasn't interested in too much except trying to run my own record company and stay off the road," he recalls. But his new venture required capital, and an Impulse contract would only help. "Warren Stevens was doing management on my behalf. He took it upon himself to approach ABC. I wasn't even interested in going in the studio at all, which happens sometimes. It happened with Miles. It was very difficult for Ed Michel to even get me in the studio."

Nonetheless, Jamal found the time between 1968 and 1972 to record five albums for Impulse: two live (*At the Top: Poinciana Revisited* and *Freeflight* [AS-9217], recorded in Montreux, Switzerland, which featured Jamal experimenting with electric piano) and three studio (*The Awakening* [AS-9194]; *Outertimeinnerspace* [AS-9226], which featured two side-long compositions; and *Tranquility* [AS-9238], a mixed bag with modal-based originals and Burt Bacharach covers).

Collectively, the albums mark a career crest for Jamal, overlapping the duration of what is celebrated as the pianist's second great trio (1966–73), with bassist Jamil Nasser and drummer Frank Gant. The Impulse titles caught Jamal in stylistic transition, fusing his signature characteristics of the fifties—elegance, economy, and shifting rhythms—with more contemporary approaches to jazz piano, and choosing more up-to-date material, like tunes composed by McCoy Tyner and Herbie Hancock. To this new mix, he added amplified instrumentation: "That concept came about because they failed to deliver the Steinway to one of my sessions. It came late, and the electric piano was there and I started using it."

In 1973, Jamal moved on to the 20th Century label, still playing plugged in and exploring more pop material.

Jamal was not the only pianist at Impulse enjoying a creative peak during this time. Four recordings—*Ptah the El Daoud* [AS-9196], *Journey in Satchidananda* [AS-9203], *Universal Consciousness* [AS-9210], and *World Galaxy* [AS-9218]—captured Alice Coltrane in full flower. She was continuing her explorations on piano, organ, and harp, playing music laced with Indian sonorities. Most of the tunes referenced her newfound spiritual path ("Shiva Loka," "Hare Krishna"); others, like "Something About John Coltrane" and "A Love Supreme," acknowledged her late husband. She recorded with an A-list of avant-friendly improvisers (saxophonists Pharoah Sanders and Frank Lowe; bassists Ron Carter, Charlie Haden, Jimmy Garrison, and Reggie Workman; drummers Rashied Ali, Ben Riley, and Jack DeJohnette), and in a variety of contexts, from small groups to full string sections, all with Impulse's blessing and budget—never mind what the jazz world was saying.

"Musicians were very late to come to Alice Coltrane," notes Michel. "Many took the attitude of 'She's just Coltrane's widow.' I didn't know whether it was a question of not being able to get past her spirituality, or the attitude that many musicians have about women. That certainly wasn't true of people who played with her, who treated her with the respect she deserved and did as they were told. Guys who wouldn't put up with anything from a lot of people would 'Yes, ma'am' her because she earned it."

As her relationship with Impulse grew, Mrs. Coltrane recalls, she found that "they never said, 'We like what you're doing and everything is good, but what about going on the charts with something the young people might like?' " With license and a budget to explore, she brought the promise of her first two albums to fruition, developing a swirling sound that locked into the spiritual air of the age and successfully integrated jazz and blues, drone-drenched ragas, Vedantic ritual chants, and even Stravinsky ("The Firebird" had been a John Coltrane favorite).

In 1972, Alice Coltrane moved herself and her family from New York City suburbia to Southern California, where she founded a center for Vedantic studies. She recorded one more title for Impulse in 1973—*Lord of Lords* [AS-9224], with a mix of classically trained string musicians and jazz players—before signing to Warner Bros. Records for a more lucrative deal. But her connection to Impulse remained strong: she continued to participate in albums featuring unreleased John Coltrane recordings, and hired ABC's former in-house counsel Bill Kaplan as her own attorney. When she departed Impulse, she left behind recordings and a reputation that enhanced the label's mystique, adding another level to The House That Trane Built.

THE AWAKENING

Ahmad Jamal / *The Awakening* / Impulse AS-9194
DATE RECORDED: February 2 and 3, 1970
DATE RELEASED: November 1970
PRODUCER: Ed Michel

Ahmad Jamal, for instance, is unsung in this sense. . . . He plays within his style but he treats each composition as a separate entity, not just as a vehicle for clichés. See, he treats each composition as something to be explored according to his style. —CANNONBALL ADDERLEY, 1972

Ed Michel had been with ABC almost a year by early 1970, producing sessions with Impulse's leading stars and reissues of those from the recent past, when it came time to fly out to New York and record Ahmad Jamal for the first time. "Everybody I knew said, 'Oh, Jamal will eat you alive. He's death on producers! He hates being told what to do.'"

"I said, 'Great. I'm not going to tell him what to do. He knows better than I do.' I met him at Plaza Sound; that was the first 'How do you do?' I said, 'It's an honor to be in the same room with you. But before we do anything else, would you try the piano and make sure you like it?' He laughed, went over and sat down and said, 'Yeah, I like it! Nice piano!' I said, 'Anything else you want me to know?' He said, 'Yeah. It's still Ramadan. I have to fast until sunset. Will you tell me when it's 5:42 so we can send out for something to eat?' I said, 'Absolutely.' That was it."

Catering plans aside, Michel's studio manner fell comfortably in line with Thiele's concept of silent support.

"My sense is, if you trust the musicians, it's their judgment that's important. If you don't trust the musicians, why are you recording them?" he once told writer Michael Jarrett. "I've always taken the point of view that the best producers are transparent. You shouldn't be aware of the fact that they are there. The less a producer does to affect the music the better."

In the case of Jamal's first studio effort for Impulse, Michel left all decisions to the pianist. "I said, 'Great. What do you want to play?' He said, 'Aren't you going to tell me?' I said, 'No. People pay a lot of money to come hear you. You know the repertoire you want to play. . . .'"

In actuality, Jamal recalls, "I had gotten off the road and was producing records [and] trying to retire, as I've tried to do many times. Very, very rarely did I work between 1969 and 1970, when I was running a record company."

Nonetheless, Jamal maintained a steady working trio—with bassist Jamil Nasser and drummer Frank Gant—the successor to the Israel Crosby–Vernell Fournier group that launched him to prominence in the late fifties. With Nasser and Gant in place in 1966, the pianist had begun exploring an expanding, updated repertoire. He had once favored obscure, lyrically based songs to a large degree; by 1969, his set lists balanced a growing number of originals with newer "standards"—popular jazz tunes like Herbie Hancock's "Dolphin Dance" and Antonio Carlos Jobim's "Wave."

The trio itself had a penchant for gear shifting and mood swings. Jamal had first made his mark with clever construction and subtle use of silence. By *The Awakening,* his sound had grown, revealing more of his already impressive range of volume and drama while retaining its trademark elegance. His take on "Stolen Moments," for instance, maintains the cool mystery at the opening of Oliver Nelson's signature tune, then restructures it, section by section, mood by mood.

Jamal's taste for episodic construction is noticeably effective on the title track. "The Awakening" builds up to a suite-like structure from a simple four-note motif, offering nods to past jazz masters from a hip, contemporary stance: with a marked fluidity, Ellingtonian flavors and Tatum-like flourishes alternate with looser, swinging sections.

"I probably wrote that in advance," Jamal reasons. "Anything that sectional I did not do on the spot. The idea of doing originals? I mean, for years all us piano players used to do covers—except for Ellington, of course. You know any Art Tatum originals? [Laughs.] But I remember Randy Weston pushing us to write our own material, and I was going with that flow of the time, to the point I'd be recording all my own stuff on albums like *Jamal Plays Jamal* [in 1974]."

The Awakening hit the stores in the late spring of 1970 with a title that fit into the spiritual flow of the day (Jamal: "I'm not at a loss ever for titles; they almost come instantaneously"). In addition, according to Michel, it distinguished itself from other Impulse albums in its brevity. "At that time, lots of our albums were twenty minutes a tune. It [*Awakening*] was an eight-tune album averaging five minutes a track. I think it became popular because it's absolutely gimmick free and none of the takes were that long."

Jamal remembers the session with fondness: "Impulse was the first time I worked with another producer. At Chess I did it all myself. Ed was the most pleasant producer I ever worked with—one of the reasons I could just sit back and write."

"We spent two days doing it," Michel adds. "At the end of the session he shook my hand and said, 'I don't get along with producers very well. You're no problem!' I said, 'Thank you very much—neither are you.'"

"She's a profoundly spiritual woman and a profoundly musical woman," states Michel. "She has—not my phrase, somebody else's phrase—a whim of tungsten. When she makes up her mind the way something is going to be done, it gets done."

NEW ARTISTS, SAME SPIRIT

Michel still sees himself primarily as a producer, not an A&R man. "When I was with Impulse was about the only time when I could sign some artists," he states, crediting the loose-and-liquid era of the seventies for the freedom he was granted to sign a few artists to the label. "There was about a fifteen-minute window of opportunity." The process, however, revealed his need to work the corporate hierarchy: "If I wanted to sign an artist I'd talk to Howard and say, '*You* bring it up with Jay. I'm just a producer.' "

Michel's signings from '69 to '71 at first leaned more to groove-driven productions than the established avant-garde path. He re-upped guitarist Mel Brown, with whom he recorded *Mel Brown's Fifth* [AS-9209] and *Big Foot Country Girl* [AS-9248]. He produced Cliff Coulter (whose *East Side San Jose* [AS-9197] was followed by *Do It Now, Worry About It Later* [AS-9216]) and, in a brief return to Impulse, Milt Jackson, whose last three albums included two live sets (*That's the Way It Is* [AS-9189] and *Just the Way It Had to Be* [AS-9230] with bassist Ray Brown and tenor saxophonist Teddy Edwards) plus a studio effort, *Memphis Jackson* [AS-9193], which featured four extended R&B-flavored romps.

But the Michel signings who proved to have the most lasting impact were three who kept Impulse's edgy and esoteric flavor: a violinist from Houston, a tenor saxophonist from Chicago, and a brother (allegedly) from another planet.

Michael White first achieved notoriety 1965 as the violin-wielding member of saxophonist John Handy's quintet in Oakland, and later became a founding member of the Fourth Way, an early fusion group that never gained national prominence. He served as a standout sideman on Pharoah Sanders's *Thembi* in 1971, before recording as a leader for Impulse in 1972 with *Spirit Dance* [AS-9215], which included message songs that played into the label's ongoing themes of universal love and racial uplift: "John

Coltrane Was Here" and "Praise Innocence," a track on which White sang with his daughters, are two examples.

From the outset, White's recordings featured an already mature blend of percussion, mood, emotive violin. His follow-up titles—*Pneuma* [AS-9221], with its airy five-part title suite, and *The Land of Spirit and Light* [AS-9241], with nylon-string guitar and Caribbean flavors—appeared in 1972 and 1973, respectively, adding gospel-vocal backup and a heavier backbeat on various numbers. Both albums benefited as well from the clear production and focused mixes listeners had come to expect from rock recordings of the day.

Saxophonist John Klemmer had established his name on Chicago's Cadet label before recording *Constant Throb* [AS-9214] for Impulse in 1972. An unabashed Coltrane devotee (the inner-sleeve design of his debut album mimicked that of *A Love Supreme*, right down to Klemmer's signature) with a penchant for electronic saxophone, he set the tone for his rock-informed work on Impulse with his use of Echoplex, phasing, electric guitar, and ethereal vocals. The live set *Waterfalls* [AS-9220] and *Intensity* [AS-9244] both arrived in 1973, and present themselves as an apex of a sort on Impulse, effectively balancing Klemmer's raspy tenor with electric guitar and bass, mood-setting keyboard effects, and R&B percussion.

Michel's idea to bring the legendary bandleader Sun Ra to Impulse grew from a boardroom challenge. In a meeting with ABC higher-ups, Michel noted that the controversial self-confessed resident of Saturn, whose space-age titles and free-driving ensemble work had heavily influenced Coltrane, seemed a natural for the label. "Make it happen" was the reply. By the time Ra had allowed his lawyer to rewrite the contract offered by ABC, Michel knew he would not be signed. "It was just too far out to happen. There were all

6. SIMILAR RIGHTS ON PLANETS OTHER THAN EARTH. Company agrees that all rights discussed in paragraph 5 above, as well as all rights of distribution and retail sales, on planets other than Earth (including but not limited to Saturn, Pluto, Jupiter, and Mars) shall belong to Sun Ra..

So who distributed to the rest of the solar system?

UNIVERSAL CONSCIOUSNESS

Alice Coltrane / *Universal Consciousness* / Impulse AS-9210

DATE RECORDED: April 6 and June 19, 1971

DATE RELEASED: September 1971

PRODUCER: Ed Michel

One day when we were at home, it was a nice afternoon, he said, "What type of music would you like to hear?" I said, "Oh, maybe something like chamber music, or maybe some South American music. . . ." And I said, "What would you like?" He said, "Something greater, something vast, something with multiple, higher dimensions." I said, "OK, what would that be?" He said, "Stravinsky." And we had the most beautiful afternoon. It had to be . . . summer of '66.

—ALICE COLTRANE

If John Coltrane could influence the musical and spiritual direction of an entire community and a record label, imagine his pull on his wife. After her husband's death in 1967, Alice Coltrane continued to play piano in the flowing, harp-like manner he originally suggested. She mastered the harp he had bought her. She continued to produce recordings in the home studio he built, releasing them on Coltrane Records, the label he had planned to start (which became a joint venture with Impulse Records). She integrated the music he had come to love—Indian ragas, Hindu chants, Stravinsky—into her own kaleidoscopic vision.

John Coltrane's unfulfilled desire to create music with strings, and Alice Coltrane's own classical studies as a Detroit teenager, inspired her fifth album. "Alice is a very schooled musician," Ed Michel states. "She knows the classical repertoire. *Universal Consciousness* was the first string album for her."

More than her previous titles, this six-track album featured the gamut of Alice Coltrane's explorations: playing Wurlitzer organ and harp, in duets (with Rashied Ali), with a rhythm section (Jimmy Garrison, Jack DeJohnette), and with strings. It was her first attempt to unite all the sounds and styles she had come to embrace in a nine-year life-altering course that began when she met John Coltrane in 1962. In her view, the album resonates with a sense of ease and flow she inherited from her husband. "I think the music sounded exploratory. I've played pieces from *Universal* in concert. [The reaction] wasn't, 'Oh my, we have to become cosmical, we have to go into some mystical experience.' The people just heard a joyfulness, a lightheartedness about it."

Perhaps the most surprising credit on the album remains "Transcriptions by Ornette

Alice Coltrane in the studio with strings, 1971.

Coleman," Alice's choice to co-arrange with her.

"That was an experience, because he's a very gentle person, and very astute. I said, 'OK, Ornette, I want you to wash these strings this way, do this.' He would just take the pen out and write and write. And when the rehearsals were done, the musicians found them to be very different from what they had been accustomed to."

Alice called the violinists "a symphony of celestial strings" in the album's liner notes. "They were all jazz-associated string players," says Michel. "John Blair, Leroy Jenkins, Julius Brand, Joan Kalisch. I mean, they knew in a jazz way how to do what she wanted. But it was very interesting in Los Angeles on later albums how Alice could take studio string players who were the cream of the crop, but still, playing free doesn't come naturally to classically trained string players. She used as her concertmaster a guy named Murray Adler—very gifted. Between Murray and Alice they opened up the string players so they could do absolutely astonishing things. One of the few times when I had to do playback was *Lord of Lords* [in 1973], because the string players couldn't believe that they had done what they had done.

"The powers of Alice Coltrane are immense. [For *Lord of Lords*] we recorded some Stravinsky. There was one point where an edit couldn't be made. Now, I thought of myself as the Charlie Parker of the razor blade. I could do things with a razor blade that are hard enough to do with digital editing. I said, 'There's no way it can be done.' She says, 'I'll go home and meditate on it.' She came back the next day and said, 'I had a wonderful meditation. I talked to John'—who she often referred to as 'the father'—'and Stravinsky and Bach and we discussed how to edit it. Stravinsky told me what to do: "Make the cut right here."' I said, 'Stravinsky's crazy! It isn't going to work!'

"I tried it and you couldn't hear the edit. It was transparent. I thought, 'I'm never ever going to argue again!'"

these clauses in the contract that didn't show up much in anybody else's contracts. Instead of signing him as a new artist, we made a distribution deal with El Saturn Records for his old recordings."

Known more by reputation than distribution, benefiting from virtually no standard sales channels, El Saturn was Ra's homegrown label: even the covers were hand-colored. The label had released his free-form music from the late fifties through the sixties. The very idea of remixing the vast catalog for release on a nationally distributed label with top-quality, eye-catching covers was avant-garde. Michel recalls that the deal originally called for twenty-four titles to be released—enough to last for years. He also recalls the first remix session.

> At that point I liked to mix at the pain threshold. It was really loud. We were mixing it quadraphonically in a relatively small room. Sun Ra was sleeping deep and snoring loud. For some reason, I stopped the tape in the middle of the tune. He came awake, wheeled his head like an owl does—all around the room, checking everything out. He said, "You Earth people sleep too much." He put his head down and started to snore again. . . .

Sun Ra's catalog finally began to appear on retail shelves in mid-'73, and it served as a capstone to Michel's first four years at Impulse. He had been as busy as Thiele had been in the prolific days of 1965–67, producing close to forty albums, not including his ongoing efforts for BluesWay. Notably, the vast majority of those titles can be called experimental or at least avant-leaning. They were supported by the healthy sales of a variety of greatest-hits packages and a few never-before-released recordings of John Coltrane that Michel found in the Impulse vault.

NEW BRICKS, SAME FOUNDATION

Impulse in the early seventies, as Michel affirms, was a house partially being built from the inside out: "Half of the sales came from the old catalog. Reissues did *very* well. This is at a time when ninety percent of pop sales were new releases and ten percent were old Mamas and Papas records, but the bulk of the pop catalog was dead meat. . . . Impulse records made money because they stayed in the catalog forever. Jazz records don't sell very much, but they don't sell very much for a long, long, long time, and the entire Impulse catalog was available all the time."

Under Michel's guidance, double albums first appeared on Impulse. The choice of artists enjoying the double-disc treatment suggests that the catalog's best-sellers in the early seventies remained unchanged from their original release years before. *The Best of John Coltrane* [AS-9200], *Gabor Szabo: His Greatest Hits* [AS-9204], and *Chico Hamilton: His Greatest Hits* [AS-9123] appeared in late 1970 and early 1971.

"At that point one didn't dig into the archives. You didn't look at unissued material," recalls Michel. "Reissues were anthologies made up out of existing album products. So there were two-fers of Coltrane material and others." But Coltrane was the exception. "If I was looking for unissued Coltrane, then it was for new releases—like *Transition*."

Transition [AS-9195], featuring music recorded by Coltrane's Classic Quartet in 1965, was Michel's first opportunity to work with unreleased session tapes that had been transported west in 1969. It was soon followed by the two-LP set *John Coltrane Live in Seattle* [AS-9202], also recorded in '65. In the process, Michel found that the state of Impulse's tape archives left much to be desired and, sadly, unaccounted for.

"Things were truly disorganized. ABC had hired two very nice girls to organize the tapes and put them in order." When certain tapes turned up missing, Michel was informed by a reliable source that specific Coltrane masters that had never been issued were thrown out because "we don't have room for all our new tapes. Why are we keeping all this old stuff? These aren't album masters anyway. . . ."

> Whenever possible I tried to have session masters stored in a more reliable place. There was a company called A Safe Place that was set up for archiving film stock, and I found out about them and they offered a very, very reasonable rate and ABC was running out of storage space. So I tried to put as much stuff as possible there.

To Michel, the inevitable disconnect between Impulse and the pop-focused decision makers at ABC was another frustrating part of the package deal he had inherited from Thiele.

> At one point I talked to the manager who ran the whole ABC sales operation. He said, "Jeez, I don't know. Some of these jazz radio stations want to get promotional

THE SATURN RECORDINGS

Sun Ra / Various Titles

DATES RECORDED: Various dates in the late 1950s and 1960s

DATES RELEASED: June 1973 through December 1975

REISSUE PRODUCER: Ed Michel

The following is adapted from Ed Michel's liner notes to Evidence ECD 222172, The Great Lost Sun Ra Albums—Cymbals & Crystal Spears, *with permission:*

If you children will gather 'round a little closer, I might just tell you something about the amazing, if short-lived, commercial/aesthetic handshake between Sun Ra and ABC Records. I believe the appropriate categorization comes from Yiddish: *meshugaas,* generally translated as "madness." "*Crazy*ness" comes a lot closer.

Impulse was sensational from my point of view. Nobody involved with the operation knew anything at all about jazz. I was doing lots and lots of new recording, and lots and lots more reissues—the only time my presence was required anyplace besides the studio was during semiannual Sales Meetings. I would be advised that I'd be given perhaps half an hour to play excerpts from upcoming new releases for the Sales and Promotion guys from the distributors.

I'd spent a bunch of time in meetings grousing about how swell it would be to do some *interesting* artist-signing, and pointed out, repeatedly, that Sun Ra had never had any representation on a "real" label. It's hard to imagine an organization more independent than Sun Ra's El Saturn—pressings in jackets individually hand-designed and -colored by the members of the Arkestra. "Legendary," "underexposed," and, indubitably, "sales potential," between them, did the job.

Remember, this is 1972, when, in terms of radio play, "underground" press exposure, and an open-minded buying market, it seemed like anything was possible. So, after some telephone conversations and a couple of deal memos went forth from ABC to Saturn, into a meeting in Jay Lasker's office went a fully enrobed Sun Ra and his Chicago-based business partner Alton Abraham. A standard Artist's Contract was presented. Alton put it in his briefcase, shook hands all 'round, and said, "We'll look it over and get back to you," and they were gone.

The following day, Alton was back with a retyped contract, turning everything on its head, with ABC, rather than Saturn, at the short end of the stick.

All the air puffed right out of the deal. I tried to explain the Inexplicable Behavior of These People, and pointed out that if it wasn't possible to make a New Recording Artist deal, perhaps it might be possible to make a Licensing Agreement for part of the Saturn catalog.

Amazingly, it worked. I still don't know why or how. So an agreement was drawn up, under which twenty-one Saturn LPs were to be made available on Impulse, along with a sampler to be drawn from those sides.

Alton and two heavy-lifting helpers brought a metal summer-camp trunk from Chicago to the Village Recorder, out of which emerged metal film cans containing, for the most part, seven-inch reels of seven-and-a-half-inch i.p.s.-speed tapes, more than a few of them mono (actually, there was one multi—eight—track tape, which had never been previously released). We transferred them to a little more state-of-the art condition, trying to denoise and clean them up, to the degree that 1972 technology would allow. New full-color covers were readied.

Nine discs saw the light of day. The rest, restored masters, new covers and all, were returned to Saturn. From a memo I wrote at The End of The Affair, they were listed (by Impulse numbers) as released:

AS-9239 *Atlantis*
AS-9242 *The Nubians of Plutonia*
AS-9243 *The Magic City*
AS-9245 *Angels and Demons at Play*
AS-9255 *Astro Black*
AS-9265 *Jazz in Silhouette*
AS-9270 *Fate in a Pleasant Mood*
AS-9271 *Supersonic Sounds*
ASD-9276 *Bad and Beautiful*

To be released (never happened):

ASD-9287 *Night of the Purple Moon*
ASD-9288 *Planet Earth*
ASD-9289 *My Brother the Wind*
ASD-9290 *Sound Sun Pleasure!*
ASD-9291 *Cosmic Tones for Mental Therapy*
ASD-9292 *We Travel the Spaceways*
ASD-9293 *Other Planes of There*
ASD-9294 *Art Forms from Dimensions Tomorrow*
ASD-9295 *Monorails and Satellites*
ASD-9296 *Cymbals*
ASD-9297 *Crystal Spears*
ASD-9298 *Pathways to Unknown Worlds*
(unnumbered sampler) *Welcome to Saturn*

I never saw a copy of the original contract, but I *do* have a copy of the termination agreement, from Da Lawyer, which, appropriately, contains the following Traditional Record Business Paragraph, which begins: "I just received notification from our royalty accounting department that a computer problem has delayed the preparation and mailing of the December 31, 1974, royalty report. However . . ."

When the ABC/Sun Ra deal fell through, before I heard it formally from Da Lawyer, I got a call from one of the underling legals who knew I cared, letting me know that it wasn't going to happen. And before I could hang up that phone, Bob Krasnow, of Blue Thumb Records, was calling me on the other one asking if I wanted to produce the Arkestra for him.

> copies of all the old Impulse albums. We only got to give them new albums!" I said, "So fifty percent of your sales are on the old albums and they're playing them all the time, and you don't want to give them copies to play?" He says, "No, you don't understand. It doesn't work that way. We've got to give them copies of new albums. . . ."

THE GREAT DIVIDE: FROM ONE SIDE . . .

The recording industry was still in major flux in the early seventies: established business structures and ways of doing business were slowly yielding to the changes brought on by the exploding profits of the rock revolution. Within each major record company, the tug of war between the old and new—the suits and the jeans—found those who sold the music (marketing, sales, promotion) increasingly on one side and those who made it (A&R and production) more and more on the other.

How jazz fit into this picture as the decade progressed, and how Impulse fit into the ABC/Dunhill frame, depended on how the music was perceived on either side of the divide. Says Michel:

> As far as Howard and Jay were concerned, I was a guy in a pointed hat who was mixing up a cauldron and throwing magical stuff into it and out would pop recordings. I remember once Jay put his arm around me and said, "Oh, you're my little money machine: like turning a crank, every time you go into the studio some dollars come out of the other side. That supports a lot of the pop stuff we have to do." I thought, "Gee, that's nice. Are you going to pay me some more?"

It was a time when ideas of musical integration—on radio, in retail, and in the studio—were being bandied about, but also resisted. "Steve Barri, one of the great bubble-gum producers, who was the head of A&R [at Dunhill], said to me, 'I don't like it when you're recording in ABC's own studios because the sounds sort of leak through the wall. It corrupts my pop guys because they all want to be jazz guys.' It was true!" Ironically, another in-house producer at ABC, Gary Katz, began working in 1971 with a rock group that was happy to pick up on any leaks of the jazz variety, and that would soon elevate the fortunes of the label: Steely Dan.

But a few at ABC did straddle the divide, with impulsive ideas of cross-pollination, including one that led to an extreme anomaly in the Impulse catalog.

"Putting Genesis on Impulse? One of the stupidest fucking ideas I'd ever heard," says Michel of *Trespass* [AS-9205], the second album by the English progressive rock band. It was a notion that came from the promotion side. "Larry Ray was the head of promotion at ABC and doing a very good job, so he had the ear of Jay Lasker. I told Larry and everybody that this was a stupid idea—Impulse was a *jazz* label. The same happened at BluesWay with [the rock trio] James Gang produced by our mutual pal Bill Szymczyk [*Yer' Album* (BLS-6034)]. It got acted on."

In hindsight, Bob Thiele's more liberal leaps of definition at Impulse seem in sync with Ray's, and given the lengthy improvisations that were typical of many progressive rock groups of the day—Genesis among them—the connection does not seem so remote. But, as Genesis had yet to reach the level of maturity and songwriting sophistication that earned the band its renown, *Trespass* "vanished without a trace," Michel says.

. . . AND THE OTHER

"I was senior vice president of sales and promotion," says Dennis Lavinthal, whose father, Lou, was then running ABC's distribution arm, ABC Record and Tape Sales. "But I was the guy who understood what was going on in the street with music. The other guys that I worked for were older and kind of removed."

Lavinthal, of the same age and cultural leaning as Michel, had joined ABC only weeks before Michel in 1969 and quickly became a generational intermediary at the company. "I was their young buck. They were teaching the business to me and I was teaching the business to them. I had very strong opinions because I was young and thought I knew everything."

Cockiness about his role at ABC was necessary, and it served Lavinthal well. "We were hot and I was doing whatever I could—sales, promotion, marketing. I used to put together the initial orders on the releases: Three Dog Night and Steppenwolf and catalog [items] like the Grass Roots and the Mamas and the Papas. That was my department: 'We're going to put out a hundred and fifty thousand. We're going to *try* to put two hundred thousand out of this record. Now we're going to ship a million records.' Whatever the numbers were, I had to sign off on that."

Sexy, sexist—that's the seventies: a 1971 advertisement suggests the cross-pollination of rock and jazz audiences.

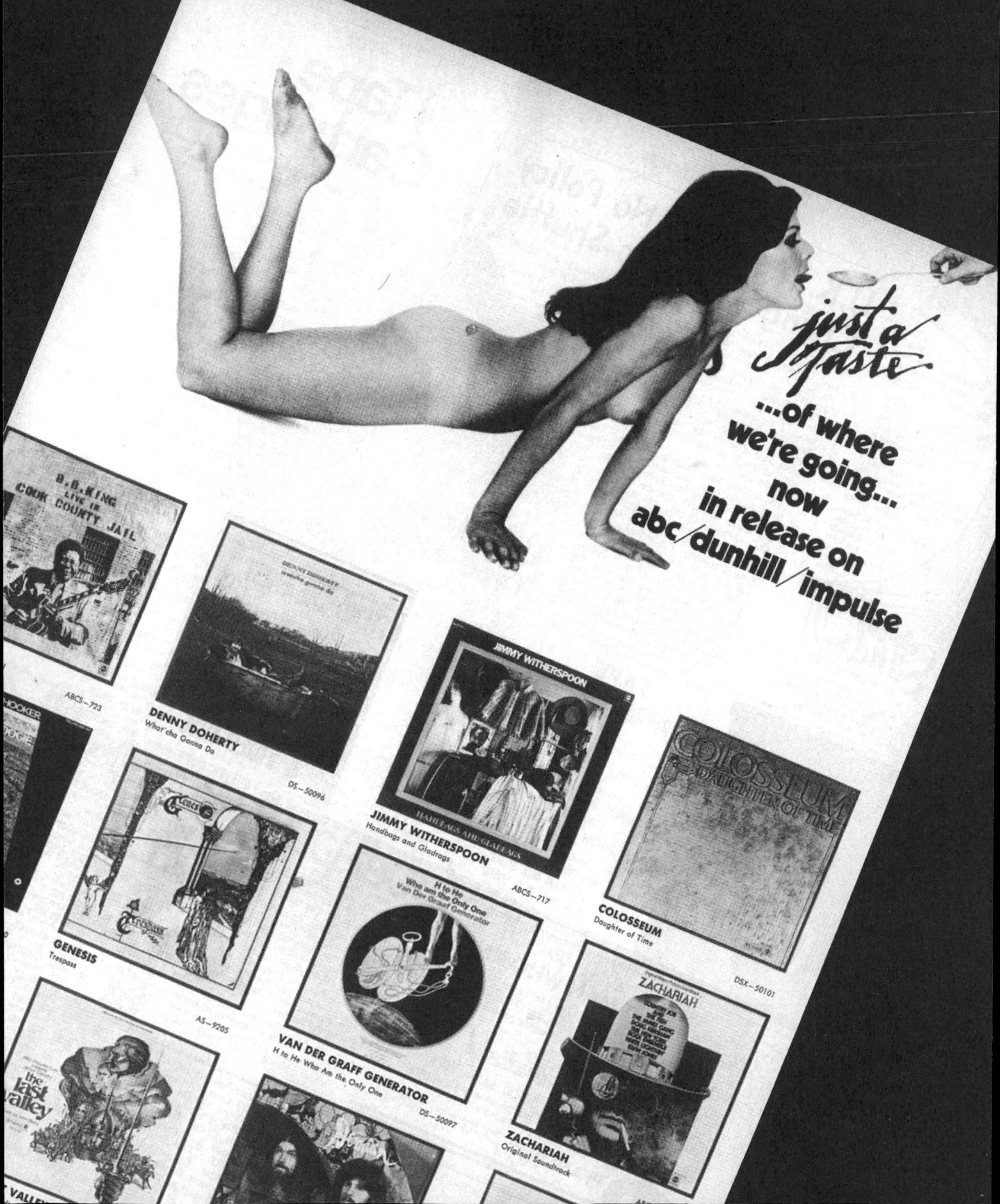

just a Taste
...of where we're going... now in release on abc/dunhill/impulse
B.B. KING LIVE IN COOK COUNTY JAIL
ABCS—723
DENNY DOHERTY
What'cha Gonna Do
DS—50096
JIMMY WITHERSPOON
JIMMY WITHERSPOON
Handbags and Gladrags
ABCS—717
COLOSSEUM DAUGHTER OF TIME
COLOSSEUM
Daughter of Time
DSX—50101
GENESIS
Trespass
AS—9205
H to He Who am the Only One Van Der Graaf Generator
VAN DER GRAFF GENERATOR
H to He Who Am the Only One
DS—50097
ZACHARIAH
ZACHARIAH
Original Soundtrack
the last valley

Jazz releases were lucky to amount to one-tenth of pop. "Thirty or forty thousand records would have been a lot for an Impulse title—from '69 on, jazz was less than five percent [of ABC's total revenue], I think. By the time ABC and Dunhill merged [under Lasker], it must have been late '71, Steely Dan was in the house and Jim Croce and [James Gang guitarist] Joe Walsh. We were starting to diversify [and] get caught up in the rock of the seventies."

In fact, ABC would launch singer-songwriter Jim Croce into the Top Ten with his first single, "You Don't Mess Around with Jim," in the late summer of '72, while Steely Dan's debut, "Do It Again," would hit in December. But it was in 1971 that, with ABC's West Coast office more in charge every day and Dunhill's sales firmly in the lead, ABC corporate decided that Lasker should assume the leadership of the music division. As a result, Larry Newton, according to Lavinthal, "quickly fell off the radar."

Newton, it turns out, had been shifted from music to film and TV, from president of ABC Records to vice president in charge of international sales for ABC Pictures in March 1970. By that summer, the music trades spoke of Lasker as ABC's new president, ready to back up Impulse releases with significant promotional support. "The jazz line would be structured like a pop company, with fewer releases and a greater concentration on promotions for mass merchandisers," Lasker told *Billboard* in September.

Yet, to Lavinthal, Impulse remained a catalog-driven effort in the eyes of ABC's newly elevated directors—echoing Newton's mid-sixties philosophy. "The theory upstairs was to be able to merchandise entire catalogs like [the classical line] Westminster and BluesWay with sixty or seventy titles of a genre at any time."

An Impulse order form from July 1970 amplifies the theory. Retailers could still order any item from the label's catalog, from AS-1, *The Great Kai and J.J.*, through AS-9197, *East Side San Jose*, except for the two folk albums, AS-24 and -25. Tellingly, on the list of Impulse's Top 40 Best Sellers, skewed to recently released titles and topped by Pharaoh Sanders's *Jewels of Thought*, were sixteen John Coltrane titles.

An Impulse retail order form lists the label's best-sellers in 1970.

impulse! abc

UNIVERSITY SERIES OF FINE RECORDINGS

ABC / Dunhill Records, Inc., 8255 Beverly Blvd., Los Angeles, California 90048

NEW RELEASES—JULY 1970

INV.	ORD.	STEREO	TITLE/ARTIST
		AS 9188	FOR LOSERS—Archie Shepp
		AS 9192	THIS RATHER THAN THAT—Buddy Montgomery
		AS 9194	THE AWAKENING—Ahmad Jamal
		AS 9195	TRANSITION—John Coltrane
		AS 9196	PTAH THE EL DAOUD—Alice Coltrane/Pharoah Sanders
		AS 9197	EASTSIDE SAN JOSE—Cliff Coulter

TOP 40 BEST SELLERS

INV.	ORD.	STEREO	TITLE/ARTIST
		AS 9190	JEWELS OF THOUGHT—Pharoah Sanders
		AS 9189	THAT'S THE WAY IT IS—Milt Jackson Quintet Featuring Ray Brown
		AS 9186	I'D RATHER SUCK MY THUMB—Mel Brown
		AS 9181	KARMA—Pharoah Sanders
		AS 9176	AT THE TOP—POINCIANA REVISITED—Ahmad Jamal
		AS 9174	THE BEST OF CHICO HAMILTON
		AS 9173	THE BEST OF GABOR SZABO
		AS 9169	THE WIZARD—Mel Brown
		AS 9161	SELFLESSNESS—John Coltrane
		AS 9156	A MONASTIC TRIO—Alice Coltrane
		AS 9154	THE MAGIC OF JU-JU—Archie Shepp
		AS 9152	CHICKEN FAT—Mel Brown
		AS 9146	THE SORCERER—Gabor Szabo
		AS 9140	OM—John Coltrane
		AS 9138	TAUHID—Pharoah Sanders
		AS 9128	JAZZ RAGA—Gabor Szabo
		AS 9125	THE GOLDEN FLUTE—Yusef Lateef
		AS 9124	COLTRANE LIVE AT THE VANGUARD AGAIN!—John Coltrane
		AS 9123	SPELLBINDER—Gabor Szabo
		AS 9120	EXPRESSION—John Coltrane
		AS 9110	MEDITATIONS—John Coltrane
		AS 9106	KULU SE MAMA—John Coltrane
		AS 9102	EL CHICO—Chico Hamilton
		AS 95	ASCENSION—John Coltrane
		AS 94	NEW THING AT NEWPORT—John Coltrane/Archie Shepp
		AS 84	1984—Yusef Lateef
		AS 77	A LOVE SUPREME—John Coltrane
		AS 73	EVERYBODY LOVES A LOVER—Shirley Scott
		AS 69	LIVE AT PEPS—Yusef Lateef

Going gold: ABC president Jay Lasker—with hands raised—acknowledges the label's new hit makers Steely Dan in 1973. Back row: booking agent Howard Rose, guitarist Denny Dias, unidentified, producer Gary Katz, ABC senior v.p. of sales and promotion Dennis Lavinthal, drummer Jim Hodder, guitarist Walter Becker, and keyboardist/singer Donald Fagen. Front row: band managers Joel Cohn and Marv Helfer, guitarist Jeff "Skunk" Baxter.

"My recollection [of Impulse] is a catalog company with Ed Michel making some quirky records and smoking some good weed," says Lavinthal. "There were some fun experimental projects that took place—a Howard Roberts album called *Antelope Freeway*. At the same time, Impulse was this avant-garde, non-melody expression of strong emotion."

Impulse titles through 1971 and into '72 prove the balance Lavinthal suggests. First-time releases from the tape library—such as John Coltrane's beautifully packaged *Sun Ship* [AS-9211], featuring music from the Classic Quartet's final session—were issued alongside sounds of spiritual focus, like Alice Coltrane's *Universal Consciousness* [AS-9210] and *World Galaxy* [AS-9218]. There were albums channeling racial pride and Afrocentrism, like Pharoah Sanders's *Black Unity* [AS-9219], and albums bristling with indignation, like Archie Shepp's *Things Have Got to Change* [AS- 9212] and *Attica Blues* [AS-9222], the latter an outcry against the massacre at the State Correctional Facility in Attica, New York.

"It seemed the sound of the whole sociopolitical revolution that started in the sixties was continuing in the seventies through Impulse," Lavinthal adds. "What we [the younger promotion and marketing staff] were trying to do was to break certain acts out of becoming the catalog thing. That's where Steve Backer came in: he moved Ed into a more commercial place."

ENTER STEVE BACKER

Blame it on the 6.6 earthquake centered in San Fernando that all Los Angeles felt on February 9, 1971. Michel remembers: "After that, Larry [Ray] and Bill [Szymczyk] got out of California. They weren't sticking around. They set up Tumbleweed Records in Denver, and Backer came in to replace Larry."

To Michel, Steve Backer was one of the great promotion men. Fresh from a more youthful environment at Verve Records, promoting Laura Nyro and Richie Havens, then at Elektra, working with the Paul Butterfield Blues Band, Backer was unprepared for the boardroom divide at ABC.

"Jay Lasker was an old-school tough guy, a Damon Runyonesque individual, and he set the tone," Backer recalls. "At the conference room table there would be sharkskin suiters with pinky rings on one side, and the guys with long hair and beads on the other. I remember after working one especially tough project, they saw how I was looking and told me to go get a *schvitz*—a steam bath. Very old school. Of course, it's been the same tightrope walk between art and commerce for the last forty years; only the hairstyles and dress codes have changed. But that was ABC then."

Backer—whose father had moonlighted as a jazz saxophonist, and who had worked as a teenager at the Cork and Bib, a Long Island nightclub that presented jazz—decided to leave a decent position with promise of advancement at Elektra because the label wasn't moving toward jazz. "This was actually the first jazz gig for me. Prior to doing this I was doing regional and national promotion for rock 'n' roll artists, and I had a pretty good reputation because I had broken a lot of records prior to coming there, like certain Carly Simon records, a couple of Doors records, a Judy Collins record. . . ."

Hired by ABC on the West Coast while based in Boston, Backer remained in the East, leaving the studio work to Michel. As a customer and a fan,

ATTICA BLUES

Archie Shepp / *Attica Blues* / Impulse AS-9222
DATE RECORDED: January 24–26, 1972
DATE RELEASED: June 1972
PRODUCER: Ed Michel

Michel makes a point; Shepp and trumpeter Roy Burrowes listen.

The headlines of September 1971 were filled with blood and rage. An uprising that had begun as a protest against inhumane prison conditions at the State Correctional Facility in Attica, New York, had led to a four-day standoff and, eventually, a full-scale assault in which thirty-nine convicts and hostages were killed—all by guards and state police. Governor Nelson Rockefeller, soon to make a bid for the presidency on the Republican ticket, had taken a hard-line, no-negotiation stance and ordered the attack.

Public outcry was immediate, especially in the African-American community, since a disproportionate number of victims were black. "My drummer, Beaver Harris, who was always a guy full of innovative ideas, came to me and said, 'Shepp, why don't we do an album about the Attica uprising?'" Archie Shepp recalls. "I thought it was a good idea, so I wrote the theme song, 'Attica Blues,' and a song that was inspired by a poem Beaver had put together, something about 'I'd rather be a plant than a man in this land.' He had his own way of writing street poetry. From that poem I wrote a song called 'Ballad for a Child,' which was sung by a guy named Carl Hull. And the poem was recited by [radical left-wing attorney] William Kunstler on the album."

Trumpeter and arranger Cal Massey got the call to arrange the album—and became a primary force behind it.

"I made it my business to know all of the people that had known Coltrane," Shepp says. "So I met Cal and had already asked him to write some music for me for what I was doing for Impulse at the time, including a thing we did called *The Cry of My People*. It's an album that hasn't ever made much noise, but I think it's one of the best albums that I've ever done, with beautiful arrangements by Massey. Romulus Franceschini did the string parts, and it had a great version of 'Come Sunday' by [singer] Joe Lee Wilson.

"So I pulled them together again with some of the best young musicians around New York and some of the best older ones. Some of them were not so well known, guys like [trombonists] Kiane Zawadi and Charles Greenlee. Charles McGhee—a very fine trumpet player. [Bassist] Jimmy Garrison, [drummer] Billy Higgins. I won't name them all, but let's see—saxophone player Roland Alexander, [guitarist] Cornell Dupree, [violinist] Leroy Jenkins, [pianist] Walter Davis Jr., and Carl Hull, who's sort of a James Brown–influenced singer, who sings the title song."

To those expecting music that reflected the intensity and volume of the public outrage over Attica, the title would have seemed the album's most provocative element. Yes, certain songs dealt with prison and prisoners ("Blues for Brother George Jackson," the incarcerated Black Panther leader killed in San Quentin), but as many focused on jazz pioneers ("Invocation to Mr. Parker," "Goodbye Sweet Pops") and the general human condition ("Ballad for a Child"). The musical mood ranged from sweet and innocent ("Quiet Dawn" was sung by Massey's twelve-year-old daughter, Waheeda) to fast and funky, but never furious.

"We geared *Attica Blues* hoping it would get wider recognition. The theme of it is blues and swing, and I was trying to do something that Impulse might put in the jukeboxes [so] that it might be heard in places outside of people's homes. I'm not so sure exactly how well this did, but it's probably the one [Impulse album] I did that made the most impression. I think Sam Rivers said at that point, 'Now Archie Shepp is playing rock 'n' roll!' [Laughs.] Some of my fellow musicians thought I was going over into Jimi Hendrix territory. I should have been so lucky. I think the fact that *Attica Blues* carried a message with it did a lot to discourage even the people who produced it from giving it too much play."

Ed Michel agrees to a degree, yet notes that *Attica Blues* was in fact issued by a company whose top brass was focused mostly on pop product and stockholder expectations.

"ABC's executives? They wouldn't have known what Attica was all about, and if they had asked me I would have said, 'Oh, that's about Governor Rockefeller,' . . . and they would have said, 'Oh, OK.' Those guys were very far removed from day-to-day reality. That's what made them good record executives."

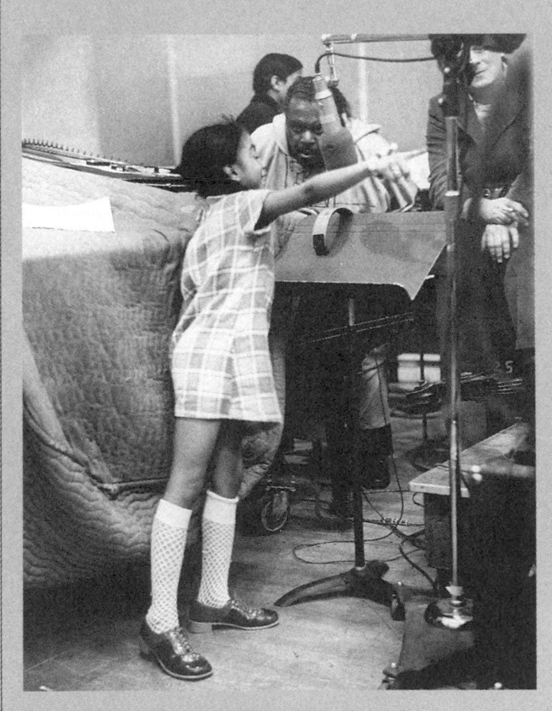

Attica, Attica!—January 1972: composer/arranger Cal Massey coaches daughter Waheeda.

Backer was thoroughly familiar with the Impulse mystique, with Coltrane at its core, and he immediately began shaping a series of popular and creatively themed multiple-disc sets.

> Coltrane, in my eyes, was the dominant force in the Impulse catalog, [so] I tried to capitalize on that with the various artist samplers we did. I did one called *Impulsively* [AS-9266-2], one called *No Energy Crisis* [AS-9267-2] when the big energy crisis was happening, one called *Irrepressible Impulses* [IMP-1972], and a whole series around instruments: a box set called *The Bass* [ASY-9284-3], *The Drums* [ASH-9272-3], and *The Saxophone* [AS-9253-3]. And we'd try to use Trane wherever possible. We had one conceptually called *Energy Essentials* [AS-9228-3], a three-record set I did with Ed. I'm really proud of the sequencing I did on the fourth side, which starts with "Acknowledgement" from *A Love Supreme*, goes into Pharoah's "The Creator Has a Master Plan," and then a cut by Michael White called "John Coltrane Was Here."

Besides the thematic, multi-artist approach, Backer initiated a series in 1972 that both celebrated the label and latched onto the double-album craze then in vogue. *Re-Evaluation: The Impulse Years* became the title for double-disc overviews of such artists as Charles Mingus, McCoy Tyner, Sonny Rollins, and Freddie Hubbard, while others, like *The Best of John Coltrane, Vol. 2* [AS-9223-2], *The Best of Pharoah Sanders* [AS-9229-2], and Alice Coltrane's *Reflection on Creation and Space* [AS-9232-2], highlighted the historical heart of the Impulse catalog.

IMPULSE ON TOUR

Of Backer's many projects at the outset of his Impulse association, one alone managed both to earn him the respect of his higher-ups and to expand his role at the label. Noting that a number of free-form rock stations in the Northeast were playing Impulse albums, Backer developed an idea: assemble Impulse's leading artists into a package tour, book it in rock clubs and college campuses, and allow the music—*performance* music—to sell itself to the young and open-eared. In 1971, when else could a college-age audience see and afford such a progressive jazz revue?

"A tour like that costs a lot of money," Backer remarks. "It is financed by the corporation and tickets are sold at very low prices. The promotion is a long-term capital investment." One reviewer wrote of a typical evening of that first ABC-subsidized "experimental regional tour," presenting Pharoah Sanders, Alice Coltrane, John Klemmer, and Michael White:

> If my own eyes had not seen that the Fillmore-like mob scene in front of [Boston's] Fenway Theatre was precipitated by a late-starting jazz concert and not one given by Miles, Herbie Mann or any other big seller, I'd never have believed it.

"The tickets were a dollar or something, and it was in the middle of January and it was freezing and still it was a mob scene," Backer says. "I got WBCN—the biggest rock station in New England, where the general manager was a huge fan of Trane—to get the word out."

Using attendance and radio play (Backer's specialty) as a measure, the tour was an unexpected success, and led to an expanded national tour with Archie Shepp added to the bill. Other jazz artists—Charles Lloyd, Miles

Davis, Rahsaan Roland Kirk, Cannonball Adderley—had already broken into the rock arena, wowing Fillmore audiences in New York and San Francisco. But no jazz revue as extensive or ambitious as the Impulse tour had been chanced on the rock circuit. It helped sell Impulse albums, and most significantly, it earned Backer a promotion to general manager of Impulse—with full signing power.

> I was quite proud when I had achieved that. Because I didn't know what I was going to do in jazz, I just knew I loved this music and wanted to work with it. And at Impulse I didn't have the feeling that there was a one-off type situation. It was more an artist development approach when I was there.

Who to sign? Again, Backer looked to the spirit of Impulse for direction.

> My thinking process was motivated by John Coltrane, and I was trying to bring this record label into his image, artist-wise. But I really wasn't looking for the next John Coltrane; I was looking for artists that were affected and impacted in certain ways by him—musically, sonically, spiritually—but who also stood on their own as individuals.
>
> Those were the first deals I ever made. There were five of them: Gato [Barbieri], Keith [Jarrett], Marion Brown, Dewey Redman, and Sam Rivers.

THE LAST WAVE

Backer's five signings—made in 1972 and 1973, and yielding worthy recordings through 1975—defined the last great avant-garde wave on Impulse. The timing could not have been better: as those with direct links to Coltrane (Alice Coltrane, Archie Shepp, Pharoah Sanders) brought their association with the label to a close, so their replacements stepped in to carry on Impulse's inherent message and musical promise.

"In my mind," Backer says, "Keith Jarrett and Gato were the more accessible part of the signings, and helped with the corporate experimentation of Dewey, Sam, and Marion, who were more difficult artists to get over." Not only did these leaders point the way for the next generation of avant-gardists, but—as the personnel listings on each album showed—they put many of them to work.

Tenor saxophonist Dewey Redman already boasted avant-garde credentials from his work with Ornette Coleman (they marched in the same Fort Worth high school band) in the late sixties and early seventies. Working with Coleman and with Charlie Haden's Liberation Music Orchestra brought Redman closer and closer to an Impulse orbit; by the time he joined Keith Jarrett's quintet, signing with Backer seemed a fait accompli. *The Ear of the Behearer* [AS-9250], his label debut in 1973 with a horns-and-strings outfit, introduced his distinctive singing-speaking tone (on alto as well as tenor), his compositional prowess (he wrote all the tracks), and his Yusef Lateef–like penchant for imported reed instruments: he played musette on the closing track, "Image (in Disguise)." Redman's second, and last, Impulse title, recorded a year later, was *Coincide* [AS-9300], on which he again played an unusual instrument (the zither) and was supported ably by avant-garde bassist Sirone.

Alto saxophonist Marion Brown was a re-signing; his 1966 album *Three for Shepp* had sold poorly, and he was not invited to do another session at the time. Back with Impulse, he proposed a three-part tribute to the poetry of Harlem Renaissance poet Jean Toomer and his own Georgia roots. The percussion-rich *Geechee Recollections* [AS-9252], recorded in 1973, offers blues-drenched melodies, with Brown's supple alto accompanied by trumpeter Leo Smith, percussionist Bill Hasson (who reads Toomer's "Karintha"), and drummer Steve McCall. The two titles that followed did not match the power of *Geechee,* but collectively, they do define a career crest. *Sweet Earth Flying* [ASD-9275], from 1974, took a cue from Miles Davis in its use of two keyboardists, Paul Bley and Muhal Richard Abrams. A year later, *Vista* [AS-9304] included a cover of Stevie Wonder's "Visions."

Of the free-blowing saxophonists active in the seventies, none paralleled the sound and musical path of Coltrane more—and therefore seemed more natural on Impulse—than Sam Rivers. Rivers was born three years before Coltrane, came up playing big-band charts, progressed to bebop, and eventually arrived at a fearless avant-garde style that challenged listeners, especially on a series of Blue Note albums from 1964 to 1967. Rivers's experimental charge, like Coltrane's, was rooted in a deep intellectual grasp of the music and its mechanics. His own arc at Impulse bears out the comparison.

Streams [AS-9251], consisting of one uninterrupted multi-sectioned live improvisation from Switzerland's Montreux Jazz Festival in 1973, featured Rivers in a trio setting (with bassist Cecil McBee and drummer Norman Connors), quickly switching among four instruments (soprano, alto, tenor, and piano!)—making it sort of Rivers's "Chasin' the Trane." Says Rivers:

> *Streams* was not even one of my best concerts during that hectic period. But it was representative of what I call "spontaneous creativity, " where everything is created on the spot—the theme, transitions, everything—making the music sound written when it wasn't. That was the first time I was able to record it, but I had been doing that for six or seven years at that point.

The next year, Rivers focused on a very different concept: a large studio group performing written music. *Crystals* [ASD-9286] can be construed as Rivers's *Africa/Brass* and his *Ascension,* presenting compositions written over fifteen years, all sharing a free and vigorous spirit, played by a brassy thirteen-piece band. Again in contrast, *Hues* [ASD-9302] was a conceptual look at shades of color and meaning, capturing more of Rivers's "spontaneous creativity." *Sizzle* [ASD-9316], a studio return in 1975, was a funky sextet date featuring Dave Holland on cello and bass, Warren Smith on vibraphone and percussion, and Ted Dunbar on guitar. It is one of Rivers's least appreciated efforts.

Comparing his four years with Blue Note to his Impulse run, Rivers states, "From the albums, you can tell the growth. I think it's the same as when I was with Blue Note. But Impulse was a sort of intermediary between Blue Note and a major label. [It had] budget, expertise. It was there at a time when musicians needed some kind of exposure and got it."

GATO AND KEITH

In 1972, Gato Barbieri and Keith Jarrett were shining brightly, two new jazz stars for the rock era: the saxophonist had just received a Grammy nod for his soundtrack to a controversial cinematic sensation starring Marlon Brando, while the pianist—and former Miles Davis sideman—had begun to release albums as both a soloist and a leader that pulled with hypnotic power.

Barbieri, first heard widely in his fellow Argentinean Lalo Schifrin's big

Philosophic Talk About Jazz Is A Bore!
After all the so-called intelligentsia beat their gums about progressive music, jazz and the perennial "Schools of Thought" one thing is sure…
Impulse Has It All In This
GATO
CHAPTER ONE: LATIN AMERICA
MICHAEL WHITE THE LAND OF SPIRIT AND LIGHT
THE LAND OF SPIRIT AND LIGHT
KEITH JARRETT FORT YAWUH
FORT YAWUH
SAM RIVERS STREAMS RECORDED IN PERFORMANCE AT THE MONTREUX JAZZ FESTIVAL
THE EAR OF THE BEHEARER DEWEY REDMAN
THE EAR OF THE BEHEARER
Mel Brown Big Foot Country Girl
BIG FOOT COUNTRY GIRL
STREAMS
THE NEW PHAROAH SANDERS
Saracho En Medio
CHARLIE HA
LIBERATION MUSIC ORCHESTRA
THE NEW PHAROAH SANDERS
EN MEDIO
Impulse Has Only One Philo
Impulse Has
impul
True But Incredible!
THE STRONGEST BULL-PEN IN MAJOR LEAGUE RECORDS.
NEW RELEASES WE COULD NOT CERTIFY GOLD
THE DAY THEY LEFT THE FACTORY.
BUT WILL WITHIN A FEW WEEKS.
POPULAR
CALIFORNIA '99
DS 50105 Andwella PEOPLE'S PEOPLE
DS 50109 Gayle McCormick
DS 50114 DANNY COX
ABCX 726 Jimmie Haskell CALIFORNIA '99
ABCS 732 Tommy Roe BEGINNINGS
PROGRESSIVE
CHICO HAMILTON HIS GREATEST HITS
AS 9209 Mel Brown's Fifth
AS 9210 Alice Coltrane UNIVERSAL CONSCIOUSNESS
AS 9211 John Coltrane SUN SHIP
AS 9213-2 Chico Hamilton HIS GREAT HITS
AS 9212 Archie Shepp THINGS HAVE GOT TO CHANGE
CLASSICAL
ABC/ATS 20009 Beverly Sills WELCOME TO VIENNA
ABC/ATS 20006 Beverly Sills DONIZETTI: ROBERTO DEVEREUX
Super Girl Beverly Sills
IMPULSE HAS IT AL
GATO
CHAPTER ONE: LATIN AMERICA
LA CHINA LEONCIA ARREO LA CORRENTINADA TRAJO
ENTRE LA MUCHACHADA LA FLOR DE LA JUVENTUD
TO BE CONTINUED
ENCUENTROS
NUNCA MAS
INDIA
VILLAGE OF THE PHAROAHS
Pharoah Sanders/AS-9254
VILLAGE OF THE PHAROAHS
MANSION WORLDS
MEMORIES OF LEE MORGAN
WENT LIKE IT CAME
VILLAGE OF THE PHAROAHS
MYTH
PHAROAH SANDERS
FEATURING VOCALIST SEDATRIUS BROWN
CHAPTER ONE: LATIN AMERICA
Gato Barbieri/AS-9248
THE SAXOPHONE
John Coltrane, Pharoah Sande
Johnny Hodges, Charlie Parke
Lester Young And Others/ASY-
e Saxophone
COLEMAN HAWKINS with BENNY CARTER
SONNY STITT / SONNY ROLLINS / JOHNNY HODGE
BEN WEBSTER / JOHN COLTRANE / ARCHIE SHEPP
LESTER YOUNG / CHARLIE PARKER / ERIC DOLPHY
ORNETTE COLEMAN / PHAROAH SANDERS
SONNY SIMMONS / JOHN GILMORE
ALBERT AYLER / JOHN KLEMMER / SAM RIVERS
MARION BROWN / DEWEY REDMAN
GATO BARBIERI
impulse!
abc

band, later on Charlie Haden's *Liberation Music Orchestra*, and most recently on Bob Thiele's Flying Dutchman label, was suddenly a hot property that year. "He was signed because of [the film soundtrack] *Last Tango in Paris,*" recalls Ed Michel, who would work and travel extensively through South America with the saxophonist.

His thrust into the public eye and his Grammy nomination belied Barbieri's avant-garde youth. He had fallen under the spell of Coltrane while still in Buenos Aires and, after arriving in New York City in the late sixties, had recorded as a leader for the modest ESP-Disk label and performed with such free players and arrangers as Don Cherry and Carla Bley. To Michel, he seemed destined for Impulse, with a gentle growl reminiscent of another Coltrane acolyte.

"Gato and Pharoah were very similar in the way they shaped musical forms. Pharoah would take an R&B lick and shake it until it vibrated to death, into freedom, and let it coalesce over a long time. Gato was not dissimilar." Each favored lengthy jams, with percussion that suggested far-off lands, and spirited saxophone solos with a leonine tone.

Barbieri's four discs for Impulse—titled *Chapter One* through *Chapter Four*—served as a virtual South American tour. The saxophonist himself speaks of them with pride and a still-thick accent. "I leave Flying Dutchman and I go to Impulse—four albums. I think it was my idea; maybe it was Michelle, my ex-wife. What I wanted to do is to touch on the most important music of Latin America. So I'll go to Buenos Aires and pick musicians. I'll go to Brazil. . . ."

"The Big Dogs [at ABC] went for it," remembers Michel. "Gato was keen for it, explaining to me that he wanted to record for Coltrane's label."

Paying for a big band is one thing. ABC's decision to invest in Gato Barbieri was generous even by rock standards: overseas recording sessions, flying musicians up from South America for a European tour. But given the warm relationship ABC had developed with the Latin American labels that carried its rock and jazz stars, the idea of recording Barbieri in Buenos Aires and Rio de Janeiro seemed a solid financial move as well. "There were bucks in South America (from the label's foreign licensees), and record companies down there would know something about the whereabouts of good recording studios," Michel wrote in the liner notes to a Barbieri collection.

The two-week trip brought forth two popular albums, *Chapter One:*

Latin America [AS-9248] and *Chapter Two: Hasta Siempre* [AS-9263], which Michel calls "Gato's initial vision." "He wanted to do a combination of what he referred to as folkloric music and tango and samba and record it all with players who weren't studio players, guys who played naturally in their tradition." (Barbieri puts it this way: "I want to be clear I invent something who is not Latin, not jazz, but is in-between.")

The first album sold exceedingly well, enough to warrant flying up an Argentinean group to record in Los Angeles in late 1973 to record further tracks for *Chapter Two: Hasta Siempre* and hiring a Latin jazz orchestra led by the legendary arranger-bandleader Chico O'Farrill the next year, which yielded *Chapter Three: Viva Emiliano Zapata* [AS-9279]. The next year, six days of recording at the Bottom Line nightclub in New York—with, among others, Ron Carter on bass and Howard Johnson on various instruments (tuba, flügelhorn, bass clarinet)—yielded *Chapter Four: Alive in New York* and an end to Barbieri's relationship with the label. Summarizing his crossover success with Impulse, Barbieri explains: "If you listen in retrospective, it's incredible. But in those days it maybe was avant-garde without being free jazz."

Un-jazz-like jazz helped propel the career of Keith Jarrett as well. In the seventies, he worked with a wide palette of moods and rhythms ranging from jumpy and jaunty to pastoral and plaintive, in solo or small-group format. He was also a one-man wave of eccentricity and profit, taking his solo piano performances into theaters and concert halls for higher fees than almost any other jazz artist before him. He answered interviewers' questions with cryptic answers that bristled at the perceived disrespect his music received. Onstage, his behavior could surprise—standing, at times gyrating, at the keys, plucking the strings inside, playing recorder or soprano sax—yet he never lost the melodic flow.

And despite standing out from the rest of the fusion-era pack by keeping his bands acoustic and free-form, Jarrett enjoyed the embrace of the rock press like no other pianist of his generation. In 1972, *Rolling Stone* ran a lengthy review celebrating three recent releases, an all-acoustic mini-wave that ran against the largely electric fusion sounds of his contemporaries. "Jarrett seems to have made the jump," reviewer Robert Palmer wrote, "from ex-Miles pianist to the most important young keyboard stylist in jazz today while nobody was looking."

Jarrett was only twenty-seven when he signed to Impulse, but with

CHAPTER ONE

Gato Barbieri / *Chapter One: Latin America* / Impulse ASD-9248
DATE RECORDED: April 17, 18, and 24, 1973
DATE RELEASED: November 1973
PRODUCER: Ed Michel

Gato Barbieri: In those days, because the jazz people they don't consider me a jazz musician. If I Latin, they don't consider me Latin. So I am here in the middle.
Ashley Kahn: Is that a good thing?
GB: Ah! It's a good thing! You know why? Because they say, "What do you play?" I say, "I play my music Gato Barbieri." I don't owe anything to anybody.

The decision to record Gato Barbieri in his native Argentina and also in Brazil was inspired, ambitious, and a good measure of ABC's support of Impulse up through 1973. The trip itself was one that proved to be worthy of Job. As related in Ed Michel's amusing liner notes to the CD collection *Latino America* [Impulse IMPD-2-236], the project faced a battery of challenges from the outset, including, in rapid succession: a band walkout, a power outage, a dearth of professional recording tape, and a power outage deliberately caused by a local electricians guild. Then there was the general political unrest. And that was just the first week.

The first stop: Buenos Aires. Well-placed grease of the folding variety, and a few well-placed friends, eventually permit three days of recording. The first two dates feature Barbieri blowing long and energetically with an Argentinean folkloric group. "I record some my songs and some other songs from the Indians," Barbieri states, referring to the indigenous musicians featured in the ten-piece lineup. "It was incredible because is the first I put people come from Argentina—there are three or four drummers, a regular rhythm section: electric bass and drums. Three different guitars and Indian harp that has only one tonality. I think it was C minor or D minor, so I had to play in that key. And the *quena* [wooden flute], the *charango* [a small ten-string guitar made from an armadillo shell], the *bombo indio* [ten tom-tom drums with goatskin heads]. They are very . . . not just brilliant. They are, 'Boom!'"

Barbieri's syntax may be confusing, but "Boom!" is easily understood. The high combustion of the session blended traditional sonorities with Barbieri's throaty tenor sax and his yelps of delight: a swirling, driving mix that echoed Pharoah Sanders at his most exultant and extended. "Please keep in mind that in the early seventies, the idea of 'world music' was not a hot button," Michel recalls, explaining that the saxophonist's motivation at the time was being a "catalyst that makes the combination of South American culture and post-Coltrane jazz sensibility a functional reality."

In his own manner of speaking, Barbieri agrees: "When I started to play there was here one, and there was here the other one. I had to come to put them together." He carried his mission into the session that followed, marrying jazz and tango, recording his tune "Nunca Mas" with a troupe fronted by the *bandoneon,* the button accordion that is the tango's signature instrument. "Buenos Aires—everything that happened there was very special," the saxophonist remarks.

Next stop: Rio de Janeiro. Brazil provided its own set of problems while band, studio, payment, and permission were negotiated. Eventually another session ensued, filled with strummed, stroked, and beaten sonorities of another native folkloric tradition. But this was not Jobim's "Corcovado" or "Desafinado."

"We go to many places to find musicians, especially not playing the bossa nova," remembers Barbieri. "Musicians of *escolas de sambas*—schools of samba. It was so beautiful in Rio in those days." The resulting samba-jazz mix was more traditional in instrumentation and song forms than the sophisticated bossa nova of the mid-seventies, and yet more edgy and modern as well, as Barbieri's tenor bristled with a proud avant-garde edge.

The collective results of the South American saga became the first two volumes of Barbieri's four-volume "Chapter" series for Impulse. *Chapter One: Latin America* achieved instant success, enough to earn ABC's assent to fly the first Argentinean group to New York for further sessions, and to accompany Barbieri on a tour of Europe. Their Montreux Jazz Festival gig in 1973 can be heard in part on *Impulse Artists on Tour* [AS-9264], which featured Impulse's top acts at the time, including John Klemmer, Michael White, Sam Rivers, and Keith Jarrett.

Barbieri's healthy sales for Impulse can be explained by a number of obvious factors, like a Grammy nomination that year for his *Last Tango in Paris* soundtrack. But Steve Backer, who was then managing Impulse, pulls back the curtain on a scene that reveals more. "I went to this ABC/Dunhill convention in Los Angeles in '73—a huge room with all the employees in it: promotion, sales, everyone. Jay [Lasker] is up front saying, 'We got this Gate-Oh Barbieri record. What do we think we can sell on this one?'

"The rumor was that he was getting paid on the gross. So if he could ship it he made money on it, even if it was returned later. Somebody says, 'How about we try 20,000?' That's about 15,000 more than Bob Thiele ever sold on Flying Dutchman. So Lasker says, 'Well, how about 30,000?' It was like a tobacco auction. Finally, he was saying, 'I'll tell you what, why don't we ship 100,000 records on Gate-Oh.'

"I'm thinking, 'Holy shit! These guys are crazy.' But to tell you the truth, a lot more records were going to be sold than if you shipped 7,000. There's going to be all sorts of visibility factors from a retail point of view. The album's going to be in end-caps [displays on the end of the record racks] and going to be filed under Gato's name instead of miscellaneous 'B.'

"And it worked. If they ended up selling 70,000, I don't care what happened to the other 30,000. For a jazz album, that's astounding!"

Keeping the record straight: Michel's list of musicians appearing on Barbieri's *Chapter One,* Buenos Aires, April 1973.

DIR. TEL. "ALVEAROTEL" BUENOS AIRES
AVENIDA ALVEAR 1891 TEL. 41 PLAZA 4031
Alvear Palace Hotel

DIRECTED BY MICHELLE BARBIERI
SOUND MAN - JUAN CARLOS MANOJAS
ASSISTANT. JORGE TAGLIANI
RECORDED - MUSIC HALL. S.A.C.I.S.I.

RAUL MERCADO. - QUENA. (INDIAN FLUTE.)
AMADEO MONGES - INDIAN HARP.
ANTONIO PANTOJA - ANAPA. ERKE. SIKU. QUENA. ERKENCHO.
ADALBERTO CEBASCO - BASS (FENDER).
DOMINGO CURA. BOMBO INDIO.
QUELO PALACIOS ACOUSTIC GUITAR.
FUMERO. - CHARANGO -
RICARDO LEW. ELECTRIC GUITAR.
POCHO LA POUBLE - TRAP DRUMS.
JORGE PADIN PERCUSSION
L ZURDO PERCUSSION

EL HOTEL NO ES REMITENTE

enough critical support, pedigree (sideman to Art Blakey, Charles Lloyd, *and* Miles Davis), and experience as a leader to allow his manager, George Avakian, to maneuver a special arrangement. Jarrett could continue to record "special projects" (solo and collaborative sessions for the Munich-based ECM label) while recording with his American-based group for Impulse. That group—Dewey Redman, Charlie Haden, drummer Paul Motian, and, at times, guitarist Sam Brown and a percussionist—was soon dubbed the American Quartet to differentiate it from his work with Swedish saxophonist Jan Garbarek.

Jarrett would stay with Impulse from 1973 through 1976 and deliver eight albums. The first four—the live Village Vanguard recording *Fort Yawuh* [AS-9240] and the studio albums *Treasure Island* [AS-9274], *Death and the Flower* [AS-9301], and *Backhand* [ASD-9305]—were all recorded from '73 to '74, with Michel producing.

"Keith is one of the guys who is a pleasure to record," Michel says. "He always knew what he wanted to do [and] it was a working band made up of brilliant players. It was a band where almost any take was good enough!"

To many, those four albums define the most consistent and influential exploratory acoustic jazz of the decade. "The Impulse quartet settings are Jarrett in his prime," declared Stephen Davis in the *New York Times* in 1975. The group was praised for its open-ended and episodic structures, which built spontaneously, often driven by a rhythmic groove. Though Jarrett was its titular leader and primary composer, the group exhibited an Ornette Coleman–like democracy: free, funky, but never follow-the-leader.

"I'm not interested in having people who believe exactly what I believe. I only care about how much they hear when they are playing," stated Jarrett of his band's sine qua non. "We all know that we're still changing if we're able to play together."

George Avakian adds: "I had explained to Ed Michel in detail my thesis that rather than having a negative effect on Impulse's sales, allowing Keith the freedom to express himself musically elsewhere in ways that were of no interest to Impulse could only broaden his image and audience —thus enhancing the value to Impulse of Keith's more conservative product. But what astonished us all was that the ECM deal (which I negotiated in German, since Manfred Eicher did not speak more than a few words of English at the time) would produce albums that would suddenly outstrip everything else he ever recorded."

4. Exceptions from exclusivity: Keith should be permitted to finish his current "serious music" album for ECM (most of it music he composed under his Guggenheim Fellowship), but he may want to do similar recording during the term of his ABC contract and ABC should realize that such recording would have virtually no effect - and might even heighten Keith's image.

Jarrett's rising fame was part of Impulse's fortune in the seventies, as was the pianist's famous aversion to the tide of plugged-in fusion bands then on the rise: John McLaughlin's Mahavishnu Orchestra. Chick Corea's Return to Forever. Wayne Shorter and Joe Zawinul's Weather Report. Jarrett was the highest-profile member of the "children of Miles" who personally experienced the rock-jazz overlap yet came out feeling that "playing electric music is bad for you and bad for people listening. . . . I think it's best to say that I do not wish to deal with electric instruments."

"Hey, I didn't like it either," admits his sideman Paul Motian. "I really wasn't into fusion, even Miles's electric stuff. I think Dewey and Charlie agreed as well."

So did Impulse. "What fusion attempted to fuse," says Michel, "I wasn't interested in putting together. I liked Zawinul as a pianist and composer and all the bass players, but thought Weather Report was pretty much a sound effects band."

"John Klemmer was as close to the idea of fusion as Impulse came, playing his horn through an Echoplex so his phrases would echo again and again," notes Backer. "[Michael] Cuscuna and I used to call him 'Klemmer . . . Klemmer . . . Klemmer . . .' " But, he adds, "Had Weather Report or Mahavishnu come my way I certainly would have signed them. I had no problem with fusion, but I would have preferred the more acoustic sound like what Chick did on *Light as Feather*, his Return to Forever album on Polydor, to preserve the identity of Impulse."

Happy times: Michael Cuscuna (left) and Steve Backer at the height of their production activities in the seventies.

THE LAST WAVE RISES . . .

Through the first half of the decade, from 1970 through 1974, jazz weathered gale-force changes: founding fathers Armstrong and Ellington died; rock continued its rapid growth, sapping revenue and resources; live venues withered away; an already thinning audience splintered, attracted to a variety of stylistic possibilities. Fusion, Funk, and Free could rightly be the names of the three possible portals to the future of the music. Impulse survived it all, maintaining its commitment to the post-Coltrane mystique and sound (mainly Doorway #3) and now and again finding a way to increase its audience.

FORT YAWUH

Keith Jarrett / *Fort Yawuh* / Impulse ASD-9240

DATE RECORDED: February 24, 1973

DATE RELEASED: November 1973

PRODUCER: Ed Michel

Can you hear me? There's absolutely no need to clap. You just clap because you felt you should—whoever did [applause, scattered laughter and chatter]. If everyone would please concentrate on the sound in this room, suddenly everything would be quiet [more laughter, chatter]. No concentration, huh?

—KEITH JARRETT
AT THE VILLAGE VANGUARD, 1973

More than a dozen years earlier, Charles Mingus chastised a Five Spot audience: "You come to me, you sit in the front row, as noisy as can be . . ." Coltrane and Cannonball played the clubs and, in interviews, complained that their music had outgrown loud and smoky venues. Miles just turned his back.

Keith Jarrett's demands for concert-hall quiet in a club—and his willingness to directly address the crowd—played into his *enfant terrible* reputation in the early seventies. He was extremely talented, prolific, prickly, and eccentric. Among his various projects, he led one of the most consistently creative acoustic quartets of the decade. Serious and dour as he seemed, Jarrett could not keep still from sheer enjoyment, according to drummer Paul Motian.

"Those yelps of delight [on *Fort Yawuh*]? Keith's. We were having a great time and he was happy and was expressing himself. We were both kind of active physically—he used to stand and crouch and I used to jump around the drums. I was happy, man. I must have spent ten years of my life with Keith Jarrett. It was great."

On a cold night in late February when Jarrett first recorded for Impulse—his sole live set for the label—his "American quartet" (Jarrett and Motian, plus Charlie Haden and Dewey Redman) was just over a year old. By the sum of their sideman experience, three of the great jazz visionaries—Miles Davis, Ornette Coleman, and Bill Evans—were all represented, and it meshed musically and personally. "I remember how much fun it was to play with the band," Motian adds. "Everyone got along, everyone played what they wanted to play. Those live tunes went on and on and on! To play something that long and be consistent and have something grow as a piece of music is great. That was happening every night."

That night in Manhattan's Village Vanguard, Jarrett's quartet included a guest artist—literally. "Danny Johnson is a painter and was a big fan of Keith's, but he was not a musician. It was Keith's idea. I'd look to my left and see him sitting on the floor next to me, playing these little bells and chimes. I never knew if he was sitting down because he was insecure about being there or what [laughs]."

Meanwhile, producer Ed Michel kept himself warm in the recording truck parked fifteen steps above the Vanguard's basement room, on Seventh Avenue South. "I wanted to be down in the club but I wanted to listen to what was going on the tape. And for a room that seems all wrong acoustically —the ceiling is too low, it's laid out funny—you can make really nice recordings there. It's one of those rooms that musicians like to be in. It affects them." ("I play different in a basement from in an attic," Jarrett said once. "These are unconscious influences that are inescapable.")

"No matter where you are—in the audience or playing—it sounds good," agrees Motian, who has recorded in the cramped club over a forty-year span. When he speaks to the audience on the performance tape, the drummer notes, "Keith tells the people not to be quiet, but to listen to the sound of the room. I enjoyed playing there more than the other places we played, like the large concert halls."

"I don't know if music like that had been played in the Vanguard before. Hearing it now I thought there was a big Japanese influence. After our tours over there—one in '72 and later in '74—I think some of that creeped into the music: Keith playing flute and all the percussion going on really gave it a Japanese flavor.

"It's interesting because the original LP I had doesn't include a lot of stuff; a lot of it's edited. They cut out some of Haden's bass solos, and [the original LP] never included Dewey's playing clarinet on 'Roads Traveled, Roads Veiled,' with Keith playing soprano [saxophone]. That was rare . . . but we were doing a *lot* of stuff—a lot of spontaneous improvisation, taking a lot of chances, and it all seemed to work. No matter what we did it sounded great. I'm surprised how good it still sounds."

What of Jarrett's chiding the audience?

"I kind of know what he felt—and I agree with him. There was a lot of spontaneous things happening and you don't want to be interrupted because it just keeps happening.

"Normally he wouldn't talk much. One time we were playing in Hamburg, and there was a pit in front of the stage for the photographers and the cameras were just clicking away. Suddenly Keith stopped and told them to get the hell out of there. Then he picked up *exactly* where he left off. Amazing."

"I remember Gato's first record," says Backer. "Over time, I think *Chapter One* sold close to 100,000 records! With titles like that, we built up the label successfully from a sales point of view, and the press was very much behind our signings."

Some artists, benefiting less from the label association than others, were unaware of Impulse's ability to profit from its range of releases. "At one point," Michel recalls, "Dewey Redman said to me, 'Ahh, what difference does it make? All those Impulse records, you could do whatever you wanted to, because they were operating it as a tax write-off.' I said, 'No, they *are* making plenty of money at it! If they weren't, they wouldn't let me make the records.'"

A change in the media certainly helped. Michel adds, "For about two years you could hear anything on the radio. I remember being in Colorado driving on vacation, and turning on a radio, hearing an Albert Ayler record and thinking, 'Wow!'"

Backer agrees that Impulse's second golden age was indeed golden—and brief. "Over all, from a [sales] volume and billing point of view, this was quite a successful period, and it lasted two or three years. But what happens with companies that have a pop division is, they run through cycles. If the cycle goes down, the top people feel the pressure to make up for the pop shortfalls, and so you feel it in the jazz end."

Much of Impulse's success was due to the respective energies of Backer, directed promotionally outward, and Michel, studio bound and production focused. "With Steve and Ed," Dennis Lavinthal remembers, "there was a real passion about the music, and I bought into their passion because I respected them. I kind of took up their cause."

. . . AND CRASHES

As 1974 wore on, it was clear that Steely Dan, Jim Croce, and Chaka Khan (with her group, Rufus) were ABC's sole hitmakers, and were pulling the company along. But together they could not offset the overextension of resources and chronic mismanagement that its other labels were suffering at the time, including multi-million-dollar contracts for superstar artists whose output never returned the investment. Part of the blame, according to Phil Kurnit, lay with ABC corporate back in New York City.

> They saw records as becoming a billion-dollar industry in the U.S. [and] said to ABC, "Do all the things you can to expand the record division and be as aggressive as possible." Lasker ran with that. For example, Lasker bought a lot of distributors so ABC really had a branch distribution system [by the mid-seventies]. They had only a little fragment of it under Newton.

Lasker began looking to import hit-producing formulas from outside the company. He began pestering Backer about a sales-topping jazz label run by the man who, ironically, had founded Impulse.

"By 1974, we were going through the down cycle," Backer says. "They were cutting their losses. Pharoah Sanders was the best-paid artist at Impulse at the time—his contract was not renewed. The pressure to equal the success of Creed Taylor at CTI put a different spin on my being able to move forward at the pace that I wanted to. I loved CTI's records—Freddie Hubbard's *Red Clay,* Grover Washington Jr.'s stuff—it was highly produced and highly glossed. The packaging was the Impulse idea taken to the extreme, but the artistry and the production work was different than everybody else in jazz at that point. CTI was the high point of the entire fusion situation."

Taylor's winning formula had been to recruit a tight cadre of jazz veterans (Milt Jackson, Stanley Turrentine, Hank Crawford, Hubert Laws, Ron Carter) with an updated repertoire of "standards" (well-known rock and funk melodies) and employ pop production standards (and budget), adding string arrangements and the like. CTI's unabashed pop sensibility earned critical reproach yet solid sales, and eventually caught Lasker's attention.

> I remember one meeting specifically, because Jay had a way of mispronouncing artists' names, and so he started by saying, "You know what, Steve? Creed Taylor is really doing well—I should have listened to you, we should have signed that Chuck Corea and Stanley Turpentine" [laughs]. I said, "Yeah, I guess we should've, Jay."

But the writing was on the wall: for the first time in the label's history, ABC brass was looking to influence the general direction of Impulse.

Before 1974 ended, Steve Backer departed ABC to pursue a leading jazz role at former CBS Records president Clive Davis's newly formed Arista Records, striking the art-commerce balance anew with a wider view than his acoustic-based approach at Impulse. He was successful almost immediately.

CRYSTALS

Sam Rivers / *Crystals* / Impulse ASD-9286
DATE RECORDED: March 4, 1974
DATE RELEASED: September 1974
PRODUCER: Ed Michel

Of the most challenging titles on the Impulse imprint—say, John Coltrane's *Ascension* or *Live in Japan,* or Albert Ayler's *Live in Greenwich Village*—Sam Rivers's second album offers the most variety, with music that can be dark and disturbing, then gushing and elegant. It's the title in his catalog that first truly celebrated Rivers the composer, arranged as a random "best of" from his extensive songbook at the time. And it's the recording that, for Rivers, immediately brings to mind a major relocation motivated by the need to find musicians who could play his own compositions.

"As far as *Crystals* goes, I moved to New York in '64 right after I did the tour with Miles Davis, because there were more musicians available who could rehearse and perform my music—that's the main reason I moved. I could have over fifty musicians ready [but] musicians in Boston were all busy."

Rivers began composing in 1955, eight years after moving to Massachusetts from Oklahoma to attend the Boston Conservatory. He developed his style on his own, absorbing music from the swing era to the days of bebop and beyond. To him, playing free seemed inevitable, yet not to the point of discarding what had gone before.

"My going into the avant-garde was not a jump. It was very gradual, because I learned everything I could about traditional music and only then did I evolve. Most musicians stay in the tradition, or they perform the avant-garde. I am good in both, as far as being able to improvise over harmonic structures. I was fortunate to be in both camps."

Crystals stands as a worthy career retrospective for Rivers, featuring compositions written over a fifteen-year span, and also as evidence of the wisdom of his move to New York: the album cover lists a staggering sixty-six musicians somehow involved in the creation of the recording. Among the better-known names—many of whom would take on leadership roles in the continuing avant-garde scene—were saxophonists Hammiet Bluiett, Anthony Braxton, and John Stubblefield; brass players Howard Johnson, Ahmed Abdullah, and Marvin Peterson; and drummers Andrew Cyrille and Billy Hart.

The album's six tracks combine written and improvised sections, urgency and modernity, and include a personal breakthrough for Rivers. " 'Tranquility' was the first atonal thing I wrote, to see how it worked. I mean, really no form, no melodies or lines, an open kind of a thing. It was all pretty much sound. From that I went on to more dense and open things. That, I would say, is my favorite track on the album."

Rivers admits to another reason behind that choice. "All the compositions were forty-five-minute compositions but had to be cut down to seven or nine minutes," he remembers. "The only one that was left as is was 'Tranquility.' The others were, like, crushed."

The one-day session required run-throughs to familiarize all with the twists and turns in Rivers's uncommon charts. "Yes, we had to rehearse—the music was all written so I could have had symphony musicians. And it wasn't my first time; I had experience with large bands. I think Ed Michel didn't have any idea what I was doing with the music, but the studio experience was very helpful, supportive. He was there because he believed in me."

Crystals reflects one perspective of Rivers's outlook on jazz: "I believe that jazz music that is written is background for improvisation—that's most important." And yet the composer made ample room for exceptions; his liner notes describe a lengthy 120-bar section, a fully composed atonal steeplechase, as being the bulk of "Tranquility." "I'm not sure you can really call it a 'jazz composition,'" he notes. "I mean, 'jazz composition' means there's improvisation involved."

The titles of the other tunes carry a similar spiritual flavor: "Exultation," "Orb," "Earth Song." Rivers says he randomly chose the tunes to record from over thirty pieces that had benefited from being "performed in the New York area, by groups . . . ranging from sextet to thirty-five musicians."

Within a year of its release, *Crystals* was being hailed as Rivers's "most immediately gripping album" by Robert Palmer in *Down Beat*. "The weight of the sound is reminiscent of the big band 'free jazz' of Sun Ra, but the composer's control is tight throughout," Palmer wrote. "It is implacably logical and rigorously structured."

Rivers offers his own simple review: "The music is clear, you know. Genuine and clear, like a crystal."

> I went to meet with [Davis] about starting a jazz division with him, and we came to terms. It seemed this would be a very aggressive thrust into the marketplace, and that I would have complete artistic latitude. I signed [avant-garde saxophonist] Anthony Braxton, and the Brecker Brothers. . . . [Tenor saxophonist] Michael Brecker and Randy [his trumpet-playing brother] added amplification to their instruments, so they were a terrific, qualified sort of fusion band that was immensely successful. They sold a quarter-million albums by their second album.

Meanwhile, back at ABC, Ed Michel continued his various studio efforts. His duties at BluesWay had crested in 1973 with the release of a whopping thirty-four albums over a two-year period, spurred by a production and licensing deal with former Vee Jay Records president Al Smith. Included were a plethora of blues musicians like Sunnyland Slim, produced by Smith; others, like Earl Hooker, Charles Brown, and Jimmy Witherspoon, produced by Michel; and John Lee Hooker, whose rock-blues efforts were overseen by Bill Szymczyk. There were also best-of's from BluesWay's first wave, plus reissues from the recently acquired catalogs of Vee Jay, featuring Jimmy Reed, and the Houston-based Duke/Peacock, with classic recordings by Bobby Bland, Junior Parker, and other R&B stars.

For Impulse, Michel balanced a year's worth of new titles by the label's leading artists (Jarrett, Barbieri, Klemmer, White, and Rivers) with in-the-can recordings from Sanders (*Village of the Pharoahs* [AS-9254], *Elevation* [AS-9261], *Love in Us All* [AS-9280]) and Shepp (*Kwanza* [AS-9262]) and a final psychedelic jazz disc from guitarist Howard Roberts (*Equinox Express Elevator* [AS-9299]). There were more best-of titles (*Re-Evaluation* two-fers on Albert Ayler, Coleman Hawkins, Yusef Lateef, and Ahmad Jamal) and the increasingly popular Coltrane gems from the vault: *Live in Japan* [AS-9246-2], *Africa/Brass Sessions, Volume 2* [AS-9272-3], and *Interstellar Space* [AS-9277].

"I knew there was more unissued stuff when I put out *Interstellar Space*—which got everybody really excited," Michel states. "But I didn't last much past that."

As Backer had felt the winds shifting, so Lasker's turn came to be buffeted. Leonard Goldenson, focused primarily on the day-to-day affairs of ABC's TV network, had left his position as chairman, leaving his assistant Marty Pompadour to deal with the record division. Spying the decrease in ABC Records' bottom line, Pompadour had taken the bold move of creating an office above Lasker: his choice was the accountant and business manager Jerry Rubenstein.

"Pompadour felt that Lasker was old hat," Phil Kurnit recalls. "He was enamored with Rubenstein, with whom he did a lot of business. Rubenstein was a very bright guy—and a C.P.A. He had something to do with Crosby, Stills, Nash and Young; Poco; and had been handling everything for Mama Cass, who had already passed away. Lasker said, 'You're in breach of contract' and walked out. It was a surprising move for Pompadour to make and it was a surprising move for Lasker to make, which proved to be Lasker's undoing in the end. And it proved Pompadour's undoing—he ultimately was out, and a large part of it was because of what happened with the record division."

The opening weeks of 1975 saw the news go public in *Billboard,* while the effect blew hard through ABC's offices.

"The whole company flushed," reports Lavinthal. "It really happened when Jerry Rubenstein came in. Here was a guy who knew very little about the music business but had a lot of clients as a business manager. This is not a story that hasn't been repeated ad infinitum in the music business over the last thirty years. Corporate guys bring in non-music people to run the record companies, and they toilet them because it's not a business that you can run with M.B.A.'s and accountants. It's a feel business."

In a matter of weeks, all ABC staff linked to Lasker were let go in a regime change.

"Jay Lasker was out, a new team was in, and I was one of Jay's boys so I was *hasta la vista,* but I wouldn't leave the studios. I was working fifty-hour days!" remembers Michel with a laugh. "I finally had to come back to the building for something and they found me to tell me I was fired. People said, 'If they knew where you were you would have been fired six weeks ago.'"

Michel remembers that he was let go sometime in early 1975. The House That Trane Built—as an active enterprise operating with the same consistent vision—effectively ended, awaiting tenants and direction from a new landlord named Rubenstein. Goldenson and ABC's shareholders would soon be forced to divest ABC of its record division. Michel and Lavinthal would continue on their respective paths in the music business. Lasker would jump to the helm at other labels, including Ariola and Motown.

Phil Kurnit sums it up: "Lasker survived, ABC ultimately didn't. Where Impulse figured into any of this, who knows?"

INTERSTELLAR SPACE

John Coltrane / *Interstellar Space* / Impulse AS-9277

DATE RECORDED: February 22, 1967

DATE RELEASED: September 1974

PRODUCER: Bob Thiele

The way [Rashied Ali] plays allows the soloist maximum freedom. I can really choose just about any direction at just about any time in the confidence that it will be compatible with what he's doing. . . . You see, he's laying down multi-directional rhythms all the time.

—JOHN COLTRANE

He was telling me that I was playing stuff like multi-directional rhythms, which I didn't have a clue as to what that was.

—RASHIED ALI

Saxophonist David S. Ware, as devoted a Coltrane acolyte as there is, is nevertheless a realist. It was one thing when Coltrane left behind the standard theme-solos-theme jazz structure. But, says Ware, when he chose to forgo regular rhythm, "when he started messing with that multi-directional time, Coltrane lost a lot of people.

"As long as you keep steady one, two, three, four—or one, two, three, four, five, six, or whatever it is—and you have cats superimposing their improvisations over that, then everything is fine.

You can get almost as avant-garde as you want to be, as long as you keep that steady pulse, right? But once you break pulse, I guarantee you, you're going to lose half of your people."

Interstellar Space, Coltrane's final studio recording, is a veritable sketchbook among larger, more complex canvases like *Meditations* and *Expression*. It features six saxophone-drums duets, all named after planets: pared-down, ecstatic performances that to some unveil the hard, analytic skeleton within the stormy flow of energy Coltrane's music had become by 1967.

"These duets are the ideal starting point for the listener who wants to understand Coltrane's last music—it's so easy to hear what he's doing," writes Lewis Porter in his Coltrane biography. "Each one begins with a theme, [then] encompasses some kind of working up to a climax followed by a calming down, which leads to a recapitulation."

One of the arguments made against avant-garde jazz, especially of Coltrane's variety, is that it is so complex that it can't be appreciated without an academic understanding of harmonic theory. Yet, as Porter argues, the range and clarity of emotion in a work like *Interstellar Space* are undeniable. He devotes a full dozen pages to the album, writing that Coltrane "succeeded precisely *because* he gave up chord changes and the restriction of a steady beat, in creating a seamless musical construction, not divisible into choruses."

Other noteworthy writers, after discovering a balance of order and improvised exploration, have focused on *Interstellar Space*. "For all its intimidating reputation as an explosion of chaos," writes Ben Ratliff, the album "is actually rather astringently planned." "This last, unfinished stage of Coltrane's music is no period of unrelieved disintegration," John Litweiler maintains. "The implications of this are enormous, for Coltrane now internalizes responsibility for structure; it's possible that future developments of his capacities of organization might have resulted in the major advances of his music."

Simply put, in the logical, repetitive use of a variety of musical motives and devices on the compositions that comprise *Interstellar Space*, the beginning of a vocabulary for a new musical language is strongly suggested, one Coltrane was planning to explore further when death ended his journey that summer. His son Ravi is one of many saxophonists—Charles Lloyd, Michael Brecker, Dave Liebman, Kenny Garrett, Joe Lovano, Charles Gayle, and David S. Ware are among the others—who would argue the case. "I believe he was reaching for a universal language through sound, trying to call together the most basic and divine qualities that are common to all human experience," Ravi Coltrane says. "It always kills me how people say John lost his mind after 1964. When they get freaked out by the exterior elements, they're missing a vast inner detail."

Another is Rashied Ali: "You can just about tell what that music was headed for—he had a handle on it. It really told you the direction he was headed in. That record [*Interstellar Space*] was one of the last things that he did. It's really something that has to be listened to and something that has to be felt. Musicians are just starting to look into the playing of this kind of a thing now."

VOL. 2
DANCING SUNBEAM
VANGUARD TAPES
NEVER BE ANOTHER YOU
WITH STANLEY TURRENTINE/BOB CRENSHAW/
THE DEDICATION SERIES/VOL. IV
DEDICATION SERIES/VOL. VI

CHAPTER 8

THE LIVES OF A LABEL; THE TENOR OF A TIME (1975–PRESENT)

I believe one can be exposed to it and respond immediately, you really don't have to know the history. I really was not that familiar with Coltrane before I met him . . . but the way it came about with me makes me think that there's hope for a lot of people.

—Bob Thiele

Historical context can mean so much. What had been the New Thing was, by the mid-seventies, much less avant. Impulse, when it was perceived as angry and in the path of Coltrane, delivered music and message that impressed and astounded. Change in music is inevitable and its velocity in the jazz realm considerable. So it's impressive that Impulse, in decline, remained vibrant and influential. And it's astounding that it proves increasingly fresh to many who, in 1975, were not yet born.

That year, The House That Trane Built was refitted—new talent, new direction—by the same man who produced John Coltrane's very first album as a leader, for Prestige in 1957. Esmond Edwards was a twenty-year industry veteran when ABC hired him. "Impulse Records, quiet for the past few months, is ready to come with five new releases," announced *Billboard* that August. The magazine noted the hiring of Edwards, who it said was expected to "mount a stronger push into contemporary mainstream jazz."

It was true. CTI's recent model of success in jazz—adored by Jay Lasker and avoided by Steve Backer—was an approach long considered by Edwards.

> I admired Blue Note: they made pretty straight-ahead records that always had that little one tune—"Song for My Father," whatever—that appealed to a broader audience. And Creed Taylor and CTI, with his Hubert Laws records and so forth, which I thought were finely crafted recordings. I never had the budget and facility to do that kind of thing. But my feeling was that the artists he recorded had already proven their jazz capabilities and if surrounding them with more "commercial" settings would increase their ability to find the wider audience they deserved—fine.

What Impulse had done in the past, Edwards believed, was limited to "hard-core fans, going to see Archie Shepp or Albert Ayler. Most of my prior record production experience was in a 'groove jazz' mode that probably appealed to a different audience—Gene Ammons and the Hammond organ groups, for example."

Edwards joined a company undergoing belt-tightening measures. The face of Impulse had long ago begun to change; orange-and-black spines were just a memory. By the time Edwards arrived, the final vestige of the classic Impulse identity—the gatefold—had vanished as well. The palpable spirit of Coltrane, and support for jazz in general, had all but disappeared. Edwards remembers: "People weren't running around with banners saying, 'Let's do something with John!' and I certainly didn't devote a lot of time to delving into the Coltrane catalog. However, I had always felt that John had a special, personal approach to the ballad. That's why we did that compilation, *The Gentle Side of John Coltrane.*"

"It was a great concept on his part. It's still in print to this day, which is pretty remarkable for a compilation," says Michael Cuscuna, whose initial duty with the Impulse catalog was to assemble and annotate the ballad-focused double album. "But it was something that really struck a chord with people."

Impulse Label 'Awakens' With An Ambitious Autumn Program

By BOB KIRSCH

LOS ANGELES—Impulse Records, quiet for the past few months, is ready to come with five releases next month featuring both established and new artists and will continue to sign artists, according to Esmond Edwards, who took over most of the Impulse production chores following the recent departure of Ed Michel.

Edwards says the ABC-distributed jazz label will "be signing sev-

jority of the upcoming Impulse releases will be new.

"I'm kind of familiarizing myself with the ABC Studios at the moment, but we expect to be going full steam within a few weeks. We've got five releases on the way and I will be doing much of the producing."

Impulse has long been recognized as one of the outstanding jazz labels,

both from the contemporary artist vantage point and in catalog strength. Under Michel, the label was one of the leaders in avant-garde jazz.

It is expected that Impulse will mount a stronger push into contemporary mainstream jazz while maintaining a Foothold in the avant-garde area.

Edwards, like his predecessors, immediately inherited album projects by artists in mid-contract. "The people that were already on Impulse when I went there represented the past thinking, though I considered them major artists—Keith Jarrett and Sam Rivers," Edwards notes. "They were just about all the artists we had left at the time I joined. It was a pretty small operation."

Esmond Edwards during his Chess Records years, 1972.

Well, a few more. Edwards oversaw Rivers's *Sizzle* [AS-9316]. He produced Jarrett's last four albums: *Mysteries* [ASD-9315], *Shades* [ASD-9322], and the unusual *Byablue* [ASD-9331] and *Bop-Be* [ASD-9334], which came from six sessions in 1975 and 1976, after Jarrett's quartet had in fact disbanded. "I was trying to fulfill my contract to Impulse . . . without being embarrassed by it," the pianist told writer Neil Tesser.

Production budgets, like packaging, were slashed. Nonetheless, Edwards managed to find a few old acquaintances whose music reflected his plans for a funkier, more accessible Impulse. "I met Jimmy Ponder at a session in New York City," says Edwards. "I thought he was a talented, underappreciated guitarist, and signed him. I heard that Sonny Criss, the highly regarded alto saxophonist, was available and signed him. Gloria Lynne was perhaps not a 'jazz singer,' but I liked her distinctive vocal quality. Of course John Handy had to be in this group. I had been a longtime fan. I was pleasantly surprised he wasn't signed."

From 1975 through 1977, Edwards produced a wealth of new titles that defined the label's new identity (listed in the Source Notes section). His signings were relegated to one- or two-off situations. He favored vocalists like Lynne and the baritone-voiced drummer Grady Tate, and was assigned special sessions with artists like keyboardist Les McCann and blues masters Bobby Bland and B.B. King. He pursued a variety of hard-bop free agents, many whom he had known for years, including Ponder, Criss, and trumpeter Blue Mitchell. In an uncanny echo of one of Creed Taylor's first Impulse productions, Edwards signed the five-trombone choir Brass Fever.

But it was Handy's catchy, dance-provoking single "Hard Work"—his first recording for Impulse—that proved the label's last commercial hurrah. "The first thing we did was 'Hard Work,' which was a pretty big

HARD WORK

John Handy / *Hard Work* / Impulse ASD-9314

DATE RECORDED: Early 1976

DATE RELEASED: June 1976

PRODUCER: Esmond Edwards

Been there, done that. It may be a cliché, but it's as accurate a summation as any of alto saxophonist John Handy's sentiment concerning jazz in general, avant-garde in particular. "Believe me, I totally appreciate that style. But I didn't want to go back to playing more artistically inclined music. If I hadn't been offered the chance to play 'Hard Work,' I wouldn't have accepted the money to sign with Impulse. I wouldn't have signed with any jazz label."

In 1975, Handy—then known for his work with Charles Mingus, and as a leader exploring the experimental edge of the jazz scene—had been away from the studio for several years. He had been rethinking music and career. With no apology, he knew he wanted more accessible music that would sell, on a label that felt the same way. "Impulse offered to do it on my terms: to be able to play that kind of music. When other people came to me they expected me to play the jazz thing. Esmond knew what I wanted because we had discussed this through the years."

Esmond Edwards had come a long way to take over Impulse in 1975. His production career had begun firmly on jazz territory, starting with Prestige sessions in the late fifties, before moving to more popular territory, producing Top Forty hits like "The 'In' Crowd" for pianist Ramsey Lewis in '65. By the time he took over the reins at Impulse, his thinking was on the same track as Handy's. "We weren't even going to consider trying to do some of the things I'd done before," Edwards says. "Certainly not some of the things John Coltrane and those guys did."

Edwards had been on staff at Columbia Records in the late sixties when he first worked with Handy, trying to mold a hit single. "In 1969, before I disappeared for a long time, Esmond and I did a 45 with [Bob Dylan's] 'Lay Lady Lay' on one side and [Blood, Sweat & Tears'] 'Spinning Wheel' on the other," Handy remembers. "So he knew that I wanted to play for more people. When I wrote 'Hard Work' I just knew it was going to happen if given a chance."

"It" did happen. Produced by Edwards and released in 1976, "Hard Work" was a surprise radio hit that caught on with its bouncy, hand-clapped groove, and caught ABC off guard. Suddenly, Impulse had its first bona fide best-selling single in fifteen years; Roy Charles's "One Mint Julep" had been the label's last charting single, in 1961.

"It was a runaway hit. They didn't know what to do with it, it came out so fast," Handy remembers. "They couldn't get it to [retail] places in time and they still sold much more than most jazz players could ever imagine."

"Anytime you have a jazz instrumental that is successful you're surprised," Edwards states. "That goes without saying. I think it was an example of the musicianship and the broad scope of his interests, from Louis Jordan all the way to Bird. He was not reluctant to explore any of those areas."

Hard Work's title track pushed sales of the album and exposed Handy's tribute to another alto saxophonist who, in the forties, had sprung to crossover success from jazz roots: "Blues for Louis Jordan."

"I was like ten or eleven when I heard recordings of 'Knock Me a Kiss,' 'Caldonia,' 'Choo Choo Ch'Boogie.' I liked 'I'm Gonna Move to the Outskirts of Town'—great blues sung by Louis Jordan. I knew all those solos because I heard them a lot. I wrote those 'Blues for Louis Jordan' lyrics literally walking out the door to the session. I knew I hit a nerve when I played some places for some older black folks and they would yell, 'Play Louis Jordan!'"

"Hard Work" paid off handsomely for Handy. "I'd always made a decent living playing straight-ahead stuff. But put it this way: I went from a $5,000 contract—that was my first front money from Impulse—to more than a million-dollar contract when I was able to leave them after the second album [*Carnival*]."

Hard Work hit at a time when the first seedlings of what would become smooth jazz were sprouting. Funky and finger-snapping recordings by saxophonist Grover Washington Jr. (*Mister Magic* in 1975) and guitarist George Benson (*Breezin'* in 1976) were selling in numbers far beyond past phenomena like *Bitches Brew*. Gato Barbieri and a number of other jazz innovators, whose music was once edgy and full of creative ferocity like Handy's, were reshaping their recordings with popular appeal in mind.

Handy is matter-of-fact about the lesson he draws from his success. "I played music that could've been on Impulse along with the Coltrane and those guys," he says. "Some of those jazz critics liked that kind of direction, but people didn't give a damn."

John Handy, 1976.

R&B/pop single," says Edwards, emphasizing the saxophonist's unabashed desire to go commercial. Handy had previously been best known as a free-blowing sideman with Charles Mingus in the sixties, and then for his spiritual sax-and-tabla excursions in the early seventies. "John is somewhat in the tradition of Dizzy Gillespie or Cannonball Adderley—he doesn't take himself too seriously. He loves playing, he likes to entertain, so he was already doing his thing and not at all embarrassed by having a hit record."

The sales boon of "Hard Work" was nowhere near enough to improve the lot of Impulse—"Jazz was something that [ABC] did like going to church on the weekend," Edwards says—or save a company locked in a downward financial spiral. "I only went there with a two-year deal, and when my contract was about to expire—when the label was about to expire—that's when ABC was sold to MCA."

MCA was then an already massive entertainment company with a record division known for its pop and rock acts. Negotiations had actually begun in 1977, and were finalized in 1979. Phil Kurnit feels that for ABC corporate, it was a move born of scorn. "They sold it to MCA to say, 'This music business is a dirty business. Everybody in this business is dirty. We're not going to have anything more to do with it. We're not going to let it affect our television revenues and our profitability and all that stuff.'"

The tally for all that Paul Anka and B.B. King and Mamas and Papas and Steppenwolf—and Coltrane?

ABC sold off its record company to MCA for what was then a fire-sale price: $30 million.

ABC . . . MCA . . . GRP . . . UMG . . . VMG . . .

The sequence of corporate initials describes the up-and-down path that brings the Impulse story up to the present. While the recorded legacies of, say, Miles Davis and Dave Brubeck enjoy the benefits that a long-standing label like Columbia Records (now part of Sony BMG Music) can offer, the Impulse catalog has been somewhat of a foster child, bouncing from one parent to another, passing through a number of reissue or reactivation programs. To wit, MCA's reissues in the early eighties were regrettable low-budget LP affairs: wafer-thin, low-grade vinyl; gatefold-less and shoddy reproductions of the original cover art.

Fortunately, that marked a low point, as the pertinent points on the Impulse timeline afterward suggest:

- 1986: In the early, halcyon days of the digital era, MCA's Ricky Schultz re-launched the Impulse name, releasing music by contemporary jazz artists like saxophonist Michael Brecker and pianist Henry Butler, on both LP and CD, featuring a bold new Impulse design scheme that resurrected the label's signature colors. The reactivated label also began producing the first round of Impulse reissues on CD, leaning on Coltrane titles, with LP liner notes reduced to squint-inducing size and less than stellar sound (reflecting the low eight-time sampling digital standard of the day). Of note was *A Tribute to John Coltrane* [MCAD-42122], a special project produced by Bob Thiele in 1987 that featured saxophonists David Murray and Pharoah Sanders with a rhythm section of McCoy Tyner, Cecil McBee, and Roy Haynes. Two years later, a three-volume *Best of Impulse* series briefly appeared on vinyl and digital formats, sporting the titles *The Impulse Collection* [MCA2-8026], *The Feeling of Jazz* [MCA2-8028], and *Fire into Music* [MCA2-8032].

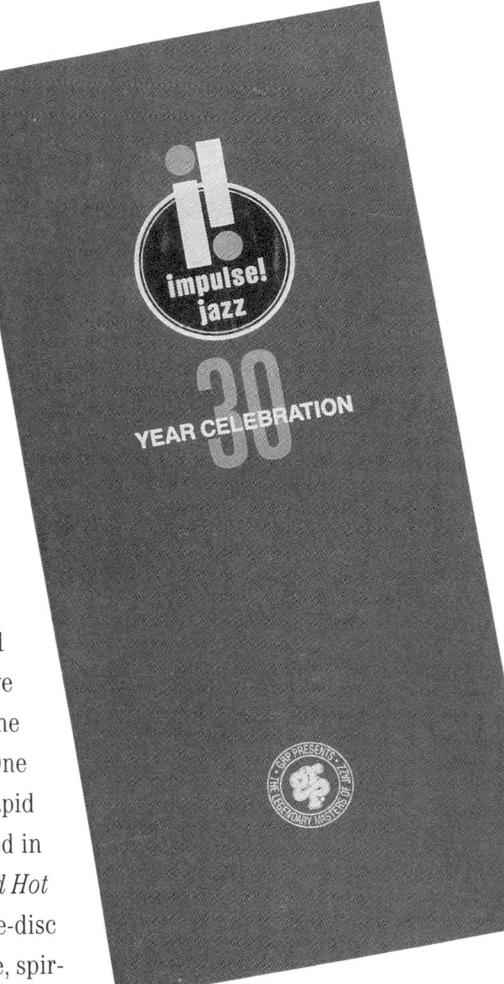

- 1990: MCA absorbed GRP, the jazz label founded by composer-keyboardist David Grusin and producer Larry Rosen, and the fortune of Impulse continued to improve. GRP took over all of MCA's jazz efforts, keeping Michael Cuscuna aboard to continue the Impulse reissue campaign. Digital sound noticeably improved, as did the packaging.

  Two releases of this period merit mention: The two-disc *Impulse Jazz: A 30-Year Celebration* [GRD-2-101] in 1991 marked the label's anniversary, joining obvious must-have tracks (Oliver Nelson's "Stolen Moments," Sanders's "The Creator Has a Master Plan," Coltrane and Hartman's "My One and Only Love") with hidden gems (Shirley Scott's "Rapid Shave," Gato Barbieri's "Cuando Vuela a Tu Lado"). Produced in 1994 by the AIDS-awareness group Red Hot Organization, *Red Hot on Impulse* [GRD-151] was another well-designed double-disc title that celebrated the label by offering its most memorable, spir-

itually focused tunes in an Impulse-inspired package. Red Hot simultaneously released *Stolen Moments* [GRD-9794], a double-disc exploration of the jazz/hip-hop overlap of the day, mixing reissued tracks by Alice Coltrane and Oliver Nelson alongside new recordings—and a few collaborations—by jazzers like Branford Marsalis, Pharoah Sanders, Ron Carter, and Joshua Redman, and such hip-hoppers as Pharcyde, MC Solaar, and Michael Franti.

- 1995–99: GRP expanded its use of the Impulse name, releasing new recordings by veterans, some already associated with the label (McCoy Tyner and Michael Brecker) and some not (Horace Silver), as well as a new generation of jazz players: pianist and vocalist Diana Krall, pianists Danilo Perez and Eric Reed, saxophonist Donald Harrison, guitarist Russell Malone—even the acid-jazz group Groove Collective. Simultaneously, Impulse became the home for the first releases of never-before-heard historic recordings (the Duke Ellington Trio in 1972) and reissues of ABC jazz recordings, many produced by Bob Thiele (Jimmy Rushing, Johnny Hartman, Betty Carter, Shirley Horn).

Thiele was brought in to help oversee a new slate of well-promoted reissues, and the press responded, celebrating the label "that dragged jazz into the era of Black Power." It was during this period that Impulse regained a signature look: recovering its orange-and-black spine, featuring removable booklets tucked in a center pocket, in a new, non-jewel-cased format. Hollis King, in-house designer for the Verve Music Group (current owner of Impulse), deserves credit for the label's modern-day appearance.

When we looked to redesign Impulse for CD format [in 1995], I was amazed at how well the old design held up. But there were two or three different versions of the Impulse design out there. The original LP covers were cardboard, and I wanted to keep that feel; they were gatefold, and I wanted that too; and I wanted to keep the orange and black, and modify the proportion of the bullet logo. Then I made a CD package with two equal spines, which didn't exist at the time, and that's how we have the Digipack we have today. One of the biggest problems for designers is how to get the ego out of the way, you know—I wanted to bring it forward but remain true to the spirit of the old package.

- 2000 to the present: A dizzying series of mergers in the late 1990s created the global media group Vivendi Universal, and effectively joined MCA with PolyGram, another major label sitting atop a jazz-rich archive. All music divisions in the conglomerate were grouped under the rubric UMG (Universal Music Group), which in turn placed all jazz-related activity in the hands of VMG: the Verve Music Group.

By the millennium, Impulse tapes were sharing archive space with historical Verve, Decca, Commodore, Mercury, EmArcy, Chess, and GRP recordings. VMG put its major living artists (Diana Krall, Wayne Shorter) on the Verve imprint, while Impulse became (primarily) a reissue label, run by a business that depends (primarily) on reissues.

"It can range from roughly sixty to eighty percent, depending on the business year," states Michael Kauffman, Verve's senior sales vice president. "When we don't have a big release, a Diana Krall or a George Benson, the catalog sales are going to be higher." Accordingly, Verve makes sure its leading catalog titles—led by Impulse—are marketed with as high a profile as possible. In 2000, Kauffman reports, "We initiated what we call our top ten Desert Island discs. There's Ella and Louis, *Getz/Gilberto,* Count Basie, and Billie Holiday. But the only person on the list twice is Coltrane: Coltrane and Hartman and *A Love Supreme*."

Beyond reissues, Verve has arrived at the idea of reserving Impulse for Coltrane-linked projects; hence *McCoy Tyner Plays John Coltrane* [314-589-183-2], a Village Vanguard set from 2001, and Alice Coltrane's *Translinear Light* [B-0002191-02], her 2004 return to commercial recording after a twenty-six-year hiatus, produced by her saxophonist son Ravi.

Beyond CDs, how else can Impulse's impact be measured? The use of various albums—especially Coltrane's—as primers in a wide range of music schools (Berklee, various conservatories and universities) is long established; increasingly common are the transcription books that publishers like Jamie Aebersold Jazz have created to accompany them. Then there is that phenomenon of the digital age: for fifteen years and counting, ever since hip-hop culture and the jazz tradition began a creative dialogue, samples of various Impulse tracks have found their way onto popular albums by a number of rappers and deejays. Some have been cleared for usage legitimately, others less formally. Some not at all.

According to an informal survey, almost a hundred hip-hop tunes have sampled Impulse gems, including tracks by such heavy hitters as Nas (using Ahmad Jamal's "I Love Music" on his "The World Is Yours"); Common (using Michael White's "Go with the Flow" on "Can I Borrow a Dollar?"); and the Pharcyde (using Johnny Hartman's "Autumn Serenade" on "Pack the Pipe"). Mixers and producers seem to favor Jamal, Pharoah Sanders, and especially John Klemmer; but they've learned to steer clear of John Coltrane. "There have been situations in the past where licenses were granted, but not in recent years," says Marilyn McLeod, who runs Jowcol, the Coltrane family office.

The family's direct involvement with the Coltrane catalog has led to an active and productive cooperation with VMG. In 2001, Alice Coltrane wrote the liner notes to a single-CD collection of her husband's inspirational numbers titled *Spiritual* [314-589-099-2]; the following year, Ravi conceived and sequenced a four-disc thematic package called *Legacy* [314-589-295-2]. Verve's commitment remains steady: the label keeps most of its vintage material in print, at times even licensing material outside its catalog for release, such as Coltrane's last recorded performance, at the Olatunji Cultural Center in New York City in 1967, and his only live performance of *A Love Supreme*.

When asked of Impulse's relative standing saleswise in the company's overall reissue picture, most Verve executives demur, unwilling to grant top-dog status to any one artist, album, or label. Yet a peek at Verve's corporate offices in Manhattan offers its own comment. On the walls of one of the company's boardrooms, overlooking sleek furniture and ultra-modern sound and video equipment, are five portraits and one gold album. All celebrate one artist alone: John Coltrane.

THE CATALOG DEVELOPER

The dust of the ABC buyout had not yet settled when MCA called in Michael Cuscuna to figure out what the company would be acquiring, and what catalog development would be possible.

"When I first went through the Impulse vaults in 1978, they had been very mistreated," Cuscuna remembers. "I was able to find a lot of good Coltrane that was still unissued, and of course I tore the place apart trying to find what I thought was the entire alternate version of *A Love Supreme* suite, with Archie Shepp and [bassist] Art Davis, but found nothing."

> Some session reels survive: for instance, the actual outtake reels from '65 [from the sessions for *The John Coltrane Quartet Plays, Transition,* and others]. But other session tapes didn't. They may have been just thrown away to make space in a warehouse somewhere, or mislaid. I would guess that they weren't stolen, because they would've surfaced in the European bootlegs if they had been.

Undaunted, Cuscuna plowed ahead, using the most pristine material available, and the Impulse catalog was developed through the eighties and nineties. Mastering engineer Erick Labson, a two-decade veteran with the Impulse catalog, still handles the analog-to-digital transfers.

"I found it very frustrating, since the original tapes are no longer available to us," Labson says. "We had to work from second-, sometimes third-generation masters. Especially in analog format [like reel-to-reel tapes], every additional copy is another generation and it introduces some sort of distortion, minor as it may be. So you get more tape hiss, and you lose clarity and detail with each subsequent tape copy. Coming off the original master is almost always the best, if you want the most original-sounding source."

That said, Cuscuna marvels at how the music on the earliest existing tape still shines through its multi-generational condition. He says he has found that Rudy Van Gelder, who engineered a majority of Impulse's sixties recordings, deserves full credit. "With anything that was recorded at Van Gelder's [studio] there's the great sigh of relief, even if it's a second-generation copy. With Rudy's stuff, it's not like you have to work to make it sound better; all you have to do is tie your hands behind your back and not fuck it up. It's that easy."

Rudy Van Gelder was, and remains, an important part of the Impulse story; he is called on to remaster recordings he originally engineered, and to help keep track of session tapes. He reports that immediately after Coltrane's death in 1967, Bob Thiele collected all the saxophonist's recordings still stored in his studio and apparently delivered them to Alice Coltrane.

> During those . . . sessions, [Thiele] had asked me to run two tapes simultaneously (big company, big budget). After Coltrane died, Bob came to the studio and said, "Rudy, I'm sorry, I have to pick up the tapes [safety copies of the Coltrane session masters]." I gave him the tapes and thought no more of it. . . . Now, years later, I realize that what he did was protect Coltrane's music. . . . The simultaneous originals I made for him are still here. . . . Thanks, Bob.

Certain masters apparently never made it to Mrs. Coltrane. Session tapes that yielded the *Coltrane* and *Ballads* albums remained in Thiele's possession until he donated them to his old high school, New Jersey's Lawrenceville School, in the early nineties. The school passed the reel-to-reel tapes to the Institute for Jazz Studies at Rutgers University, which returned them to the Verve Music Group for later reissue.

Arguably the one person most familiar with how different labels approached organizing and cataloging their respective tape vaults is reissue producer Michael Cuscuna. "The session reels from two 1962 sessions? It's a comment on his disorganization," he says. "Under no circumstances was Thiele stealing tapes. Most major companies, not Blue Note or Prestige, but if Columbia or ABC-Paramount went in to do a session, they'd run two machines because they can afford the tape costs. Those reels Thiele had were B reels from the second machine. How they ended up in his office, then in his apartment, and then in the stuff he sent to his high school, I have no idea."

The discovery of these session masters led to the release of "Deluxe Editions" of *Coltrane* and *Ballads* in 2002. "But in '98," reports Ken Druker, Verve's head of catalog development, "we put out the popular Classic Quartet box with a great booklet and eight discs and called it *The Complete Impulse Studio Recordings*. So after we released the Deluxe Editions, of course the e-mails started: Why did we hold [this material] back in '98? Do we know what the word 'complete' means? [Laughs.] You can't win."

More recently a much-publicized jazz auction was held in New York City in February 2005. The effort by the auction house to attract appropriate and worthy items mysteriously turned up thirty-three Coltrane session tapes. The tape boxes were marked "Impulse" and included such long-lost recordings as the complete session of the sextet version of *A Love Supreme* from December 10, 1964. Other sessions included in these tapes: the complete Coltrane-Hartman date; the full *Coltrane* album session (with even more outtakes than found on Thiele's reel); an unreleased quartet session from the day before the Coltrane-Hartman album was recorded; and unused studio tracks for *Impressions*.

In a 1971 interview, Thiele revealed how these tapes left the Impulse library in the first place: "Just before leaving ABC I made a tape copy of everything that [John and I] recorded, and had the company give it to Alice Coltrane. I knew that people forget, tapes are even lost, you know the damnedest things can happen at record companies. So I turned everything over to Alice and let her at least take care of the editing. She has time, she has a studio in her house, so she has really been going through everything I recorded with him."

How these recordings ended up with Coltrane's Philadelphia relatives (with whom he remained in touch after starting a new family with Alice) may never be clear. But neither is the idea that anything inappropriate occurred. As of this writing, unsurprisingly, Verve is in the process of re-securing the tapes, with an eye toward future issue of the performances.

A MILLION VIBRATIONS

The majority of those who steered Impulse along its forty-year course—Esmond Edwards, Steve Backer, Ed Michel, Creed Taylor—have settled into a life of semi-repose.

Taylor keeps an office in Manhattan where he is currently working on a number of jazz audio-video projects that explore new formats like high-definition TV. Backer, also in the New York City area, continues his activities, recently helming the revived Savoy record label, and is called on intermittently to lend his expertise to catalog projects, often teaming with Michael Cuscuna (the two worked together on the *Classic Quartet* box set for Verve). Michel, living in Hawaii, is also sought after time and again for various reissue projects and, in a professional full circle, recently returned to gigging as a bassist, playing with local bop-base groups.

Cuscuna is based in Connecticut, licensing material from various jazz catalogs for his own jazz imprint, Mosaic, and continues to be the man the sun sees least. Hours in tape archives and studios assure his reign as the top hands-on reissue specialist. Edwards calls northern California home, and enjoys a life far from the studio and the music business, yet is still generous and helpful when an inquisitive researcher comes knocking.

Until the day he died from kidney failure in 1996, Bob Thiele never stopped hustling or listening. Through the seventies and in later years that were less fruitful, he kept Flying Dutchman afloat and finally sold the label to his final American distributor, RCA. He managed to secure funding for a series of labels well into the nineties, with colorful names like Doctor Jazz and Red Baron. Occasionally, as on the Red Baron album *Sunrise, Sunset* in 1991, he revisited one of Coltrane's ideas, forming his own "classic quartet" as "the Bob Thiele Collective," a group featuring David Murray in the saxophone chair with pianist John Hicks, bassist Cecil McBee, and drummer Andrew Cyrille.

Thiele's son, Bob Jr., recalls that as he began to pursue his own career in songwriting in the late seventies, his father remained ever-curious, with an ear for the avant-garde edge. "He took me one night to see [alto saxophonist] Arthur Blythe. Arthur was playing free jazz. And at least commercially it seemed like it had little if any relevance to me. But I remember nine months or a year later when his record came out, every single review I read was incredible—they were all saying how it was one of the most important jazz records to come along since the age of Coltrane. And I was like, how did he know? That was his gift. He heard something in Arthur Blythe that I certainly didn't."

When John Coltrane passed away in 1967, he left behind a family, an increasing circle of followers, and a golden trove of recordings that still helps pay the bills for the company with the good fortune to own the Impulse catalog. His musical influence is pervasive and easy to mark, inside the jazz circle and beyond.

To Bob Thiele and many who crossed Coltrane's path, he was a catalyst who opened up a door where none had been before. "He carried me on into jazz music. I think I would have just faded away—I was a swing cat, you know," Thiele stated a few years before he died. "Even to this day I thank Coltrane for being."

The Impulse story survives well beyond recording dates and catalog numbers, and the Thiele-Coltrane relationship had implications that outlasted them both. In the context of the music business, it represents that occasional, magical occurrence: one man setting aside preconceptions, listening with fresh ears, and growing from the experience.

"I just became more and more excited about making records—all kinds of records," Thiele said in the mid-eighties. "I listen to Coltrane, and I still listen to Bix Beiderbecke, and I listen to Louis Armstrong's Hot Five, I listen to everything. Coltrane just opened it up."

Coltrane was one who led by example and suggestion—never by directive. His way was not to show *the* way ahead, but one possibility, inspiring all to their own paths. "Seek not to follow in the footsteps of men of old," wrote the Japanese poet Matsuo Bashō in the seventeenth century. "Seek what they sought."

I hold to a feeling: had Coltrane been able to appreciate all the sounds Impulse eventually housed, he would have (1) been pleased to have been part of that singular, variegated spectrum, and (2) agreed with the poet and shrugged off any credit. "I don't think people are necessarily copying me," he said in 1964, the year he created music that earned him two Grammy nominations and gained induction into *Down Beat*'s Hall of Fame. "People reach the same end by making a similar discovery at the same time."

That same year, Coltrane claimed on the cover of *A Love Supreme* that "one thought can produce millions of vibrations." Time has proved him correct: his own ideas and recordings have vibrated in that very quantity. The House That Trane Built—as a record label, a musical approach, and a more inclusive way of hearing the world—continues to stand.

The legacy lives on: a 1998 magazine advertisement that says it all.

EPILOGUE

TRANSLINEAR LIGHT

Alice Coltrane / *Translinear Light* / Impulse B-0002191-02
DATE RECORDED: April 28–29, 2000; April 14, 2002; April 27–28, 2004
DATE RELEASED: September 28, 2004
PRODUCER: Ravi Coltrane

Unlike Coltrane's generation of musicians, who were expected to push jazz forward—and did—his son's generation is being asked to save jazz from extinction by keeping the faith, which might prove the greater task.

—FRANCIS DAVIS, 1996

It's an early afternoon in February at Capitol Records' Studio B in Hollywood, a room filled with history and meaning. Sinatra, Nat Cole, and the Beach Boys recorded many of their classics there, but to four-year-old William Coltrane, the studio is about ample running space and swivel chairs that need testing. To thirty-eight-year-old Ravi Coltrane, William's father and a working saxophonist of gathering renown who is now wearing the twin hats of producer and performer, the legendary studio is a second choice: "It's slightly awkward and impersonal—if only the sight lines were better."

To sixty-seven-year old Alice Coltrane, Ravi's mother and William's grandmother, it is simply another room with another piano. "Nervous—me? No. This is very comfortable," she says softly, patiently noodling on a Steinway in an isolation booth, as a swarm of family, friends, and fellow musicians are all to and fro. "But the men I think may have some issues."

Mrs. Coltrane is re-entering the frenetic record business, preparing to create music for *Translinear Light*, her first commercial album in twenty-six years. Truth be told, she is allowing, rather than actively instigating, her return to the spotlight. "Well, I told my children I'm so happy to do this, but I'm not starting a second career!"

In 2004, Alice Coltrane's life of semiretirement finds her home most often, focused on contemplation and inner growth. She has maintained that direction for forty years, revealing a conviction far more constant and solid than many of the spiritual adventurers of her age (including many musicians). It seems only natural that her album be released on the one label she and her husband helped define.

Mother and son sit on opposite sides of the dinner table north of Los Angeles. Ravi reminds his mother of a moment in 2002 when she held court to a line of well-wishers after she sat in with his quartet at Joe's Pub in Manhattan. "You can remember easily the lines of people standing outside your dressing room just waiting to say hello or thank you after that concert."

"My son's been trying to tell me that for a while. I never considered myself to be so remembered like John Coltrane," counters Alice. "But for myself, I'm sure there must be a few people."

"She's being modest," shrugs Ravi, used to such humility. "But," he quickly adds, "reaching all the Alice Coltrane fans is not even close to the primary motivation for me wanting to do these types of things with my mother.

"My earliest memories of her are her playing music, either piano or organ or harp, or playing recordings. I'd come home from school and she'd just be sitting at the organ, playing hymns and things. It was like, you go home and your dad's reading the paper or watching the television. That's what music was for her. It was this sustenance that was a part of her daily existence.

"I always felt like there was a gap that was widening—any idea of us being two professional working musicians at the same time was just evaporating. I was getting deeper and deeper into music and each year she would say she was more and more retired from music. I think about those times I had opportunities to play professionally with my mother, but I was new to it and not ready. I wanted some document that I'll always be able to share with my kids. I don't want to have a day of regret, saying, 'I never did this with my mom.' "

Back in the studio, Ravi is a blur. What was intended as a one-session album has evolved into much more. Ultimately, *Translinear Light* is culled from multiple studio visits: eight tracks recorded in 2000, '02, and '04. The album will present Alice in a variety of settings (duo, trio, and quartet) and accompaniment: Ravi on tenor and soprano sax and percussion; Alice's youngest son, Oranyan, on alto; bassists Charlie Haden and James Genus; drummers Jack DeJohnette and Jeff Watts; and the Sai Anantam Singers, a choir from her ashram.

"It would *not* be retro Alice Coltrane, this sort of nostalgic seventies-sounding record. Scratch that," says Ravi. "And you don't want to have it sound like 'Let's make it a hip-hop record.' It still has to be an Alice Coltrane record—to balance that sort of forward-thinking, present-day sense, but also have a little bit of historical influence there."

Son and mother agreed the fulcrum would be "songs of praise that would extend from the church music that she had played growing up, to Negro spirituals, to John Coltrane's music, and her spiritual music from the seventies. It would also extend to some of the Eastern, Indian-influenced music she's involved with today. Between all these areas, we found some nice, complementary pieces."

The album combines them with new tunes, traditional Indian numbers, Hindu chants, hymnal standards, and long-celebrated pieces revived from Alice's Impulse recordings.

Translinear Light was produced and programmed "to honor John . . . because he's the inspirer," according to his widow. In autumn of 2004, it was released to positive reviews that made liberal use of the word "overdue" and frequent mention of the special relationship between John Coltrane and the label he helped make famous. As a legion of curious consumers—familiar with Alice Coltrane or not at all—bought the CD and removed the plastic wrapping, there it was once more: the feeling of expectant surprise that Impulse had once delivered, album after album, with uncanny consistency, for a solid, fifteen-year spell.

Capitol Studios, Hollywood, April 27, 2004: Alice Coltrane at the mixing console with (left to right) drummer Jack DeJohnette, engineer Steve Genewick, and grandson William.

ACKNOWLEDGMENTS

Books, like jazz, are most always collective efforts, with many deserving applause. Please join me in acknowledging:

Dave Dunton, an agent with an uncanny ability to know the answers before the questions arise.

All at W. W. Norton who devoted time and expertise to pull this together smoothly, positively: my editor, Maribeth Payne; A. Courtney Fitch (whose initial initial I am convinced stands for "after hours"), Nancy Palmquist, Don Rifkin, and Graham Norwood; plus a truly inspired design team that wove together images and text, maintaining and updating the Impulse feel: Julia Druskin, Debra Morton-Hoyt, Dana Sloan, and Charles Brock of the DesignWorks Group, Inc.

All at the Verve Music Group who provide access and support. In the east, Ron Goldstein, Ken Druker, Bryan Koniarz, Nate Herr, Regina Joskow, Marc Lipiner, and Mark Smith. A special tip of the hat to Hollis King, the keeper of the orange and black, and his staff, including Sherniece Smith and many others. In the archives out west: Randy Aronson.

A copy editor born to jazz, the nonpareil Pierre Gardez, who made sure all things jibe while filtering out the jive—and who deserves his own book deal! Also Ted Panken and Hal Miller, for looking over facts and text.

A number of immediate believers across the pond: first, the Granta family in London—George Miller, Gail Lynch, Sarah Wasley, and Louise Campbell. In Paris, Milan, Osaka, Barcelona, Hamburg, and London, respectively: Daniel Richard, Luca Formenton, Yasuhiro Fujioka, Julian Vinuales, Marlies Helder, and Nathan Graves.

A special line here to all who serve at the paper- and vinyl-crammed shelves at the Institute of Jazz Studies on the Rutgers campus in Newark: Dan Morgenstern, Ed Berger (thanks for the Benny tip!), Vincent Pelote, Tad Hershorn, Esther Smith and her crew.

Another special line for Bob Belden, for being a go-to repository of original Impulse LPs, and for so many other reasons.

Yet another for the men who created the finely focused chapter-opening images: Jack Vartoogian and Jim Whitaker.

All the lensmen whose work helped define the original Impulse look: the late Joe Alper (thanks, George and Jaye!) and three men whose friendship has become an unexpected lagniappe of these book projects: Jim Marshall, Chuck Stewart, and Pete Turner.

Those who provided many of the images that help convey the Impulse story: Michael, Jonathan Hyams, and Helen Ashford at the Michael Ochs Archives. Jason Elzy and Walter Boholst at Warner Bros./Rhino. Greta Rucker and Julia Swidler at the BMG part of Sony BMG. Tom Evered at Blue Note/EMI. Gordon Joshua Murray at *Billboard* magazine. Howard Rosen and Jim Shields at Evidence Music. George Boziwick at the New York Public Library. And for capturing that certain élan in the author's photo, Marc PoKempner, my Chicago running partner.

Radio folk, presenters, bookers, musicians, and others extending support along the way: Josh Jackson; Bill Bragin at Joe's Pub; Dave Liebman; Ravi, Michelle, and Alice Coltrane, and Marilyn McLeod; Joel Chriss; Steve Bensusan; Mike Byers; Ginny Urus; George Gilbert; Joan Hardie.

New friends: Fran Attaway, Steve Backer, Alan Bergman, Curtis Fuller, Ed Michel, Creed Taylor, John Sinclair, Don Hunstein, John Dixon, and Jim Dickson (the last two whose ideas and memories were invaluable in providing context and flavor). Old buddies: Andrew Caploe and Dave Brendel. Venerable veterans: George Avakian, Bill Kaplan, Sid Feller, Orrin Keepnews, Michael Cuscuna, and Gary Giddins. Tireless transcribers and researchers: Michael Heller, Todd Nicholson, Amanda Replogle, Justin Padro, Kieran McGee, and, when not gracing the floorboards, Abigail Royle.

For first believing this subject to be worthy of extended coverage: Chris Porter and Lee Mergner at *JazzTimes*, and Andrew Male at *MOJO*.

And to all those not listed yet deserving credit for making this study a reality—please forgive the omission.

This history is dedicated to all the musicians whose timeless sounds contributed to the Impulse legacy, and compelled me to get this done. Thank you—may this effort send hungry ears back your way.

DISCUS PERSONAE

Steve Backer—Initially director of East Coast promotion and publicity for ABC in 1971. Success in promoting Impulse to a younger, rock-oriented audience led to his role as general manager of the label. Signed, among others, Keith Jarrett, Gato Barbieri, and Dewey Redman to the label. Departed ABC in 1973 to join Clive Davis at Arista Records, establishing a jazz division for the new label.

Alan Bergman—In-house counsel for ABC from 1965 to 1969, focused on the legal affairs of ABC-Paramount Records, including Impulse. Primary contact for business issues for John Coltrane during this time.

Sam Clark—First president of ABC-Paramount Records, 1955–64. Originally a record distributor in Boston, was recruited by Leonard Goldenson to research the possibility of a record division for the ABC-Paramount entertainment corporation, then to actually create and run it.

Michael Cuscuna—Jazz producer and reissue specialist; began his career as a late-night deejay in the late 1960s. First researched and helped produce Impulse reissues in 1977 and has been involved with many of the label's back-catalog efforts since then.

Esmond Edwards—Veteran jazz producer and photographer whose first production was John Coltrane's first album as a leader, *Coltrane,* for the Prestige label. As in-house producer at ABC Records from 1975 to 1977, was in charge of Impulse, steering the label in a more commercial, R&B-flavored direction.

Leonard Goldenson—Originally head of United Paramount Theaters, became chairman and founder of the ABC-Paramount corporation, which was established after United Paramount purchased the ABC Network in 1951. Though primarily focused on ABC Television, oversaw all divisions of the entertainment/media conglomerate from 1951 to 1986. Initiated the AmPar Record Corporation in 1955, which led to the creation of ABC-Paramount Records and eventually Impulse.

Bill Kaplan—First in-house counsel hired specifically for ABC-Paramount Records, serving from 1961 to 1967. Currently represents the Coltrane family and estate.

Phil Kurnit—In-house counsel for ABC from 1963 to 1966, focused on the legal and business affairs of ABC-Paramount Records, including Impulse.

Jay Lasker—One of the founders of Dunhill Records; his success with the Mamas and the Papas—and later Steppenwolf and Three Dog Night—led to a leading role in the West Coast office of ABC-Paramount. Eventually assumed the top position at ABC Records, serving as president from 1970 to 1975.

Dennis Lavinthal—Hired as Jay Lasker's assistant at Dunhill Records in 1969; became senior vice president for sales and promotion at ABC. Though more focused on rock and pop releases, acted as a buffer between the higher-ups and the less commercial, more creative efforts at Impulse and BluesWay. Departed in 1975 after a regime change at the label.

Harry Levine—Originally a talent booker for the Paramount Theaters chain, helped establish the AmPar Record Corporation with Sam Clark in 1955, becoming vice president of the ABC-Paramount label, with a focus on artists and music. Original booster of the plan to create Impulse Records.

Ed Michel—Journeyman producer and musician, hired in 1969 by ABC as an in-house producer, focused on Impulse and BluesWay. Oversaw hundreds of sessions, as well as reissues and first issues of material from the Impulse vaults. Departed in 1975 after a regime change at the label.

Larry Newton—Originally ABC-Paramount's national director of sales; became company president in 1965 and held the position until 1970. Brokered the Ray Charles deal in 1960 and led the company's expansion into distribution and the rock era.

Howard Stark—Originally part of the marketing team at ABC-Paramount, managed Impulse (and other ABC labels) after Bob Thiele 's decision to go freelance in 1968. Eventually moved himself and Impulse to Los Angeles, where he became general manager of ABC-Dunhill. Ceded the running of Impulse to Steve Backer in 1971. Departed ABC in 1975 after a regime change at the label.

Bill Szymczyk—Producer hired by ABC Records in 1968. Oversaw hits by B.B. King, rock albums by the James Gang, and various co-productions with Ed Michel for Impulse. Departed ABC and California in 1971 to start the short-lived label Tumbleweed Records.

Creed Taylor—Originally an in-house producer with ABC-Paramount from 1955 to 1960, overseeing all jazz recordings and other styles of music as well. Initiated the concept for a separate, independent jazz label called Pulse—later changed to Impulse—which was launched in early 1961. Within months was recruited to take over Verve Records, where he found commercial success first with bossa nova, then with pop-jazz albums by the likes of Wes Montgomery. Eventually created his own label in 1970, Creed Taylor International (CTI), fine-tuning the pop-jazz overlap into a best-selling and highly influential sound.

Bob Thiele—Veteran jazz and pop music producer whose diverse and impulsive taste in jazz—and willingness to follow the direction of his label stars, especially John Coltrane—helped define Impulse's musical identity beginning in late 1961. Duties included producing albums for ABC-Paramount, Impulse and BluesWay, before he went freelance in late 1968. Eventually left Impulse to form his own label, Flying Dutchman, in mid-1969. Also published *Jazz* magazine—later *Jazz and Pop*—from 1961 to 1970.

Rudy Van Gelder—Legendary jazz recording engineer whose studios in New Jersey, first in Hackensack (in the 1950s) and then in Englewood Cliffs (from 1960 to the present), were the site of countless recordings issued on a variety of labels. Van Gelder's was the primary studio for Impulse from the outset to 1967; Van Gelder himself was John Coltrane's engineer of choice.

SOURCE NOTES

INTRODUCTION

1 *"The music of a well-ordered age"*: Herman Hesse, *Magister Ludi* (New York: Bantam Books, 1969): 20.
1 *"That's where it's at"*: Bob Thiele, quoted by George Hoefer, "The Record Men: Bob Thiele" (*Jazz,* January 1966): 22.
2 *"In school, I"*: Daniel Richard, conversation with author, April 12, 2003.
2 *"There was a certain"*: Gary Giddins, interview with author, MiniDisc recording, August 8, 2003.
2 *"The branding was terrific"*: Don Heckman, interview with author, MiniDisc recording, June 4, 2003.
3 *"Those gatefolds were"*: John Sinclair, interview with author, MiniDisc recording, April 28, 2003.
4 *"profitably encompass"*: Nat Hentoff, "Raising Wax Criteria" (*Down Beat,* October 20, 1966): 10.
4 *"it seemed as though"*: Ed Michel, interview with author, MiniDisc recording, June 23, 2003.
4 *"Impulse will always"*: Gary Burton, interview with author, MiniDisc recording, August 5, 2003.
5 *"Impulse was there"*: Ed Michel, interview.
7 *"If there was"*: Archie Shepp, interview with author, MiniDisc recording, September 7, 2003.
7 *"John was the one"*: Alice Coltrane, interview with author, MiniDisc recording, October 20, 2003.
8 *"The whole record industry"*: Bob Thiele, quoted by Robert Palmer, "From the Inside Out: Bob Palmer Interviews Bob Thiele," *Coda* (June 1971): 34.
9 *"Coltrane was the jewel"*: Creed Taylor, interview with author, MiniDisc recording, May 19, 2003.
10 *"Impulse was a record"*: Ed Michel, interview.

CHAPTER 1 / THE MAN BEHIND THE SIGNATURE: CREED TAYLOR (1954–1961)

13 *"Historians may remember"*: Burt Korall, Dom Cerulli, and Mort L. Nasatir, *The Jazz Word* (1960; reprint, New York: Da Capo Press, 1987): 1.
13 *"He likes jazz"*: Hugh Hefner (*Playboy*, June 1957).
14 *"I think the seed"*: Creed Taylor, interview.
14 *equally struggling Bethlehem Records*: For more on this enterprising company—"one of the most consistently satisfying labels in jazz"—see Michael Erlewine et. al. (editors), *All Music Guide to Jazz,* 3rd edition (San Francisco: Miller Freeman Book, 1998): 1,326.
15 *"I read* Billboard": Creed Taylor, interview.
15 *Founded in 1955*: Interesting discussions on the creation and early years of the ABC-Paramount Corporation can be found in: Charlie Gillett, *The Sound of the City: The Rise of Rock and Roll* (New York: Pantheon Books, 1983): 62–63; and Michael Lydon, *Ray Charles: Man and Music* (New York: Penguin Putnam, 1998): 166.
16 *The Am-Par Record Corporation*: ABC's first in-house counsel, Bill Kaplan, offers his take on the inspiration behind creating a music division: "Goldenson felt, 'We should have a record company because my two rivals, RCA and CBS, have them.' He was using Sam Clark as a consultant as to what record company he should buy, because Sam was the head of a big wholesale distributorship in Boston. Leonard finally said, 'Sam, would you just start up a company for us and head it?'" Bill Kaplan, interview with author, MiniDisc recording, June 21, 2003.
16 *"At the start"*: Phil Kurnit, interview with author, MiniDisc recording, May 21, 2003.
16 *"In the fifties"*: Larry Newton, interview with author, MiniDisc recording, February 19, 2001.
16 *"I started on"*: Sid Feller, interview with author, MiniDisc recording, February 17, 2001.
17 *"The first real"*: Ibid.
17 *ABC-Paramount saw little success*: *ABC-Paramount Album Discography, Part 1* (www.bsnpubs.com/abc/abc100.html).
17 *Don Costa was hired*: Costa would go on to nurture the careers of ABC's top sellers like Paul Anka and Eydie Gormé—and later, after leaving ABC, become a favorite arranger for Frank Sinatra.
17 *"They sold everything"*: Creed Taylor, interview.
17 *"Paul Anka came"*: Sid Feller, interview.
19 *"We spent a lot"*: Ibid.
19 *"It was similar"*: Larry Newton, interview.
19 *"I did a whole"*: Creed Taylor, interview.
20 *"Jazz was my mission"*: Ibid.
20 *"I started with Decca"*: Fran Attaway, interview with author, MiniDisc recording, July 23, 2003.
20 *"I could spend"*: Ibid.
21 *"These meetings would"*: Ibid.
21 *"This was around"*: Grachan Moncur III, interview with author, audiocassette recording, February 19, 2001.
21 *"Sam Clark, Harry Levine"*: Alan Bergman, interview with author, MiniDisc recording, May 14, 2003.
22 *"Sam was a classy"*: Phil Kurnit, interview.
22 *"Harry was worth"*: Ibid.
22 *"Harry and I"*: Creed Taylor, interview.
22 *"They came by"*: Ibid.
23 *"We came up with"*: Ibid.
23 *"He would say"*: Ibid.
23 *"He was a great"*: Larry Newton, interview.
23 *one of the first major labels*: "ABC-Paramount did . . . beat all the major labels to the market with stereo records, having them in the catalog as early as June, 1958 . . . the first ABC-Paramount stereo issues were ACS-218 [*Eydie Gormé Vamps the Roaring '20s*], 219 [*More College Drinking Songs*], 221 [*Heavenly Songs in Hi-Fi*—Ferrante & Teicher], and 223 [*Sing a Song of Basie*]. (*ABC-Paramount Album Discography, Part 2,* www.bsnpubs.com/abc/abc200.html.)

23 *"It just came"*: Creed Taylor, interview.
23 *"Here they were"*: Ibid.
24 *"I arranged for"*: Fran Attaway, interview.
24 *"Why does a painter"*: Creed Taylor, interview.
24 *"When I was just"*: Pete Turner, interview with author, MiniDisc recording, May 10, 2003.
25 *"Creed was exceptional"*: Ibid.
27 *The 33 ⅓ rpm*: "Lieberson Cites Col. Disk Sale Leadership" (*Billboard*, December 23, 1957): 15.
27 *In 1959, the Kingston Trio*: Joel Whitburn, *The Billboard Book of Top 40 Hits*, 6th edition (New York: Billboard Books, 1996): 814.
27 *as* Billboard*'s singles charts reveal*: Per *The Billboard Book of Top 40 Hits*, 6th edition, p. 814: ABC-Paramount's four no. 1's were: by Frankie Avalon ("Venus" and "Why"), Paul Anka ("Lonely Boy"), and Lloyd Price ("Stagger Lee"), versus Columbia's two—by Johnny Horton ("The Battle of New Orleans") and Guy Mitchell ("Heartaches by the Number")—and RCA's pair: by Elvis Presley ("A Big Hunk o' Love") and the Browns ("The Three Bells").
28 *"Tangerine"*: Charles oversaw the release of music by a few favorite artists on his Tangerine label, notably Percy Mayfield and Jimmy Scott, but his own recordings were released on the ABC-Paramount label. Today, all the music originally released on ABC is still owned by Charles's estate and continues to be licensed by specialty reissue labels like Rhino and Shout Factory.
28 *"I'm sure part"*: Bill Kaplan, interview.
28 *"After Ray Charles"*: Sid Feller, interview.
29 *"I had thought"*: Creed Taylor, interview.
29 *"Very serious music"*: Ibid.
29 *"I sensed that"*: Fran Attaway, interview.
29 *"I always thought"*: Creed Taylor, interview.
30 *"We shared an office"*: Fran Attaway, interview.
30 *"She had great taste"*: Creed Taylor, interview.
30 *"I remember he"*: Margo Guryan, interview with author, MiniDisc recording, August 1, 2003.
31 *"It all started"*: Creed Taylor, interview.
31 *"Harry was an invaluable"*: Ibid.
31 *"The late '50s"*: June Bundy, "Late '50s Bid for Posterity, Fame as Real 'Jazz Age'" (*Billboard*, March 9, 1959): 1.
31 *"Jazz is now"*: Irving Townsend, "The Ten Best Friends of Jazz" (*Down Beat*, August 20, 1959): 89.
32 *"We had a big company"*: Larry Newton, interview.
32 *"Catalog"*: Bill Kaplan, interview.
33 *"Creed was an enormous"*: Margo Guryan, interview.
33 *"That's when Larry"*: Creed Taylor, interview.
36 *"Atlantic sent me"*: Ray Charles and David Ritz, *Brother Ray: Ray Charles's Own Story* (1978; reprint, New York: Da Capo Press, 2004), 193–94.
36 *"To my mind"*: Ibid., 192–93.
36 *"If you didn't"*: Creed Taylor, interview.
36 *"There were certain"*: Ibid.
37 *"Kai Winding was"*: Ibid.
37 *"the most unique"*: Ibid.
37 *"I liked arrangers"*: Ibid.
37 *"The first four records"*: Margo Guryan, interview.
38 *"We only had one"*: Sid Feller, interview.
39 *"I tried to juxtapose"*: Creed Taylor, interview.
39 *"They were slick"*: Gary Giddins, interview.
39 *"I can remember"*: Jaimoe [John Lee Johnson], interview with author, MiniDisc recording, March 22, 2003.
39 *"I don't think"*: Creed Taylor, interview.
42 *"In the sixties"*: Ibid. Lacking any demographic data, it's exceedingly difficult to measure Impulse's specific impact on the African-American community in 1961. Charles topped the R&B charts with "One Mint Julep," but the fact that he was already a noted R&B star at that point argues against crediting either musical style or label. In any event, the single's success in retail and on radio inarguably helped in putting Impulse in front of a broad, multi-hued audience.
42 *"knocked me out"*: Eliot Tiegel, interview with author, DAT recording, April 16, 2001.
42 *"It was overwhelming"*: Bruce Lundvall, interview with author, MiniDisc recording, August 12, 2003.
43 *"They were priced"*: George Avakian, interview with author, MiniDisc recording, April 1, 2003.
43 *"Impulse made an immediate"*: Sid Feller, interview.
43 *"A real pattern"*: Creed Taylor, interview.
46 *"Oliver was another story"*: Ibid.
47 *"He had that eruptive"*: Jimmy Heath, interview with author, audiocassette recording, February 8, 2000.
47 *"I first met Coltrane"*: Creed Taylor, interview.
48 *under contract to Prestige*: In 1960 and 1961, Oliver Nelson and Eric Dolphy were signed to Prestige; J.J. Johnson to Columbia; Freddie Hubbard to Blue Note; and Bill Evans to Riverside. Intriguingly, of the jazz artists who recorded for ABC-Paramount—from Urbie Green to Lambert, Hendricks and Ross—Taylor recalls that most had been signed to multi-album contracts.
48 *"The financial aspects"*: Phil Kurnit, interview.
48 *"I felt more secure"*: Creed Taylor, interview.
48 *"The Shaw Agency"*: Bill Kaplan, interview.
48 *"a smart businessman"*: Creed Taylor, interview.
49 *"So John came in"*: Ibid.
49 *"They worked out"*: Ibid.
49 *"It wasn't as if"*: Bill Kaplan, interview.
49 *"I know that"*: John Coltrane, interview with Ralph J. Gleason, tape recording, May 2, 1962.
49 *"I didn't say anything"*: Creed Taylor, interview.
50 *"It was a pretty tight"*: Ibid.
50 "Africa/Brass": Ibid.
50 *"We play 'Greensleeves'"*: John Coltrane, interview with Ralph J. Gleason.
51 *Metro-Goldwyn-Mayer*: "Granz Sells but Holds" (*Down Beat*, February 2, 1961): 11.
51 *"I got the call"*: Creed Taylor, interview.
51 *"I thought I could"*: Ibid.
54 *"I mean, I* had": Ibid.
54 *"I was floating"*: Ibid.
54 *"I was staggered"*: Margo Guryan, interview.
56 *"got ahold of"*: John Carisi quoted in Larry Hicock, *Castles Made of Sound: The Story of Gil Evans* (New York: Da Capo Press, 2002): 124–25.
56 *"We just kind of"*: Creed Taylor, interview.
56 *"At first there"*: Ibid.
56 *"Look—I'm being"*: Ibid.

CHAPTER 2 / THE RE-EDUCATION OF BOB THIELE (1961–1962)

59 *"For me, there are three"*: Jerry Wexler quoted in Richard Buskin, *Inside Tracks* (New York: Avon Books, 1999): 26.
59 *"A New York"*: Sid Feller, interview.
59 *"An ingenious A&R"*: Archie Shepp, interview.
59 *"He had what"*: Dan Morgenstern, interview with author, DAT recording, April 9, 2001.
60 *"Sheepshead Bay aristocracy"*: Bob Thiele, *What a Wonderful World: A Lifetime of Recordings* (New York: Oxford University Press, 1995): 7.
61 *"The reason this"*: Ibid., 28.
62 *"I suppose I"*: Ibid., 42.
62 *"budding record business"*: Ibid., 45.
64 *"Brunswick [Records]"*: Ibid., 52.
64 *"Sam Clark [the president]"*: Creed Taylor, interview with author, DAT recording, November 11, 2001.
65 *"What a lot"*: Bob Thiele, interview with Michael Jarrett, audiocassette, Winter 1995.
65 *"I must confess"*: Bob Thiele, quoted by Robert Palmer, *Coda,* 31.
65 *"Those [pop] records"*: Bob Thiele, interview with Michael Jarrett.
65 *"The finished product"*: Ibid.
66 *"It was all"*: Ibid.
66 *"resident 'jazz freak'"*: *What a Wonderful World,* 119.
66 *"I was already working"*: Bob Thiele, interview with Michael Jarrett.
66 *"I don't think"*: Bob Thiele, quoted by Robert Palmer, *Coda,* 31.
66 *"evenings in hell"*: Rudy Van Gelder, interview with author, MiniDisc recording, June 2, 2004.
67 *"at first extremely"*: *What a Wonderful World,* 120.
67 *"Typical of most"*: Ibid., 119.
67 *"I'll never forget this"*: Bob Thiele, quoted in *Blue Trane,* TV documentary produced by Philippe Koechlin and Domique Cazenare, Canal Plus (France), 1992, videocassette.
70 *"Once I was"*: Bob Thiele, quoted by Robert Palmer, *Coda,* 31.
70 *"The best thing"*: Ibid.
71 *"You want to record"*: Alan Bergman, interview.
71 *"The [Impulse] budget"*: Bob Thiele, interview with Michael Jarrett.
71 *"Bob did certainly"*: Alan Bergman, interview.
74 *"The New Wave of Folk"*: Impulse's brief foray into folk music promised as wide-ranging a vision of the music as it did with jazz. Recorded on the strength of Brown's tune "Lizzie Borden"—a Top 50 hit for the Chad Mitchell Trio in early '62—*Alarums and Excursions* featured comical songs more in tune with Allan Sherman's or Tom Lehrer's satirical sense than Oscar Brand's sincerity or bawdiness. Though the idea was short-lived, Thiele's instinct accurately pointed to a common audience for forward-looking, non-mainstream music of the early sixties. Jazz and folk were then equally popular on college campuses, and George Wein's parallel jazz and folk festivals in Newport suggested a similar overlap.
74 *"I had conversations"*: Phil Kurnit, interview.
74 *"I always level"*: Bob Thiele, quoted by Robert Palmer, *Coda,* 32.
74 *"Thiele really envisioned"*: Phil Kurnit, interview.
75 *"I love musicians"*: Bob Thiele, quoted by Robert Palmer, *Coda,* 32.
75 *"Jazz recording was"*: Bob Thiele, interview with Michael Jarrett.
75 *"My first major"*: Dick Katz, interview with author, MiniDisc recording, July 30, 2003.
77 Down Beat *magazine's pages*: The two articles at the center of the dispute were John Tynan, "Take 5" (*Down Beat,* November 23, 1961): 40, and Leonard Feather, "Feather's Nest" (*Down Beat,* February 15, 1962): 17.
77 *"John Coltrane and Eric Dolphy"*: Don DeMicheal, "John Coltrane and Eric Dolphy Answer the Jazz Critics" (*Down Beat,* April 12, 1962.)
77 *"Both* Ballads *[A(S)-32] and"*: *What a Wonderful World,* 123. Note that Thiele errs in the title of the Coltrane-Hartman album; it is of course *John Coltrane and Johnny Hartman.*
80 *"Impulse was interested"*: Pauline Rivelli and Robert Levin (editors), *Black Giants* (New York: World Publishing, 1970): 34.
80 *"I think that [Coltrane]"*: Bob Thiele, quoted by Frank Kofsky, "The New Wave: Bob Thiele Talks to Frank Kofsky" (*Coda,* May/June 1968): 4.
81 *trombonist Curtis Fuller*: Lost in the wash of time is the certainty as to who brought Fuller into the Impulse fold on an exclusive basis. Given the date of the trombonist's initial session (November 15, 1961) and Creed Taylor's penchant for trombonists, it is likely Taylor had at least set the wheels in motion for a Fuller contract with Impulse.
84 *"During that time"*: Chico Hamilton, interview.
84 *"It was a dynamite"*: Ibid.
84 *"I didn't ever keep"*: Freddie Hubbard, interview with author, MiniDisc recording, June 2, 2003.
85 *"He wanted me"*: Curtis Fuller, interview.
85 *"It was just"*: Ibid.
88 *"The contract was"*: McCoy Tyner, interview with author, MiniDisc recording, August 8, 2003.
88 *"For example, when"*: Bob Thiele, quoted by Robert Palmer, *Coda,* 33.
88 *"John [Coltrane] was there"*: McCoy Tyner, interview.
89 *"It was kind"*: Ibid.
89 *"He was glad"*: Ibid.

CHAPTER 3 / INTUITION AND IMPULSE (1963–1964)

93 *"At Impulse, he"*: Bob Thiele Jr., interview with author, MiniDisc recording, May 26, 2004.
93 *"There was this"*: Gary Giddins, interview.
94 *"Thiele knew each"*: Michael Cuscuna, liner notes to *Impulse Jazz.*
94 *"Thiele was an old-timer"*: Gary Giddins, interview.
94 *"In the early days"*: Bob Thiele, quoted by Robert Palmer, *Coda,* 34.
95 *"We had Max Roach"*: Larry Newton, interview.
95 *"People like Coltrane"*: Bob Thiele, quoted by Robert Palmer, *Coda,* 34.
96 *"I was sneaking"*: Ibid., 32.
100 *"You talk to"*: Larry Newton, interview.

100 *reissue of Lambert, Hendricks and Ross's*: Billy Taylor's *My Fair Lady Loves Jazz* [A(S)-72] was another ABC jazz title from the 1950s reissued on Impulse that year.
100 *Hard-swinging organ combos*: David Rosenthal, *Hard Bop: Jazz & Black Music, 1955–1965* (New York: Oxford University Press, 1992): 63.
100 *inner-city jukeboxes*: Ibid., 68.
103 *"We called it"*: Ibid., 116.
103 *"There was no science"*: Phil Kurnit, interview.
103 *"They talk now"*: Ibid.
103 *"It was up"*: Sid Feller, interview with author, telephone, November, 30, 2001.
105 *"the promotion guy"*: Joel Dorn, interview with author, DAT recording, June 22, 2001.
105 *"I don't know"*: Bob Thiele, quoted by Phil Johnson, "They Couldn't Help Acting on Impulse" (*The Independent* [UK], February 3, 1995): 26.
106 *"It was actually"*: Phil Kurnit, interview.
106 *four leading vibraphonists*: Gary McFarland's *Point of Departure* [A(S)-46] featured a sextet with bassist Steve Swallow and drummer Mel Lewis; Terry Gibbs's *Take It from Me* [A(S)-58] was highlighted by guitarist Kenny Burrell, bassist Sam Jones, and drummer Louis Hayes; Milt Jackson's *Jazz 'N' Samba* [A(S)-70] was a mix of musical styles; Lionel Hampton's *You Better Know It!!!* [A(S)-78] included the mallet man playing piano on "Swingle Jingle."
106 *four swing-era stalwarts*: Ben Webster—former tenor man with Duke Ellington—was brought into the Impulse fold weeks before relocating to Europe at age fifty-five, yielding the fine quartet outing *See You at the Fair* [A(S)-65], which featured Roger Kellaway and Hank Jones trading off on piano. *Everybody Knows Johnny Hodges* [A(S)-61] was essentially the core of the Ellington band, sans the Duke, showcasing the group's legendary alto saxophonist in a title role. Tenor saxophonist Paul Gonsalves, another Ellington sideman (Thiele's "Ducal" jones was boundless), recorded two discs for Impulse: *Cleopatra Feelin' Jazzy* [A(S)-41], which twisted two trends of the day (jazz soundtrack treatments and the new Elizabeth Taylor movie), and *Tell It the Way It Is!* [A(S)-55], a rootsy, almost soul-jazz outing that included the Hodges original "Impulsive." Clark Terry reprised the label's self-referential tune on his first Impulse album, *The Happy Horns of Clark Terry* [A(S)-64], which found the trumpeter in the company of Webster, Kellaway, and alto man Phil Woods, among others.

One album cover anomaly worth mentioning from this group: Gonsalves's *Cleopatra Feelin' Jazzy,* for an unexplained reason, did not sport Impulse's signature gatefold cover, and was the sole release until the mid-'70s to be denied that honor.
106 *three bebop/hard-bop veterans*: J.J. Johnson's cool and moody *Proof Positive* [A(S)-68] was a mostly quartet session that left ample room for the trombonist's improvisations and Harold Mabern's piano. Art Blakey's *A Jazz Message* [A(S)-45] grouped the drummer not with his Messengers, but with pianist McCoy Tyner, bassist Art Davis, and alto and tenor saxophonist Sonny Stitt, who grabbed the spotlight. *Message* came close on the heels of Stitt's own (and only) album as sole leader for Impulse: *Now!* [A(S)-43], a sprightly and swinging set sparked by his crystal tone, and supported by Hank Jones's piano, Milt Hinton's bass, and Al Lucas's drums.
106 *big-band arranger*: Oliver Nelson's *More Blues and the Abstract Truth* [A(S)-75] stands out today more for the soloists brought in for the session—Ben Webster, Phil Woods, pianist Roger Kellaway, and trumpeter Thad Jones—than for the tunes, as had been the case with Nelson's initial triumph for Impulse.
106 *style-hopping summits*: Sonny Stitt and Paul Gonsalves's *Salt and Pepper* [A(S)-52], the disc that rounded out Stitt's three-session deal with Impulse, is considered his best for the label. Essentially a two-tenor jam session utilizing workhorses like "Perdido," Stitt's own "Surfin'," and a title track jointly composed by the two saxophonists, the album brings to mind the classic encounters made famous by Norman Granz—which Creed Taylor had found little time for. Of particular note here is Stitt's limber and loquacious turn on alto on "Star Dust."
106 *"They were relaxed dates"*: Hank Jones, interview with author, MiniDisc recording, November 23, 2004.
107 *"You never knew"*: Bob Thiele, interview with Michael Jarrett.
107 *"It was still"*: *What a Wonderful World,* 72.
108 *"At that time"*: Ibid., 68.
109 *"Bob wrote this piece"*: Alice Coltrane, interview with author, MiniDisc recording, June 1, 2001.
109 *"came out of"*: Chico Hamilton, interview.
109 *"I had a son"*: *What a Wonderful World,* 69.
109 *"I was kind of caretaker"*: Alan Bergman, interview.
109 *"My salary was"*: *What a Wonderful World,* 73.
110 *"Impulse appears to be"*: Fred Norsworthy, "Modern Jazz in New York, 1963" (*Coda,* March, 1964): 30.
111 "Norsworthy's ramblings": Bob Thiele, "Letters to the Editor" (*Coda,* April/May 1964): 17.
112 *"I was initially"*: Bob Thiele, interview with Michael Jarrett.
112 "[*Mingus*] *was a real*": Ibid.
112 *According to Mingus biographer*: Gene Santoro, *Myself When I Am Real: The Life and Music of Charles Mingus* (New York: Oxford University Press, 2001): 220.
113 *"Impulse went to"*: Charles Mingus, liner notes to *The Black Saint and the Sinner Lady,* Impulse A(S)-35.
116 *"The late* [*trumpeter*] *Don Cherry"*: Yusef Lateef, interview with author, MiniDisc recording, June 28, 2001.
116 *"I was free"*: Ibid.
116 *"Bob came up"*: McCoy Tyner, interview.
117 *"I was so young"*: Ibid.
118 *"It was certainly"*: Bob Thiele, quoted by Frank Kofsky, *Coda,* 6.
118 *"I like extended"*: John Coltrane quoted by Kitty Grimes, "John Coltrane Talks to Jazz News" (*Jazz News* [UK], December 27, 1961): 13.
119 *"In early 1964"*: George Avakian, e-mail to author, October 30, 2005. It should be noted that Coltrane's idea of recording one style of music for Impulse, while releasing another style on another label, was the very concept Avakian would make happen in 1972 when—as Keith Jarrett's manager—

he would negotiate the pianist's contract with Impulse, while allowing him to record for ECM as well. Avakian adds: "The Coltrane-Impulse situation made for three or four weeks of interesting speculation at the time. But when I looked even more closely at when those conversations had taken place in the summer of 1964, I was reminded that if the Impulse contract option had not been picked up, Trane's first recording for me would surely have been *A Love Supreme*, for some other label, probably World Pacific, since I had an excellent rapport with [World Pacific chief] Dick Bock."

122 *"Its length was practically"*: *What a Wonderful World*, 127.
123 *"We not only"*: Bob Thiele, interview with Michael Jarrett.
123 *"See, ABC was"*: Alan Bergman, interview.
123 *"Phonogram was in Germany"*: Phil Kurnit, interview.
123 *"There were no"*: Alan Bergman, interview.
128 *"It wasn't a"*: Bill Kaplan, interview.
129 *"If you made it"*: Larry Newton, interview.
129 *"This was still at"*: Phil Kurnit, interview.
129 *"By '65, Sam Clark"*: Bill Kaplan, interview.
129 *"Thiele became less important"*: Phil Kurnit, interview.

CHAPTER 4 / THE NEW THING AND IMPULSE (1965–1966)

131 *"By comparison, the Ornette"*: Joe Goldberg, *Jazz Masters of the Fifties* (1965; reprint, New York: Da Capo Press, 1983): 189.
131 *"I heard many things"*: Max Roach, quoted by Steve Rowland (producer), "Remembering Trane," radio documentary, 1987.
131 *"Some of his solos"*: Archie Shepp, interview.
132 *"It* was *assertive"*: Roger McGuinn, interview with author, DAT recording, March 8, 2001.
132 *"The Black Panthers"*: Frank Lowe, interview with author, DAT recording, April 4, 2001.
132 *"I'm playing their suffering"*: Nat Hentoff, "The Life Perspectives of the New Jazz" (*Down Beat,* Music '66): 23.
132 *"The voice becomes"*: LeRoi Jones, "Strong Voices in Today's Black Music" (*Down Beat,* February 10, 1966): 15.
133 *"I think* Fire Music*"*: Gary Giddins, interview.
133 *"In those days"*: Bob Thiele, quoted in Ted Fox, *In the Groove: The People Behind the Music* (New York: St. Martin's Press, 1986): 196.
133 *"I dislike war"*: John Coltrane, interview with Kazuki Tsujimoto, tape recording, July 9, 1966.
133 *"Maybe it sounds angry"*: John Coltrane, interview with Carl-Erik Lindgren, tape recording, March 22, 1960.
134 *"What he became"*: Alice Coltrane, interview.
134 *"I figured I"*: John Coltrane, interview, Frank Kofsky, August 1966; reprinted in Pauline Rivelli and Robert Levin (editors), *The Black Giants* (New York: World Publishing Company, 1970): 31.
135 *"That was the"*: Frank Foster, interview with author, DAT recording, September 6, 2001.
135 "Ascension *blew everybody"*: Dave Liebman, interview with author, DAT recording, April 16, 2001.
138 *"The Impulse record"*: LeRoi Jones, "Strong Voices in Today's Black Music" (*Down Beat,* February 10, 1966): 48.
139 "[*Coltrane*] *brought me"*: Bob Thiele, quoted in *In the Groove,* 192–95.
139 *ESP-Disk*: The list of artists recorded by the lawyer Bernard Stollman for his ESP label from 1963 through the end of the decade—from Sun Ra and Ornette Coleman to Albert Ayler, Pharoah Sanders, Marion Brown, Roswell Rudd, and others—made it a de facto farm team for Impulse. If Bob Thiele was indeed aware of the upstart label that bravely printed its covers in Esperanto rather than English, he never mentioned it to associates or friends, or in interviews.
139 *"Schoenfeld [the writer]"*: Bob Thiele, "Jazz Is Mugged by 'New Thing'" (*Jazz,* June 1964): 34.
140 *the publication's letters column*: See "Letters to the Editor" in the May–October 1965 issues of *Jazz* magazine.
140 *"the rankling racket"*: Jean P. LeBlanc, "The Happy Sound Is Dying" (*Esquire,* April 1966): 144.
140 *"The jazz revolution"*: Nat Hentoff, "The New Jazz" (*Newsweek,* December 12, 1966): 101.
140 *"Impulse, Blue Note"*: Don Heckman, "Breakthrough '66" (*Down Beat,* Music '67): 17.
143 *Other swing-era headliners*: Coleman Hawkins's *Wrapped Tight* [A(S)-87] swings delightfully with Barry Harris on piano, Snooky Young on trumpet, Urbie Green on trombone, and arrangements on half the tunes from Manny Albam. Trombonist Lawrence Brown's *Inspired Abandon* [A(S)-89] was yet another energetic dip into Ellingtonia with Johnny Hodges and other Duke's men (a worthy Chapter Two to *Everybody Knows Johnny Hodges*). Drummer Louis Bellson, whose *Thunderbird* [AS-9107] evoked his month-long after-hours residency at Las Vegas's Thunderbird nightspot, featured a hard-driving octet and included spirited covers of tunes by Ellington, Thad Jones, and Neal Hefti, with arrangements by the Argentinean pianist and composer Lalo Schifrin. In 1966, the recently rediscovered piano pioneer Earl Hines fronted the full Ellington band to stellar results on *Once Upon a Time* [AS-9108]. Alto saxophone legend Benny Carter, then based in Los Angeles, got a chance to reprise his '61 Impulse debut with *Additions to Further Definitions* [AS-9116], recording "Doozy" and sharing solos with fellow alto saxophonist Bud Shank. *Spanish Rice* [S-9127] combined noted trumpeter Clark Terry with young arranger Chico O'Farrill and yielded a big-band exercise made memorable by its unusual lineup (two guitars, four trumpets, much Latin percussion) and the brevity of the less-than-three-minute tracks, including reconceived takes of "Peanut Vendor" and "Tin Tin Deo" as well as originals.
143 *"As a matter"*: Hank Jones, interview.
143 *"It fit right"*: Ibid.
143 *"Thiele has taken"*: Nat Hentoff, "The Jazz Record Scene" (*Down Beat,* Music '66): 50.
147 *"It may be that"*: Nat Hentoff, "Raise Waxing Criteria" (*Down Beat,* October 20, 1966): 10.
147 My People: A 1963 theatrical production produced by Duke Ellington, *My People* featured music inspired by the civil rights movement ("King Fit the Battle of Alabam'") and added songs from his "Black, Brown and Beige." It included his orchestra of the day and various vocalists, and was later reissued on Thiele's Red Baron label.

147 *"I first became"*: Michael Cuscuna, interview with author, telephone, December 26, 2004.
147 *"I don't know"*: Ibid.
147 *"Blues is perhaps"*: "ABC to Bow a Blues Label; Taps 4 Names" (*Billboard,* December 17, 1966): 1.
150 *"The whole blues"*: Alan Bergman, interview.
150 *"Impulse was a special"*: Chico Hamilton, interview.
151 *contract artists like*: Yusef Lateef's last few Impulse titles included *1984* [A(S)-84], *Psychicemotus* [A(S)-92], *A Flat, G Flat and C* [AS-9117], and *The Golden Flute* [AS-9125], all of which continued his successful mixing of earthy blues with exotic instrumentation (including the ethereal theremin on *A Flat*), foreign sounds and classical influences (his take on Satie's "First Gymnopedie" off *Psychicemotus* is Third Stream fusion at its best), and even swing-era standards (he covered Nat Cole's "Straighten Up and Fly Right" on *The Golden Flute*).

From '65 through '66, Chico Hamilton steamed ahead with a sound that freely plucked what it needed from Latin, boogaloo, and the more avant-garde styles around. As sidemen Charles Lloyd and Gabor Szabo left to pursue their own careers, the drummer recorded albums featuring an eight-piece session group, *Chic Chic Chico* [A(S)-82], and with new reedman Sadao Watanabe, *El Chico* [AS-9102], both in 1965. In 1966 he recorded *The Further Adventures of El Chico* [AS-9114], featuring alto saxophonist Charlie Mariano. *The Dealer* [AS-9130], Hamilton's last for Impulse, stands out for featuring the recording debut of guitarist Larry Coryell and showing off Archie Shepp's piano playing on "For Mods Only." "A lot of guys came out of my band: Charles, Gabor, Larry—I groomed these guys, man. I let them find themselves, you know," Hamilton says today of his talent-recruiter role while at Impulse (Chico Hamilton, interview).

Thiele's instinct to avoid repetition certainly held true for Shirley Scott, who persisted as Impulse's soul-jazz leader with three more albums through 1966. Surprisingly, none featured her husband's complementary tenor. *On a Clear Day* [AS-9109] found her in a simple but swinging trio setting with bassist Ron Carter and drummer Jimmy Cobb (both recent Miles Davis sidemen), while *Soul Duo* [AS-9133] pitted her with Thiele's favorite trumpeter, Clark Terry. *Girl Talk* [AS-9141], Scott's contract-ending title for Impulse, placed her in a trio setting again.
151 *quirky, one-of-a-kind one-offs*: As if to make up for Stanley Turrentine's absence on his wife's albums, Thiele recorded the emerging tenor saxophonist with Scott in a cooking quartet context on the groove-grinding *Let It Go* [AS-9115]. It was Turrentine's sole hiatus from a ten-year run with Blue Note, and one of five intriguing one-offs on Impulse that highlighted well-known beboppers or hard-boppers from '65 through '66. Zoot Sims's *Waiting Game* [AS-9131] is a sax-and-strings outing that took place in London, featuring a twenty-five-piece orchestra and Gary McFarland's lush (though not flowery) arrangements. *Greek Cooking* [AS-9143] survives as a somewhat dated attempt to place Phil Woods's fluid alto within the context of a Greek strings-and-percussion ensemble; bouzoukie player Iordanis Tsomidis is the surprise star, transcending mediocre material (primarily movie themes and a Mamas and Papas cover). Thiele continued his penchant for concept-driven albums that sought a hook to grab audience attention with drummer Dannie Richmond's *"In" Jazz for the Culture Set* [AS-98]. The album alluded to the Pop Art movement with a wall of Campbell's soup cans on its cover, and was an ambitious (if overly cerebral) effort to collapse highbrow and popular culture together. Tunes by Bob Dylan and Chuck Berry and a handful of originals were tackled, modern-jazz style, by a small Mingus-styled band: Richmond and pianist Jaki Byard (both Mingus sidemen) plus guitarists Toots Thielemans and Jimmy Raney and bassist Cecil McBee.
151 *"I was newly"*: Alan Bergman, interview.
153 *"to go with"*: Sonny Rollins, quoted by Fred Miles, "Tapeing the Artists," (*Abundant Sounds,* July 1964, vol. 2, no. 3).
153 *"Everybody sort of"*: Sonny Rollins, quoted by Eric Nisenson, *Open Sky: Sonny Rollins and His World of Improvisation* (New York: St. Martin's Press, 2000): 178–79.
156 *Rollins's flirtation with the avant-garde*: Thanks to Ted Panken for the reminder of Sonny's more experimental work on RCA.
156 *"It turned out"*: Sonny Rollins, quoted by Eric Nisenson, *Open Sky,* 179.
156 *"I was kind"*: Ibid.
156 *"Early in the game"*: Bill Kaplan, interview.
156 *"John's contract provided"*: Ibid.
157 *"This is what"*: Ibid.
157 *"If John called"*: Alan Bergman, interview.
157 *"During the period"*: Bob Thiele, quoted by Robert Palmer, *Coda,* 32.
158 *"It's a lot"*: "The New Jazz" (*Newsweek,* December 12, 1966): 104.
158 *"The term 'free'"*: Archie Shepp, interview.
158 *one-offs with New Thing*: Archie Shepp's sideman, trombonist Roswell Rudd, stepped out with his American debut as a leader with *Everywhere* [AS-9126], a set of lengthy originals that introduced newer avant-garde arrivals (alto saxophonist Robin Kenyatta) and free-jazz veterans (bassist Charlie Haden, drummer Beaver Harris). Marion Brown's *Three for Shepp* [AS-9139] was an obvious followup to Shepp's Coltrane tribute of '64, divided between covers of Shepp compositions and Brown originals. Pharoah Sanders's *Tauhid* [AS-9138] caught the music, especially "Upper and Lower Egypt," that first attracted Coltrane to the tenor man from Little Rock, Arkansas.
158 *"Bob Thiele approached"*: Pharoah Sanders, interview with author, MiniDisc recording, June 1, 2003.
158 *"Thiele has not"*: Nat Hentoff, "The Jazz Record Scene" (*Down Beat,* Music '66): 50.
158 *"I keep wondering"*: Nat Hentoff, "Raising Wax Criteria" (*Down Beat,* October 20, 1966): 10.
158 *"One can just"*: Martin Williams, "A Modest Proposition" (*Down Beat,* December 14, 1966): 13.

CHAPTER 5 / BETWEEN JAZZ AND A HARD PLACE (1965–1967)

163 *"Jazz has had a peculiar"*: Ralph Gleason, *Celebrating the Duke: And Louis, Bessie, Billie, Bird, Carmen, Miles, Dizzy*

and Other Heroes (1975; reprint, New York: Da Capo Press, 1995): 149–50.

164 *"had a difficult time"*: Bob Thiele, quoted by Robert Palmer, *Coda,* 32.

164 *"I remember going"*: Bob Thiele Jr., interview.

164 *"They turned these"*: Bob Thiele, quoted by Robert Palmer, *Coda,* 32.

165 *"Some large companies"*: Ibid.

166 *"What I tried"*: Bob Thiele, quoted by William Ruhlmann, "Bob Thiele Produced Them All" (*Goldmine,* December 11, 1992): 4.

167 *"Playing pop songs"*: Gabor Szabo quoted by Pauline Rivelli, "Gabor Szabo" (*Jazz,* August '66): 30.

167 *"Gabor called me up"*: Larry Coryell, interview with author, MiniDisc recording, August 16, 2003.

167 *"because they were"*: Ibid.

168 *"The only real solos"*: Ibid.

168 *"That record is good"*: Ibid.

169 *"I'd get bored"*: Gary McFarland quoted by Dan Morgenstern, "Gary McFarland: Theme and Variations" (*Down Beat,* February 24, 1966): 25.

169 *five projects*: *Latin Shadows* [A(S)-93], with Shirley Scott's organ sound brightening an otherwise forced mix of material ("Downtown," "Can't Get Over the Bossa Nova," "Soul Sauce") with a string section and Latin percussion. *Tijuana Jazz* [AS-9104] (featured Clark Terry, other brass, and rhythm, in a project that seemed as inspired by Mexico as by Herb Alpert's success). *Profiles* [AS-9112] (a live-at-Lincoln Center performance of McFarland originals by an all-star jazz orchestra). *Simpatico* [AS-9122] (a co-headlined and pop-focused project with Gabor Szabo, with the arranger's lugubrious, multi-tracked vocals on various originals like "Ups and Downs" and Beatles tunes). The last and most memorable of McFarland's titles was *The October Suite: Steve Kuhn Plays the Compositions of Gary McFarland* [AS-9136]. On it, Coltrane's first pianist, classically trained and still thinking modally, tackled a series of impressionistic tunes written specifically for a session elevated by a string section on half the tracks, and winds on the rest.

172 *"You know we"*: Alan Bergman, interview.

172 *"ABC Records was"*: Ibid.

172 *"The Paramount Theater"*: Phil Kurnit, interview.

173 *"Ray Charles was"*: Alan Bergman, interview.

173 *"Those quote, gold albums"*: Bill Kaplan, interview.

173 *renew his Impulse contract*: Yasuhiro Fujioka et al., *John Coltrane: A Discography and Musical Biography* (*Studies in Jazz,* no. 20) (Lanham, Md.: Scarecrow Press, 1993): 292.

174 *"Alice Coltrane remembers"*: Alice Coltrane (related by Jowcol staff) and Ravi Coltrane, telephone conversations with author, July 14, 2005.

178 *"If we were"*: Bob Thiele, quoted by Frank Kofsky, *Coda,* 9.

179 *"I had talked"*: Alan Bergman, interview.

179 *"I don't know"*: Bob Thiele, quoted in *Blue Trane*.

179 *"We were all crushed"*: Bill Kaplan, interview.

179 *"I do remember"*: Ibid.

180 *"He was our leader"*: Archie Shepp, interview.

180 *"At that point"*: Alice Coltrane, interview.

180 *"I had never"*: Bill Kaplan, interview.

180 *"I'm sure that"*: Alan Bergman, interview.

180 *"I've had some"*: Bob Thiele, quoted by Frank Kofsky, *Coda,* 9–10.

CHAPTER 6 / IMPULSE AFTER TRANE (1967–1969)

183 *"The changes in"*: Martin Williams, "John Coltrane: Man in the Middle" (*Down Beat,* December 17, 1967): 114.

183 *"Once John had"*: Alice Coltrane, interview. According to Thiele, Coltrane had other plans in addition to those carried out by his widow. "His goal, shortly before he died, was to get a loft in the Village and he wanted to set up a place where people could come in, listen to his music being created—in other words, people could attend rehearsals, no admission, just the price of Coca-Cola. . . . This was definitely an ambition of his" (Bob Thiele, quoted by Frank Kofsky, *Coda,* 8). Given the loft scene that would flower in downtown Manhattan through the seventies, led in part by Rashied Ali and Ornette Coleman, Coltrane could be influential even through intention—at least prescient.

185 *"I never really"*: Alice Coltrane, interview.

185 *"My experience with Bob"*: Ibid.

185 *"Now, you will not"*: Ibid.

189 *"John meditated a lot"*: Ibid.

189 *"Before the sixties"*: Ibid.

189 *"I think you'll find"*: Marion Brown, quoted by Robert Palmer, liner notes to *Live in Greenwich Village: The Complete Impulse Recordings,* IMPD-2–273, 1998.

189 *Unlike the music*: For more on this distinction between Coltrane and Ayler, see Robert Palmer's excellent liners to the CD collection *Live in Greenwich Village: The Complete Impulse Recordings*. For more on the relationship between the two saxophonists, see Valerie Wilmer, *As Serious as Your Life* (London: Serpent's Tail, 1992): 106–11.

192 *"Albert Ayler had"*: Alice Coltrane, interview.

192 *"The music I bring"*: Albert Ayler, LP, "Message from Albert," *New Grass* (Impulse AS-9175, 1968).

196 *"You have to make"*: *As Serious as Your Life,* 108–9.

196 *"About the same time"*: Archie Shepp, interview.

197 *"John was very interested"*: Alice Coltrane, interview.

197 *"He did see"*: Ibid.

197 *"That's always been"*: Archie Shepp, interview.

198 *"I was trying"*: Ibid.

199 *"I fought for the"*: Bob Thiele, quoted by Robert Palmer, *Coda,* 32.

199 *"The unanimous reaction"*: Ibid.

199 *"I could sense"*: *What a Wonderful World,* 139.

200 *"Flying Dutchman Productions"*: "Thiele's Tie with Impulse" (*Billboard,* December 14, 1968): 3.

200 *"We are looking"*: "Impulse, BluesWay Broadening" (*Billboard,* March 8, 1969): 6.

200 *Jamal himself established a trio*: "Jamal Plans All-Trade Expansion" (*Billboard,* May 24, 1969): 8.

201 *"Despite the prolific"*: *What a Wonderful World,* 138.

201 *"It was the same"*: Ibid.

201 *ABC restructured*: "ABC Revamps Set-Up to 4 Separate Units" (*Billboard,* January 25, 1969): 3.

203 *acquired distribution rights to Riverside Records*: The

famed jazz label—one of the most important independents to come out of the fifties—had flourished from 1954 to 1964, producing classic recordings by Thelonious Monk, Cannonball Adderley, Bill Evans, and Wes Montgomery. Three years after the label went belly up, on August 5, 1967, *Billboard* printed a headline reading "ABC Will Distribute Riverside Globally," and explained that Bob Thiele would be in charge of repackaging the catalog for release. Small surprise that as a number of Riverside titles began reappearing in 1968, the Impulse releases diminished to a mere eighteen sessions that year.

204 *Newton was hailed*: "ABC to Step Up Buying Pace; Re-Signs Newton" (*Billboard,* December 23, 1967): 2.

204 *"California means a fresh"*: Eliot Tiegel, "Individuality Stressed in ABC's New Thrust at Market by Stark" (*Billboard,* October 18, 1969): 3.

204 *"Howard [Stark] became"*: Phil Kurnit, interview.

208 *"has set up three"*: "Thiele Bows 3 Labels; Sets Distrib. Deal With Philips" (*Billboard,* April 26, 1969): 1.

208 *"I resigned"*: *What a Wonderful World,* 139.

208 *"American distributor"*: "Thiele Picks Label's U.S. & Intn'l. Distribs" (*Billboard,* July 12, 1969): 3.

208 *The first Flying Dutchman releases*: The first wave of Flying Dutchman releases included Steve Allen's *Soulful Brass 2,* the Bob Thiele Emergency's *Head Start,* Spontaneous Combustion's *Come and Stick Your Head In,* the John Carter/Bobby Bradford Quartet's *Flight for Four,* the Tom Scott Quartet's *Jazz to Hair,* Stanley Crouch's *Ain't No Ambulances for No Nigguhs Tonight,* and Robert Scheer's *A Night at Santa Rita,* an audio documentary about a prison.

209 *"In the last several years"*: Paul Ackerman, "Total View" (*Billboard,* special Flying Dutchman insert, October 18, 1969): FD-3.

209 *"was probably the greatest"*: Bob Thiele, quoted by Frank Kofsky, *Coda,* 10.

CHAPTER 7 / IMPULSE OUT WEST (1969–1975)

211 *"Bob Thiele was"*: Michael Cuscuna, interview.

211 *"To quote a friend"*: Ed Michel, interview.

213 *"Between Steppenwolf"*: Ibid.

214 *"The [Impulse cover] design"*: Ibid.

214 *local talent base in Los Angeles*: The first wave of Ed Michel's L.A.-based productions yielded Emil Richards's live recording *Spirit of 1976* [AS-9182], Mel Brown's *I'd Rather Suck My Thumb* [AS-9186], Chris Coulter's *East Side San Jose* [AS-9197], and Dave MacKay and Vicki Hamilton's *Rainbow* [AS-9198].

215 *"The Coltrane and"*: Ed Michel, interview.

215 *"A gentleman all"*: Alice Coltrane, interview.

215 *"Nice man"*: Ahmad Jamal, interview with author, MiniDisc recording, April 15, 2003.

215 *"A nice man but"*: Archie Shepp, interview.

217 *"The sessions were"*: Ed Michel, interview.

217 *The* Jewels of Thought *session*: Ibid.

217 *"I realized looking"*: Ibid.

218 *"They were just great"*: Pharoah Sanders, interview.

218 *"This was during"*: Ibid.

218 *"I was running"*: Ed Michel, interview with Michael Jarrett, audiocassette, Fall 1995.

219 "Billboard *described it*": "Impulse Producers Giving Acts Double-Edged Effect" (*Billboard,* July 25, 1970): 10.

219 *"I dislike recordings"* Ed Michel, interview with Michael Jarrett.

222 *"During that period"*: Ahmad Jamal, interview.

222 *"That concept came"*: Ibid.

223 *"Musicians were very"*: Ed Michel, interview with author.

223 *"they never said"*: Alice Coltrane, interview.

226 *"She's a profoundly"*: Ibid.

226 *"When I was"*: Ed Michel, interview with Michael Jarrett.

227 *"It was just"*: Ed Michel, interview with author.

230 *"At that point"*: Ed Michel, interview with Michael Jarrett.

230 *"Half of the sales"*: Ed Michel, interview with author.

231 *"At that point"*: Ibid.

231 *"we don't have room"*: Ibid.

231 *"Whenever possible"*: Ibid.

231 *"At one point"*: Ibid.

234 *"As far as Howard"*: Ibid.

234 *"Steve Barri"*: Ibid.

235 *"Putting Genesis"*: Ed Michel, e-mail to author, March 13, 2005.

235 *"vanished without a trace"*: Ibid.

235 *"I was senior vice president"*: Dennis Lavinthal, interview with author, MiniDisc recording, June 1, 2003.

235 *"We were hot"*: Ibid.

237 *"Thirty or forty thousand"*: Ibid.

237 *"quickly fell off"*: Ibid.

237 *Newton, it turns out*: "Executive Turntable" (*Billboard,* March 7, 1970): 6.

237 *ABC's new president*: "Impulse Producers Giving Acts Double-Edged Effect" (*Billboard,* July 25, 1970): 10.

237 *"The jazz line"*: Eliot Tiegel, "New Marketing Approaches Key ABC/Dunhill 55-LP Sales Meet" (*Billboard,* September 12, 1970): 3.

237 *"The theory upstairs"*: Dennis Lavinthal, interview.

238 *"My recollection [of Impulse]"*: Ibid.

238 *"It seemed the sound"*: Ibid.

239 *"After that, Larry"*: Ed Michel, interview with author.

239 *"Jay Lasker was"*: Steve Backer, interview.

239 *"This was actually"*: Ibid.

242 *"Coltrane, in my eyes"*: Ibid.

243 *"A tour like"*: Steve Backer, quoted by Michael Ullman, *Jazz Lives: Portraits in Words and Pictures* (Washington, D.C., New Republic Books, 1980): 218.

243 *"If my own"*: James Isaacs review, written for the *Cambridge Phoenix,* Winter 1972, confirmed by Isaacs and quoted by Steve Backer, liner notes to *Irrepressible Impulses,* Impulse IMP-1972, 1972.

243 *"The tickets were"*: Steve Backer, interview.

244 *"I was quite proud"*: Ibid.

244 *"My thinking process"*: Ibid.

244 *"In my mind"*: Ibid.

246 "Streams *was not even*": Sam Rivers, interview with author, MiniDisc recording, March 31, 2005.

246 *"From the albums"*: Ibid.

248 *"He was signed"*: Ed Michel, interview with author.

248 *"Gato and Pharoah"*: Ibid.

248 *"I leave Flying"*: Gato Barbieri, interview with author, MiniDisc recording, May 24, 2003.
248 *"The Big Dogs"*: Ed Michel, liner notes to *Latino America,* Gato Barbieri, Impulse, IMPD-2–236, 1997.
248 *"There were bucks"*: Ibid.
249 *"I want to be"*: Gato Barbieri, interview.
249 *"If you listen"*: Ibid.
249 *"Jarrett seems to"*: Robert Palmer, "Keith Jarrett: From 'Ex-Miles Pianist' to Important Stylist" (*Rolling Stone,* December 21, 1972): 66.
252 *"Keith is one"*: Ed Michel, interview with author.
252 *"The Impulse quartet"*: Stephen Davis, "In League with the Giants" (*New York Times,* September 28, 1975, Arts section): 6.
252 *"I'm not interested"*: Keith Jarrett, quoted by Robert Palmer, "The Inner Octaves of Keith Jarrett" (*Down Beat,* October 24, 1974): 17.
253 *"playing electric music"*: Ibid.
253 *"Hey, I didn't"*: Paul Motian, interview with author, MiniDisc recording, April 3, 2005.
253 *"What fusion attempted"*: Ed Michel, interview with author.
253 *"John Klemmer was as close"*: Steve Backer, interview.
256 *"I remember Gato's"*: Ibid.
256 *"At one point"*: Ed Michel, interview with author.
256 *"For about two"*: Ibid.
256 *"Over all, from a [sales] volume"*: Steve Backer, interview.
256 *"With Steve and Ed"*: Dennis Lavinthal, interview.
256 *other labels were suffering*: William Knoedelseder, *Stiffed* (New York: HarperCollins, 1993): 9.
257 *"They saw records"*: Phil Kurnit, interview.
257 *"By 1974, we"*: Steve Backer, interview.
257 *"I remember one"*: Ibid.
260 *"I went to meet"*: Ibid.
260 *"I knew there was"*: Ed Michel, interview with author.
261 *"Pompadour felt that"*: Phil Kurnit, interview.
261 *the news go public*: Bob Kirsch, "Jerry Rubenstein: New ABC Records Chairman Is an Astute Businessman Who's Not Unknown to Trade" (*Billboard,* January 18, 1975): 3.
261 *"The whole company"*: Dennis Lavinthal, interview.
261 *"Jay Lasker was out"*: Ed Michel, interview with author.
261 *"Lasker survived"*: Phil Kurnit, interview.

CHAPTER 8 / THE LIVES OF A LABEL; THE TENOR OF A TIME (1975–PRESENT)

265 *"I believe one"*: Bob Thiele, quoted by Robert Palmer, *Coda,* 31–32.
265 *"Impulse Records, quiet"*: Bob Kirsch, "Impulse Label 'Awakens' with an Ambitious Autumn Program" (*Billboard,* August 16, 1975): 6.
266 *"I admired Blue Note"*: Esmond Edwards, interview with author, MiniDisc recording, April 5, 2005.
266 *"hard-core fans"*: Ibid.
266 *"People weren't running"*: Ibid. Noted jazz researcher, educator, and Coltrane-ologist David Wild offers another perspective on Impulse's archival activity during this time: "Back in the early seventies, I started working on transcribing early Coltrane solos, with some vague idea of making a book out of it. As part of that process I rather naïvely sent off letters to different people, asking questions about Coltrane and the recordings. One went to Ed Michel, at that point head of the Impulse label, and about two years later, in early '76, I got a letter from Ed's successor, Esmond Edwards, asking me to call.

"It seems the Japanese licensees were frustrated by the lack of new Coltrane releases; they wanted new product. Steve Diener, Esmond's superior in the organization, quoted them as saying something like 'we could sell x units of a recording of Coltrane sneezing.' Esmond was not familiar enough with the material [and] they needed someone to sort through the material and identify stuff to release.

"Over Thanksgiving 1976, Impulse flew my wife and me out to L.A. from Michigan, and we spent three days in a studio at the Beverly Boulevard location, playing through the tapes that remained in the vault, cataloging what was there. Interestingly, Michael Cuscuna was in the next studio producing a session with [comedian] Martin Mull, and stuck his head in. I recognized his name from articles he'd done in *Down Beat* and liner notes. I remember his first question was whether we'd found the Archie Shepp *A Love Supreme* session. Of course we hadn't; a lot of the original reels were gone from the vault.

"Working remotely from Ann Arbor, I later delivered Esmond a list of titles for a proposed Vanguard LP. I suggested titling it *Spiritual,* but Esmond called it *The Other Village Vanguard Tapes* [AS-9325]. After that LP was released there was another reorganization at ABC and Esmond departed. Nobody replaced him, but Cuscuna started handling projects on a freelance basis, and we worked together on the next couple of releases—I did the research as an adjunct to getting to write the liner notes for each release.

"That weekend was the beginning of a relationship that was active until the late eighties and still exists; the most recent liner notes I did for Impulse were for *The Olatunji Concert: The Last Live Recording* [314–589–120–2] in 2001" (e-mail to author, October 13, 2005).
266 *"It was a great"*: Michael Cuscuna, interview.
267 *"I was trying"*: Keith Jarrett, quoted by Neil Tesser, liner notes to Keith Jarrett, *Mysteries: The Impulse Years, 1975–1976,* Impulse, IMPD 4–189, 12.
267 *"I met Jimmy Ponder"*: Esmond Edwards, interview.
267 *wealth of new titles*: Vocalists: Gloria Lynne, *I Don't Know How to Love Him* [ASD-9311]; Betty Carter, *What a Little Moonlight Can Do* [ASD-9321]; Grady Tate, *Master Grady Tate* [ASD-9330]; Bobby Bland and B.B. King, *. . . Together Again* [ASD-9317]. Hard-boppers: Jimmy Ponder, *Illusions* [ASD-9313] and *White Room* [ASD-9327]; Sonny Criss, *Warm and Sonny* [ASD-9312] and *The Joy of Sax* [ASD-9325]; Lucky Thompson, *Dancing Sunbeam* [ASD-9507]; Blue Mitchell, *African Violet* [ASD-9328] and *Summer Soft* [ASD-9347]; Les McCann, *The Music Lets Me Be* [AS-9329]. The five-trombone choir Brass Fever: *Brass Fever* [ASD-9308] and *Time Is Running Out* [ASD-9319].
267 *"The first thing"*: Esmond Edwards, interview.
270 *"Jazz was something"*: Ibid.
270 *"They sold it"*: Phil Kurnit, interview.
270 *what was then a fire-sale price*: *Stiffed*, 9.
272 *"that dragged jazz"*: Phil Johnson, "They Couldn't Help Acting on Impulse" (*The Independent* [UK], February 3, 1995): 26.

272 *"When we looked"*: Hollis King, e-mail to author, April 2, 2005.
273 *"It can range"*: Michael Kauffman, interview with author, DAT recording, October 16, 2001.
274 *"There have been situations"*: Marilyn McLeod, telephone conversation with author, April 12, 2005.
275 *"When I first"*: Michael Cuscuna, interview.
275 *"I found it"*: Erick Labson, interview with author, DAT recording, July 31, 2001.
275 *"With anything that"*: Michael Cuscuna, interview.
276 *"During those . . . sessions"*: Rudy Van Gelder, facsimile to author, January 15, 2002.
276 *"The session reels"*: Michael Cuscuna, interview.
276 *"But in '98"*: Ken Druker, telephone conversation with author, April 17, 2005.
276 *thirty-three Coltrane session tapes*: For a full listing and analysis of these long-lost tapes, see: Barry Kernfeld, "John Coltrane in Rudy Van Gelder's Studio," Part 1 (*Names & Numbers*, April 2005): 2–7, and Part 2 (*Names & Numbers*, July 2005): 3–9, errata 14–15. *Names & Numbers* is a Dutch publication, printed in English, and for subscriptions lists as a contact Gerhard Hoogeveen, Reine Claudestraat 15, 1326 JC Almere, The Netherlands. E-mail: gehojazz@planet.nl. Much thanks to Mr. Kernfeld for this information.
277 *"Just before leaving"*: Bob Thiele, quoted by Robert Palmer, *Coda*, 32.
278 *"He took me"*: Bob Thiele Jr., interview.
278 *"He carried me"*: Bob Thiele, heard on radio special *Tell Me How Long Trane's Been Gone*, part 2 of 5, Steve Rowland and Larry Abrams co-producers, 2001.
279 *"I just became"*: Bob Thiele, quoted in Ted Fox, *In the Groove*, 195.
279 *"I don't think people"*: John Coltrane, quoted in Leonard Feather, "Coltrane Shaping Musical Revolt" (*New York Post*, October 18, 1964): 54.

ALBUM PROFILES

Please note that the release dates of the profiled albums were mostly drawn from *Schwann Long Playing Record Catalog* (now titled *Schwann Spectrum*), the monthly publication listing all recorded music titles in print. These dates are approximate, and when it was possible to use another source, *Schwann* often proved to be late by one month. Yet no other reliable record exists to help determine when specific Impulse titles first appeared, save for reviews and advertisements. It is interesting to note that for the most part, the standard time from studio to release for an Impulse album was six months, sometimes as little as two or three!

RAY CHARLES / *GENIUS + SOUL = JAZZ*

34 *"If you want to tell"*: This quote and remaining Ray Charles quotes in this album profile from interview with author, MiniDisc recording, June 24, 2003.
34 *"You've got Clark"*: This quote and remaining Creed Taylor quotes in this album profile from interview with author.
35 *"It was in"*: Quincy Jones, interview with author, MiniDisc recording, August 23, 2003.

GIL EVANS / *OUT OF THE COOL*

41 *"made the album in an afternoon"*: Stephanie Stein-Crease, *Gil Evans: Out of the Cool* (Chicago: Acapella Books, 2002): 235.
41 *the three previous sessions*: Ibid.
41 *" 'La Nevada' was not"*: Ibid., p. 236
41 *"When he is not"*: John S. Wilson, "Halting Path of the Jazz Arranger" (*New York Times*, March 26, 1961).

OLIVER NELSON / *THE BLUES AND THE ABSTRACT TRUTH*

44 *"That's my title"*: This quote and remaining Creed Taylor quotes in this album profile from interview with author.
44 *"Me, Phil Woods"*: This quote and remaining Freddie Hubbard quotes in this album profile from interview with author.

JOHN COLTRANE / *AFRICA/BRASS*

52 *"I certainly thought"*: This quote and remaining Creed Taylor quotes in this album profile from interview with author.
52 *"All I remember"*: This quote and remaining Freddie Hubbard quotes in this album profile from interview with author.
52 *"I have an African"*: John Coltrane, interview with Ralph J. Gleason, tape recording, May 2, 1962.
52 *"Rehearsal time was"*: This quote and remaining McCoy Tyner quotes in this album profile from interview with author.
53 *"In 1965 we"*: Roger McGuinn, interview with author, March 8, 2001.
53 *"We never heard Coltrane"*: Phil Lesh, interview with author, September 5, 2001.

JOHN COLTRANE / *LIVE AT THE VILLAGE VANGUARD*

69 *"The melody not"*: John Coltrane, quoted by Nat Hentoff, liner notes to *Live at the Village Vanguard*, Impulse A(S)-10, 1962.
69 *"I was living"*: Archie Shepp, interview with author, MiniDisc recording, September 7, 2003.
69 *"It's basically a blues"*: Ibid.
69 *"More like waitin'"*: Ira Gitler, "Double View of Coltrane 'Live'" (*Down Beat*, April 26, 1962): 24.
69 *"Sputtering inconclusiveness"*: Pete Welding, Ibid.
69 *"musical mega-nova"*: *What a Wonderful World*, 120–21.
69 *"one of those crucial"*: Gary Giddins, *Visions of Jazz* (New York: Oxford University Press, 1998): 476.

BENNY CARTER / *FURTHER DEFINITIONS*

73 *"considered by many"*: Monroe Berger, Ed Berger, and James Patrick, *Benny Carter: A Life in American Music*, 2nd edition (Lanham, Md: Scarecrow Press, 2001): 275.
73 *"I was in New York"*: This quote and remaining Benny Carter quotes in this album profile from interview with Ed Berger, radio station WBGO, June 2001.
73 *"At that time"*: This quote and remaining Phil Wood quotes in this album profile (save for the one below) from interview with author, MiniDisc recording, September 26, 2005.
73 *"Hawk's entrance on"*: Phil Woods, liner notes to Benny

Carter, *Another Time, Another Place,* Evening Star ES-104, 1996. Thanks to Ed Berger for this!

THE ELLINGTON SAXOPHONE ENCOUNTERS

78 *"Duke Ellington came to me"*: Coleman Hawkins, quoted by Stanley Dance, liner notes to *Duke Ellington Meets Coleman Hawkins,* Impulse A(S)-26, 1963.
79 *"I was really honored"*: John Coltrane, quoted by Stanley Dance, liner notes to *Duke Ellington and John Coltrane,* Impulse A(S)-30, 1963.
79 *"Up until the Ellington"*: Bob Thiele, quoted by Frank Kofsky, *Coda,* 4–5.
79 *"From then on"*: Ibid.

CURTIS FULLER / *CABIN IN THE SKY*

82 *"Thiele said"*: This quote and remaining Curtis Fuller quotes in this album profile from interview with author, MiniDisc recording, July 26, 2003.

FREDDIE HUBBARD / *THE ARTISTRY OF FREDDIE HUBBARD*

86 "*[Bob Thiele] called it*": This quote and remaining Freddie Hubbard quotes in this album profile from interview with author.

McCOY TYNER / *INCEPTION*

90 *"What really motivated"*: McCoy Tyner, interview.
91 *"Bob Thiele came"*: Ibid.
91 *"I had been doing"*: Ibid.
91 *"He's the one"*: Ibid.
91 "Inception—*I wrote*": Ibid.
91 *"Playing with Elvin"*: McCoy Tyner, quoted by Nat Hentoff, liner notes to *Inception,* Impulse A(S)-39, 1962.
91 *"Melodic inventiveness"*: John Coltrane, quoted by Nat Hentoff, Ibid.

JOHN COLTRANE AND JOHNNY HARTMAN

98 *"Then the English"*: This quote and remaining Johnny Hartman quotes in this album profile from John S. Wilson, "Hartman Singing in 'Voices of Jazz'" (*New York Times,* May 21, 1982): C18.
98 *"I had the idea of the vocal"*: Bob Thiele, quoted by Frank Kofsky, *Coda,* 13.
99 *"Johnny Hartman"*: John Coltrane, quoted by Frank Kofsky, *Black Giants,* 34.
99 *"After the show"*: In the 1982 interview, Hartman identified Coltrane's pianist as Cedar Walton, not McCoy Tyner, and also placed Van Gelder's studio in Hackensack, rather than Englewood Cliffs, New Jersey. With almost twenty years from session to interview, the singer's memory lapses are hardly surprising.
99 *"I remember Johnny"*: *What a Wonderful World,* 124.
99 *"At a later date"*: Michael Cuscuna, liner notes to *John Coltrane and Johnny Hartman,* GRD-157, 1995.
99 *"a version of 'Afro Blue'"*: Ibid.
99 *"revitalized the careers"*: Will Friedwald, *Jazz Singing: America's Great Voices from Bessie Smith to Bebop and Beyond* (New York: Collier Books, 1990) 270–71.
99 *"at the time"*: Ibid.

CHARLES MINGUS / *THE BLACK SAINT AND THE SINNER LADY*

114 *"You haven't been told"*: Korall, Cerulli, and Nasatir, *The Jazz Word*: 17.
114 *"talented, successful and angry"*: "Crow Jim" (*Time,* October 19, 1962).
114 *"Volatile"*: John S. Wilson, "Maturing Artist" (*New York Times,* November 3, 1963).
114 *"A Volcano Named"*: Nat Hentoff, "A Volcano Named Mingus" (*HiFi/Stereo Review,* December 1964): 52.
115 *"New Folk Band"*: *Myself When I Am Real,* 210.
115 *"my living epitaph"*: Charles Mingus, liner notes to *The Black Saint and the Sinner Lady,* Impulse A(S)-35, 1963.
115 *"I'm doing what"*: Stanley Dance, "Mingus Speaks" (*Jazz,* November–December, 1963): 11.
115 *"The sessions for* Black Saint": Bob Thiele, interview with Michael Jarrett.
115 *"I write compositions"*: Charles Mingus, quoted by Nat Hentoff, *HiFi/Stereo Review,* 54.
115 *"Each man's particular"*: Ibid.
115 *"When a Mingus"*: Hentoff, Ibid., 55.
115 *"as Mingus's parents"*: *Myself When I Am Real,* 210.
115 *"Black Saint who suffers"*: Dr. Edmund Pollack, liner notes to *The Black Saint and the Sinner Lady*.
115 *"From every experience"*: Ibid.

ARCHIE SHEPP / *FOUR FOR TRANE*

120 *"Let me explain"*: Archie Shepp, interview.

JOHN COLTRANE / *A LOVE SUPREME*

124 *"When he was"*: Alice Coltrane, interview. Though the three original double-sided pages of sheet music paper that comprise John Coltrane's *A Love Supreme* manuscript were auctioned in February 2005 to an unknown bidder, the rights to publish their image have been retained by the Coltrane family. The images published herein are being published with the express permission of Alice Coltrane and Jowcol Music.

JOHN COLTRANE / *ASCENSION*

136 *"I made a thing"*: John Coltrane, interview with Alan Grant, WABC broadcast, unknown date, 1965.
136 *"The ensemble passages"*: Lewis Porter, *John Coltrane: His Life and Music* (Ann Arbor: University of Michigan Press, 1998): 263.
137 *"We used to get"*: Alan Bergman, interview.
137 *"We used to listen"*: Gary Giddins, interview.
137 *"I [had] sent"*: *What a Wonderful World,* 128.
137 *"When we found"*: Gary Giddins, interview.

PEE WEE RUSSELL / *ASK ME NOW!*

144 *"It was highly"*: This quote and remaining Russell George quotes in this album profile from interview with author, MiniDisc recording, April 14, 2003.

144 *"was a great catalyst"*: This quote and remaining Ronnie Bedford quotes in this album profile from interview with author, MiniDisc recording, April 15, 2003.

145 *"What happened is"*: This quote and remaining George Avakian quotes in this album profile from interview with author.

EARL HINES / *ONCE UPON A TIME*

148 *"There are a few"*: Dan Morgenstern, *Living with Jazz* (New York: Pantheon, 2004): 162.

148 *"A triumph"*: Ibid.

149 *"decided to summon"*: Uncredited cover copy, Earl Hines, *Once Upon a Time,* Impulse A-9108, 1966.

SONNY ROLLINS / *ALFIE*

154 *"The method is unusual"*: Joe Goldberg, "The Further Adventures of Sonny Rollins" (*Down Beat,* August 26, 1965): 21.

154 *"a very good understanding"*: Sonny Rollins, quoted by Nat Hentoff, liner notes, *Alfie,* Impulse IMPD-224, 1997.

155 *"I hope to compose"*: Ibid.

155 *"I enjoyed writing"*: Sonny Rollins, quoted by Eric Nisenson, *Open Sky,* 181.

ODDS & TRENDS—PART I

160 *"There was just"*: Michael Cuscuna, interview.

161 *"It could go"*: Ibid.

STEVE KUHN / *THE OCTOBER SUITE*

170 *"I'm looking at it"*: Steve Kuhn, interview with author, MiniDisc recording, December 22, 2004.

ODDS & TRENDS—PART II

176 *"I then half-heartedly"*: *What a Wonderful World,* 64.

177 *Richards and his Microtonal Blues*: Rock footnote: Emil Richards's Microtonal Blues Band included legendary session guitarist Tommy Tedesco, as well as percussionist Joey Porcaro, whose sons Jerry and Steve would found the rock group Toto in 1978.

JOHN AND ALICE COLTRANE / *COSMIC MUSIC*

186 *"O.K., this was"*: Alice Coltrane, interview.

187 *"There were problems"*: Bill Kaplan, interview.

187 *"Once* [Cosmic Music] *was available"*: Alice Coltrane, interview.

187 *"The fervor on"*: Mike Zwerin, "Cosmic Music" (*Rolling Stone,* February 1, 1969).

187 *"Some people didn't"*: Alice Coltrane, quoted by Edwin Pouncey, "Enduring Love" (*The Wire,* April 2002): 40.

ALBERT AYLER / *MUSIC IS THE HEALING FORCE OF THE UNIVERSE*

190 *"Suddenly here I was"*: This quote and remaining Ed Michel quotes in this album profile from interview with author.

ELVIN JONES AND RICHARD DAVIS / *HEAVY SOUNDS*

194 *"It was one"*: This quote and remaining Elvin Jones quotes in this album profile from interview with author, MiniDisc recording, August 31, 2002.

194 *"Bob said, 'Why'"*: This quote and remaining Richard Davis quotes in this album profile from interview with author, MiniDisc recording, May 24, 2004.

CHARLIE HADEN / *LIBERATION MUSIC ORCHESTRA*

202 *"I wanted to be part"*: This quote and remaining Carla Bley quotes in this album profile from interview with author, MiniDisc recording, August 9, 2003.

202 *"I was real concerned"*: This quote and remaining Charlie Haden quotes in this album profile from interview with author, MiniDisc recording, February 18, 2004.

PHAROAH SANDERS / *KARMA*

206 *"I call what"*: This quote and remaining Leon Thomas quotes in this album profile from *Black Giants,* 116.

206 *"I met Leon"*: This quote and remaining Pharoah Sanders quotes in this album profile from interview with author.

HOWARD ROBERTS / *ANTELOPE FREEWAY*

220 *"At the end"*: This quote and remaining Bill Szymczyk quotes in this album profile from interview with author.

221 *"a fun recording"*: Chip Stern, "Best of 2003" (*Audiophile,* January 2004).

AHMAD JAMAL / *THE AWAKENING*

224 *"Ahmad Jamal, for instance"*: Cannonball Adderley, interview with Denver deejay Jack Winter, tape recording, February 1972.

224 *"Everybody I knew"*: Ed Michel, interview with author.

224 *"My sense is"*: Ed Michel, interview with Michael Jarrett.

225 *"I said, 'Great'"*: Ed Michel, interview with author.

225 *"I had gotten"*: This quote and remaining Ahmad Jamal quotes in this album profile from interview with author.

225 *"At that time"*: Ed Michel, interview with author.

225 *"We spent two"*: Ibid.

ALICE COLTRANE / *UNIVERSAL CONSCIOUSNESS*

228 *"One day when"*: This quote and remaining Alice Coltrane quotes in this album profile from interview with author.

228 *"Alice is a very schooled"*: This quote and remaining Ed Michel quotes in this album profile from interview with author.

229 *"we recorded some Stravinsky"*: In a switch from her role OK-ing the use of her late husband's music, Alice Coltrane herself recalls approaching the family of Igor Stravinksy when she wanted to record his music. "I had gotten a letter from Mrs.

Stravinsky once, because years ago I would do excerpts from either the 'Firebird' suite or 'The Rite of Spring,' and she said, 'Oh no, my husband would never play excerpts from any of his works.' I wrote back to her and I told her that I held Mr. Stravinsky in the highest regard, and I would never present anything musically that was a disservice or dishonor to him or his family, and I appreciate her informing me that he would prefer only the entire work to be performed, and not portions of his work. So I stopped recording [Stravinsky's music in excerpt], but I have performed an excerpt at [the Manhattan cathedral] St. John the Divine" (interview with author).

SUN RA: THE SATURN RECORDINGS

232 *"If you children"*: Ed Michel, www.edmicheljazzproducer.com/sun_ra_notes%201.htm.

ARCHIE SHEPP / *ATTICA BLUES*

240 *"My drummer, Beaver Harris"*: This quote and remaining Archie Shepp quotes in this album profile from interview with author.
241 *"ABC executives"*: Ed Michel, interview with author.

GATO BARBIERI / *CHAPTER ONE*

250 *"In those days"*: This quote and remaining Gato Barbieri quotes in this album profile from interview with author.
251 *"Please keep in mind"*: Ed Michel, liner notes to *Latino America,* Gato Barbieri, Impulse, IMPD-2–236, 3.
251 *"I went to this ABC/Dunhill"*: This quote and remaining Steve Backer quotes in this album profile from interview with author.
251 *"The rumor was that"*: An accounting—so to speak—of excesses invited by the sales bonus arrangement certain ABC executives enjoyed is offered in William Knoedelseder's investigative account of improprieties in the music business, *Stiffed* (9): "One former ABC president, Jay Lasker, had negotiated an employment contract based on sales. The problem was the contract defined 'sales' as what was manufactured and shipped to the distribution centers, not what was actually sold to customers. As a result, Lasker pressed records far in excess of any market demand, eventually filling up ABC's own warehouses and having to lease more space from independent distributors, which he paid for by giving the distributors the equivalent in free records."

Knoedelseder clearly lays a major part of the blame for the demise of ABC Records on Lasker's self-profiting scheme. Says Dennis Lavinthal of his former boss and his habit of inflating sales predictions at company meetings: "That was all kind of like a rehearsed game that Jay was playing because the people in the room all worked for him. I remember us taking runs on certain Impulse records—Klemmer and Alice Coltrane—and trying to sell a lot more records than we had before by trying to get some of what was called underground radio airplay on the records. I know we were selling lots of records, so this whole rap about the warehouses and the returns and everything, I don't know if that was true. I don't know what that game was. I was too young and naïve to figure that out" (Dennis Lavinthal, interview with author).

KEITH JARRETT / *FORT YAWUH*

254 *"Can you hear me?"*: Keith Jarrett, addressing audience, *Keith Jarrett: The Impulse Years, 1973–1974,* Impulse IMPD5–237, 1997.
254 *"You come to me"*: Charles Mingus, quoted in *The Jazz Word,* 16.
254 *"Those yelps of delight"*: This quote and remaining Paul Motian quotes in this album profile from interview with author.
255 *"I wanted to be"*: Ed Michel, interview with author.
255 *"I play different"*: Keith Jarrett, quoted by Leonard Lyons, *The Great Jazz Pianists* (New York: Da Capo Press, 1983): 298.

SAM RIVERS / *CRYSTALS*

258 *"As far as"*: Sam Rivers, liner notes to *Crystals,* Impulse ASD-9286, 1974.
259 *"All the compositions"*: This quote and remaining Sam Rivers quotes in this album profile from interview with author.
259 *"most immediately gripping"*: Robert Palmer, "Sam Rivers: An Artist on an Empty Stage" (*Down Beat,* February 13, 1975): 33.

JOHN COLTRANE / *INTERSTELLAR SPACE*

262 *"The way [Rashied Ali] plays"*: John Coltrane, quoted by Nat Hentoff, liner notes to *Live at the Village Vanguard Again!* Impulse A(S)-9124, 1968.
262 *"He was telling me"*: Rashied Ali, interview with author.
262 *"when he started"*: David S. Ware, interview with author, MiniDisc recording, June 23, 2001.
263 *"These duets are"*: *John Coltrane: His Life and Music,* 277.
263 *"succeeded precisely* because": Ibid., 288.
263 *"For all its intimidating"*: Ben Ratliff, *The New York Times Essential Library—Jazz: A Critic's Guide to the 100 Most Important Recordings* (New York: Times Books, 2002): 189.
263 *"This last, unfinished"*: John Litweiler, *The Freedom Principle: Jazz After 1958* (1984; reprint, New York: Da Capo Press, 1990): 102–3.
263 *"I believe he"*: Ravi Coltrane, interview with author.
263 *"You can just"*: Rashied Ali, interview with author.

JOHN HANDY / *HARD WORK*

268 *"Believe me, I totally"*: This quote and remaining John Handy quotes in this album profile from interview with author, MiniDisc recording, April 8, 2005.
268 *"We weren't even"*: This quote and remaining Esmond Edwards quotes in this album profile from interview with author.

EPILOGUE: ALICE COLTRANE / *TRANSLINEAR LIGHT*

280 *"Unlike Coltrane's generation"*: Francis Davis, *Like Young* (New York: Da Capo Press, 2001): 174.
All quotes from Ravi and Alice Coltrane from interviews with author, MiniDisc recordings, February 19 and 20, 2004.

IMPULSE RECORDS DISCOGRAPHY, 1961–1977

Please note: Until Impulse began to print a P line (a copyright statement including the year) on all of its releases in 1969, the most reliable record of an album's release date was the *Schwann Long Playing Record Catalogue*, a monthly publication that relied on the record labels to accurately report when a title had been manufactured and distributed to retail. That system was not a perfect one, nor was the accuracy of the album cover information–the song titles below reflect what was printed on the covers, including such errors as John Coltrane's tune "Niema" (rather than "Naima") on Archie Shepp's *Four for Trane*.

As well, Impulse's catalog numbering process was, at times, less than reliable: note the skipped-over numbers AS-9172, 9177, and 9179 as Bob Thiele was preparing to leave ABC in late 1968/early 1969. As curious are a few numbering anomalies—such as Coltrane's *Selflessness* AS-9161 and Archie Shepp's *Three for a Quarter, One for a Dime* AS-9162; both albums sport cover designs that imply a release date years after other titles immediately before and after in catalog sequence.

Sources: The archives of the Institute of Jazz Studies, Rutgers University, Newark, New Jersey; those of the Verve Music Group, New York, New York; and the personal collection of Bob Belden. Additional online corroboration from www.jazzdisco.org/impulse.

CATALOG # AND YEAR OF RELEASE	TITLE AND ARTIST	TRACKS
A(S) 1 1961	*The Great Kai and J.J.* Kai Winding and J.J. Johnson	This Could Be the Start of Something; Georgia on My Mind; Judy; Blue Monk; Alone Together; Side by Side; I Concentrate on You; Theme From "Picnic"; Trixie; Going, Going, Gong!; Just for a Thrill
A(S) 2 1961	*Genius + Soul = Jazz* Ray Charles	From the Heart; I've Got News for You; Moanin'; Let's Go; One Mint Julep; I'm Gonna Move to the Outskirts of Town; Stompin' Room Only; Mister C.; Strike Up the Band; Birth of the Blues
A(S) 3 1961	*The Incredible Kai Winding Trombones* Kai Winding	Speak Low; Lil Darlin'; Doodlin'; Love Walked In; Mangos; Impulse; Black Coffee; Bye, Bye, Blackbird; Michie (Slow); Michie (Fast)
A(S) 4 1961	*Out of the Cool* The Gil Evans Orchestra	La Nevada; Where Flamingos Fly; Bilbao; Stratusphunk; Sunken Treasure
A(S) 5 1961	*The Blues and the Abstract Truth* Oliver Nelson	Stolen Moments; Hoe-Down/Cascades; Yearnin'; Butch and Butch; Teenie's Blues
A(S) 6 1961	*Africa/Brass* The John Coltrane Quartet	Africa; Greensleeves; Blues Minor
A(S) 7 1961	*Art Blakey and the Jazz Messengers* Art Blakey and the Jazz Messengers	Alamode; Invitation; Circus; You Don't Know What Love Is; I Hear a Rhapsody; Gee Baby, Ain't I Good to You
A(S) 8 1961	*Percussion Bitter Sweet* Max Roach	Praise for a Martyr; Mendacity; Man from South Africa; Garvey's Ghost; Mama; Tender Warriors
A(S) 9 1962	*Into the Hot* The Gil Evans Orchestra	Moon Taj; Pots; Angkor Wat; Bulbs; Barry's Tune; Mixed
A(S) 10 1962	*Live at the Village Vanguard* John Coltrane	Spiritual; Softly as in a Morning Sunrise; Chasin' the Trane

CATALOG # AND YEAR OF RELEASE	TITLE AND ARTIST	TRACKS
A(S) 11 1962	*The Quintessence* Quincy Jones and His Orchestra	Quintessence; Robot Portrait; Little Karen; Straight, No Chaser; For Lena and Lennie; Hard Sock Dance; Invitation; The Twitch
A(S) 12 1962	*Further Definitions* Benny Carter and His Orchestra	Honeysuckle Rose; The Midnight Sun Will Never Set; Crazy Rhythm; Blue Star; Cotton Tail; Body and Soul; Cherry; Doozy
A(S) 13 1962	*Soul Trombone and the Jazz Clan* Curtis Fuller	The Clan; In the Wee Small Hours of the Morning; Newdles; The Breeze and I; Dear Old Stockholm; Ladies' Night
A(S) 14 1962	*Statements* Milt Jackson Quartet	Statement; Slowly; A Thrill from the Blues; Paris Blues; Put Off; A Beautiful Romance; Sonnymoon for Two; The Bad and the Beautiful
A(S) 15 1962	*Count Basie and the Kansas City Seven* Count Basie and the Kansas City Seven	Oh, Lady, Be Good; Secrets; I Want a Little Girl; Shoe Shine Boy; Count's Place; Senator Whitehead; Tallyho, Mr. Basie!; What'cha Talkin'?
A(S) 16 1962	*It's Time* Max Roach, His Chorus and Orchestra	It's Time; Another Valley; Sunday Afternoon; Living Room; Profit; Lonesome Lover
A(S) 17 1962	*The Song Is Paris* Jackie Paris	Duke's Place; If Love Is Good to Me; Jenny; My Very Good Friend in the Looking Glass; 'Tis Autumn; Nobody Loses All the Time; Everybody Needs Love; Cherry; Thad's Blues; Tonight; Cinderella
A(S) 18 1962	*Inception* McCoy Tyner Trio	Inception; There Is No Greater Love; Blues for Gwen; Sunset; Effendi; Speak Low
A(S) 19 1962	*Jazz Goes to the Movies* Manny Albam and His Orchestra	Exodus; High Noon; Paris Blues; Dolce Vita; Majority of One; Green Leaves of Summer; The Guns of Navarone; El Cid; Slowly
A(S) 20 1962	*2 3 4* Shelly Manne	Take the "A" Train; The Sicks of Us; Slowly; Lean on Me; Cherokee; Me and Some Drums
A(S) 21 1962	*Coltrane* John Coltrane Quartet(te)	Out of This World; Soul Eyes; Inch Worm; Tunji; Miles' Mode
A(S) 22 1962	*Cabin in the Sky* Curtis Fuller	The Prayer/Taking a Chance on Love; Cabin in the Sky; Old Ship of Zion; Do What You Wanna Do; Honey in the Honeycomb; Happiness Is a Thing Called Joe; Savannah; Love Turned the Light Out; In My Old Virginia Home; Love Me Tomorrow; The Prayer
A(S) 23 1962	*Out of the Afternoon* Roy Haynes Quartet	Moon Ray; Fly Me to the Moon; Raoul; Snap Crackle; If I Should Lose You; Long Wharf; Some Other Spring
A(S) 24 1963	*Alarums and Excursions* Michael Brown	The John Birch Society; Starr Faithfull's Last Letter; Lizzie Borden; The Blood-Red Rose; Run to Your Momma; Zion (Salt Lake City); Ruth Snyder; Diamonds of Dew; Robert E. Lee; Mary, the Queen of Scots; Lost in the Woods; I Like a Fun'ral
A(S) 25 1963	*Morality* Oscar Brand	Spent My Money on Sally Brown; The Morning Dew; Sixteen Next Sunday; Billy the Kid; The Devil's in the Women; Tomorrow We'll Be Sober; The Willow Garden; Talking Morality Blues; A Dodgin' (The Dodger); The Pale Moonlight; Rye Whiskey; The Old Traveler's Song; Passing Through

CATALOG # AND YEAR OF RELEASE	TITLE AND ARTIST	TRACKS
A(S) 26 1963	*Duke Ellington Meets Coleman Hawkins* Duke Ellington and Coleman Hawkins	Limbo Jazz; Mood Indigo; Ray Charles' Place; Wanderlust; You Dirty Dog; Self Portrait (of the Bean); The Jeep Is Jumpin'; The Ricitic
A(S) 27 1963	*The Artistry of Freddie Hubbard* Freddie Hubbard	Caravan; Bob's Place; Happy Times; Summertime; 7th Day
A(S) 28 1963	*Desafinado: Coleman Hawkins Plays Bossa Nova and Jazz Samba* Coleman Hawkins Sextet	Desafinado; I'm Looking Over a Four Leaf Clover; Samba Para Bean; I Remember You; One Note Samba; O Pato; Um Abraco No Bonfa; Stumpy Bossa Nova
A(S) 29 1963	*Passin' Thru* Chico Hamilton Quintet	Passin' Thru; The Second Time Around; El Toro; Transfusion; Lady Gabor; Lonesome Child
A(S) 30 1963	*Duke Ellington & John Coltrane* Duke Ellington and John Coltrane	In a Sentimental Mood; Take the Coltrane; Big Nick; Stevie; My Little Brown Book; Angelica; The Feeling of Jazz
A(S) 31 1963	*George Wein & the Newport All-Stars* George Wein and the Newport All-Stars	At the Jazz Band Ball; The Bends Blues; Crazy Rhythm; Slowly; Ja-Da; Keepin' Out of Mischief Now; Blue Turning Grey Over You; Lulu's Back in Town
A(S) 32 1963	*Ballads* John Coltrane Quartet	Say It (Over and Over Again); You Don't Know What Love Is; Too Young to Go Steady; All or Nothing at All; I Wish I Knew; What's New; It's Easy to Remember; Nancy
A(S) 33 1963	*Reaching Fourth* McCoy Tyner Trio	Reaching Fourth; Goodbye; Theme for Ernie; Blues Back; Old Devil Moon; Have You Met Miss Jones
A(S) 34 1963	*Today and Now* Coleman Hawkins Quartet	Go Lil Liza; Quintessence; Don't Love Me; Love Song from "Apache"; Put on Your Old Grey Bonnet; Swingin' Scotch; Don't Sit Under the Apple Tree
A(S) 35 1963	*The Black Saint and the Sinner Lady* Charlie Mingus	Solo Dancer; Duet Solo Dancers; Group Dancers; Trio and Group Dancers; Single Solos and Group Dance; Group and Solo Dance
A(S) 36 1963	*Americans in Europe—Volume 1* Various Artists	No Smokin', Low Life—Kenny Clarke Trio; I Can't Get Started—Idrees Sulieman Quartet; Freeway, Pyramid—Bill Smith Quintet; 'Round Midnight—Bud Powell Trio
A(S) 37 1963	*Americans in Europe—Volume 2* Various Artists	My Buddy Run Rabbits, Why Daughter How Are You—The Traditional Americans in Europe; Rose Room—Albert Nicholas Quartet; Wine, Whiskey and Gin Head Woman—Champion Jack Dupree; Lots of Talk for You—Curtis Jones; All the Things You Are, I Remember Clifford—Don Byas Quintet
A(S) 38 1964	*The Body and the Soul* Freddie Hubbard	Body and Soul; Carnival; Chocolate Shake; Dedicated to You; Clarence's Place; Aries; Skylark; I Got It Bad and That Ain't Good; Thermo
A(S) 39 1963	*Nights of Ballads and Blues* McCoy Tyner	Satin Doll; We'll Be Together Again; 'Round Midnight; For Heaven's Sake; Star Eyes; Blue Monk; Groove Waltz; Days of Wine and Roses

CATALOG # AND YEAR OF RELEASE	TITLE AND ARTIST	TRACKS
A(S) 40 1963	*John Coltrane and Johnny Hartman* John Coltrane and Johnny Hartman	They Say It's Wonderful; Dedicated to You; My One and Only Love; Lush Life; You Are Too Beautiful; Autumn Serenade
A(S) 41 1963	*Cleopatra Feelin' Jazzy* Paul Gonsalves	Caesar & Cleopatra Theme; Antony and Cleopatra Theme; Bluz For Liz; Cleo's Blues; Action in Alexandria; Cleo's Asp; Cleopatra's Lament
A(S) 42 1963	*Impressions* John Coltrane	India; Up 'Gainst the Wall; Impressions; After the Rain
A(S) 43 1963	*Now!* Sonny Stitt	Surfin'; Lester Leaps In; Estralita; Please Don't Talk About Me When I'm Gone; Touchy; Never-Sh!; My Mother's Eyes; I'm Getting Sentimental Over You
A(S) 44 1964	*Gordon Jenkins Presents My Wife the Blues Singer* Beverly Jenkins	You Don't Know My Mind; The Blues Ain't Nothin' but a Woman Cryin' for Her Man; Please Mr. Miller/Freight Train Blues; It's a Low Down Dirty Shame; Daylight Savings Blues; Western Union Man; Rain Is Such a Lonesome Sound; My Last Goodbye to You; Big Four Blues
A(S) 45 1964	*A Jazz Message* Art Blakey Quartet	Café; Just Knock on My Door; Summertime; Blues Back; Sunday; The Song Is You
A(S) 46 1964	*Point of Departure* Gary McFarland Sextet	Pecos Pete; Love Theme from "David and Lisa"; Sandpiper; Amour Tormentoso; Schlock-House Blues; I Love to Say Her Name; Hello to the Season
A(S) 47 1964	*Soul Sisters* Gloria Coleman Quartet featuring Pola Roberts	Que Baby; Sadie Green; Hey Sonny Redd; Melba's Minor; Funky Bob; My Lady's Waltz
A(S) 48 1964	*Live At Newport* McCoy Tyner	Newport Romp; My Funny Valentine; All of You; Monk's Blues; Woody'N You
A(S) 49 1964	*Illumination!* Elvin Jones/Jimmy Garrison Sextet	Nuttin' Out Jones; Oriental Flower; Half and Half; Aborigine Dance in Scotland; Gettin' on Way; Just Us Blues
A(S) 50 1964	*Live at Birdland* John Coltrane	Afro-Blue; I Want to Talk About You; The Promise; Alabama; Your Lady
A(S) 51 1964	*For Members Only* Shirley Scott Trio	Southern Comfort; Blue Piano; Freedom Dance; Toys in the Attic; Blues for Members; I've Grown Accustomed to Her Face; Marchin' to Riverside; We're Goin' Home
A(S) 52 1964	*Salt and Pepper* Sonny Stitt and Paul Gonsalves	Salt and Pepper; S'posin'; Theme from "Lord of the Flies"; Perdido; Stardust
A(S) 53 1964	*After the Lights Go Down Low and Much More!!!* Freda Payne	After the Lights Go Down Low; Sweet Pumpkin; Blue Piano; The Things We Love to Do; Awaken My Lonely One; Sweet September; I Cried for You; 'Round Midnight; Out of This World; Lonely Woman; I Wish I Knew; It's Time
A(S) 54 1964	*Mingus, Mingus, Mingus, Mingus, Mingus* Charlie Mingus	II B.S.; I X Love; Celia; Mood Indigo; Better Get Hit in Yo' Soul; Theme for Lester Young; Hora Decubitus

CATALOG # AND YEAR OF RELEASE	TITLE AND ARTIST	TRACKS
A(S) 55 1964	*Tell It the Way It Is!* Paul Gonsalves	Tell It the Way It Is!; Things Ain't What They Used to Be; Duke's Place; Impulsive/Rapscallion in Rab's Canyon; Body and Soul
A(S) 56 1964	*Jazz 'Round the World* Yusef Lateef	Abana; India; You, So Tender and Wistful; Yusef's French Brother; The Volga Rhythm Song; Trouble in Mind; The Good Old Roast Beef of England; Raisins and Almonds; Utopia; Ringo Awake
A(S) 57 1964	*I Just Dropped By to Say Hello* Johnny Hartman	Charade; In the Wee Small Hours of the Morning; Sleepin' Bee; Don't You Know I Care; Kiss & Run; If I'm Lucky
A(S) 58 1964	*Take It from Me* Terry Gibbs	Take It from Me; El Fatso; Oge; Pauline's Place; 8 Lbs., 10 Ozs.; Gee Dad, It's a Deagan; All the Things You Are; Honeysuckle Rose
A(S) 59 1964	*Man from Two Worlds* Chico Hamilton	Man from Two Worlds; Blues Medley: Little Sister's Dance, Shade Tree, Island Blue; Forest Flower, Sunrise; Forest Flower, Sunset; Child's Play; Blues for O.T.; Mallet Dance; Love Song to a Baby
A(S) 60 1964	*Mingus Plays Piano: Spontaneous Compositions and Improvisations* Charlie Mingus	Myself When I Am Real; I Can't Get Started; Body and Soul; Roland Kirk's Message; Memories of You; She's Just Miss Popular Hybrid; Orange Was the Color of Her Dress, Then Silk Blues; Meditations for Moses; Old Portrait; I'm Getting Sentimental Over You; Compositional Theme Story: Medleys, Anthems and Folklore
A(S) 61 1964	*Everybody Knows Johnny Hodges* Johnny Hodges	Everybody Knows; The Jeep Is Jumpin'; 310 Blues; Main Stem; I Let a Song Go Out of My Heart/Don't Get Around Much Anymore; A Flower Is a Lovesome Thing; Papa Knows; Open Mike
A(S) 62 1964	*Alexandria the Great* Lorez Alexandria	Show Me; I've Never Been in Love Before; Satin Doll; My One and Only Love; Over the Rainbow; Get Me to the Church on Time; The Best Is Yet to Come; I've Grown Accustomed to His Face; Give Me the Simple Life; I'm Through With Love
A(S) 63 1964	*Today and Tomorrow* McCoy Tyner	Contemporary Focus; Night in Tunisia; T 'N A Blues; Autumn Leaves; Three Flowers; When Sunny Gets Blue
A(S) 64 1964	*The Happy Horns of Clark Terry* Clark Terry	Rockin' in Rhythm; In a Mist; Return to Swahili; Ellington Rides Again: Don't Get Around Much Anymore, Perdido, I'm Beginning to See the Light; Impulsive; Do Nothin' Till You Hear from Me; Jazz Conversations; High Towers
A(S) 65 1964	*See You at the Fair* Ben Webster	See You at the Fair; Over the Rainbow; Our Love Is Here to Stay; In a Mellow Tone; Lullaby of Jazzland; Stardust; Fall of Love; While We're Dancing; Someone to Watch Over Me
A(S) 66 1964	*Crescent* John Coltrane Quartet	Crescent; Wise One; Bessie's Blues; Lonnie's Lament; The Drum Thing
A(S) 67 1964	*Great Scott!!* Shirley Scott Trio	A Shot in the Dark; Great Scott; The Seventh Dawn; Hoe Down; Shadows of Paris; Five O'Clock Whistle; The Blues Ain't Nothin' but Some Pain; I'm Gettin' Sentimental Over You; Make Someone Happy
A(S) 68 1965	*Proof Positive* J.J. Johnson	Neo; Lullaby of Jazzland; Stella by Starlight; Minor Blues; My Funny Valentine; Blues Waltz
A(S) 69 1965	*Live at Pep's* Yusef Lateef	Sister Mamie; Number 7; 12 Tone Blues; See See Rider; The Magnolia Triangle; The Weaver; Slippin' Slidin'

CATALOG # AND YEAR OF RELEASE	TITLE AND ARTIST	TRACKS
A(S) 70 1964	*Jazz 'N' Samba* Milt Jackson	Blues for Juanita; I Got It Bad and That Ain't Good; Big George; Gingerbread Boy; Jazz 'N' Samba; The Oo-Oo Bossa Noova; I Love You; Kiss and Run; Jazz Bossa Nova
A(S) 71 1964	*Four for Trane* Archie Shepp	Syeeda's Song Flute; Mr. Syms; Cousin Mary; Niema [*sic*]; Rufus
A(S) 72 1965	*My Fair Lady Loves Jazz* [Reissue of ABC-177] Billy Taylor Trio with Quincy Jones	Show Me; I've Grown Accustomed to Her Face; With a Little Bit of Luck; The Rain in Spain; Get Me to the Church On Time; Wouldn't It Be Loverly?; I Could Have Danced All Night; On the Street Where You Live
A(S) 73 1965	*Everybody Loves a Lover* Shirley Scott	Everybody Loves a Lover; Little Miss Know It All; Sent for You Yesterday; Shirley; Blue Bongo; The Lamp Is Low; The Feeling of Jazz
A(S) 74 1965	*The Voice That Is!* Johnny Hartman	The More I See You; A Slow Hot Wind; Let Me Love You; Funny World; These Foolish Things; My Ship; The Day the World Stopped Turning; Joey, Joey, Joey; Sunrise, Sunset; Waltz for Debbie; It Never Entered My Mind
A(S) 75 1965	*More Blues and the Abstract Truth* Oliver Nelson	Blues and the Abstract Truth; Blues O'Mighty; Theme from "Mr. Broadway"; Midnight Blue; The Critic's Choice; One for Bob; Blues for Mr. Broadway; Goin' to Chicago Blues
A(S) 76 1965	*More of the Great Lorez Alexandria* Lorez Alexandria	But Beautiful; Little Boat; Dancing on the Ceiling; It Might as Well Be Spring; Once; The Wildest Gal in Town; Angel Eyes; This Could Be the Start of Something Big; No More; That Far Away Look
A(S) 77 1965	*A Love Supreme* John Coltrane	Acknowledgement; Resolution; Pursuance; Psalm
A(S) 78 1965	*You Better Know It!!!* Lionel Hampton	Ring Dem Bells; Vibraphone Blues; Tempo's Birthday; Sweethearts on Parade; Pick a Rib; Trick or Treat; Cute; Swingle Jingle; Taste of Honey
A(S) 79 1965	*McCoy Tyner Plays Ellington* McCoy Tyner	Duke's Place; Caravan; Solitude; Searchin'; Mr. Gentle and Mr. Cool; Satin Doll; Gypsy; Without a Song
A(S) 80 1965	*Happiness* Russian Jazz Quartet	Waltz; Remember; Journey from Moscow; Composition in the Form of Blues; Secret Love; Dedication to M.J.Q.
A(S) 81 1965	*Queen of the Organ* Shirley Scott	Just in Time; Squeeze Me; Rapid Shave; The Theme
A(S) 82 1965	*Chic Chic Chico* Chico Hamilton	Chic Chic Chico; Corrida de Toros; Tarantula; What's New; St. Paddy's Day Parade; Carol's Walk; Swampy; Fire Works
A(S) 83 1966	*Sing a Song of Basie* [Reissue of ABC-222] Lambert, Hendricks and Ross	Down for Double; Fiesta in Blue; Down for the Count; Blues Backstage; Avenue C; Everyday; It's Sand, Man; Two for the Blues; One O'Clock Jump; Little Pony
A(S) 84 1966	*1984* Yusef Lateef	1984; Try Love; Soul Sister; Love Waltz; One Little Indian; Listen to the Wind; Warm Fire; Gee! Sam Gee; The Greatest Story Ever Told
A(S) 85 1965	*The John Coltrane Quartet Plays* John Coltrane	Chim Chim Cheree; Brazilia; Nature Boy; Song of Praise

CATALOG # AND YEAR OF RELEASE	TITLE AND ARTIST	TRACKS
A(S) 86 1965	*Fire Music* Archie Shepp	Hambone; Los Olvidados; Malcolm, Malcolm, Semper Malcolm; Prelude to a Kiss; The Girl from Ipanema
A(S) 87 1966	*Wrapped Tight* Coleman Hawkins	Wrapped Tight; Intermezzo; Out of Nowhere; Indian Summer; Red Roses for a Blue Lady; Marcheta; Beautiful Girl; She's Fit; And I Still Love You; Bean's Place
A(S) 88 1966	*Dear John C.* Elvin Jones	Dear John C.; Smoke Rings; Love Bird; Feeling Good; Anthropology; This Love of Mine; Fantazm; Ballade; Everything Happens to Me
A(S) 89 1965	*Inspired Abandon* Lawrence Brown's All Stars with Johnny Hodges	Stompy Jones; Mood Indigo; Good Queen Bess; Little Brother; Jeep's Blues; Do Nothin' Till You Hear from Me; Ruint; Sassy Cue
A(S) 90 1966	*The New Wave of Jazz* Various Artists	Nature Boy; Holy Ghost; Blue Free; Hambone; Brilliant Corners
A(S) 91 1965	*Sonny Rollins on Impulse!* Sonny Rollins	On Green Dolphin Street; Everything Happens to Me; Hold 'Em Joe; Blue Room; Three Little Words
A(S) 92 1965	*Psychicemotus* Yusef Lateef	Psychicemotus; Bamboo Flute Blues; Semiocto; Why Do I Love You?; First Gymnopedie; Medula Sonata; I'll Always Be in Love With You; Ain't Misbehavin'
A(S) 93 1966	*Latin Shadows* Shirley Scott	Latin Shadows; Downtown; Who Can I Turn To?; Can't Get Over the Bossa Nova; This Love of Mine; Perhaps, Perhaps, Perhaps; Soul Sauce; Hanky Panky; Noche Azul; Drreamsville; Feeling Good
A(S) 94 1966	*New Thing at Newport* John Coltrane and Archie Shepp	Introduction; One Down, One Up; Rufus (swung his face at last to the wind, then his neck snapped); Le Matin des Noire; Scag; Call Me by My Rightful Name
A(S) 95 1966	*Ascension* John Coltrane	Ascension (Part 1); Ascension (Part 2)
A(S) 96 1966	*Ask Me Now!* Pee Wee Russell Quartet with Marshall Brown	Turnaround; How About Me?; Ask Me Now; Some Other Blues; I'd Climb the Highest Mountain; Licorice Stick; Prelude to a Kiss; Baby You Can Count on Me; Hackensack; Angel Eyes; Calypso Walk
A(S) 97 1966	*On This Night* Archie Shepp	The Mac Man; In a Sentimental Mood; Gingerbread, Gingerbread Boy; On This Night; The Original Mr. Sonny Boy Williamson; Pickaninny
A(S) 98 1966	*"In" Jazz for the Culture Set* Dannie Richmond	High Camp; Sweet Little Sixteen; Freedom Ride; The Spider; Blowin' in the Wind; Pfoofnick; The Berkeley Underground; Mister Nashville; John Kennedy Memory Waltz
A(S) 99 1966 (maybe 1964)	*Definitive Jazz Scene, Volume 1* Various Artists	Solitude—Ellington and Hawkins; Trey of Hearts—Count Basie; Single Petal of a Rose—Ben Webster; Tippie—Terry Gibbs; Lisa and Pam—Shirley Scott; Big Nick—John Coltrane; Avalon—Shelly Manne; Freedom—Charlie Mingus; Hammer-Head Waltz—Clark Terry; Flapstick Blues—McCoy Tyner
A(S) 100 1966 (maybe 1965)	*Definitive Jazz Scene, Volume 2* Various Artists	Without a Song—Ray Charles; The Blues Ain't Nothin' but Some Pain—Shirley Scott; Moon Over My Annie—Lionel Hampton; Night Lights—Oliver Nelson; Gloria—J.J. Johnson; Dear Old Stockholm—John Coltrane; You'd Be So Nice to Come Home To—McCoy Tyner; Blues Company—Manny Albam; Anything I Do—Tommy Flannagan

CATALOG # AND YEAR OF RELEASE	TITLE AND ARTIST	TRACKS
A(S) 9101 1966	*Definitive Jazz Scene, Volume 3* Various Artists	Vilia—John Coltrane Quartet; The Chased—Archie Shepp Trio; One for Phil—Oliver Nelson's Septet; Five Spot After Dark—McCoy Tyner Trio; Big Noise from Winnetka—Chico Hamilton Trio; March for Igor—Russian Jazz Quartet; Time After Time—Shirley Scott Quartet; That Five—Four Bag—Elvin Jones Quartet
A(S) 9102 1966	*El Chico* Chico Hamilton	El Chico; People; Marcheta; This Dream; Conquistadores; El Moors; Strange; Helena
A(S) 9103 1966	*It Serves You Right to Suffer* John Lee Hooker	Shake It; Country Boy; Bottle Up; You're Wrong; Sugar Mama; Decoration Day; Money; It Serves You Right to Suffer
A(S) 9104 1966	*Tijuana Jazz* Gary McFarland and Co. with Clark Terry	South of the Border; Acapulco at Night; Fantastic, That's You; Limehouse Blues; Tijuana; Marcheta; Granny's Samba; Soul Bird; Mexicali Rose; Ira Schwartz's Golden Dream; Mary Jane; Sweet Georgia Brown
A(S) 9105 1966	*Gypsy '66* Gabor Szabo	Yesterday; The Last One to Be Loved; The Echo of Love; Gypsy '66; Flea Market; Walk On By; If I Fell; Gypsy Jam; I'm All Smiles
A(S) 9106 1966	*Kulu Se Mama* John Coltrane	Kulu Se Mama; Vigil; Welcome
A(S) 9107 1966	*Thunderbird* Louis Bellson	Little Pixie; Nails; Serenade in Blues; Back on the Scene; No More Blues; Cottontail; Softly with Feeling
A(S) 9108 1966	*Once Upon A Time* Earl Hines	Once Upon a Time; Black and Tan Fantasy; Fantastic, That's You; Cottontail; The Blues in My Flat; You Can Depend on Me; Hash Brown
A(S) 9109 1967	*On a Clear Day* Shirley Scott	On a Clear Day You Can See Forever; What'll I Do?; Cold Winter Blues; All Alone; What the World Needs Now Is Love; Corcovado; Days of Wine and Roses; Instant Blues
A(S) 9110 1966	*Meditations* John Coltrane	The Father, the Son and the Holy Ghost; Compassion; Love, Consequences, Serenity
A(S) 9111 1966	*Alfie: Original Music from the Score* Sonny Rollins	Alfie's Theme; He's Younger Than You; Street Runner with Child; Transition Theme for Minor Blues or Little Malcolm Loves His Dad; On Impulse; Alfie's Theme Differently
A(S) 9112 1966	*Profiles* Gary McFarland	Winter Colors—An Early Morning River Stroll, Grey Afternoon, January Jubilee; Willie; Sage Hands; Bygones and Boogie-Boogie (Boogie and Out); Mountain Heir; Milo's Other Samba
A(S) 9113 1966	*Michelle* Oliver Nelson	Island Virgin; These Boots Are Made for Walkin'; Jazz Bug; Together Again; Flowers on the Wall; Yesterday; Once Upon a Time; Michelle; Do You See What I See?; Fantastic, That's You; Beautiful Music; (Land of Meadows) Meadowland
A(S) 9114 1966	*The Further Adventures of El Chico* Chico Hamilton	Got My Mojo Working; Who Can I Turn To?; That Boy with That Long Hair; Daydream; The Shadow of Your Smile; Evil Eye; Monday, Monday; Manila; My Romance; Stella by Starlight
A(S) 9115 1966	*Let It Go* Stanley Turrentine	Let It Go; On a Clear Day You Can See Forever; Ciao, Ciao; 'Taint What You Do (It's How You Do It); Good Lookin' Out; Sure As You're Born (Theme from "Harper"); Deep Purple

CATALOG # AND YEAR OF RELEASE	TITLE AND ARTIST	TRACKS
A(S) 9116 1966	*Additions to Further Definitions* Benny Carter	Fantastic, That's You; Come On Back; We Were in Love; If Dreams Come True; Prohibido; Doozy; Rock Bottom; Titmouse
A(S) 9117 1966	*A Flat, G Flat and C* Yusef Lateef	Warm Hearted Blues; Nile Valley Blues; Robbie; Psyche Rose; Chuen Blues; Feather Comfort; Blind Willie; Feelin' Alright; Sound Wave; Kyoto Blues
A(S) 9118 1967	*Archie Shepp Live in San Francisco* Archie Shepp	Keep Your Heart Right; The Lady Sings the Blues; Sylvia; The Wedding; Wherever June Bugs Go; In a Sentimental Mood
A(S) 9119 1966	*Roll 'Em Shirley Scott Plays the Big Bands* Shirley Scott	Roll 'Em; For Dancers Only; Little Brown Jug; Stompin' at the Savoy; Ain't Misbehavin'; Sophisticated Swing; Sometimes I'm Happy; A Tisket A Tasket; Things Ain't What They Used to Be; Tippin' In
A(S) 9120 1967	*Expression* John Coltrane	Ogunde; To Be; Offering; Expression
A(S) 9121 1967	*East Broadway Run Down* Sonny Rollins	East Broadway Run Down; Blessing in Disguise; We Kiss in a Shadow
A(S) 9122 1966	*Simpático* Gary McFarland with Gabor Szabo	The Word; Nature Boy; Norwegian Wood; Hey, Here's a Heart; Cool Water; Ups and Downs; Yamaha Mama; You Will Pay; Spring Song; She's a Cruiser; Simpático
A(S) 9123 1966	*Spellbinder* Gabor Szabo	Witchcraft; It Was a Very Good Year; Gypsy Queen; Bang, Bang; Cheetah; My Foolish Heart; Yearning; Autumn Leaves; Speak to Me of Love
A(S) 9124 1967	*Live at the Village Vanguard Again!* John Coltrane	Naima; Introduction to My Favorite Things; My Favorite Things
A(S) 9125 1966	*The Golden Flute* Yusef Lateef	Road Runner; Straighten Up and Fly Right; Oasis; (I Don't Stand) A Ghost of a Chance with You; Exactly Like You; The Golden Flute; Rosetta; Head Hunters; Smart Set
A(S) 9126 1967	*Everywhere* Roswell Rudd	Everywhere; Yankee No-How; Respects; Satan's Dance
A(S) 9127 1966	*Spanish Rice* Clark Terry and Chico O'Farrill	Peanut Vendor; Angelitos Negros; El Cumbanchero; Joonji; Que Sera; Mexican Hat Dance; Spanish Rice; Say Si Si; Macarena; Tin Tin Deo; Contigo en la Distancia; Happiness Is
A(S) 9128 1967	*Jazz Raga* Gabor Szabo	Walking on Nails; Mizrab; Search for Nirvana; Krishna; Raga Doll; Comin' Back; Paint It Black; Sophisticated Wheels; Ravi; Caravan; Summertime
A(S) 9129 1967	*Sound Pieces* Oliver Nelson	Sound Piece for Jazz Orchestra; Flute Salad; The Lady from Girl Talk; The Shadow of Your Smile; Patterns; Elegy for a Duck
A(S) 9130 1967	*The Dealer* Chico Hamilton	For Mods Only; Trip; Baby, You Know; Larry of Arabia; Thoughts; Jim-Jeannie
A(S) 9131 1967	*The Waiting Game* Zoot Sims	Old Folks; I Wish I Knew; Once We Loved; It's a Blue World; September Song; Over the Rainbow; Stella by Starlight; One I Could Have Loved (Theme from "13"); You Go to My Head; Does the Sun Really Shine on the Moon?

CATALOG # AND YEAR OF RELEASE	TITLE AND ARTIST	TRACKS
A(S) 9132 1967	*Happenings* Hank Jones and Oliver Nelson featuring Clark Terry	Broadwalk Samba; Winchester Catheral; Mas Que Nada; Lullaby of Jazzland; Jazztime, USA; Cul-de-Sac; Happenings; Lou's Good Dues Blues; Fugue Tune; Spy with a Cold Nose; Funky but Blues
A(S) 9133 1967	*Soul Duo* Shirley Scott with Clark Terry	Soul Duo; Until I Met You (Corner Pocket); This Light of Mine; Joonji; Up a Hair; Taj Mahal; Clark Bars
A(S) 9134 1967	*Mama Too Tight* Archie Shepp	Portrait of Robert Thompson (as a young man); Prelude to a Kiss; The Break Strain—King Cotton; Dem Basses; Mama Too Tight; Theme for Ernie; Basheer
A(S) 9135 1967	*Nine Flags* Chico O'Farrill	Live Oak; Patcham; Aromatic Tabac; Dry Citrus; Royal Saddle; Panache; Green Moss; Manzanilla; Clear Spruce; Lady from Nine Flags
A(S) 9136 1967	*The October Suite: Steve Kuhn Plays the Compositions of Gary McFarland* Steve Kuhn	One I Could Have Loved; St. Tropez Shuttle; Remember When; Traffic Patterns; Childhood Dreams; Open Highway
A(S) 9137 1967	*The College Concert of Pee Wee Russell and Henry Red Allen* Pee Wee Russell and Red Allen	Blue Monk; I Want a Little Girl; Body and Soul; Pee Wee's Blues; 2 Degrees East, 3 Degrees West; Graduation Blues
A(S) 9138 1967	*Tauhid* Pharaoh Sanders	Upper Egypt & Lower Egypt; Japan; Aum, Venus, Capricorn Rising
A(S) 9139 1967	*Three for Shepp* Marion Brown Quartet	New Blue; Fortunato; The Shadow Knows; Spooks; West India; Delicado
AS 9140 1968	*Om* John Coltrane	Om, Part 1; Om, Part 2
AS 9141 1967	*Girl Talk* Shirley Scott	Girl Talk; Come Back to Me; We'll Be Together Again; Love Nest; Swingin' the Blues; Keep the Faith, Baby; Chicago, My Kind of Town; On the Trail; You're a Sweetheart
AS 9142 1967	*Sweet Love, Bitter (Soundtrack)* Mal Waldron	Loser's Lament; Della; Hillary; Espresso Time; Keel; Smokin'; Delia's Dream; The Search; Candy's Ride; "Bread"; Eagle Flips Out; Brindle's Place; Sleep Baby Sleep
AS 9143 1967	*Greek Cooking* Phil Woods featuring Iordanis Tsomidis	Zorba the Greek; A Taste of Honey; Theme from Antony & Cleopatra; Got a Feelin'; Theme from Sampson and Delilah; Greek Cooking; Nica
AS 9144 1967	*The Kennedy Dream: A Musical Tribute to John Fitzgerald Kennedy* Oliver Nelson and His Orchestra	Let the Word Go Forth; A Genuine Peace; The Rights of All; Tolerance; The Artists' Rightful Place; Jacqueline; Day in Dallas; John Kennedy Memory Waltz
AS 9145 1967	*Intercollegiate Music Festival, Volume 1* Various Artists	Machu Picchu, You Turn Me On Sump'n Fierce!, Forever Lost in My Mind's Eye, And So We Swang—Ohio State University Jazz Workshop Band; Kharisma for Keiko, New Jass—San Francisco State College Quintet; Joyful Noise, Thou Swell—Joey DeVito
AS 9146 1967	*The Sorcerer* Gabor Szabo	The Beat Goes On; Little Boat; Lou-ise; What Is This Thing Called Love?; Space; Stronger Than Us; Mizrab; Comin' Back

CATALOG # AND YEAR OF RELEASE	TITLE AND ARTIST	TRACKS
AS 9147 1967	*Spirit of '67* Pee Wee Russell and Oliver Nelson and His Orchestra	Love Is Just Around the Corner; This Is It; Memories of You; Pee Wee's Blues; The Shadow of Your Smile; Ja-Da; A Good Man Is Hard to Find; Bopol; I'm Coming Virginia; Six and Four
AS 9148 1968	*Cosmic Music* John Coltrane	Manifestation; Lord, Help Me to Be; Reverend King; The Sun
AS 9149 1967	*Swing Low, Sweet Cadillac* Dizzy Gillespie	Swing Low, Sweet Cadillac; Mas Que Nada (Pow, Pow, Pow); Bye; Something in Your Smile; Kush
AS 9150 1967	*A Lovely Bunch of Al "Jazzbo" Collins and Bandidos* Al Collins	Sonny Cool; Goldilox and the Three Bears; Jazz Mass; The Three Little Pigs; The Power of the Flower; Little Red Riding Hood; Jack and the Beanstalk; The Swearing In of the Bandidos
AS 9151 1968	*Wind, Sky and Diamonds* Gabor Szabo	San Franciscan Nights; A Day in the Life; Twelve-Thirty; To Sir with Love; White Rabbit; Guantanamera; Saigon Bride; The End of Life; Lucy in the Sky with Diamonds; Are You There?; W.C. Fields
AS 9152 1967	*Chicken Fat* Mel Brown	Chicken Fat; Greasy Spoon; Home James; Anacrusis; Hobo Flats; Shanty; Sad But True; I'm Goin' to Jackson; Slalom
AS 9153 1967	*Live from Los Angeles* Oliver Nelson's Big Band	Miss Fine; Milestones; I Remember Bird; Night Train; Guitar Blues; Down by the Riverside; Ja-Da
AS 9154 1968	*The Magic Of Ju-Ju* Archie Shepp	The Magic of Ju-Ju; You're What This Day Is All About; Shazam; Sorry 'Bout That
AS 9155 1967	*Live in Greenwich Village* Albert Ayler	For John Coltrane; Change Has Come; Truth Is Marching In; Our Prayer
AS 9156 1968	*A Monastic Trio* Alice Coltrane	Ohnedaruth; Gospel Trane; I Want to See You; Lovely Sky Boat; Oceanic Beloved; Atmic Peace
AS 9157 1967	*It's What's Happening* Clark Terry	Electric Mumbles; Secret Love; Take Me Back to Elkhart; Take the 'A' Train; Tee Pee Time; Grand Canyon Suite
AS 9158 1967	*Impressions of New York* Rolfe and Joachim Kuhn Quartet	Arrival; The Saddest Day; Reality; Predictions
AS 9159 1968	*Light My Fire* Bob Thiele and His New Happy Times Orchestra with Gabor Szabo, Tom Scott, and the California Dreamers	Forest Flower; Rainy Day Woman #12 & 35; Krishna; Fakin' It; Eight Miles High; Sophisticated Wheels
AS 9160 1968	*Heavy Sounds* Elvin Jones and Richard Davis	Raunchy Rita; Shiny Stockings; M.E.; Summertime; Elvin's Guitar Blues; Here's That Rainy Day
A(S) 9161 1968 (maybe 1972)	*Selflessness Featuring My Favorite Things* John Coltrane	My Favorite Things; I Want to Know About You; Selflessness
AS 9162 1969	*Three for a Quarter, One for a Dime* Archie Shepp	Three for a Quarter (Part 1); One for a Dime (Part 2)

CATALOG # AND YEAR OF RELEASE	TITLE AND ARTIST	TRACKS
AS 9163 1968	*Honeysuckle Breeze* Tom Scott with the California Dreamers	Never My Love; She's Leaving Home; Naima; Mellow Yellow; Baby I Love You; Today; North; Blues for Hari; Deliver Me
AS 9164 1968	*Bill Plummer and the Cosmic Brotherhood* Bill Plummer	Journey to the East; Pars Fortuna (Part of Fortune); The Look of Love; Song Plum; Arc 294; Lady Friend; Antares
AS 9165 1968	*Love Cry* Albert Ayler	Love Cry; Ghosts; Omega; Dancing Flowers; Bells; Love Flower; Zion Hill; Universal Indians
AS 9166 1968	*Journey to Bliss* Emil Richards and the Microtonal Blues Band	Maharimba; Bliss; Mantra; Enjoy, Enjoy; Journey to Bliss—Part 1; Journey to Bliss—Part 2; Journey to Bliss—Part 3; Journey to Bliss—Part 4; Journey to Bliss—Parts 5 and 6
AS 9167 1968	*More Sorcery* Gabor Szabo	Los Matadoros; People; Corcovado; Lucy in the Sky with Diamonds; Comin' Back; Spellbinder
AS 9168 1968	*Soulful Brass* Oliver Nelson and Steve Allen	Torino; Sound Machine; Goin' Out of My Head; Can't Take My Eyes Off You; Spooky; 125th Street and 7th Avenue; Green Tambourine; (Sittin' on) The Dock of the Bay; Goin' Great; Things I Should Have Said; Go Fly a Kite; Melissa; Last Night (Was a Bad Night)
AS 9169 1968	*Wizard* Mel Brown	Ode to Billie Joe; Swamp Fever; Blues After Hours; African Sweets; Stop; Chunk a Funk; Miss Ann; W-2; Withholding
AS 9170 1969	*The Way Ahead* Archie Shepp	Damn If I Know (The Stroller); Frankenstein; Fiesta; Sophisticated Lady
AS 9171 1969	*Rural Still Life* Tom Scott	Rural Still Life #26; Song #1; Freak In; With Respect to Coltrane; Just Messin' Around; Body and Soul
AS 9172	***No Release***	
AS 9173 1968	*The Best of Gabor Szabo* Gabor Szabo	Spellbinder; Witchcraft; Gypsy Queen; Paint It Black; Sophisticated Wheels; Yesterday; Walk On By; The Beat Goes On; Little Boat (O Barquinho)
AS 9174 1969	*The Best of Chico Hamilton* Chico Hamilton	Forest Flower: Sunrise; Forest Flower: Sunset; People; Chic Chic Chico; Conquistadores (The Conquerors); Who Can I Turn To (When Nobody Needs Me); Evil Eye; Larry of Arabia
AS 9175 1969	*New Grass* Albert Ayler	Message from Albert; New Generation; Sun Watcher; New Ghosts; Heart Love; Everybody's Movin'; Free at Last
AS 9176 1969	*At the Top: Poinciana Revisited* Ahmad Jamal	Have You Met Miss Jones; Poinciana; Lament; Call Me; Theme From "Valley of the Dolls"; Frank's Tune; How Insensitive
AS 9177	***No Release***	
AS 9178 1969	*Ornette at 12* Ornette Coleman	C.O.D.; Rainbows; New York; Bells and Chimes
AS 9179	***No Release***	
AS 9180 1969	*Blues for We* Mel Brown	Twist and Shout; Blues for We; Ob-La-Di, Ob-La-Da; Son of a Preacher Man; Set Me Free; Frekey Zeke; Indian Giver; Stranger on the Shore

CATALOG # AND YEAR OF RELEASE	TITLE AND ARTIST	TRACKS
AS 9181 1969	*Karma* Pharoah Sanders	The Creator Has a Master Plan; Colors
AS 9182 1970	*Spirit of 1976* Emil Richards	Spirit of 1976; Peek-a-Boo; All Blue; One Tooth Grin; Like Me; 10 to 5; Jordu
AS 9183 1970	*Liberation Music Orchestra* Charlie Haden	The Introduction; Song of the United Front; The Fifth Regiment; The Four Generals; Long Live the Fifteenth Brigade; Ending to the First Side; Song for Che; War Orphans; The Interlude (Drinking Music); Circus '68 '69; We Shall Overcome
AS 9184 1970	*Dave Mackay and Vicky Hamilton* Dave Mackay and Vicky Hamilton	Now; See You Later; Jacque the Junkman; Jersey Bounce; Like Me; Samba for Vicky; Blues for Hari; Elephant Song; Moon Rider; Here
AS 9185 1969	*Huntington Ashram Monastery* Alice Coltrane	Huntington Ashram Monastery; Turiya; Paramahansa Lake; Via Sivanandagar; IHS; Jaya Jaya Rama
AS 9186 1970	*I'd Rather Suck My Thumb* Mel Brown	I'd Rather Suck My Thumb; Scorpio; Eighteen Pounds of Unclean Chitlings; You Got Me Hummin'; Do Your Thing; Troubles; Dixie
AS 9187 1970	*Crisis* Ornette Coleman	Broken Shadows; Comme Il Faut; Song for Che; Space Jungle; Trouble in the East
AS 9188 1970	*For Losers* Archie Shepp	Stick 'Em Up; What Would It Be Without You; Abstract; I Got It Bad; Un Croque Monsieur
AS 9189 1970	*That's the Way It Is* Milt Jackson	Frankie and Johnny; Here's That Rainy Day; Wheelin' and Dealin'; Blues in the Bassment; Tenderly; That's the Way It Is
AS 9190 1970	*Jewels of Thought* Pharoah Sanders	Hum-Allah-Hum-Allah-Hum-Allah; Sun in Aquarius, Part I; Sun in Aquarius, Part II
AS 9191 1970	*Music Is the Healing Force of the Universe* Albert Ayler	Music Is the Healing Force of the Universe; Masonic Inborn, Part 1; A Man Is Like a Tree; Oh! Love of Life; Island Harvest; Drudgery
AS 9192 1970	*This Rather Than That* Buddy Montgomery	Willy Nilly Blues; Beautiful Love; Didn't We; Winding Up
AS 9193 1970	*Memphis Jackson* Milt Jackson with the Ray Brown Big Band	Uh-Huh; One Mint Julep (one way); One Happy Day; Memphis Junction; Queen Mother Stomp; Braddock Breakdown; A Sound for Sore Ears; Enchanted Lady; One Mint Julep (the other way); Picking Up the Vibrations
AS 9194 1970	*The Awakening* Ahmad Jamal	The Awakening; I Love Music; Patterns; Dolphin Dance; You're My Everything; Stolen Moments; Wave
AS 9195 1970	*Transition* John Coltrane	Transition; Dear Lord; Suite—Prayer and Meditation: Day, Peace and After, Prayer and Meditation: Evening, Affirmation, Prayer and Meditation: 4 A.M.
AS 9196 1970	*Ptah, the El Daoud* Alice Coltrane	Ptah, the El Daoud; Ramakrishna; Blue Nile; Mantra

CATALOG # AND YEAR OF RELEASE	TITLE AND ARTIST	TRACKS
AS 9197 1970	*East Side San Jose* Clifford Coulter	Do It Again; East Side San Jose; Prayer Garden; Cliff's Place; Sal Si Puedes (Get Out If You Can); Big Fat Funky Shirley; Alum Rock Park
AS 9198 1970	*Rainbow* Dave Mackay and Vicky Hamilton	Happying (Flip's Blues); Will o' the Wisp; If I Ask You; 4 Ira; See My Rainbow; Peek-a-Boo; Free; Silent; A Time for Love; Reach Out
AS 9199 1970	*Summun Bukmun Umyun* Pharoah Sanders	Summun, Bukmun, Umyun; Let Us Go into the House of the Lord
AS 9200-2 1970	*The Best of John Coltrane: His Greatest Years* John Coltrane	Africa; Softly as in a Morning Sunrise; Soul Eyes: After the Rain; Afro-Blue; Alabama; My Favorite Things; Bessie's Blues; Psalm (A Love Supreme Part 4); Kulu Se Mama; Naima; Om
AS 9202-2 1971	*Live in Seattle* John Coltrane featuring Pharoah Sanders	Cosmos; Out of This World (Part One); Out of This World (Part Two); Evolution (Part One); Evolution (Part Two); Tapestry in Sound
AS 9203 1971	*Journey in Satchidananda* Alice Coltrane featuring Pharoah Sanders	Journey in Satchidananda; Shiva-Loka; Stopover Bombay; Something About John Coltrane; Isis and Osiris
AS 9204-2 1971	*His Great Hits* Gabor Szabo	Sophisticated Wheels; Simpatico; My Foolish Heart; Twelve Thirty; Krishna; Mountain Heir; Gypsy '66; Evil Eye; If I Fell; Spring Song; Lady Gabor; People; Search for Nirvana; White Rabbit; El Toro; Yearning; Space; Spellbinder
AS 9205 1971	*Trespass* Genesis	Looking for Someone; White Mountain; Visions of Angels; Stagnation; Dusk; The Knife
AS 9206 1971	*Thembi* Pharoah Sanders	Astral Traveling; Red, Black and Green; Bailophone Dance; Morning Prayer; Thembi; Love
AS 9207 1971	*Antelope Freeway* Howard Roberts	Antelope Freeway, Part 1; That's America fer Ya; Dark Ominous Clouds; De Blooz; Sixteen Track Fireman; The Ballad of Fazzio Needlepoint; Five Gallons of Astral Flash Could Keep You Up for Thirteen Weeks; Santa Clara River Bottom; Road Work
AS 9208 1971	*The Last Album* Albert Ayler	Untitled Duet; Again Comes the Rising of the Sun; All Love; Toiling; Desert Blood; Birth of Mirth; Water Music
AS 9209 1971	*Mel Brown's Fifth* Mel Brown	Time for a Change; Good Stuff; Seven Forty-Seven (Airport Blues); Luv Potion; Drifting Blues; Cheap at Half Price; Home Mage; Gimme a Little Slack
AS 9210 1971	*Universal Consciousness* Alice Coltrane	Universal Consciousness; Battle at Armageddon; Oh Allah; Hare Krishna; Sita Ram; The Ankh of Amen-Ra
AS 9211 1971	*Sun Ship* John Coltrane	Sun Ship; Dearly Beloved; Amen; Attaining; Ascent
AS 9212 1971	*Things Have Got to Change* Archie Shepp	Money Blues; Dr. King, the Peaceful Warrior; Things Have Got to Change
AS 9213-2 1971	*His Great Hits* Chico Hamilton	Helena; Manila; Got My Mojo Working; Corrido de Toros; That Boy with the Long Hair; Man from Two Worlds; Fireworks; El Moors; Transfusion; Mallet Dance; Lonesome Child; Blues for O.T.

CATALOG # AND YEAR OF RELEASE	TITLE AND ARTIST	TRACKS
AS 9214 1972	*Constant Throb* John Klemmer	Constant Throb—Part 1; Constant Throb—Part 2; Neptune; Let Me Touch the Wind; California Jazz Dance; Rainbows; Crystaled Tears; Precious Leaf
AS 9215 1972	*Spirit Dance* Michael White	Spirit Dance; The Tenth Pyramid; John Coltrane Was Here; Ballad for Mother Frankie White; Samba; Unlocking the Twelfth House; Praise Innocence
AS 9216 1972	*Do It Now, Worry About It Later* Clifford Coulter	Ridin' on Empty; Yodelin' in the Whatchamaname Thang; Do It Now; Worry About It Later; Mr. Peabody; VJC; Before the Morning Comes
AS 9217 1972	*Freeflight* Ahmad Jamal	Introduction; Effendi; Dolphin Dance; Manhattan Reflections; Poinciana
AS/AQ 9218 1972	*World Galaxy* Alice Coltrane	My Favorite Things; Galaxy Around Olodumare; Galaxy in Turiya; Galaxy in Satchidananda; A Love Supreme
AS/AQ 9219 1972	*Black Unity* Pharoah Sanders	Black Unity—Part 1; Black Unity—Part 2
AS/AQ 9220 1972	*Waterfalls* John Klemmer	Prelude 1; Waterfall 1; Utopia: Man's Dream; There's Some Light Ahead; Centrifugal Force; Prelude 2; Waterfall 2
AS/AQ 9221 1972	*Pneuma* Michael White	Pneuma; Ebony Plaza; Journey of the Black Star; The Blessing Song
AS/AQ 9222 1972	*Attica Blues* Archie Shepp	Attica Blues; Invocation: Attica Blues; Steam—Part 1; Invocation to Mr. Parker; Steam—Part 2; Blues for Brother Geoge Jackson; Invocation: Ballad for a Child; Ballad for a Child; Goodbye Sweet Pops; Quiet Dawn
AS 9223-2 1972	*The Best of John Coltrane: His Greatest Years, Vol. 2* John Coltrane	Greensleeves; India; Opening sections of Ascension; Miles' Mode; Big Nick; The Promise; Chim Chim Cheree; Ascension; The Father and the Son and the Holy Ghost; Manifestation; Ogunde
AS/AQ 9224 1972	*Lord of Lords* Alice Coltrane	Andromeda's Suffering; Sri Rama Ohnedaruth; Excerpts from The Firebird; Lord of Lords; Going Home
AS/AQ 9225 1972	*Infinity* John Coltrane	Peace on Earth; Living Space; Joy; Leo
AS 9226 1972	*Outertimeinnerspace* Ahmad Jamal	Bogota; Extensions
AS/AQ 9227 1972	*Live at the East* Pharoah Sanders	Healing Song; Lumkili (Part 1); Lumkili (Part 2); Memories of J.W. Coltrane
ASD 9228 1972	*Impulse Energy Essentials* Various Artists	Hora Decubitus—Charles Mingus; Garvey's Ghost—Max Roach; Mama Too Tight—Archie Shepp; Aries—Freddie Hubbard; Teenie's Blues—Oliver Nelson; Spiritual—John Coltrane; Bulbs—Cecil Taylor; New Blue—Marion Brown; Nuttin' Out Jones—Elvin Jones/Jimmy Garrison; East Broadway Run Down—Sonny Rollins; Acknowledgement from A Love Supreme—John Coltrane; The Creator Has a Master Plan—Pharoah Sanders; John Coltrane Was Here—Michael White; Opening selections of Ascension (Edition 1)—John Coltrane; Holy Ghost—Albert Ayler; Song for Che—Charlie Haden's Liberation Music Orchestra; Galaxy Around Olodumare—Alice Coltrane; Leo—John Coltrane

CATALOG # AND YEAR OF RELEASE	TITLE AND ARTIST	TRACKS
AS 9229-2 1972	*The Best of Pharoah Sanders* Pharoah Sanders	Upper Egypt; The Creator Has a Master Plan (Part 1); The Creator Has a Master Plan (Part 2); Hum-Allah-Hum-Allah-Hum-Allah; Colors; Let Us Go into the House of the Lord; Thembi
AS 9230 1973	*Just the Way It Had to Be* Milt Jackson featuring Ray Brown	Listen, Hear; SKJ; Who Can I Turn To; If I Were a Bell; The Very Thought of You; Bags' Groove
AS/AQ 9231 1973	*Cry of My People* Archie Shepp	Rest Enough (Song to Mother); A Prayer; All God's Children Got a Home in the Universe; The Lady; The Cry of My People; African Drum Suite (Part 1); African Drum Suite (Part 2); Come Sunday
AS/AQ 9232-2 1972/73	*Reflection on Creation and Space* Alice Coltrane	Blue Nile; The Sun; Concluding section of Galaxy Around Olodumare; Galaxy in Turiya; Medley: Journey in Satchidananda, Galaxy in Satchidananda; Battle at Armageddon; Lovely Sky Boat; A Love Supreme; Sri Rama Ohnedaruth; Andromeda's Suffering; I Want to See You; Sita Ram; Oh Allah; Excerpts from The Firebird
AS 9233 1972	*Wisdom Through Music* Pharoah Sanders	High Life; Love Is Everywhere; Wisdom Through Music; The Golden Lamp; Selflessness
IMP 1972 1972 *(special promotional release)*	*Irrepressible Impulses* Various Artists	Astral Traveling—Pharoah Sanders; Dear Lord—John Coltrane; Galaxy in Turiya—Alice Coltrane; Crystaled Tears—John Klemmer; Wave—Ahmad Jamal; Worry 'Bout It Later—Cliff Coulter; Attica Blues—Archie Shepp; Larry of Arabia—Chico Hamilton; Blue Nile—Alice Coltrane; Frankie and Johnny—Milt Jackson; Money Blues—Archie Shepp
AS 9234-2 1973	*Re-Evaluation: The Impulse Years* Charles Mingus	Better Get Hit in Yo' Soul; Mood Indigo; Body and Soul; Hora Decubitus; The Black Saint and the Sinner Lady; Freedom; Theme for Lester Young; She's Just Miss Popular Hybrid; II B.S.
AS 9235-2 1973	*Re-Evaluation: The Impulse Years* McCoy Tyner	Inception; Welcome; Contemporary Focus; One Down, One Up; Effendi; Blue Monk; Serenity; Monk's Blues; Have You Met Miss Jones; Sun Ship; Autumn Leaves; You'd Be SO Nice to Come Home To
AS 9236-2 1973	*Re-Evaluation: The Impulse Years* Sonny Rollins	Hold 'Em Joe; Blessing in Disguise; East Broadway Run Down; Alfie's Theme; Three Little Words; On Green Dolphin Street; Blue Room; On Impulse
AS 9237-2 1973	*Re-Evaluation: The Impulse Years* Freddie Hubbard	The 7th Day; Body and Soul; Aries; Stolen Moments; Chocolate Shake; Thermo; Skylark; Bob's Place; Cascades; Clarence's Place; Carnival (Manha de Carnaval); Hoe-Down; Caravan
AS/AQ 9238 1973	*Tranquility* Ahmad Jamal	I Say a Little Prayer; The Look of Love; When I Look in Your Eyes; Illusions Opticas; Nothing Ever Changes My Love for You; Emily; Tranquility; Free Again; Manhattan Reflections
AS 9239 1973	*Atlantis* Sun Ra	Mu; Lemuria; Yucatan; Bimini; Atlantis
AS/AQ 9240 1973	*Fort Yawuh* Keith Jarrett	(If the) Misfits (Wear It); Fort Yawuh; De Drums; Still Life, Still Life
AS/AQ 9241 1973	*Land of Spirit and Light* Michael White	Land of Spirit and Light; Fatima's Garden; Fiesta Dominical; O Ancient One; Lament (Mankind)

CATALOG # AND YEAR OF RELEASE	TITLE AND ARTIST	TRACKS
AS 9242 1973	*Nubians of Plutonia* Sun Ra	Plutonian Nights; The Golden Lady; Star Time; Nubia; Africa; Watusa; Aiethopia
AS/AQ 9243 1973	*The Magic City* Sun Ra	The Magic City; The Shadow World; Abstract Eye; Abstract "I"
AS/AQ 9244 1973	*Intensity* John Klemmer	Rapture of the Deep; Love Song to Katherine; Prayer for John Coltrane; Waltz for John Coltrane; (C'mon an') Play with Me; Sea of Passion; Last Summer's Spell
AS 9245 1974	*Angels and Demons at Play* Sun Ra	Tiny Pyramids; Between Two Worlds; Music from the World Tomorrow; Angels and Demons at Play; Urnack; Medicine for a Nightmare; A Call for All Demons; Demon's Lullaby
AS 9246-2 1973	*Live—Concert in Japan* John Coltrane	Introduction (Meditations); Leo (Part 2); Peace on Earth, Parts 1 and 2; Leo (Part 3)
AS/AQ 9247 1973	*En Medio* Gary Saracho	Sunday's Church; Happy Sad; Rose for a Lady; Senor Baker; Conquest de Mejico
AS/AQ 9248 1973	*Chapter One: Latin America* Gato Barbieri	Encuentros; India; La China Leoncia Arreo la Correntinada Trajo Entre la Muchachada; Nunca Mas; To Be Continued
AS/AQ 9249 1973	*Big Foot Country Girl* Mel Brown	Need Love; Home Folks; Red Cross Store; Little Girl, Don't You Know; Big Foot Country Girl; Goin' Down Slow; Stinging Bea
AS/AQ 9250 1973	*The Ear of the Behearer* Dewey Redman	Innerconnection; Imani; Walls-Bridges; P.S.; Boody; Sunlanding; Image (in Disguise)
AS/AQ 9251 1973	*Streams* Sam Rivers	Tenor Sax Section; Flute Section; Piano Section; Soprano Sax Section
AS/AQ 9252 1973	*Geechee Recollections* Marion Brown	Once Upon a Time; Karintha; Buttermilk Bottom; Introduction; Tokalokloka; Ending
ASH 9253-3 1973	*The Saxophone* Various Artists	Body and Soul—Coleman Hawkins; All the Things You Are—Don Byas; Stardust—Sonny Stitt; Three Little Words—Sonny Rollins; I Let a Song Go Out of My Heart/Don't Get Around Much Anymore—Harry Carney; Someone to Watch Over Me—Ben Webster; Out of this World—John Coltrane; Rufus—Archie Shepp; Jumpin' with Symphony Sid—Lester Young; Confirmation—Charlie Parker; Mendacity—Eric Dolphy with Max Roach; Song for Che—Ornette Coleman; Offering—John Coltrane; Mantra—Pharoah Sanders with Alice Coltrane; Gettin' on My Way—Sonny Simmons with Elvin Jones; T 'N' A Blues—John Gilmore with McCoy Tyner; Ghosts—Albert Ayler; Prelude and Waterfall I—John Klemmer; Once Upon a Time (A Children's Tale)—Marion Brown; Innerconnection—Dewey Redman; Encore—Sam Rivers; Encontros—Gato Barbieri
AS/AQ 9254 1973	*Village of the Pharoahs* Pharoah Sanders	Village of the Pharoahs (Parts 1, 2 and 3); Myth; Mansion Worlds; Memories of Lee Morgan; Went Like It Came
AS/AQ 9255 1973	*Astro Black* Sun Ra	Astro Black; Discipline "99"; Hidden Spheres; The Cosmo-Fire

CATALOG # AND YEAR OF RELEASE	TITLE AND ARTIST	TRACKS
AS 9256-2 1973	*Ellingtonia: Re-Evaluation: The Impulse Years* Duke Ellington and Various Artists	The Jeep Is Jumpin'—Duke Ellington and Coleman Hawkins; A Flower Is a Lovesome Thing—Johnny Hodges; Take the Coltrane—Duke Ellington and John Coltrane; Caravan—McCoy Tyner; In a Mellotone—Ben Webster; Once Upon a Time—Earl Hines; Things Ain't What They Used to Be—Paul Gonsalves; Do Nothin' Till You Hear from Me—Clark Terry; Good Queen Bess—Lawrence Brown; Open Mike—Johnny Hodges; In a Sentimental Mood—Duke Ellington and John Coltrane; Cottontail—Earl Hines; Solitude—McCoy Tyner; Jeep's Blues—Lawrence Brown; Wanderlust—Duke Ellington and Coleman Hawkins; 310 Blues—Johnny Hodges; Mood Indigo—Lawrence Brown; Rockin' in Rhythm—Clark Terry
AS 9257-2 1973	*Re-Evaluation: The Impulse Years* Albert Ayler	Zion Hill; New Ghosts; Drudgery; Love Cry; Sun Watcher; Oh! Love of Life; Water Music; Holy Ghost; Universal Indians; Again Comes the Rising Sun; For John Coltrane
AS 9258-2 1973	*Re-Evaluation: The Impulse Years* Coleman Hawkins	Out of Nowhere; Solitude; Self-Portrait (of the Bean); Um Abraco No Bonfa; The Midnight Sun Will Never Set; Wrapped Tight; Samba Para Bean; Put On Your Old Grey Bonnet; Mood Indigo; She's Fit; Don't Sit Under the Apple Tree; Indian Summer; O Pato; Swingin' Scotch; Slowly; Go Lil Liza
AS 9259-2 1973	*Re-Evaluation: The Impulse Years* Yusef Lateef	Straighten Up and Fly Right; Kyoto Blues; (I Don't Stand a) Ghost of a Chance with You; Nile Valley Blues; Sound Wave; Psychicemotus; Blind Willie; Warm Fire; Twelve Tone Blues; Golden Flute; Exactly Like You; Raisins and Almonds; Feelin' Alright; Feather Comfort; Sister Mamie; Trouble in Mind; Number 7; One Little Indian
AS 9260-2 1973	*Re-Evaluation: The Impulse Years* Ahmad Jamal	Wave; Emily; Dolphin Dance; Patterns; Insensatez; Manhattan Reflections; Stolen Moments; Bogota; Tranquility; Poinciana
AS/AQ 9261 1974	*Elevation* Pharoah Sanders	Elevation; Greeting to Saud; Ore-S-Rere; The Gathering; Spiritual Blessing
AS/AQ 9262 1974	*Kwanza* Archie Shepp	Back Back; Spoo Pee Doo; New Africa; Slow Drag; Bakai
AS/AQ 9263 1974	*Chapter Two: Hasta Siempre* Gato Barbieri	Encontros Parts One and Three; Latino America; Marissea; Para Nosotros; Juana Azurduy
AS/AQ 9264 1974	*Impulse Artists on Tour* Various Artists	Encuentros—Gato Barbieri; Roads Traveled, Roads Veiled—Keith Jarrett; Free Love—John Klemmer; Hues of Melanin—Sam Rivers; Fiesta Dominical—Micheal White
ASD 9265 1975	*Jazz in Silhouette* Sun Ra	Enlightenment; Saturn; Velvet; Ancient Aiethopia; Hours After; Horoscope; Images; Blues at Midnight
ASD 9266-2 1975	*Impulsively!* Various Artists	La China Leoncia Arreo la Correntinada Trajo Entre la Muchachada la Flor de la Juventud, India—Gato Barbieri; De Drums, Still Life Still Life—Keith Jarrett; Fiesta Dominical, The Land of Spirit and Light—Michael White; Big Foot Country Girl, Need Love—Mel Brown; (C'mon an') Play with Me, Love Song to Katherine—John Klemmer; Senor Baker, Parts 1 and 2—Gary Saracho; We Shall Overcome—Charlie Haden; Boody, Sunlanding—Dewey Redman; Karintha, Parts 1 and 2—Marion Brown; Astro Black, Abstract "I"—Sun Ra; Leo—John Coltrane; Streams (tenor saxophone, flute sections) Sam Rivers

CATALOG # AND YEAR OF RELEASE	TITLE AND ARTIST	TRACKS
AS 9267-2 1974	*No Energy Crisis* Various Artists	Para Nosotros—Gato Barbieri; Preytude—Michael White; Cosmos—John Coltrane; Change Has Come—Albert Ayler; Basheer—Archie Shepp; The Tree of the Forbidden—John Klemmer; Tokolokoloka (Part 2)—Marion Brown; Suite for Molde—Sam Rivers; Red, Black and Green—Pharoah Sanders; The Cosmo-Fire—Sun Ra; Interconnection—Dewey Redman
AS/AQ 9268 1974	*Father Music, Mother Dance* Michael White	Father Music, Mother Dance; Reiko; Commin' From; Way Down Inside; Water Children; Mary's Waltz
ASD 9269 1974	*Magic and Movement* John Klemmer	Blood of the Sun (Primary Pulse); Blood of the Sun (Secondary Pulse); Blood of the Sun (Tertiary Pulse); How Cum Ya Got ta Rip Off Your Brothers?; Free Love; The Tree of Forbidden Fruit (Alpha Branch); The Tree of Forbidden Fruit (Beta Branch); The Tree of Forbidden Fruit (Gamma Branch)
ASD 9270 1974	*Fate in a Pleasant Mood* Sun Ra	The Others in Their World; Space Mates; Lights of a Satellite; Distant Stars; Kingdom of Thunder; Fate in a Pleasant Mood; Ankaton
ASD 9271 1974	*Supersonic Sounds* Sun Ra	India; Sunology; Advice to Medics; Super Bronze; Soft Talk; Sunology (Part 2); Kingdom of Not; Portrait of the Living Sky; Blues at Midnight; El Is a Sound of Joy; Springtime in Chicago; Medicine for a Nightmare
ASD 9272-3 1974	*The Drums* Various Artists	A La Mode—Art Blakey; Mama—Max Roach; No Smokin'—Kenny Clarke; Thermo—Philly Joe Jones with Freddie Hubbard; Afternoon of a Basie-ite—Sid Catlett with Lester Young; Cottontail—Jo Jones with Benny Carter; Sattement—Connie Kay with Milt Jackson; Snap, Crackle—Roy Haynes; The Berkeley Underground—Dannie Richmond; Brainwashed—Buddy Rich; Thunderbird—Louis Bellson; Cherokee—Shelly Manne; Jim-Jeanie—Chico Hamilton; Comin' Back—Bernard "Pretty" Purdie with Gabor Szabo; Shiny Stockings—Elvin Jones; The Drum Thing—Elvin Jones with John Coltrane; Gospel Trane—Rashied Ali with Alice Coltrane; Ghosts—Milford Graves with Albert Ayler; Spooky Drums Number Two—Baby Dodds; Rufus—Joe Chambers with Archie Shepp; Magic of Juju—Beaver Harris, Norman Connors, and Ed Blackwell with Archie Shepp; Pots—Sonny Nurray with Cecil Taylor; Late Evening Prayer—Alphonse Mouzon with John Klemmer; Angles (Without Edges)—Paul Motian with Keith Jarrett; Hues of Melanin—Barry Altschul with Sam Rivers
ASD 9273 1974	*Africa Brass Sessions, Vol. 2* John Coltrane	Song of the Underground Railroad; Greensleeves; Africa
ASD 9274 1974	*Treasure Island* Keith Jarrett	The Rich (and the Poor); Blue Streak; Fullsuvolivus (Fools of All of Us); Treasure Island; Introduction—Yaqui Indian Folk Song; Le Mistral; Angles (Without Edges); Sister Fortune
ASD 9275 1974	*Sweet Earth Flying* Marion Brown	Sweet Earth Flying (Parts 1–5); Eleven Light City (Parts 1–4)
ASD 9276 1975	*The Bad and the Beautiful* Sun Ra	The Bad and the Beautiful; Ankh; Just in Time; Search Light Blues; Exotic Two; On the Blue Side; And This Is My Beloved
ASD 9277 1974	*Interstellar Space* John Coltrane	Mars; Venus; Jupiter; Saturn
ASD 9278-2 1974	*His Greatest Years, Volume 3* John Coltrane	Dear Lord; Chasin' the Trane; Up 'Gainst the Wall; Crescent; Nature Boy; Welcome; Cosmos; Dedicated to You; Expression; Living Space

CATALOG # AND YEAR OF RELEASE	TITLE AND ARTIST	TRACKS
ASD 9279 1974	*Chapter Three: Viva Emiliano Zapata* Gato Barbieri	Milonga Triste; Lluvia Azul; El Sublime; La Podrida; Cuando Vuelva a Tu Lado; Viva Emiliano Zapata
ASD 9280 1974	*Love in Us All* Pharoah Sanders	Love Is Everywhere; To John
ASD 9281 1974	*Go with the Flow* Michael White	Go with the Flow; The Lady Sirro; In the Silence (Listen); Spaceslide; Her; Moondust Shuffle; Go with the Flow
ASD 9282-2 1974	*The Impulse Years* Milt Jackson	Frankie & Johnny; I Love You; One Mint Julep; Sermonette; Braddock Breakdown; Who Can I Turn To; Queen Mother Stomp; A Beautiful Romance; If I Were a Bell; Enchanted Lady; Here's That Rainy Day; Gingerbread Boy; Evening in Paris; Put Off; Bags' Groove
ASD 9283-2 1974	*The Impulse Years* Elvin Jones	Pursuance from A Love Supreme; Impressions; Your Lady; Vigil; Shiny Stockings; Attaining; All or Nothing at All; Dear John C.; We Kiss in a Shadow; Aborigine Dance in Scotland; Concluding Section of Serenity
ASD 9284-3 1974	*The Bass* Various Artists	Plucked Again—Jimmy Blanton with Duke Ellington; Tricotism—Oscar Pettiford with Lucky Thompson; The Plain but Simple Truth—Pettiford With Thompson; Very Thought of You—Ray Brown with Milt Jackson; II BS—Charles Mingus; Teenie's Blues—Paul Chambers with Oliver Nelson; Gloria's Step—Scott LaFaro with Bill Evans; Jazz Conversations—Milt Hinton with Clark Terry; The Sicks of Us—George Duvivier with Shelly Manne; Song of Praises—Jimmy Garrison with John Coltrane; Long Wharf—Henry Grimes with Roy Haynes; Song for Che—Charlie Haden with the Liberation Music Orchestra; Walls-Bridges—Sirone with Dewey Redman; Syeeda's Song Flute—Reggie Workman with Archie Shepp; Sophisticated Lady—Ron Carter with Archie Shepp; Black Unity—Stanley Clarke and Cecil McBee with Pharoah Sanders; Summertime—Richard Davis with Elvin Jones; The Chased—David Izenson with Archie Shepp; Love—Cecil McBee with Pharoah Sanders
ASD 9285-2 1974	*Ellingtonia: Re-Evaluations, Volume 2* Duke Ellington and Various Artists	Black and Tan Fantasy—Earl Hines; Cottontail—Louis Belson; Come Sunday—Archie Shepp; Mood Indigo—Charles Mingus; The Feeling of Jazz—Duke Ellington and John Coltrane; Satin Doll—McCoy Tyner; Main Stem—Johnny Hodges; Do Nothin' Till You Hear from Me—Lawrence Brown; Action in Alexandria—Paul Gonsalves; You Dirty Dog—Ellington and Coleman Hawkins; Single Petal of a Rose—Ellington; Prelude to a Kiss—Pee Wee Russell; Ring Dem Bells—Lionel Hampton; East St. Louis Toodle-Oo—Steely Dan
ASD 9286 1974	*Crystals* Sam Rivers	Exultation; Tranquility; Postlude; Bursts; Orb; Earth Song
ASD 9287–9298	***Sun Ra titles never issued***	
ASD 9299 1975	*Equinox Express Elevator* Howard Roberts	Unfolding In; Timelaps; TTTT; Growing National Concern; 2 d.b., Eyes of Blue; (The Single) (On This Side); Real Freak of Nature Historical Monument; Slam; Harold J. Ostly, the County Tax Assessor; Unfolding (on Itself)
ASD 9300 1975	*Coincide* Dewey Redman	Seeds and Deeds; Somnifacient; Meditation Submission Purification; Joie de Vivre; Funcitydues; Phadan-Sers; Qow
ASD 9301 1975	*Death and the Flower* Keith Jarrett	Death and the Flower; Prayer; Great Bird

CATALOG # AND YEAR OF RELEASE	TITLE AND ARTIST	TRACKS
ASD 9302 1975	*Hues* Sam Rivers	Amber; Turquoise; Rose; Chartreuse; Mauve; Indigo; Onyx; Topaz; Ivory Black; Violet
ASD 9303 1975	*Chapter Four: Alive in New York* Gato Barbieri	Milonga Triste; La China; Lluvia Azul; Baihia
ASD 9304 1975	*Vista* Marion Brown	Maimoun; Visions; Vista; Moment of Truth; Bismillahi 'Rrahmani 'Rrahim; Djini
ASD 9305 1975	*Backhand* Keith Jarrett	Inflight; Kuum; Vapallia; Backhand
ASD 9306-2 1975	*The Gentle Side of John Coltrane* John Coltrane	Soul Eyes; What's New; Welcome; Nancy; My Little Brown Book; Lush Life; Wise One; Alabama; My One and Only Love; I Want to Talk About You; Dear Lord; After the Rain; In a Sentimental Mood; Spiritual
ASD 9307-2 1975	*Dancing Sunbeam* Lucky Thompson	Tom Kattin'; Old Reliable; Deep Passion; Translation; Tricrotism; Bo-Bi My Boy; A Lady's Vanity; Op Meets Lt; NR #2; Once There Was; Dancing Sunbeam; NR #1; Little Tenderfoot; The Plain but the Simple Truth; Mister Man; Good Luck
ASD 9308 1975	*Brass Fever* Brass Fever	Lady Marmalade; Djingi; Sunshine Superman; Back at the Chicken Shack; Bach Bone
ASD 9309	***No release***	
ASD 9310 1976	*Club Date* Yusef Lateef	Rogi; Oscalypso; Gee! Sam Gee; Brother John; P-Bouk; Nu-Bouk
ASD 9311 1976	*I Don't Know How to Love Him* Gloria Lynne	Shelter of Your Love: I Don't Know How to Love Him; Out of This World; We Are the Dreamers; Thank You Early Bird; I'm Through with Love; I'll Be Passing By This Way Again; Visions; How Will I Know
ASD 9312 1976	*Warm and Sonny* Sonny Criss	Cool Struttin'; The Way We Were; That's the Way of the World; Bumpin'; Sweet Summer Breeze; Memories; Blues for Willie
ASD 9313 1976	*Illusions* Jimmy Ponder	Funky Butt; Energy III; Jennifer; Do It Baby; Illusions; Sabado Sombrero
ASD 9314 1976	*Hard Work* John Handy	Hard Work; Blues for Louis Jordan; Young Enough to Dream; Love for Brother Jack; Didn't I Tell You; Afro Wiggle; You Don't Know
ASD 9315 1976	*Mysteries* Keith Jarrett	Rotation; Everything That Lives Laments; Flame; Mysteries
ASD 9316 1976	*Sizzle* Sam Rivers	Dawn; Flare; Flame; Scud
ASD 9317 1976	*Together Again . . . Live* B.B. King and Bobby Bland	Let the Good Times Roll; Medley: Stormy Monday Blues, Strange Things Happen; Feel So Bad; Medley: Mother-in-Law Blues, Mean Old World; Everyday (I Have the Blues); Medley: The Thrill Is Gone, I Ain't Gonna Be the First to Cry
ASD 9318 1976	*Metamorphosis* Marcus Wade	Metamorphosis; Sugar Loaf Sunrise; Would You Like to Ride; Journey to Morocco; Poinciana; Feelings; Funk Machine; Daniel

CATALOG # AND YEAR OF RELEASE	TITLE AND ARTIST	TRACKS
ASD 9319 1976	*Time Is Running Out* Brass Fever	Time Is Running Out; Takin' It to the Streets; Boogie On Reggae Woman; Mr. Tambourine Man; Dancing Machine; Pressure Drop; Summertime; Funky Carnival
ASD 9320	***No release***	
ASD 9321-2 1976	*What a Little Moonlight Can Do* [Reissue of Peacock-90 and ABC-363] Betty Carter	You're Driving Me Crazy; I Can't Help It; By the Bend of the River; Blue's Blues; Foul Play; You're Getting to Be a Habit with Me; Isle of May; But Beautiful; All I've Got; Make It Last; Bluebird of Happiness; Something Wonderful; What a Little Moonlight Can Do; There's No You; I Don't Want to Set the World on Fire; Remember; My Reverie; Mean to Me; Don't Weep for the Lady; Jazz (Ain't Nothing but Soul); For You; Stormy Weather; At Sundown; On the Alamo
ASD 9322 1976	*Shades* Keith Jarrett	Shades of Jazz; Southern Smiles; Rose Petals; Diatribe
ASD 9323	***No release***	
ASD 9324 1977	*Carnival* John Handy	Carnival; Alvina; Watch Your Money Go; I Will Leave You; Love's Rejoicing; Make Her Mine; All the Things You Are; Christina's Little Song
ASD 9325 1977	*The Other Village Vanguard Tapes* John Coltrane	Chasin' the Trane; Spiritual; Untitled Original; India; Greensleeves; Spiritual (alternate take)
ASD 9326 1977	*Joy of Sax* Sonny Criss	You've Lost That Lovin' Feeling; Don't You Worry 'Bout a Thing; You Are So Beautiful; Turn Me Loose; Stolen Moments; Have a Talk with God; Midnight Mellow
ASD 9327 1977	*White Room* Jimmy Ponder	If You Need Someone to Love (Let Me Know); Going Back to Country Living; Easy; Bro' James; White Room; Quintessence; So in Love
ASD 9328 1977	*African Violet* Blue Mitchell	Mississippi Jump; Ojos de Rojo; Sand Castles; African Violet; As; Square Business; Forget
ASD 9329 1977	*Music Let's Me Be* Les McCann	Street Dance; Beyond Yesterday; My Darling, My Darling; Ruby Jubilation; My Name Is Francis; Vallarta; Music Let's Me Be
ASD 9330 1977	*Master Grady Tate* Grady Tate	Differerntly; Ain't No Love in the Heart of the City; Funiculi, Funicula; The Hungry Years; I Don't Know How to Look for Love; Dream Love; Give a Little Bit; Without the One I Love; A Song of Life
ASD 9331 1977	*Byablue* Keith Jarrett	Byablue; Konya; Rainbow; Trieste; Fantasm; Yahllah; Byablue
ASD 9332 1977	*First Meditations* Keith Jarrett	Meditations: Love, Compassion, Joy, Consequences, Serenity
ASD 9333 1977	*Change, Change, Change: Live at the Roxy* Les McCann	Change, Change, Change; I Don't Want to Say Goodbye to a Brother; North Carolina; Rid of Me; I Never Thought That You Would Go; Song of Love; The Roller

BIBLIOGRAPHY

JAZZ: THE FIFTIES TO THE SEVENTIES

BOOKS

Buskin, Richard. *Inside Track*. New York: Avon Books, 1999.

Coryell, Julie and Laura Friedman. *Jazz-Rock Fusion*. New York: Delacorte Press, 1978.

Davis, Francis. *Like Young*. New York: Da Capo Press, 2001.

Erlewine, Michael, et al., eds. *All Music Guide to Jazz*. San Francisco: Miller Freeman Books, 1998.

Fox, Ted. *In the Groove: The People Behind the Music*. New York: St. Martin's Press, 1986.

Friedwald, Will. *Jazz Singing: America's Great Voices from Bessie Smith to Bebop and Beyond*. New York: Collier Books, 1990.

Giddins, Gary. *Visions of Jazz*. New York: Oxford University Press, 1998.

Gleason, Ralph J. *Celebrating the Duke: And Louis, Bessie, Billie, Bird, Carmen, Miles, Dizzy and Other Heroes*. New York: Da Capo Press, 1995.

Goldberg, Joe. *Jazz Masters of the Fifties*. 1965; reprint, New York: Da Capo Press, 1983.

Hentoff, Nat. *The Jazz Life*. 1961; reprint, New York: Da Capo Press,1978.

———, and Albert J. McCarthy, eds. *Jazz*. 1959; reprint, New York: Da Capo Press, 1975.

Jones, LeRoi (Amiri Imamu Baraka). *Black Music*. 1967; reprint, New York: Da Capo Press, 1998.

———. *Blues People*. New York: William Morrow, 1963.

Keepnews, Orrin. *The View from Within: Jazz Writings, 1948–1987*. New York: Oxford University Press, 1988.

Korall, Burt, Dom Cerulli, and Mort L. Nasatir, eds. *The Jazz Word*. 1960; reprint, New York: Da Capo Press, 1987.

Morgenstern, Dan. *Living with Jazz*. New York: Pantheon, 2004.

Ratliff, Ben. *The New York Times Essential Library—Jazz: A Critic's Guide to the 100 Most Important Recordings*. New York: Times Books, 2002.

Rivelli, Pauline, and Robert Levin, eds. *The Black Giants*. New York: World Publishing Company, 1970.

Rosenthal, David. *Hard Bop: Jazz and Black Music, 1955–1965*. New York: Oxford University Press, 1992.

Shipton, Alyn. *A New History of Jazz*. London: Continuum, 2001.

Sidran, Ben. *Black Talk*. 1971; reprint, New York: Da Capo Press, 1983.

———. *Talking Jazz: An Oral History*. New York: Da Capo Press, 1995.

Snitzer, Herb. *Jazz: A Visual Journey*. Clearwater, Fla.: Notables Inc., 1999.

Taylor, Arthur. *Notes and Tones: Musician-to-Musician Interviews*. New York: Da Capo Press, 1993.

Walser, Robert, ed. *Keeping Time: Readings in Jazz History*. New York: Oxford University Press, 1999.

Wilmer, Val. *Mama Said There'd Be Days Like This*. London: The Women's Press, 1989.

Williams, Martin T. *Jazz Masters in Transition, 1957–1969*. 1970; reprint, New York: Da Capo Press, 1982.

———. *The Jazz Tradition*. New York: Oxford University Press, 1970.

———, ed. *Jazz Panorama: From the Pages of* The Jazz Review. New York: Crowell-Collier Press, 1962.

ARTICLES

Bundy, June. "Late '50s Bid for Posterity Fame as Real 'Jazz Age.'" *Billboard* (March 9, 1959): 1.

"Crow Jim." *Time* (October 19, 1962).

Gabree, John. "The World of Rock." *Down Beat* (August 23, 1967): 18–20.

Townsend, Irving. "The Ten Best Friends of Jazz." *Down Beat* (August 20, 1959): 89.

JOHN COLTRANE

BOOKS

Fujioka, Yasuhiro, et al. *John Coltrane: A Discography and Musical Biography* (*Studies in Jazz,* no. 20). Lanham, Md.: Scarecrow Press, 1993.

Kahn, Ashley. *A Love Supreme: The Story of John Coltrane's Signature Album*. New York: Viking/Penguin, 2002.

Porter, Lewis. *John Coltrane: His Life and Music*. Ann Arbor: University of Michigan Press, 1998.

Thomas, J. C. *Chasin' the Trane: The Music and Mystique of John Coltrane*. Garden City, N.Y.: Doubleday, 1975.

Woideck, Carl, ed. *The John Coltrane Companion: Five Decades of Commentary*. New York: Simon & Schuster, 1998.

ARTICLES (CONTEMPORANEOUS)

Clouzet, Jean, and Michel Delorme. "Entretien avec John Coltrane." *Les Cahiers du Jazz* (France) (VIII, 1963).

Coleman, Ray. "Coltrane: Next Thing for Me—African Rhythms." *Melody Maker* (July 11, 1964): 6.

Coltrane, John. "Coltrane on Coltrane." *Down Beat* (September 29, 1960): 26–27.

Dawbarn, Bob. "I'd Like to Play Your Clubs." *Melody Maker* (November 25, 1961): 8.

DeMicheal, Don. "John Coltrane and Eric Dolphy Answer the Jazz Critics." *Down Beat* (April 12, 1962): 20–23.

———. "The Monterey Festival," *Down Beat* (November 9, 1961): 13.

Feather, Leonard. "Coltrane Shaping Musical Revolt." *New York Post* (October 18, 1964): 54.

———. "Feather's Nest," *Down Beat* (February 15, 1962): 17.

———. "For Coltrane the Time Is Now." *Melody Maker* (December 19, 1964): 10.

"Finally Made." *Newsweek* (July 24, 1961).
Gardner, Barbara. "John Coltrane." *Down Beat* (Music 1962).
Gitler, Ira. "'Trane on the Track." *Down Beat* (October 16, 1958): 16–17.
———, and Pete Welding. "Double View of Coltrane 'Live.'" *Down Beat* (April 26, 1962).
Gleason, Ralph J. "Coltrane Not for Those Who Want a Popular Tune." *Des Moines Register* (March 26, 1960).
———. "Coltrane on Jazz Solos." *New York Journal-American* (July 15, 1961).
———. "Coltrane's Sax Blows Instant Art." *San Francisco Chronicle* (November 24, 1963): 30.
———. "John Coltrane Here: A Major Artist." *San Francisco Chronicle* (September 15, 1960).
———. "Weinstock vs. Gleason on Coltrane." *Los Angeles Mirror-News* (March 28, 1960).
Hendricks, Jon. "John Coltrane." *Saturday Review* (November 1964).
Hennessey, Mike. "Coltrane: Dropping the Ball and Chain from Jazz." *Melody Maker* (August 14, 1965): 6.
Hultin, Randy. "I Remember 'Trane." *Down Beat* (Music 1968): 104–5.
"John Coltrane Talks to Jazz News." *Jazz News* (December 27, 1961): 13.
Kofsky, Frank. "John Coltrane: Interview by Frank Kofsky." *Jazz & Pop* (September 1967): 23–31.
———. "The New Wave: Bob Thiele Talks to Frank Kofsky About John Coltrane." *Coda* (May 1968): 2–10.
Nelsen, Don. "Exploring the Jazz Legacy of John Coltrane." *New York Times* (September 29, 1974): 8–10.
———. "'Trane Stops in the Gallery." *Sunday News* (New York) (May 15, 1960).
Pekar, Harvey. "Impressions." *Down Beat* (August 29, 1963): 22.
Postif, Francois. "John Coltrane." *Jazz Hot* (France) (January 1962).
Quersin, Benoit. "La Passe Dangereuse." *Jazz* (France) (January 1963).
Spellman, A.B. "Trane + 7 = A Wild Night at the Gate." *Down Beat* (December 30, 1965): 15–44.
Welding, Pete. "My Favorite Things." *Down Beat* (June 22, 1961): 30–31.
Williams, Martin. "Africa/Brass." *Down Beat* (January 18, 1962): 29–32.
———. "Coltrane Triumphant." *Saturday Review* (January 16, 1965): 73–74.
———. "Coltrane Up to Date." *Saturday Review* (April 30, 1966): 67.
Wilson, John S. "Coltrane's 'Sheets of Sound.'" *New York Times* (August 13, 1967).
Woodfin, Henry. "Coltrane's Progress." *Sounds & Fury* (October 1965).

ARTICLES (POSTHUMOUS)

Christon, Lawrence. "This Trane Keeps A-Rollin': Twenty-Five Years After John Coltrane's Death, Jazz and Pop Musicians Remain in the Long Shadow of the Saxophonist's Innovation and Influence." *Los Angeles Times* (July 12, 1992).
Cook, Richard. "John Coltrane: A Spiritual 'Trane Ride from the Birdland Blues to A Love Supreme." *New Musical Express* (December 25, 1982): 60–77.
Crouch, Stanley. "Titan of the Blues: John Coltrane." *Village Voice* (October 6, 1987): 90.
Davis, Francis. "Coltrane at 75: The Man and the Myths." *New York Times* (September 23, 2001).
Donloe, Darlene. "Living with the Spirit and Legacy of John Coltrane." *Ebony* (March 1989): 46–50.
Garland, Phyl. "Requiem for 'Trane." *Ebony* (November 1967): 67–74.
Giddins, Gary. "Metamorphosis: Chasing 'Chasin' the Trane' Down the Corridors of Its History." *Village Voice* (October 7, 1997): 67–68.
Heckman, Don. "A Legacy Supreme: John Coltrane Broke the Bounds of Traditional Improvisation. Three Decades After His Death, When You Listen to Jazz of the '90s, You Can Still Hear the Influence of This Tenor Legend." *Los Angeles Times* (July 13, 1997).
Kopulos, Gordon. "John Coltrane: Retrospective Perspective." *Down Beat* (July 22, 1971): 14–40.
McDonald, Michael Bruce. "Traning the Nineties, or the Present Relevance of John Coltrane's Music of Theophany and Negation." *African American Review* (vol. 29, no. 2, 1995): 275–82.
Norris, John. "The Final Legacy." *Coda* (May/June 1968): 18–20.
Palmer, Robert. "A Tribute to John Coltrane's Spirit." *New York Times* (September 25, 1987).
Priestley, Brian. "Countdown to Ecstasy." *Wire* (December 1985): 39.
Ruhlmann, William. "Going to Extremes: John Coltrane on Record." *Goldmine* (June 23, 1995): 18–144.
"Still a Force in '79: Musicians Talk About John Coltrane." *Down Beat* (July 12, 1979): 20–45.
Williams, Martin. "John Coltrane: Man in the Middle." *Down Beat* (December 17, 1967): 114.

OTHER SELECTED IMPULSE MUSICIANS

BOOKS

Carr, Ian. *Keith Jarrett: The Man and His Music*. London: Grafton Books, 1991.
Hicock, Larry. *Castles Made of Sound: The Gil Evans Story*. New York: Da Capo, 2002.
Jones, Quincy. *Q: The Autobiography of Quincy Jones*. New York: Doubleday, 2001.
Nisenson, Eric. *Open Sky: Sonny Rollins and His World of Improvisation*. New York: St. Martin's Press, 2000.
Palmer, Richard. *Sonny Rollins: The Cutting Edge*. New York: Continuum, 2004.
Santoro, Gene. *Myself When I Am Real: The Life and Music of Charles Mingus*. New York: Oxford University Press, 2001.
Stein-Crease, Stephanie. *Gil Evans: Out of the Cool*. Chicago: Acapella Books, 2002.

ARTICLES

"At Home with Oliver Nelson." *Jazz* (July 1966): 15–18.
Conover, Willis. "What Makes Gary Run." *Jazz* (May 1965): 8–11.

Delehant, Jim. "Confessions of a Non-Purist." *Down Beat* (September 21, 1967): 22–23.
DeMicheal, Don. "Gabor Szabo: Jazz and the Changing Times." *Down Beat* (October 5, 1967).
Goldberg, Joe. "The Further Adventures of Sonny Rollins." *Down Beat* (August 26, 1965): 21.
Hentoff, Nat. "A Volcano Named Mingus." *HiFi/Stereo Review* (December 1964): 52–55.
Hoefer, George. "Larry Coryell: Now!" *Down Beat* (June 29, 1967): 17–19.
Morgenstern, Dan. "Gary McFarland: Theme and Variations." *Down Beat* (February 24, 1966): 25.
Palmer, Robert. "Sam Rivers: An Artist on an Empty Stage." *Down Beat* (February 13, 1975): 33.
Pouncey, Edwin. "Enduring Love: Alice Coltrane." *Wire* (April 2002): 36–44.
Rivelli, Pauline. "Gabor Szabo." *Jazz* (August 1966): 8–30.
———. "Jazz + Rock = Larry, Jim, Chris & Bobby." *Jazz* (November 1966): 22–26.
Wilson, John S. "Hartman Singing in 'Voices of Jazz.'" *New York Times* (May 21, 1982): C18.
———. "Maturing Artist." *New York Times* (November 3, 1963) (re Charles Mingus).

ABC-PARAMOUNT, DUNHILL, AND IMPULSE

BOOKS

Gillett, Charlie. *The Sound of the City: The Rise of Rock and Roll*. New York: Pantheon Books, 1983.
Knoedelseder, William. *Stiffed*. New York: HarperCollins, 1993.
Lydon, Michael. *Ray Charles: Man and Music*. New York: Penguin Putnam, 1998.

ARTICLES

"ABC to Bow a Blues Label; Taps 4 Names." *Billboard* (December 17, 1966): 1.
"ABC-Paramount Bows Jazz Label—Impulse." *Billboard* (December 5, 1960): 3–14.
"ABC-Para Parley Sets New Mark." *Billboard* (January 30, 1965): 4.
"ABC-Paramount Success Saluted." *Music Reporter* (August 24, 1959): 1–14.
"ABC-Paramount Will Reactivate Apt Label." *Billboard* (January 9, 1965): 3.
"ABC Revamps Set-up to 4 Separate Units." *Billboard* (January 25, 1969): 3.
"ABC to Step Up Buying Pace; Re-signs Newton." *Billboard* (December 23, 1967): 4.
"ABC Will Distribute Riverside Globally." *Billboard* (August 5, 1967): 1.
Cuscuna, Michael. "The Story of Impulse!" Liner notes to 2-CD package *Impulse! Jazz: A 30-Year Celebration*, GRD-2–101, 1991.
Hentoff, Nat. "The Jazz Record Scene." *Down Beat* (Music 1966): 50.
———. "Raising Wax Criteria." *Down Beat* (October 20, 1966): 10.
"Impulse, BluesWay Broadening." *Billboard* (March 8, 1969): 6.
"Impulse Producers Giving Acts Double-Edged Effect." *Billboard* (July 25, 1970): 10.
"Jerry Rubenstein: New ABC Records Chairman Is an Astute Businessman Who's Not Unknown to Trade." *Billboard* (January 18, 1975): 3.
Johnson, Phil. "They Couldn't Help Acting on Impulse." *The Independent* (UK) (February 3, 1995): 26.
Kirsch, Bob. "Impulse Label 'Awakens' with an Ambitious Autumn Program." *Billboard* (August 16, 1975): 6.
"New Marketing Approaches Key ABC/Dunhill 55-LP Sales Meet." *Billboard* (September 12, 1970): 3.
Norsworthy, Fred. "Modern Jazz in New York, 1963." *Coda* (March 1964): 30.
"The Record Companies Rap." *Down Beat* (Music Handbook 1974): 12–18.
Thiele, Bob. "Letters to the Editor." *Coda* (April/May 1964): 17.
Tiegel, Eliot. "Individuality Stressed in ABC's New Thrust at Market by Stark." *Billboard* (October 18, 1969): 3.
Williams, Martin. "A Modest Proposition." *Down Beat* (December 14, 1966): 13.

WEB SITES

ABC-Paramount Album Discography, Part 1, www.bsnpubs.com/abc/abc100.html.
ABC-Paramount Album Discography, Part 2, www.bsnpubs.com/abc/abc200.html.
Edwards, David, Patrice Eyries, and Mike Callahan. *ABC-Paramount Records Story,* www.bsn.pubs.com/abc/abcstory.html.
Tan, Kelvin. "Act on Impulse!" *Lindy Hop Ensemble* (Singapore), www.lindyhopensemble.com/blackspeak/impulse.htm.

CREED TAYLOR

ARTICLES

Considine, J.D. "That 70's Jazz (for the Discriminating Rapper)." *New York Times* (March 31, 2002).
Hoefer, George. "The Record Men: Creed Taylor." *Jazz* (January 1965): 19–21.
Panken, Ted. "The Right Groove: Creed Taylor." *Down Beat* (October 2005): 59–61.

BOB THIELE

BOOKS

Thiele, Bob. *What a Wonderful World: A Lifetime of Recordings*. New York: Oxford University Press, 1995.

ARTICLES

Ackerman, Paul. "Total View." *Billboard* (Special Flying Dutchman insert, October 18, 1969): FD-3.
Hoefer, George. "The Record Men: Bob Thiele." *Jazz* (January 1966): 22.

Kofsky, Frank. "The New Wave: Bob Thiele Talks to Frank Kofsky." *Coda* (May/June 1968): 3–10.
Milkowski, Bill. "Irons in the Fire." *Pulse!* (June 1990).
Palmer, Robert. "From the Inside Out: Bob Palmer Interviews Bob Thiele." *Coda* (June 1971): 31–34.
Rozzi, James. "Bob Thiele: Once Again Flying Dutch." *Coda* (September/October 1992): 11–16.
Ruhlmann, William. "Bob Thiele Produced Them All." *Goldmine* (December 11, 1992): 44–50.
Thiele, Bob. "Jazz Flashbacks." *Jazz* (November/December 1962): 15.
"Thiele Bows 3 Labels; Sets Distrib. Deal with Philips." *Billboard* (April 26, 1969): 1.
"Thiele Picks Label's U.S. & Intn'l. Distribs." *Billboard* (July 12, 1969): 3.
"Thiele's Tie with Impulse." *Billboard* (December 14, 1968): 3.
Watrous, Peter. "Bob Thiele, 73, Record Producer for Jazz Legends" (obituary). *New York Times* (February 1, 1996).

STEVE BACKER

BOOKS

Ullman, Michael. *Jazz Lives: Portraits in Words and Pictures.* Washington, D.C.: New Republic Books, 1980.

ARTICLES

Sutherland, Sam. "Steve Backer Still Bucking the System." *Billboard* (September 11, 1982): 10–31.
Tesser, Neil. "Steve Backer: Arista's Jazz Godfather." *Radio Free Jazz* (November 1978): 11–12.
Watrous, Peter. "Steve Backer: One Man's Faith in Jazz, in Words and Action." *New York Times* (February 18, 1997): 15.

THE NEW THING: POLITICS, JAZZ, AND THE AVANT-GARDE

BOOKS

Jost, Ekkehard. *Free Jazz.* 1981; reprint, New York: Da Capo Press, 1994.
Kofsky, Frank. *Black Nationalism and the Revolution in Music.* New York: Pathfinder Press, 1970.
Litweiler, John. *The Freedom Principle: Jazz After 1958.* 1984; reprint, New York: Da Capo Press, 1990.
Saul, Scott. *Freedom Is, Freedom Ain't: Jazz and the Making of the Sixties.* Cambridge, Mass.: Harvard University Press, 2003.
Wilmer, Val. *As Serious as Your Life: John Coltrane and Beyond.* London: Serpent's Tail, 1977.

ARTICLES

Chernus, Roy. "Coltrane/Tyner and the 'New Thing.'" *New York Arts Journal* (November/December 1978, no. 12).
"*Down Beat*'s Music 1962—7th Annual Yearbook."
"*Down Beat*: Music 1966—11th Yearbook."
Feather, Leonard. "Feather's Nest" (column on "anti-jazz"). *Down Beat* (February 15, 1962): 40.
Heckman, Don. "Breakthrough '66." *Down Beat* (Music 1967): 17.
Hentoff, Nat. "The Life Perspectives of the New Jazz." *Down Beat* (Music 1966): 23.
———. "The New Jazz." *Newsweek* (December 12, 1966): 101.
Hyams Ericsson, Marjorie. "Experimentation in Public: The Artist's Viewpoint." *Down Beat* (April 8, 1965): 15.
"Jazz Is Mugged by 'New Thing' (a response)." *Jazz* (June 1965): 34–35.
Jones, LeRoi. "Strong Voices in Today's Black Music." *Down Beat* (February 10, 1966): 15.
Kofsky, Frank. "Revolution, Coltrane and the Avant-Garde." *Jazz* (Part I: July 1965): 13–26; (Part II: August 1965): 18–22.
LeBlanc, Jean P. "The Happy Sound Is Dying," *Esquire* (April 1966): 144.
Qamar, Nadi. "Titans of the Saxophone." *Liberator* (April 1966): 21–22.
"Racial Prejudice in Jazz—Part I." *Down Beat* (March 15, 1962): 20–26.
"Racial Prejudice in Jazz—Part II." *Down Beat* (March 29, 1962): 22–25.
Schoenfeld, Herm. "Jazz Mugged by 'New Thing.'" *Variety* (April 24, 1965): 49.
Smith, Steve. "The Sound and the Fury: Archie Shepp." *JazzTimes* (May 2001): 46–165.
Tynan, John. "Take 5." *Down Beat* (November 23, 1961): 40.
Wilson, John S. "Jazz and the Anarchy of the Avant Garde." *New York Times* (April 24, 1966): 30–31.

INDEX

Note: Page numbers in *italics* indicate illustrations; page numbers followed by an "n" indicate endnotes.